1992.

Ecce Caffin

D0733087

Northwest Coast Indians built some of the most beautiful Native North American houses. Surrounded by totem poles, this home is part of a reconstructed Haida village at the University of British Columbia's Anthropology Museum in Vancouver, British Columbia. (R. Shanks)

Cover Photo: David Smith of the Coastal Pomo Indian Dancers wearing the orange and black flicker headband of the California Indian people. (R. Shanks)

Beautiful Mary Ann Rabesca, a Dene' Indian, models for the Native Women's Association of Northwest Territories. She wears a Dene' (Athabaskan) caribou hide jacket and mukluks with snowshoes. (Dept. of Information, Govt. of Northwest Territories—Tessa Macintosh)

THE NORTH AMERICAN INDIAN TRAVEL GUIDE

Ralph Shanks
and
Lisa Woo Shanks, editor

Iroquois gus-to-weh headdress,
Six Nations Reserve, Ontario.

COSTAÑO BOOKS   **BOX 355**   **PETALUMA, CALIFORNIA 94953**

COSTAÑO BOOKS
P.O. BOX 355
PETALUMA, CALIFORNIA 94953

By the same author:
Lighthouses of San Francisco Bay
Lighthouses and Lifeboats on the Redwood Coast

FIRST EDITION

Copyright © 1986 by Ralph Shanks and Lisa Woo Shanks

All rights reserved

Library of Congress Catalog Card Number 86-70680
ISBN 0-930268-07-5

California Indian Baskets: Pomo, Yuki, Western Mono (left to right).

*"But what can I teach them?" I asked.
"Teach them that we are people,"
the California Indian elder replied.
And so I have tried.*

This book is dedicated to the North American Indian people with deep appreciation.

California Indian Baskets: Maidu, Pomo, Wintun (left to right).

Aztec dancers from Mexico carry feathered shields and wear tropical bird feather headdresses that Montezuma and Cortez would recognize. (R. Shanks)

THE NORTH AMERICAN INDIAN TRAVEL GUIDE

TABLE OF CONTENTS

Note: For best results use your GUIDE in conjunction with a current Road Atlas.

Seneca-Cayuga Tribal office facade detail, patterned after wampum belt designs. Miami, Oklahoma. (R. Shanks)

The unforgettable Papago symbol of "I'itoi and the path of life". If you begin at I'itoi and follow the path, you end up at the circle. This symbol is carried by the lead dancer in the chelkona dance. (R. Shanks)

INTRODUCTION
THE ROAD TO INDIAN COUNTRY

A PERSONAL NOTE

The memories lingered in his mind. The trip from the Eastern Woodlands, across the Great Plains through the Southwestern deserts to the Pacific had been a long one. He walked within the palisade walls of the Cherokee village past the council house and the sacred fire. The women greeted him as they wove their baskets along the cool waters of the stream. He saw the men carving a dugout canoe while a teenage boy prepared for a hunt. One of the people invited him to a dance that evening and he sat in the ceremonial grounds with no light but the fire and no sound but the singing. Only at sunrise did the music and dancing end and the people rest.

Later, on the Plains, he came over the rise to see dozens of tepees in the valley below. There was singing and dancing there, too, but of a different kind. The dancers poured by him in an endless line of colorful feathers, fringed shawls, beaded moccasins, and hair roaches made of deer hair. The people were generous, giving away blankets to those they wished to honor. There was a feast and gambling games that continued long into the night.

A warm breeze touched his face and another memory flooded his mind. What was it? Oh yes, the feel of the desert wind atop the Southwestern mesa when he was with the Hopi. They had all eaten wafer thin bread made of blue corn that the Hopis had grown in their fields below. He went to the plaza and saw the masked gods climb from the underground kiva. They had danced by him just a few feet away—were they men or spirits?

Finally he reached the Pacific Ocean. On the beach beneath the towering trees of the rain forest, the Indian people cooked salmon on cedar sticks. Later, he helped launch the canoe, its animal head prow pointed up the river beyond the totem poles of the village. The sharp pointed paddles of the oarsmen struck the water soundlessly as they pulled away from the rocky beach. It was cold now and the rain began to fall. The time for memories was over.

Some adventurer or fur trader must have written that account of long gone days in America or Canada, you might expect. But actually, I experienced these events recently. And there were many more. But for a long time I thought such adventures were impossible.

As a boy I often wandered about an old Indian village site, hunting arrowheads and longing to meet the people who had called this place home. I spent time reading countless books on Indians. I was sad to be told that many tribes had few survivors and most practiced little of their old ways. It seemed that there would be few chances to meet Indian people and even if I ever did would there be much they could tell me? I had to content myself with old photographs, historians' accounts, and a few arrowheads. For many years I felt a sense of loss, falsely believing that most Native American and Canadian cultures had vanished. I had childhood friends who were Indians but we talked only of our shared non-Indian world of school and sports. Why talk of something that's supposedly no longer there?

Later, as an adult I got my first indication that most Indian cultures still survive. Just because Indian people had learned the advantages of modern technology and schooling did not mean that the wisdom and benefits of time tested Indian ways of life are forgotten.

Today a Native American may be a successful lawyer, nurse, teacher, business owner, or skilled worker who has traveled, reads good books, and generally feels at ease in contemporary American society. But that does not mean that person is no longer Indian. The Creek doctor may be a stomp dancer on weekends, the Pomo nurse a skilled basket weaver in her spare moments, the Hopi museum curator a composer of traditional Hopi religious songs, the Sioux businessman a frequent pow-wow singer and the Iroquois university professor a medicine man in training.

Non-Indians often travel to Indian communities and see modern homes, TV antennas, automobiles and trucks and conclude that all traditional Indian ways must be gone. But return during special events and you will gain a more accurate impression. The people usually know the ancient songs and dances, the traditional arts and crafts, and can often comfortably speak English and Paiute or Cherokee or Pomo. You may even see old time Indian houses reconstructed and delicious Indian foods being offered to guests. Just because most Indian people have learned to function well in the modern world does not mean that the old ways are not practiced and held in honor. It's just that being a modern Native American means that you learn to function well in two worlds.

Indian people realize, as did everyone's ancestors, that a car is a more efficient means of transport than a horse, that TV is fun to watch, that books are a pleasure to read, and that you can usually make a better living as a doctor, skilled construction worker, or government worker than as a hunter and trapper or sheep herder. Indians can still dress in some of the most beautiful costumes the world has ever known, can still sing songs that have pleased the ear and the earth for centuries, can dance with a skill and grace you'll never forget, and create art that is world renowned. It's just that these things must be combined with the chores of everyday survival in today's complex and demanding societies.

Indians are both modern citizens and people fortunate to have hundreds of unique, living tribal heritages. Remember that Indians are people first and foremost, subject to the same hopes and fears as are humans of every race. Enjoy the traditional activities, but keep in mind, too, the people you see colorfully dancing are all potential friends, neighbors, co-workers, employees, and employers.

It is also important to realize that Indian people are not vanishing. Writers who speak of "last members" of various tribes do Indian people a disservice. Very few tribes are actually extinct and most of those were simply absorbed into other tribes (or non-Indian races) so that genetically even they still exist. In fact, the vast majority of Indian and Eskimo tribes still function, quite alive and increasing in numbers.

Indian and Eskimo populations in North America probably hit its low point after the influenza epidemic of 1918. By then the population was reduced to about a quarter of what it had been when Columbus arrived. Since about 1920, with improved health care and education, the Native North American population has continued to increase. The rise has been most spectacular since the 1960's and continues to grow rapidly today. The present Indian and Eskimo population in Canada, Greenland, and the United States may already surpass what it was in 1492, and certainly will top it by the year 2000. In other words, there will soon be more Indian and Eskimo people alive than any previous time in history.

Indian population figures are impressive. The 1980 US Census reports nearly 1,500,000 Indian, Eskimo, and Aleut citizens. Canada has over 300,000 citizens legally recognized as Indians and Inuit (Eskimo) plus an estimated 1,000,000 more people of predominately Indian and Eskimo ancestry. Thousands

of Eskimos also live in Greenland. Total Eskimo population is well over 100,000 people. Total Aleut population is about 10,000 people. Thus, we have a rapidly growing Native North American population today which exceeds three million people.

Indian people constitute one of the major ethnic groups in the world. In addition to the 3 million Indians in the US and Canada, another 40 million Indians live in Latin America. If you also include the 165 million Mestizos (people predominately Indian but with some non-Indian ancestry), we have a total of well over 200 million Indians in the world! The political, economic, and cultural impact of this many people has great potential. Latin American Indian leaders have been the first to perceive this potential and conferences have been held toward developing Indian bonds across national boundaries, especially with the goal of defeating poverty. Total North and South American Indian population exceeds that of every country in Europe, except the Soviet Union, and tops such major Asian nations as Japan and Korea combined. But let's return to the US and Canada.

Along with this increase in numbers, there has also been a cultural renaissance as well. Due to official government policy, disruptions by war and disease, and the effects of coping with a rapidly changing world, most Indian and Eskimo cultures suffered neglect for a time. For most groups, rock bottom was hit around the 1950's. In some cases, just a few dedicated individuals or families kept traditions alive. But along with the important new respect for minority people that came out of the Civil Rights Movement of the sixties, there also was a new appreciation for everyone's heritage. No one responded better than Indian and Eskimos, and today most groups proudly continue their traditions.

Today it is possible to attend outstanding Native American events with Indian people from every cultural area in North America: California, Southwest, Great Plains, Great Basin, Eastern Woodlands, Southeast, Northwest Coast, Arctic, and Subarctic. In every region of the US and Canada it is possible today to hear the beautiful songs, see the great dances, and meet the fine people whose ancestors originally owned your part of North America. Even in the cases where the tribe native to your home town no longer sponsors public events, culturally similar neighboring groups will give you a good insight into traditional Indian life in your area.

Most Indians do not live on reservations, especially in states like California with cities offering jobs. As a result, many Indian events are now also held in urban areas and are close at hand for large numbers of people. When ceremonies are held on the reservation, large numbers of urban Indians return for the festivities. We have met Indian people at remote reservations who turned out to be neighbors of ours, vacationing just as we were. Many of the reservation events also serve as a homecoming reunion for tribal members from all over the country.

CULTURAL AREAS

Anthropologists group Indian and Eskimo people into ten great "cultural areas". A cultural area is a geographical region where most Indians lived in a life style similar to one another. While no two tribes lived identical lives (and there is remarkable variation within cultural areas), the concept is useful in beginning to gain an understanding of traditional Indian life. Just remember that a cultural area is not an Indian concept and no group ever thought of themselves as living in a cultural area. The idea is "anthropological shorthand", useful to point out some prominent characteristics of each region of the continent.

CALIFORNIA CULTURAL AREA—This area is unique in many ways. First, it is the only one that corresponds closely to a state boundary. Central California was the heart of this region, where Indian people lived in bark, tule, or earthcovered houses. The people were hunters and gatherers, and the most important foods were the acorn, seeds, and fish. Medically sophisticated with complex ceremonial systems, California Indians made one of the world's great discoveries: they learned to live in relative peace. The strength of character, gentle kindness, and deep religious beliefs of many California Indian people soon becomes obvious to the visitor.

California was the most densely populated portion of pre-Columbian America. Today spectacular traditional dances are still performed, several villages have been reconstructed, fine museums abound, and some excellent art and crafts are made. Basketry reached its highest development in the world here. There are Indian doctors, both men and women, who continue to practice, and among a number of groups traditional religions thrive. The roundhouse (or dancehouse) is a center of religious life for many tribes. Anthropologists have called Indian California the most complex ethnographic area in the world and it remains a fascinating Native American region.

NORTHWEST COAST CULTURAL AREA—This cultural area extends along the Pacific Coast from Oregon through Washington and British Columbia to southern Alaska. It is world famous for its magnificent wood carvings including totem poles, large sea-going dugout canoes, spacious beautiful houses, and colorful masked dances. Salmon was the most important food and cedar the preferred wood for carving. Some anthropologists have called the Indian cultures here the most advanced non-agricultural societies in the world.

Today canoe racing is an active and exciting traditional sport. Salmon cooked Northwest Coast Indian style is a gourmet's delight. Many public events center around canoe races, often accompanied by a salmon bake and dancing. Reconstructed houses and villages, great museums (some of the best are tribally owned and operated), and high quality arts and crafts all combine to make the Pacific Northwest well worth a visit.

SOUTHWEST CULTURAL AREA—This area is comprised of Arizona, New Mexico, and northern Mexico. Traditional Native American activities are highly visible here. Agriculture was well developed in this arid region with special crops and innovative desert farming. Pueblo and Hopi villages, richly costumed ceremonies, magnificent pottery, other arts and crafts, and ancient ruins combine to make this a thriving portion of Indian America. There are many museums and arts and crafts stores.

Ancient religions form the core of many Indian communities. Many Indian nations here have fine cultural centers, motels, and restaurants. Events are frequent and well attended. Tribal councils often oversee multi-million dollar business corporations and a number of groups have model scholarship programs for their young people.

SOUTHEASTERN CULTURAL AREA—Southeastern Indians developed sophisticated political systems, agriculture, and artwork rivaling the ancient civilizations of Mexico. The boundaries of this region correspond closely to those of the Old South. Early in the 19th century most Southeastern Indians were brutally removed to Oklahoma due to political agitation by land greedy settlers. The forced evacuation of the tribes was called the "Trail of Tears" due to the tragic loss of Indian lives on the road west.

However, once in Oklahoma, Southeastern tribes responded by establishing independent nations complete with capitol buildings, schools, churches, farms and newspapers. As a result, the Creek, Cherokee, Choctaw, Chickasaw, and Seminole became known as the "Five Civilized Tribes". Later, other Indian Nations were settled in Oklahoma and Indian led government continued until their land was taken again in the late 19th Century.

Despite hardships, the Indian people of Oklahoma have long been and remain leaders among Native American people. Today many have achieved high positions in government, education, law, arts, business, literature, and other fields. Tribal governments here are often among the best run in North America.

Much traditional life remains among Southeastern Nations in Oklahoma. The Cherokee have completely reconstructed a historic village and offer tours led by Native American college students. Special festivals feature traditional activities and both Indian and non-Indian owned museums provide educational opportunities. Importantly, traditional religions are still practiced, particularly by the Creek, Seminole, Yuchi and some of the Cherokee. Opportunities exist to attend "stomp dances", an enjoyable and interesting form of traditional American Indian dancing unique to the eastern half of America.

Some Indians remained in the South, among them the Seminole in Florida, Choctaw in Mississippi, Cherokee in North Carolina, Catawba in South Carolina, and various groups in Louisiana. Some of these groups have carefully preserved many of the best aspects of their traditional life and have at the same time developed modern facilities for visitors. By combining a visit to Oklahoma with trips to some of the tribes still in the South, you can gain insight into the highly developed Southeastern Indian cultures.

GREAT PLAINS CULTURAL AREA—No group of Native Americans has influenced world-wide recognition of Native Americans as have the Plains Indian people. Plains Indian tribes inhabit the Great Plains of the US and Canada. In Europe, the international symbol for a campground is the Plains Indian tepee, perhaps the world's most widely known form of tent. From among the many differing Indian cultures, movies and television have generally chosen the Plains Indians as subjects for their dramas. This has been a mixed blessing. It has brought world-wide fame, but it has also resulted in much inaccurate information.

One particular misconception needs correction: that the Plains Indian people were a bloody, warlike group. Before the Euro-Americans arrived, life on the Plains was actually relatively peaceful. The noted anthropologist George E. Hyde discovered that aboriginal Pawnee houses were dispersed over a wide area of the Plains much like modern farms, allowing each family close access to its fields. Later, after Plains tribes received guns and horses and came under competition from European settlers for scarce resources the Pawnee were constantly under attack from hostile tribes. As a result, Pawnee houses became tightly clustered in protective groups. First encounters with the Dakota (Sioux) likewise indicated a fairly peaceful people. Indeed, Minnesota Sioux were driven west by tribes made war-like by European contacts. Later the Dakota became enmeshed in numerous wars, but their original nature seems to have been a peaceful one.

Plains cultures combined buffalo hunting with agriculture. The houses were usually earthcovered lodges or skin tepees. Eventually a life centering around the horse evolved. During the 19th Century most Plains tribes engaged in now famous battles with both Euro-Americans and other Indians. Today Plains Indian people live largely in the Midwest. Although many deeply religious ceremonies are held, the general public can most easily share in the exciting Plains culture through visits to pow-wows and tepee encampments.

EASTERN WOODLANDS CULTURAL AREA—This cultural area is located in what is now the northeastern United States and adjacent Canada. It extends west to include the Great Lakes. In the great American novels by James Finimore Cooper, northeastern Indian people star as some of the main characters. The Six Nations of the Iroquois, the most powerful Indian confederacy ever formed, was such an inspired form of government that Benjamin Franklin, Thomas Jefferson, and other founding fathers of the Republic are said to have been influenced by the Iroquois example when writing the US constitution. It was northeastern Indians who saved the Pilgrims lives by feeding them and teaching them Indian farming methods. The crops and game of the New England Algonquin Indians have become the basis of our modern Thanksgiving: turkey, pumpkin pie, corn on the cob, cranberries, and squash. All these were originally Indian foods and all were given freely by generous northeastern Indian people.

The Eastern Woodlands people were farmers, hunters, and fishermen. Homes were often longhouses or wigwams covered with bark, mats or skin. Iroquois and Delaware sacred dances featured fascinating masked beings. Our modern game of lacrosse, today's canoes, toboggans, snow shoes, and the most common style of moccasin shoes are inventions of Eastern Woodlands Indian people. Woodwork achieved high development here.

It may come as a surprise to some of our non-Indian readers, but most eastern Indian nations are alive and well today. Very much a part of modern America and Canada, high steel workers of the Mohawk and other Indian nations built New York City's tallest buildings. Most groups also carefully retain old traditions.

A Sioux Chief stands proudly atop the red catlinite cliffs of Pipestone National Monument in Minnesota. He holds a ceremonial pipe made of soft catlinite stone quarried from these very rocks. (Minnesota Office of Tourism, St. Paul)

Iroquois nations in New York, Ontario, and elsewhere all have outstanding celebrations open to the public which include some traditional dancing. Many Eastern Woodlands groups were driven west but still hold fine events in their new homes in Oklahoma, Minnesota, Kansas, Iowa, or Wisconsin.

GREAT BASIN and PLATEAU CULTURAL AREAS—This is the mountain rimmed high desert interior of the eastern portions of Washington, Oregon, California, southern Idaho, western Utah, and all of Nevada. Anthropologists were slow to realize the creative inventiveness of the region's original peoples. But the visitor is quick to appreciate the warmth, wit, and resourcefulness of modern Indian residents. Although there have been two hundred years of heavy influence from Plains tribes, most Great Basin Indian people retain a character uniquely their own.

The Great Basin is not generous in plant and animal resources when compared to other regions. Agriculture was almost impossible, although the Nuwuvi (southern Paiute), farmed quite successfully. Salmon runs in the north, pine nut harvests in the west, and rabbit hunts everywhere provided important foods. Nutritious roots were more important here than anywhere else and root festivals and pine nut festivals are still held. Houses were made of brush, mats or skins, depending on climate and available materials.

Today pow-wows are common with the best feature often being the fascinating traditional stick games (also called hand games, for details see TRIBAL LISTING: FLATHEAD). Traditional baby cradles of basketry covered with leather and elaborately beaded are seen at these celebrations. No baby ever had a finer home and skilled craftswomen are as proud of their art as the mothers are of the lovely babies they hold.

SUBARCTIC CULTURAL AREA—The Subarctic cultural area is comprised of non-coastal Northwest Territories and the Yukon in Canada and interior Alaska. Tribes here speak Athabaskan languages and often refer to themselves by the name Dene'. Hunting, trapping, and fishing were, and are, common ways of life. Drum dancing is a common musical form. Beautiful traditional Dene' Indian clothing of designer quality is made. Dene' moose or caribou hide moccasins, mukluks, jackets and the like are sold today and are of great beauty.

ARCTIC CULTURAL AREA—The Eskimo people of the coastal far north now often prefer to be called Inuit. These people based their life largely on the sea and developed rich artistic abilities. Inuit carvings, prints, and other artwork are prized. Dancing, music and games are exciting traditional events at many vil-

lages. Today the Inuit are developing many businesses in the North, including hotels, restaurants, and museums aimed at visitors. The opportunities to visit the Land of the Eskimo are greater and more exciting now than ever before.

ON THE ROAD TO INDIAN COUNTRY

It is important to understand that this book is written for both Indian and non-Indian people. We have seen traditional Indian cultures being admired and enjoyed by people of all races. Every tribe has unique contributions which increases our joy in living and our appreciation of the world. The great variety of Indian heritage is one thing that makes it so special. There is no one Indian or Eskimo culture, but rather hundreds of rich cultures. Indian people are well known for their magnificent art, dance, and clothing styles. But Indian people also have made and are currently making important contributions to agriculture, medicine, philosophy, architecture, religion, education, technology and much more. This book will discuss some of these contributions along with some of today's important issues.

My wife, Lisa, and I have spent the last five years traveling throughout most of the United States and into Canada visiting Indian people, events, and cultural institutions. We have tried to come as students, not so much to ask questions but to learn by the Indian way of listening and observing. If given a choice between finding out a fact or building a friendship we always tried to choose friendship. Before going to visit a Native American group I read many books and often telephoned the tribal office for advice on when to visit and what to see. Indian friends or anthropologists had helpful suggestions. If you were taking a trip to China, Italy, or Kenya you would similarly want to prepare yourself to do your best to be a good guest. Some of the more traditional Indian cultures are as different from Euro-American life in the US and Canada as any of those three countries. So you'll enjoy yourself the most and your trip will be more meaningful if you read as much as possible first.

But before you conclude that a trip to Indian Country is going to require years of reading and a personal friendship with dozens of Native Americans let me reassure you. Remember when I mentioned there has been a renaissance among Native North American people? Today many Indian groups are going all out to welcome visitors. Tribally owned resorts, inns, motels, restaurants, cultural centers, museums, arts and crafts shows, RV parks and campgrounds are all found in Indian Country. Of particular interest are many reconstructed traditional dwellings and even entire villages. Many of the cultural centers or tribal

The Oneida Nation Museum's reconstructed village. The framework of a partially completed longhouse can be seen at the left. A palisade fence surrounds the village for defense. (Oneida Nation Museum)

Longhouses in winter. This beautiful scene is at Ska-Nah-Doht Indian Village in Ontario. (Ska-Nah-Doht: Lower Thames Valley Conservation Authority)

Zuni Pueblo's dancers have appeared at every one of Gallup, New Mexico's Inter-Tribal Ceremonials since 1922. (Inter-Tribal Ceremonial Association)

The Inter-Tribal Ceremonials feature outstanding Native American dancing and art annually near Gallup, New Mexico. Here, a Pima dance group from Arizona's Gila River Reservation does the Basket Dance. (Inter-Tribal Ceremonial Association)

offices provide booking services for speakers or traditional dance groups for public performances. Thus, some Indian speakers or dance groups may even be able to come to your community. As detailed throughout the book there are countless special events such as ceremonial dances, pow-wows, fiestas, fund raisers, arts and crafts shows where visitors are welcome.

BEING A GOOD GUEST IN INDIAN COUNTRY

We have tried to list only public events in this book. Many events, in part, even depend on your coming for success as a larger crowd helps defray expenses. But there are some sacred ceremonies open to initiated members only and some private family occasions, too. The events listed in this book are virtually all public ones, but if you have doubts, tribal offices or cultural centers are good places to turn to for advice. The Bureau of Indian Affairs also can be helpful. Indian Centers located in major cities are also very helpful in learning about local Indian events where everyone is welcome.

Events vary in expected behavior. Many traditional Indian people believe that everyone who comes with a good heart helps make the event a success. A respectful, dignified attitude is usually appropriate. For sacred events, behave with the same respect you would at church or temple. Quiet, unobtrusive behavior is usually a good idea so as not to interfere with proceedings. Most Indian people are generous, gracious hosts and I have often been thanked for attending events and for my interest in the tribal culture. Many Indian people have said what matters is that you are Indian in your heart. The color of your skin does not matter.

Most Indian festivities prohibit or frown on alcohol or drugs and some reservations ban them completely. Dignified dress is usually a good idea as you're not at the beach, but often at a religious service.

At some of the big Indian events cameras are everywhere and you sometimes wonder if Kodak or Fuji might be sponsoring things. But at other times cameras or tape recorders are prohibited. Usually the people in charge will announce if photography is not permitted (the Hopi post signs). *But it is always important to ask those in charge if pictures or taping are allowed before photographing, taping or sketching.* It's always good form to ask permission before taking an individual's picture. Many times I've asked someone to pose for me. When I turn around there is a whole line of people, both Indian and non-Indian, taking a picture too. (Some events thoughtfully have a special time for photos and then ask that all picture taking occur only then. This is a good idea that seems to make everyone happy.) I usually offer to send the person a print if they would like one. It is a gift to be allowed to take someone's photo and they should, of course, be thanked graciously.

Finally, be sure and talk to Indian people with the same dignity and respect you would want yourself. Never use works like "brave", "squaw", "papoose", and other racist terms derived from the movies. Indian people also get tired of obviously ignorant questions, such as, "Do you live in a tepee?", "Do Indians still scalp people?" and so on. Your reading will make such questions unnecessary.

But enough "don'ts", let's spend the rest of the book focusing on "do's". Just watch your Indian hosts and take your cues from them about proper behavior. If you're confused, a polite inquiry should be all that's needed.

Many Indian events are free and those that charge an admission fee are almost always reasonably priced. Admission is rarely over a few dollars, plus sometimes photography and parking fees. Many pow-wows and other events operate at a loss and are supported financially by the tribe, individuals, or occasionally by local community groups. What money is earned usually goes to pay the drummers and singers or as prizes for the dancers if there is a contest. Dance groups are usually paid, as well. Sometimes donations are requested and I always try to donate generously. After all, you are getting several hours of high quality dancing and music and consider what you might have to pay for this in New York or San Francisco.

DANCES & CEREMONIES

When attending Indian events, an attitude of dignity and respect is a good start. An important distinction of most Indian events is whether they are sacred or social occasions. Some are a mixture of both. Sacred events or dances generally mean that the activities are aimed at accomplishing religious goals and a reverent attitude is proper. Often, photographs and taping are prohibited at these times. Some sacred activities are closed to non-Indians and Indians of other tribes, but many are open to courteous, respectful guests. Sacred events are not for show, but are of profound meaning and great importance to participants. The good will of each person attending is important and everyone needs to come with a good heart.

Social dancing and events are done for pleasure and most pow-wow activities fall into this category. It is still important to be respectful and a good, unobtrusive guest. Pictures and taping are usually allowed, but always check with those in charge first.

Since pow-wows are so common, a bit of detail about them may be helpful. There are both inter-tribal pow-wows and those sponsored by a particular tribe or band. Inter-tribal pow-wows generally have songs which are shared by people of various tribes, while tribally sponsored pow-wows may have these plus real tribal songs or even solely tribal songs. Tribally sponsored pow-wows are especially rewarding because they usually have dances and songs unique to the sponsoring Indian tribe.

Typically pow-wows are social occasions, sometimes with competitive dancing. If it is a competition pow-wow, the dancing is divided into age and sex categories and by dance type. For example, there will be "men's straight dancing", a more traditional dance style done with great dignity. The men's straight dancers often wear very traditional and impressive costumes. "Men's fancy dancing" usually features younger men in costumes with very large bustles, especially in Oklahoma. Complicated dance steps and a more rapid dancing is characteristic.

There are similar women's categories, although on the average the women dancers tend toward the dignity of the straight dancer style. Round dances and other dances where both men and women dance are also done. There are dances for girls and for boys too, and you'll see the next generation of dancers coming along. Sometimes a blanket dance is done. Donations are requested to help pay "the drum" (those who are singing), or to help raise money for someone in need, such as a sick elder. Everyone donates by placing money on a blanket set out for this purpose during the next song.

You may also see "give aways", when a family honors those who have helped them by giving away blankets or other items. There may also be an "honoring dance" where in a solemn and dignified manner friends and relatives dance around the grounds behind the person being honored.

At certain times you will be expected to stand, such as during an honoring dance and during the grand entry when the flag song is sung. Men usually remove their hats and a quiet, respectful attitude is appropriate.

Some pow-wows also have unique tribal songs and dances and these are a sign of really good pow-wows. Elders may also sing fine, old time songs seldom heard in public and these too are a special treat.

Some Indian people criticize competitive pow-wows because they tend to overlook real tribal dancing in favor of competitive Plains-type dances of a standard form. However, better pow-wows are now including more tribal dancing and trying to broaden the dances to include such dance types as stomp dances, California Indian dances, Iroquois dances, Pueblo dances, Northwest Coast dancing and the like.

For some tribes pow-wows *are* their old time dancing, but for most Indian groups tribal events or special performances offer the best opportunity to see real traditional dancing. This is because many tribes never did any pow-wow dancing until recent years, although Plains tribes have done the grass dance (from which pow-wow dancing is descended) for centuries.

For Indian people in the East, South, Southwest, California, Northwest Coast, Subarctic, and Arctic regions, other types of dancing are the real traditional dances. Let's look at each of these cultural areas.

CALIFORNIA—This dancing is highly distinctive with two major regional styles. In Central California, orange flicker-feather headbands and sacred "Big head" costumes are worn by men. Generally a wrap of buckskin, tule reeds, or animal skins is worn at the waist. Necklaces of abalone or clam shell and wooden whistles are worn around the neck. Large beaded belts are often worn, too, replacing early feathered belts. The Pomo, Miwok, Nomlaki, and Maidu all dance using these costumes. The Maidu also wear a bear dance outfit during their June bear dances. California dances used to be seen only in central California but increasingly dance groups are traveling to Oklahoma and elsewhere. Their beautiful songs and dances are very popular among Indians and non-Indians alike.

Central California Indian women dancers, especially among the Pomo and Miwok, wear lovely long dresses of cloth or buck cloth. These are often decorated with finely worked shells and beads. The Pomo women sometimes wear headpieces made of a roll of fur with petite orange flicker feather shafts and beads dangling from them. The effect makes a European queen's crown seem half as beautiful.

In Northwestern California (Humboldt, Trinity, and Del Norte counties), the Hupa, Karuk and to a lesser degree Yurok and Tolowa still perform their unique dances. The white deerskin dance, using albino deerskins and wolf hair headdresses, is famous. Less well known but equally impressive are the brush dance and the jump dance. Brilliant red head bands

California Indian music and dance is unexcelled in North America and includes fascinating instruments. Pomo dancer David Smith holds a pair of split stick clappers to accompany the beat of the singing. In the background another Pomo dancer blows a whistle made of a pair of hollow reeds. (R. Shanks)

Bill Franklin, Miwok elder, has done much to bring Miwok culture to others. He and his family and friends have an excellent traditional Miwok dance group that performs at central California Indian events. Mr. Franklin wears the exquisitely beautiful California Indian headband of orange flicker feather shafts with the black tips of the feathers still attached. (R. Shanks)

Many California Indian young people are learning the ancient songs thanks to such dedicated families as the Brown family of Lake County, California. These boys and girls are grandchildren of Malvina Brown, a charming lady who has worked hard to pass on her Pomo heritage to her children and grandchildren. Robinson Rancheria Land Celebration, Lake County, California, 1983. (R. Shanks)

Cahuilla singers with gourd rattles in hand present traditional bird songs to an appreciative audience at the annual Malki Museum Fiesta at Morongo Indian Reservation near Banning, California. (R. Shanks)

A beautiful young Pomo woman wears a traditional California Indian dress decorated with abalone shells and a headpiece of fur with flicker feather and bead pendants. Point Arena Coastal Pomo Dancers. (R. Shanks)

Jim Skye Iroquois Dancers wearing Iroquois gus-to-weh headdress, finger woven sashes, leggings, and moccasins of Eastern Woodland tradition. Schoharie Museum, New York. (Association for the Advancement of Native North American Arts and Crafts)

of woodpecker feathers are worn by the men along with all kinds of finery. The women wear beautiful basketry caps and lovely skirts decorated with shell and pine nut beads.

Major musical instruments are the split stick clapper, whistles, deerhoof rattles, foot drum, and (in Northwestern California) the rectangular hand drum. Central California Indian people usually go barefoot as they dance to keep in close contact with the earth. Both public performances and sacred dancing are done today. Dancing is done: (1) inside a ceremonial roundhouse, (2) outdoors in front of the dance house, or (3) within a brush enclosure. In Northwestern California, a round sunken amphitheater is built with benches around the rim. Dancing may also be done in the open at sacred locations.

EASTERN WOODLANDS—Traditional dancing continues both at religious ceremonies and at public celebrations sponsored by the Iroquois, Passamaquoddy, Sac & Fox, Ojibwa, and others. Among the Iroquois, religious dancing is done in the longhouse, closed to the public on some reserves but open to guests on others. The easiest way to see fine Iroquois and other Eastern Woodlands dancing is at special public events or regularly scheduled cultural presentations.

Traditional dance costumes are quite beautiful with lovely beaded leggings and dresses ornamented with old time Iroquois or Algonquian designs. The men often wear the gus-to-weh headdresses, one of native North America's artworks. Public dancing is often done outdoors with dancers moving in a long line while singers sit nearby. Water drums and rattles made of cow horn, elm bark, or a snapping turtle accompany the singing. Eastern Woodlands music and dance is outstanding, although unfortunately some groups have been adopting Plains clothing, music and dance at the expense of their own culture. Still, there are good opportunities to see high quality Eastern Woodlands dances. Many eastern Indian people are working hard to preserve their irreplaceable traditions.

The term "longhouse" deserves explanation. It has three meanings today, two of which pertain to the Eastern Woodlands. Originally, it referred most commonly to the bark covered dwellings of the Iroquois and their neighbors in the northeast. These Iroquois old time longhouses were shaped like the quonset huts of World War II fame. They can be seen today at several reconstructed Iroquois and Huron villages. The modern Iroquois use the term longhouse to refer to the long, narrow frame buildings used today for

ceremonials. These are modern style structures, but inside the traditional dancing and singing of the Longhouse Religion continues. The third meaning of the word is used in Washington State, British Columbia and Alaska. A longhouse in this region refers to Northwest Coast style traditional dwellings, whether ancient or modern. Usually these plank or board buildings are good sized with large traditional paintings on the walls. Often totem poles are attached or raised nearby.

NORTHWEST COAST—Indian people in western Washington, British Columbia, and southern Alaska are renowned for their carved wooden masks, finely woven capes, and colorful button blankets. Dancing is done both indoors (it's often rainy here and some dances are supposed to be done only in the winter) or outside, often near the sea. The Kwakiutl, Nootka, Makah, Tlingit, Tsimshian, Coast Salish and others dance and sing the ancient music. Hearing the echoing drum inside the longhouse, watching the clapping beaks of the bird masks open and rapidly close, while everything is accompanied by hauntingly beautiful music of the Northwest Coast is unforgettable.

Religious "Spirit Dancing" is not generally done for the public, but a number of important Indian nations in the area do sponsor public events where traditional Northwest Coast dancing may be seen. These events are often a combination of dancing, singing, dugout canoe races, a salmon bake (cooked the delicious Indian way), and arts and crafts show.

SOUTHEAST—Indian dancing and music continues today, thriving in Oklahoma, Mississippi, and Florida. Perhaps the most characteristic dance form is the stomp dance. The most important religious event is the Green Corn ceremony. Creek, Yuchi, Cherokee, Seminole, Shawnee, Choctaw, Natchez and others all still do these ancient dances.

The stomp dance actually extends from Florida to Maine along the east coast, but is most prominent among Southeastern tribes. Typically beginning late in the night, stomp dances frequently last until sunrise. Often part of religious ceremonies, stomp dances must have been common among the ancient mound builders. Some of the dance patterns correlate with the designs on ancient mound builder pottery as the dances might be seen from a higher elevation, as from the top of a mound. The dancers move in a line behind a leader who not only sets the pace and path of the dance, but leads the singing, too. Dancers repeatedly answer the leader's musical chant with pleasing refrains.

In the Papago chelkona dance participants carry the symbol of I'itoi and the path of life as well as images of thunder clouds and sea gulls. This exquisite dance features interesting dance patterns and calming music. (R. Shanks)

The dances are called "stomp dances" because the participants gracefully stomp their feet in short steps in time to the music. Women generally wear leg rattles about their lower legs, usually made of terrapin (turtle) shells, or lacking these, made of tin cans. Pebbles are placed in the shells or cans and the sound is pleasing and rhythmic, especially with the terrapin leg rattles. Dancing is usually done around a fire. During more important dances, the women wear beautiful dresses, made colorful by ribbonwork. From the back of their heads, hair ornaments with long ribbons trailing down add a touch of beauty. The men dress simply, usually wearing ribbonshirts or street clothes, occasionally topped by a cowboy hat with an attached feather or two. The stomp dance season runs from May through October and the dances are generally held in tribal town squares, although some dances occur in Oklahoma pow-wows late in the evening after the Plains dancing is over.

The sacred Green Corn Dance is the high point of the Ceremonial year and includes the beautiful feather dance where men carry white crane feathers atop poles. A variety of other interesting dances are performed during Green Corn. (For details SEE: TRIBAL LISTINGS—CREEK.)

Southeastern dancing makes the days of the mound builders come alive again and is a favorite among many Native Americans and other music lovers.

PLAINS—Plains Indian dancing is the best known and most commonly seen type of Indian dances. Most people will see pow-wow competition dancing with its elaborately beautiful costuming. Plains people did and still do other types of dances as well, including the sacred sun dance. Because we have described pow-wows elsewhere, we should mention that some fine Plains tribal dancing continues and magnificent old warrior society dances and songs are being revived. The Comanche and Kiowa have been among the leaders in this area and are to be congratulated on preserving songs and dances unique to their people. Many tribes host huge celebrations attracting thousands of visitors, both Indian and non-Indian. Crow Fair, the Pawnee Homecoming Pow-wow, and various Sioux events are examples of big time pow-wows. The Anadarko, Oklahoma area is rich in southern Plains dancing.

SOUTHWEST—Southwestern Indian music is as varied as the many tribes which live in this arid region. Hopi and Pueblo, Pima and Papago, Mojave and Cocopah, Apache and Navajo, Walapai and others all have dancing quite different from one another. Hopi and Pueblo dancing is characterized by large men's choruses, drumming, and elaborately costumed religious dancing. The Hopi and Pueblo are gracious about welcoming guests, but are quite strict about prohibiting photos or taping at sacred dances. Some Pueblo social dancing can be photographed, but check first.

The Hopi and Zuni are famous for their masked Kachina and Shalako dances where the participants represent spiritual beings. In the well known Hopi Snake Dance, men dance with snakes in their mouths. Yet it must be remembered that this is a religious rite, not a performance. The Hopi and Pueblo people are farmers and since rain is a rare commodity in the Southwest, many ceremonies center around ensuring good crops.

The Apache mountain spirit dancers (often called crown dancers) rank among the best in North America with their masks, altar-like headdresses, and distinctive head and arm movements. Their Navajo neighbors also have unforgettable dancing and music, and with its high pitch singing is unmistakable among all North American Indian people. You'll be captivated by the Navajo chants.

The Papago and Pima have their lovely dances, too, and the women can be seen in long, flowing dresses often carrying finely coiled baskets on their heads. The Papago "skipping and scraping (or Chelkona) dance" where participants carry seagull, cloud, and lightning effigies is a favorite.

The Walapai, Mojave, and Cocopah all do bird songs with very graceful dancing and pleasing music. Watch for the fine gourd rattles of the men and the beaded shoulder collars of the women.

PLATEAU and GREAT BASIN—In the Plateau and Great Basin country there are some fine Native American events. During handgames beautiful traditional songs are sung. Bear dances with the rasp like sounds of the bear are a specialty of the Ute. Pow-wow dancing is everywhere. Some groups proudly preserve unique tribal songs which can be heard nowhere else. Root celebrations are important among many of this region's Indian nations as they were major food sources. Large tepee encampments are held by the Yakima, Colville and others, and the Walker River Paiute hold an annual pine nut festival.

SUBARCTIC—The Subarctic region of interior Alaska, the Yukon, and Northwest Territories still has local Indian celebrations with very good music and drumming. Drum dances are representative here.

ARCTIC—In the Arctic, the Inuit or Eskimo people are very famous for their masked dances, large hand drums, and their unique music. Many villages sponsor periodic dances where visitors are welcome.

MEXICO—Mexican Indian dancing is increasingly being performed in the US. Aztec dancers perform everywhere from Wisconsin Dells to Albuquerque. Los Voladores, Mexican flying dancers who dive off a high pole and whirl around it hanging from ropes, have performed at the Indian Pueblo Culture Center in Albuquerque. Sedona, Arizona, has Tlaquepaque Day when Huichol, Yaqui, and other Mexico tribes arrive for festivities and dancing.

INDIAN TIME

Some Indian groups are very punctual in starting events at the announced time. Some other events may begin at the specified time, but later activities will pretty much occur according to no fixed schedule. At other events, festivities may begin hours after the advertised time. It is important to have a flexible attitude about when events are scheduled to start and when they actually begin.

Native American people often joke about "Indian time". This is in reference to the fact that some Indian events begin much later than the announced time. As one Pomo elder said, "If we're late please forgive us, remember we're on Indian time today." While some may find lateness a frustration, the best approach is to go on Indian time yourself. Slow down your pace and accept that events will occur at some time during the day or night and just relax. You'll soon find yourself in a pleasantly relaxed state and will have a better time than by being on "hurry up whitemen's time."

INDIAN HUMOR

You'll probably hear Indian humor at some events. Some of the very best humorists are Native Americans, remember Will Rogers, a Cherokee? Indian humor is often self-effacing. Example: I once asked a Cherokee craftswoman if I could take her picture weaving a basket. She laughed and said, "Sure, put it in the funny papers!" I replied, "Well, if I do, it will be right next to my picture!" We both laughed and it is a happy memory. Notice that the butt of each of our jokes was ourselves, not the other person.

Some pow-wow announcers are quite funny and you'll hear some Indian humor that way. But the best is always the kidding between two or three people. You catch on after a while and learn how to do it. Be patient, careful, and listen like any good student. Indian humor is little known outside the Indian community, but it is unexcelled in warmth, good natured feelings, and wit.

BUYING ARTS AND CRAFTS

Today Native American and Canadian people work both in traditional and contemporary art styles. Some artists combine Native American techniques with those from other continents to produce unique results. Native American people are unsurpassed worldwide in their ability to produce beautiful and meaningful artwork. Arts and crafts are important sources of income for many Indian people, in part because such employment allows a person to remain closer to a traditional lifestyle than do many other jobs. But beyond this, many Native American people gain a great deal of personal satisfaction from creating beautiful and often functional arts and crafts.

Tribal culture centers, museum gift shops, Indian operated shops, individual Indian artists booths at pow-wows and other events, tribal crafts associations, and the like are great places to shop. Hundreds of these places are listed in this book. Prices are often cheaper since there is not the overhead or large markup of an expensive shop in a high rent district.

Be sure to research your area of interest. Read some of the many good books that cover nearly all aspects of Indian products. Visit museums and cultural centers to see fine examples of the type of work that interests you. Talk with knowledgeable people about the subject. The following magazines will also be very helpful. All list many dealers in Indian art.

INDIAN ARTS AND CRAFTS MAGAZINES

INDIAN TRADER MAGAZINE, a monthly newsmagazine lists many art shows, pow-wows, and other special events. Articles focus on Indian arts and crafts, history, contemporary issues, and outstanding Native American artists. One of your best sources of current activities in the world of Indian arts and crafts. To subscribe write: 603 South Second St, Box 1421, Gallup, NM 87301. Phone (505) 722-6694.

INDIAN ART MAGAZINE, a quarterly magazine, provides current information on galleries, museum exhibits, auctions, and books. Beautifully printed articles deal with major collections, museums, development and transitions in arts and crafts, etc. Emphasis on fine old collectors' items. To subscribe write: 7314 East Osborn Dr, Scottsdale, AZ 85251.

AMERICAN INDIAN BASKETRY, a quarterly magazine, covers basketry of past and present. Very useful to those interested in this highly advanced Native American art form. To subscribe write: Box 66124, Portland, OR 97266.

Also see the listing for the INDIAN ARTS AND CRAFTS

A selection of North American Indian music available from Canyon Records. (Copyright Canyon Records. Used with permission. Courtesy of Raymond Boley.)

ASSOCIATION under NEW MEXICO—ALBUQUERQUE.

INDIAN AND ESKIMO MUSIC ON RECORDS AND TAPES

There is a good selection of Native North American music recordings available today. These are generally of high quality. There are both long playing records and tapes available, although tapes are beginning to replace records at some companies. Plains, Southwest, and Plateau music is plentiful and there is a moderate supply of Eastern Woodlands and Southeastern music available commercially. However, there is a shortage of California, Northwest Coast, Subarctic and Eskimo records and tapes. Perhaps one or more of the producers will take steps to fill this need. The first six producers listed here all have catalogs.

Listening to Indian and Eskimo music gives great pleasure and emotional release. These are songs that have come from this land and whose roots are deep in North American history. Happy listening.

CANYON RECORDS
4143 North Sixteenth St
Phoenix, AZ 85016
(602) 226-4823
Canyon Records is the largest producer of Indian music in the US. They have a catalog and large retail store. Their recordings are of high quality and consist of both traditional and contemporary Indian music. They are very strong on Plains, Southwest, and Prairie Province music. Some unusual selections include Yakima, Caddo, Pima, and Papago music. Canyon Records also carries the recordings of several other producers as well. All of Canyon's recordings I've heard have been of high quality. Also SEE: ARIZONA—PHOENIX.

Papago high school students from Arizona present the traditional chelkona dance. A girl gracefully carries a basket made of yucca atop her head. These attractive, flowing gowns are traditional. (R. Shanks)

FOLKWAYS RECORDS
632 Broadway, 9th floor
New York, NY 10012
(212) 777-6606

Indian and Eskimo music is just one part of Folkways large line of products. Ask for their "Recordings of North American Indians" brochure. Folkways offers some rare Northwest Coast and Eskimo music. Their Seneca Social Dance Music and Nootka songs are among my favorites, but a few of their records were made long ago and may be below your standards of quality. Their newer recordings I've heard have been excellent, however.

INDIAN HOUSE
Box 472
Taos, NM 87571
(505) 776-2953

Indian House is very strong on high quality Southwestern recordings, with a large selection of Navajo and Pueblo records and tapes. Also, plenty of Plains (especially Kiowa, Sioux and Ponca) recordings are available as well. A real treat are the four recordings of Stomp Dances of the Creek, Yuchi, and Seminole. They have a catalog and take phone orders. All Indian House recordings I've heard have been of high quality.

INDIAN RECORDS
Box 47
Fay, OK 73646
(405) 887-3316

Indian Records specializes in Plains and Plateau music. They have a large selection of tapes and some records from the Sioux and Crow, west to the Warm Springs and Umatilla. The Indian House recordings I have heard have all been of good quality. Mail order catalog.

IROQRAFTS
RR 2
Ohsweken Ontario, Canada NOA IMO
(416) 765-4206

Located on the Six Nation's Grand River Indian Reserve, this business is owned by Guy Spittal, an Iroquois. Mr. Spittal is a singer of traditional Iroquois songs and he and several others have combined their talents to produce a three volume record series called Iroquois Social Dance Songs. These are high quality records with explanatory text and this is a delight for those wanting Eastern Woodlands music. Send two dollars for their catalog of fine Woodlands arts and crafts which includes the record listings.

LIBRARY OF CONGRESS
MUSIC DIVISION—RECORDING LABORATORY
Washington, DC 20540
(202) 287-5000

The Library of Congress sells a series of records of Native American music. A few are early recordings of fair quality, but by far most of their records are of excellent quality. They cover much of the US including Delaware, Cherokee, Paiute, Seneca, and many others. Write for their catalog of American Indian music.

LOWIE MUSEUM OF ANTHROPOLOGY
103 Kroeber Hall
University of California
Berkeley, CA 94720
(415) 642-3681

Lowie Museum has an outstanding collection of tapes on California Indian music available. The five tape series is called a "Sampler of California Indian music". These tapes cover the three main cultural regions of the state—central, northwestern, and southern California. High quality selections of Pomo, Yokuts, Wintun, Yurok, Tolowa, Cahuilla, Western Mono, and other tribes music are presented.

CLIFF DWELLINGS and INDIAN MOUNDS

The United States is blessed with two spectacular types of archeological wonders. The first of these are the cliff dwellings and other stone and adobe buildings found primarily in Arizona, Colorado, New Mexico, and Utah. Whole communities of these fascinating structures may be seen today. Cliff dwellings are located on sheer cliffs on the faces of massive rock monoliths in desert and forest country. Some are four stories high while others contain hundreds of rooms. Other Southwest ruins are on flat plains and are Biblical appearing structures looking like ruins from ancient Babylon. There are fortress-like towers, subterranean ceremonial chambers (called kivas), vast irrigation canal systems, astronomical observatories, apartment houses, amphitheaters and much more. All types can be explored today. Check the listings for the four states mentioned above.

The Southwest is not the only part of the country with enchanting marvels of ancient Indian builders. Much of the eastern half of America is dotted with scattered Indian mounds and other earthworks. These mounds and other earthen structures were built by laboriously hauling baskets of soil and rock to create some of the wonders of the new world. The ancient Indian people built mounds reaching a hun-

Boulder House in Hovenweep National Monument is a good example of the intriguing defensive towers you can visit. Ancient Indians built these hundreds of years ago. (National Park Service)

dred feet in height and assuming many different shapes. Some were the bases of sacred temples while others became the tombs of great leaders. Some were conical, while others were flat topped. Mounds were even constructed in the form of animals—bears, serpents, birds, deer, or panthers. These are called "effigy mounds" and are found primarily in Iowa, Wisconsin, Ohio and neighboring states. Temple and burial mounds and other earthworks are most common in Illinois, Georgia, West Virginia, Alabama, Mississippi, Tennessee, Indiana, Ohio, and Oklahoma. Check the listings for all these and neighboring states and you'll find many mounds to visit.

MUSEUMS AND PARKS: A NEW POTENTIAL

Increasingly, better parks and museums are hiring Indian employees to serve as directors, curators, interpreters, planners, rangers, maintenance people, etc. Traditional Indian people are invaluable as cultural consultants and staff members. Many are willing and qualified to assume such duties. Their lifelong training by traditional Indian educational methods cannot be replaced by an academic degree. The concept of non-Indians alone presenting Indian culture is outdated and inadequate. Ideas, philosophies, beliefs, rituals, and a thousand other details not even dreamed of by most non-Indians tend to be overlooked or misinterpreted without Indian guidance. Fortunately many of the institutions listed here have already hired Indian staff members and established Indian Advisory Boards.

In our book we have given special emphasis to tribally owned museums and cultural centers. They are direct expressions of the people and provide unique insights into the Indian Way. Hopefully, one day nearly every Indian and Inuit group in North America will have their own cultural heritage center. Knowledgeable private donors and responsive government agencies already help with funding as do many tribal governments and Indian associations. Such museums and centers say, "This is who we are and this is what we would like you to know about us."

Indian people of North America have always produced outstanding leaders. Among them are the chiefs of the Five Civilized Tribes of Oklahoma. Five distinguished leaders are at an Inter-Tribal Council Meeting at the Cherokee Capitol in Tahlequah, Oklahoma. From left to right are: Chief Hollis Roberts of the Choctaw Nation, Chief Claude Cox of the Creek (Muscogee) Nation, Chief Wilma Mankiller of the Cherokee Nation, Chief Ed Tanyan of the Seminole Nation, and Governor Overton James of the Chickasaw Nation. Chief Wilma Mankiller is the first Native American woman to become chief of a large US Indian tribe. (Creek Nation Communications Center—Helen Chalakee)

Indian people have become leaders in the field of law. The Native American Rights Fund (NARF) has won major Supreme Court victories benefiting thousands of Indian and Inuit people. Arlinda Locklear, at left, was the first Indian woman attorney to argue a case before the Supreme Court. She is a Lumbee, a major tribe in North Carolina. Henry Sockbeson, a Penobscot, is also an outstanding attorney on NARF's Washington, DC, staff. (Native American Rights Fund—Boulder, Colorado)

SOME MAJOR TRENDS AND ISSUES IN INDIAN COUNTRY

INDIAN OWNED AND OPERATED BUSINESSES

Indian owned businesses are many and varied. These include lumber mills, hotels, resorts, canneries, commercial fishing, mini-marts, shopping centers, bingo enterprises, smoke shops, tour services, river rafting, mineral and oil extracting, farming, cattle and sheep ranching, office and warehouse ownership and leasing, garment making, manufacturing (furniture, dolls, clocks, etc.), industrial parks, etc.

Many tribes have developed skilled, well trained Indian business and professional leaders who competently manage such enterprises. There have been some failures, just as there are in non-Indian operated businesses. But year by year the number, size, and profitability of these Indian owned and operated businesses increases.

Indian businesses are often among the most imaginative and innovative around. Witness Lummi aquaculture, Apache jojoba processing, and Choctaw manufacturing. For those who doubt the business ability of Native Americans, plan a stay at such four star rated hotels as the Kah-Nee-Tah lodge in Oregon or the Sheraton Anchorage Hotel in Alaska. Both are Native American owned and operated, the former by the Warm Springs tribe and the latter by the Eskimo people. Many other fine Indian motels, hotels, and inns are listed in the GUIDE.

One recent business many tribes have entered is operating bingo recreational enterprises. These are generally highly profitable and create jobs where they are desperately needed. In some cases, the new bingo enterprise has transformed reservations from discouraged, impoverished places to places of hope, high employment and pride. Profits are invested in developing other reservation businesses such as retail stores, manufacturing companies and agricultural lands. College and technical school scholarships are provided as well. It seems better to have gambling money create needed jobs for Indian families than to slip away to organized professional gamblers and disappear from the community. Increased job opportunities and business development is a major goal on many reservations. See Ojibwa listings in Minnesota and Choctaw listings in Mississippi for additional information on Indian business.

INDIAN AGRICULTURE

Ever since the New England Algonquin tribes saved the Pilgrims' lives by teaching them Native American agriculture and introducing them to Indian crops, Indians have been renowned for their ability in farming. A tribute to this is a typical Thanksgiving dinner of turkey, pumpkin pie, cranberry sauce, corn bread, and sweet potatoes, all entirely Native American in origin. Although not all tribes had the need to farm, those that did were often quite sophisticated. The Hohokam and other ancient people of the Southwest (ancestors of the Pima and Papago), had complex, extensive irrigation systems with canals over miles of desert land. Some of these canals can still be seen today. The Cahuilla of southern California dug huge walk-in wells which supplied water in the desert.

The Papago method of dry farming the Arizona desert was very impressive. This practice is now being studied by scientists as a solution to the arid Southwest's water shortage. Special crops of beans and other plants were developed which could grow very quickly immediately after brief desert downpours. Fields were cleared, planted, and left to await the rain. Carefully located by Native American farmers, the water ran down to the right spot and watered the fields. The quick growing plants then matured on this minimal rainfall and a crop was harvested. Some Papago farmers still farm this way and its potential is exciting.

The Hopi of northern Arizona have developed special strains of corn that can actually grow in sand dunes. The corn plants have deep roots which go far below the surface to reach moisture deep in the dune.

Modern Apaches in Arizona import (from the Cochimi tribe in Mexico) and gather the desert jojoba (ho-HO-buh) bean so popular in shampoos and for industrial uses as a substitute for whale oil. Jojoba is a desert plant and grows well in Arizona and is an ideal crop which can be grown without irrigation. Other arid adapted plants are being experimented with and may revolutionize agriculture by reducing the dependency on irrigation water. Many Southwest Indian groups, with large areas of desert land, are among the leaders in such research and development.

FISHERIES

In the Pacific Northwest, commercial fisheries are a major industry and Native Americans have struggled to establish rights to a significant percentage of the harvest. Tribes such as the Quinault Nation operate their own canneries and many individual Indian people own commercial fishing boats. The Lummi Nation actually farms the ocean. Its aquaculture farm has been featured in many news articles. Northwest

Chief Phillip Martin of the Mississippi Band of Choctaw has led his people to economic and educational progress by attracting industry to their reservation and encouraging higher education. Here he confers with Voncile Bull at the Choctaw Greeting Card plant. (Mississippi Band of Choctaw Communications Program)

Business development is stressed among the six reservations of the Minnesota Chippewa Tribe, and the Ojibwa people have built excellent business enterprises. At White Earth Reservation, Ojibwa assistant manager Rob Steck works at Ojibwa Forest Products, a tribally owned lumber business. (White Earth Tribal Council—Norma Felty)

Creating jobs and reducing unemployment is a major goal of many tribal governments. Among the most successful are the Mississippi Band of Choctaw. The Choctaw Industrial Park on the Reservation near Philadelphia, Mississippi, has attracted some of America's largest corporations and a number of plants operate here. This is a wire harness plant, a part of Chahta Enterprises. (Communications Program—Mississippi Band of Choctaw Indians)

Many Indians are successful commercial fishermen in the Pacific Northwest. The joy of a career on the sea is evident in this Northwest Coast Indian fisherman's face. (Northwest Indian Fisheries Commission—Steve Robinson)

Indian tribes in the Pacific Northwest manage one of the most important fisheries in the United States. Careful planning and a strong emphasis on protecting fish habitat results in increased fish resources for everyone. Here, a watershed planning meeting is held under the guidance of the Indian Fisheries Commission of Olympia, Washington. Indian and non-Indian fisheries people are now working together to manage fish harvests. (Northwest Indian Fisheries Commission—Steve Robinson)

Coast Indian nations are considered leaders in the field of fisheries management.

The fisheries management activities of the Pacific Northwest Indian people are exciting. Seventeen tribes have established hatcheries which currently release over 32 million fish annually to the benefit of commercial and sport fishermen. Individual tribes engage in creative efforts to restore fish habitats, reintroduce fish to barren streams, eliminate migration barriers and fight pollution.

For example, the Tulalip Tribe, Trout Unlimited and the Forest Service recently joined forces to remove sediment and debris to rehabilitate a major stream. The stream is now habitable again and fish have returned to spawn. The Nisqually Tribe has been working with Weyerhaeuser Timber to restock extremely remote areas using helicopters equiped with 400 gallon buckets. Young salmon are flown to remote headwaters to restore fish populations. The Skagit System Co-op made up of the Swinomish, Upper Skagit, and Sauk-Suiattle tribes, is developing a superior broodstock of steelhead which will return from the sea to their river homes for faster spawning. Hopefully, fish survival rates will improve and the population will increase.

There are many other innovative fisheries management activities of the Pacific Northwest Indian tribes and nations. Many of these Native American directed programs go far beyond routine fisheries management requirements and strive for excellence in the field. As Northwest Indian Fisheries Commission Chairman Billy Frank, a Nisqually, explains, "The fish is our heritage. It is who we are. We must all help the salmon in his struggle to survive." For more information SEE: WASHINGTON—OLYMPIA and TRIBAL LISTINGS—LUMMI.

INDIAN FOODS AND RESTAURANTS

A number of the tribes listed operate excellent restaurants offering both Indian and non-Indian foods. The Hopi, Pueblo, Ojibwa, Cherokee, Pima, Eskimo, Miccosukee, and others all have restaurants, most with delicious tribal specialties. At pow-wows, ceremonials, and other celebrations inter-tribal favorites such as fry bread, Indian tacos, and the like are served. At very traditional events you may be lucky enough to be offered Miwok acorn mush, Quinault salmon, Navajo mutton, Hopi piki bread, Stockbridge-Munsee hull corn soup, and other less common but gourmet quality treats. Some groups annually have deep pit barbecues where foods are cooked in underground ovens and the beef will be among the most tender and flavorsome you've ever had. Native American cooking seems on the verge of becoming a well known and popular cuisine. In Washington state, Tillicum Village is a model of what a fine Indian restaurant can be as are the Southwest's Hopi Culture Center restaurant and the Indian Pueblo Cultural Center restaurant in Albuquerque. There are an increasing number of Native American cookbooks written by qualified Indian home economists and chefs.

A large percentage of everyday foods were originally developed by Indian people in North and South America. Foods that came from the Indian people include corn, tomatoes, potatoes, cranberries, beans, squash, pumpkins, pineapple (yes, they were planted in Hawaii), avocados, salmon, abalone, turkeys, strawberries, and much more. The Southwest Museum of Los Angeles has a large poster illustrating Native American food contributions. The list seems to go on forever. Food must have been plain indeed before the Indian cooks and farmers helped improve it!

EDUCATION

Including Native American studies and language programs in our schools is important to Indian and non-Indian people alike. Most history classes concentrate on only the last 300 years of US and Canadian history, while the lives of the people who have occupied the continent for the preceding 20,000 to 50,000 years are largely ignored. Indian and Eskimo people learned a great deal in such a long period. There are important lessons about ecology, medicine, food resources, agriculture, architecture, philosophy, religion, tools, public speaking, art, and the like which need to be taught to everyone in our schools and colleges. Our education has long been biased toward a European perspective and is consequently weakened by ignoring the insights and contributions of Indians, Inuit, and other non-Europeans.

For Indian and Inuit youngsters, ethnic studies programs can greatly increase their chances for success in school. The Makah Nation of Washington began teaching the Makah language in the public schools with excellent results. The Makah children's test scores in English showed a marked increase after having enrolled in Makah language and culture classes. In fact, for the first time in the school system's history, Indian children outscored white youngsters in English achievement tests. The Makah classes both helped Indian children grasp language construction and rules and spurred their interest in education.

It is important, too, that Native American and Native Canadian people be on the teaching staff, the school board, and hired as consultants to teach special pro-

Education begins early for many young Native
Americans. These are some of Creek Nation's recent
graduates in the Head Start program. Both Indian
and non-Indian youngsters participate. (Creek Nation
Communications Center—Elliot Barnett)

Yanush Tubby wears a Choctaw shirt for the annual
Choctaw Tribal Thanksgiving Feast near
Philadelphia, Mississippi. Tribes such as the Choctaw
stress the importance of education for their young
people. (Mississippi Band of Choctaw Indians—
Communication Program)

grams. I know of school districts with large Indian populations with no Indian teachers and no Indian school board members. There is bitterness toward the school districts and this hurts children's educations. With so many young Native Americans graduating from college these days such a situation is shamefully inexcusable. Better school districts seek qualified Native American and Canadian teachers, offer Indian studies programs, and hire talented Indian and Eskimo community members to teach special programs.

Leaders of the Indian community should be encouraged and supported in their efforts to obtain seats on the school boards. Such school districts have better results. It says something to a youngster when she or he sees Native North American people teaching, conducting special programs, and managing the school district. It says we are a part of the educational process and there is a future in the system for us.

THE ELDERS AND SPIRITUAL LEADERS

One of many good qualities Indians can teach non-Indians is deep respect for the elders. This respect will become apparent right away to newcomers at Indian and Inuit events. The old people hold a high position in most tribes and their wisdom, knowledge, and beliefs are honored. Elders are welcomed not only as participants, but as leaders and they respond with dignity and guidance. The elders often serve as cultural historians, passing on the heritage of a people. Usually middle aged and young people learn as much as they can from the elders for they know that one day they will be elders. Then they must keep the knowledge and pass it on. In many tribes, certain families take special responsibility to do this and to them we all owe a great debt of gratitude.

Many tribes also have spiritual leaders. These are usually, but not always, elders and may be men or women. Becoming a spiritual leader takes many years, certainly as long as becoming an ordained clergyman or medical doctor. Some spiritual leaders are ceremonial leaders, others Indian doctors, some teachers of both Indians and non-Indian students, while others may be all of the above. Spiritual leaders generally have exceptional knowledge and are highly respected in the Indian community and by non-Indian friends. Often they are very influential in tribal decisions and opinion making.

VETERANS AND YOUNG PEOPLE

Two other groups deserve special mention. First, the military veterans of so many tribes returned from World War II and later wars with a knowledge of the world and self confidence that enabled them to become valuable leaders of their people. Some of the events listed in this book, especially in Oklahoma, were started by returning veterans. They have continued their tribal leadership to this day.

Finally, the Indian and Inuit young people deserve mention. So many are working hard in school and college today. They are a credit both to their tribes and to the US and Canada. Already many have become respected professional, government, and business leaders. Yet most make the effort to keep the traditions of their tribes alive, too.

We have met hundreds of fine Indian people and the happiest seem to be those who enjoy and appreciate the traditional tribal way as well as what is good in contemporary US and Canadian society. The dances, songs, prayers, and old stories offer strength and help. But so do books, colleges, health programs, good jobs and a secure place in the world. We need both worlds.

RELIGION

There are shared beliefs among many Native American religions, but there is also great variation from one tribe to another. There are also variations in the degree of Christianization of tribes from one to another as well as differences in how much, if any, of the tribal religion is practiced. The differences range from tribes such as the Hopi where nearly everyone participates in some way in the traditional religion to some groups where no ancient religious ceremonies continue. Most Indian groups fall somewhere in between and some Indian people practice both Christian beliefs and those of their ancestors.

Religion was everywhere in traditional Indian life and today many Native Americans feel that much in the world is sacred. Spiritual life and activity is evidenced in all aspects of nature, human behavior, many material objects, and human activities. Among non-Indians, games, for instance, are just games. But among Indian traditionalists a foot race, a dice game, a stickball game, or an Indian football game may have great religious significance. Among the Seneca-Cayuga of Oklahoma, it is believed that Our Creator gave the Iroquois people certain games to enjoy and He watches when they are played. Our Creator's presence at these games makes them special and unusually enjoyable. Thus, not only games but many other seemingly ordinary facets of daily life often have religious meaning.

Most ancient ceremonies are still done because they are believed to bring either important benefits or to

Geneva Mattz, Yurok elder, sits by the round doorway of an old time redwood plank house. She wears the distinctive basketry cap of Northwestern California. Mrs. Mattz is a cultural historian and teacher who has inspired many educators and students to appreciate California Indian cultures. Requa, California. (R. Shanks)

Elders are very important in Indian cultures and respect for their wisdom runs deep. Laura Fish Somersall, a Wappo, is one of the last fluent speakers of the Wappo language. She has worked diligently with linguists to preserve this central California tribe's language. Here, she weaves an exquisite basket of willow, sedge, and bullrush root. The Pomo and Wappo are unexcelled worldwide in the art of basketry. Santa Rosa, California. (R. Shanks)

Many Indian and Inuit people are active Christians. Newton Indian Methodist Church in eastern Oklahoma is one of 70 predominantly Creek Indian Churches scattered throughout the Creek Nation. Services are bilingual in English and Muscogee (Creek). (Creek Nation Communication Center—Gary Robinson)

Many Native Americans are accomplished musicians and some tribes have bands that present concerts. John Amos is a renowned fiddler in the Bogue Chitto Community on the Choctaw Reservation in Mississippi. A good fiddler is an indispensable part of any Choctaw house dance. (Mississippi Band of Choctaw Indians—Communications Program)

ward off disasters. Often these benefits are for all the world's people so that their successful completion benefits humans of all races.

One moving Indian religious event is the Maidu Bear Dance in northern California. Both Indian and non-Indian guests are invited to share in portions of the ceremony which results in spiritual and health benefits for all participants. At many other events just attending as an observer with a good heart helps the event's spiritual goals and benefits you as well. Unfortunately, some religious events (or portions of them) are open to members only. But most Indian people are good hosts who welcome those who come with dignity and respect.

RELIGIOUS FREEDOM

A major issue over the years has been the right of Indian freedom of religion. The worst examples of interference were such cases as the Spanish missions where ceremonies were often suppressed, the Canadian government's confiscation of Northwest Coast arts and the banning of potlatches there, and the vigorous interference of American missionaries which resulted in the banning (for a time) of many reservation dances.

Today such interference is much reduced, and probably completely gone in most areas. But in prisons, Native Americans often are denied the use of traditional religious facilities such as sweatlodges and access to medicine men vital to practicing some tribal religions. It is not difficult for prison authorities to make such accommodations and the requests are no less valid than when a prisoner requests that a minister or priest offer him communion.

CHRISTIANITY AND TRADITIONAL INDIAN RELIGIONS

In some Indian communities there is a split between Christian Indian people and those who practice the traditional tribal religions. This is unfortunate because both groups have fine people involved. There is a need to respect both religious perspectives since neither is likely to disappear. Both true Christianity and true Indian traditional religions stress accepting all people in a compassionate and understanding manner. Both traditional Indian tribal religions and Christianity have vital lessons and great philosophies to teach us all.

Some progress is being made today. When Wintu tribal spiritual leader Grant Towendolly died, the funeral was conducted by both traditional Indian religious leaders and a Methodist pastor. Both had been

part of Mr. Towendolly's life. Afterward, the Methodist pastor stated that the words of the Indian spiritual leaders were the most meaningful he had ever heard spoken at any funeral, a high compliment.

At a predominately Mohawk Catholic Church in the northeast, one Christian parish sponsors a traditional Iroquois dance group where the old songs and dances are performed. Christian Indian people thus retain benefits of both spiritual perspectives.

Pima Indian author Anna Moore Shaw, a devout Presbyterian leader, in her beautiful book, "A Pima Past", describes how meaningful and important it was for her to hear the ancient Pima songs sung once again.

SOME PROBLEMS IN INDIAN COUNTRY

There are, despite considerable progress by so many tribes, still major problems facing many Indian people. These include poverty, inadequate health care, unemployment, alcoholism, lack of affordable housing, juvenile delinquency, and the like.

Indian people themselves are doing much to help. Urban and reservation non-profit organizations which are Indian led and staffed by Indian professionals operate in many places. But money is a constant problem and nowhere have Federal spending cutbacks hurt more than among the Native American people. There is currently a real funding crisis and effective, well run Indian programs have had to close or cut back services when tax money has been redirected from domestic to military spending. Lack of Federal money has created a major crisis.

Lack of investment capital is another major problem on many reservations and American, Canadian, and foreign business leaders need to make efforts to work with tribal leaders to help develop businesses on impoverished reservations. Indian people respond enthusiastically to good job opportunities, especially those which allow a person to live close enough to a reservation that is home. Many reservations offer a willing, highly trainable work force desperate for decent jobs.

Health care available to Indian people in some areas is inadequate. Understaffed and overworked medical people are characteristic in a number of reservation situations. In response to such problems, the Creek Nation of Oklahoma recently won the right to administer funds for its own health program (the director is a Creek graduate of Harvard Medical School) rather than have a branch of the government operate the program. The results have been excellent.

Urban Indians particularly face a loss of Bureau of Indian Affairs services when they move to the cities seeking employment. Urban Indian job seekers need additional services, not less, as they struggle in a new environment. There needs to be an updating of our laws regarding health care, education, social services, and job placement for urban Indian people as the Native American population is becoming increasingly urbanized.

In situations where strong, well led tribal governments have been encouraged to chart their own course, progress is being made on these and other problems. Indian people want to solve problems themselves, but they need to be able to plot their own future and they need the strong financial backing of government sponsored (but tribally operated) programs. From the private sector, investment capital and new business ventures need to be made under joint direction with tribal officials.

All business and government endeavors must be made with Indian guidance, advice, and leadership to achieve success. As noted elsewhere, Indian businesses, agriculture, and fisheries are among the most innovative in the country. Indian run government programs really do make a difference in improving people's lives. It's just that there aren't enough business enterprises or enough fully developed government programs to meet such vast needs.

Too many Indian people suffer from serious health problems, unbelievably bad housing, reservation unemployment rates that often exceed those of inner-cities, high suicide rates, devastating alcoholism problems, and more. But now for the first time there are also large numbers of highly skilled, educated Indian men and women with the dedication and ability to solve these monstrous problems. But they do need the financial, political, and spiritual support of the non-Indian majority in the US and Canada.

INDIAN SELF-DETERMINATION: A BIRTHRIGHT FOR THE FUTURE

Through the centuries a major issue for Indian people has been the right to control their own lives and land. This was the issue when Phillip lead the Wampanoags against the English in New England in the first major Indian war and it is still the issue of many law suits today. Quite simply, Indian tribes want to be able to determine what to do with their lives, lands, and spiritual life. Indians are unique in having distinct legal status in a number of areas, derived from historic treaty rights.

It is very important to remember that throughout history the US and England have dealt with the tribes as independent nations. Treaties were made and ratified by Congress much in the same manner as with France, Mexico or Japan. Many legal guarantees have come out of these treaties which give the Indian tribes special status under US and Canadian laws. These result in certain tribal rights of taxation, court systems, land use, business activities, and so on. Infringement on these rights of tribal sovereignty weakens tribal governments and hurts the Indian people.

US and Canadian government and business policies need to be structured to strengthen tribal self-determination and leadership. Only where predominantly Indian leadership exists have Indian economic, social, and educational programs worked best. Non-Indians are useful and valued staff members, but decision making must be in Indian hands. Certainly Indians recognize their ties to non-Indians through US or Canadian citizenship, inter-marriage, friendships, and other commonalities. But all of us need to remember that Indian tribes have unique legal and cultural reasons which require that Indian self-determination and tribal independence be supported and strengthened.

The Native American Rights Fund of Boulder, Colorado, has been a leader in providing legal services to Indian tribes across America. NARF lawyers are primarily Native Americans and rank with the best in the country. Native American Rights Fund has an outstanding record of achieving legal victories for Indian and Eskimo people. (Native American Rights Fund)

Choctaw Greeting Enterprise, a branch of American Greetings Corporation, is one of the largest producers of greeting cards in North America. It is located on the Mississippi Choctaw Reservation. (Mississippi Band of Choctaw Indians—Communications Program)

Many tribes hold annual princess contests and select one of their talented and beautiful young women to reign at selected social occasions during the year. This is charming Kathie Henry who was selected Choctaw princess for 1985-86 in Mississippi. (Mississippi Band of Choctaw Indians—Communications Program)

USING YOUR GUIDE

Every effort has been made to achieve accuracy in your "North American Indian Travel Guide". We have traveled thousands of miles in the US and Canada over a seven year period visiting dozens of Indian groups and attending many activities. For groups we couldn't visit, we have made use of the telephone and written inquiries. Hundreds of people were interviewed, both formally and informally. Countless tribal officials, traditional leaders, cultural center staffs, government officials, museum and park personnel, tourist offices, and other just plain nice people all helped with information and advice. The superb kindness and cooperation of Indian traditionalists and tribal office staff deserves special appreciation.

The book is organized so that you can conveniently locate events either geographically or by tribe. The geographical section on the United States is followed by Canada's listings. After Canada is the Tribal Listing section. All sections are organized alphabetically.

Cross check the geographical section with the tribal section. You'll find exciting related listings that way. We hope, too, you'll use the GUIDE like any other book and just enjoy reading through it. Included are frequent accounts of interesting information and stories about Indian and Eskimo history, cultural sites, and events. All geographical listings here are found in the better road atlases we consulted.

We have emphasized phone numbers over addresses for many cultural centers and tribal offices since the hard working staffs often lack the time to respond to written inquiries. If you want to know the date of an event, a brief courteous phone call is generally the best method.

A few cautions are also in order. First, phone numbers and addresses sometimes change. Events sometimes get cancelled at the last minute, and dates change. Typographical errors can occur and misinformation can be accidentally included. Before making a long distance call you might want to double check the number with directory assistance. Before making a trip, always check to make sure the event is still going to happen or that the date hasn't been changed. All we can say is that we and hundreds of Indian and non-Indian people have all tried our best to bring you the best information ever assembled on contemporary Indian and Eskimo activities and cultural resources.

It should also be noted that on some large reservations there are few fences along the roads. This is called "open range", and night driving can be hazardous. Hitting a cow or a sheep can result in a tragic accident. Minimize night driving or avoid it. A few reservations also have problems, as do many American communities, with teenage gangs and drunk drivers. Avoid situations where you might be vulnerable, such as isolated, dark areas.

Remember, too, that you are dealing with hundreds of different cultures. Appropriate dress and behavior will vary somewhat from one tribe to another. Dignified clothing (no shorts on either sex, no bare midriffs, etc.) is required at some tribe's sacred dances. At other events, casual clothing is often permitted. It's best to dress with dignity; you can go change if casual dress proves appropriate. Notice what your Indian hosts are wearing and take your cue from them. Finally, always ask permission before photographing, sketching, or taping.

In these introductory pages we have tried to give you a perspective on both contemporary and traditional Native North American cultures. We hope our orientation has been of value to you. It seems fitting at this point to recommend the writings of Dr. James. H. Howard. Dr. Howard understood better than almost anyone the links between contemporary and traditional Indian life. You can do no better than to read his books and articles. Especially helpful are the following: SHAWNEE! (Ohio Univ. Press), THE SOUTHEASTERN CEREMONIAL COMPLEX AND ITS INTERPRETATION (Missouri Archeological Society), and OKLAHOMA SEMINOLES (Oklahoma Univ. Press). More than just accounts of specific groups, they teach understanding of the continuity between yesterday and today in Indian cultural life.

If you have suggestions to improve the next GUIDE please let us know. We'd like to add more events, cultural centers, Indian centers, museums, Indian owned businesses, etc. If there are revisions you'd recommend we make, please also tell us. We want the GUIDE to serve you and hope that it will become a living thing with many future editions.

As we write this we are thinking of the Pomo prayer song to take you safely on your journey. God bless you, drive carefully, and go with a good heart.

Etidluie, Cape Dorset Inuit artist, at the beginning stage of creating an Eskimo sculpture. (Dept. of Information, Govt. of Northwest Territories—B. Wilson)

NORTH AMERICAN INDIAN CULTURAL AREAS

CONTEMPORARY LOCATIONS OF INDIAN TRIBES
IN THE UNITED STATES

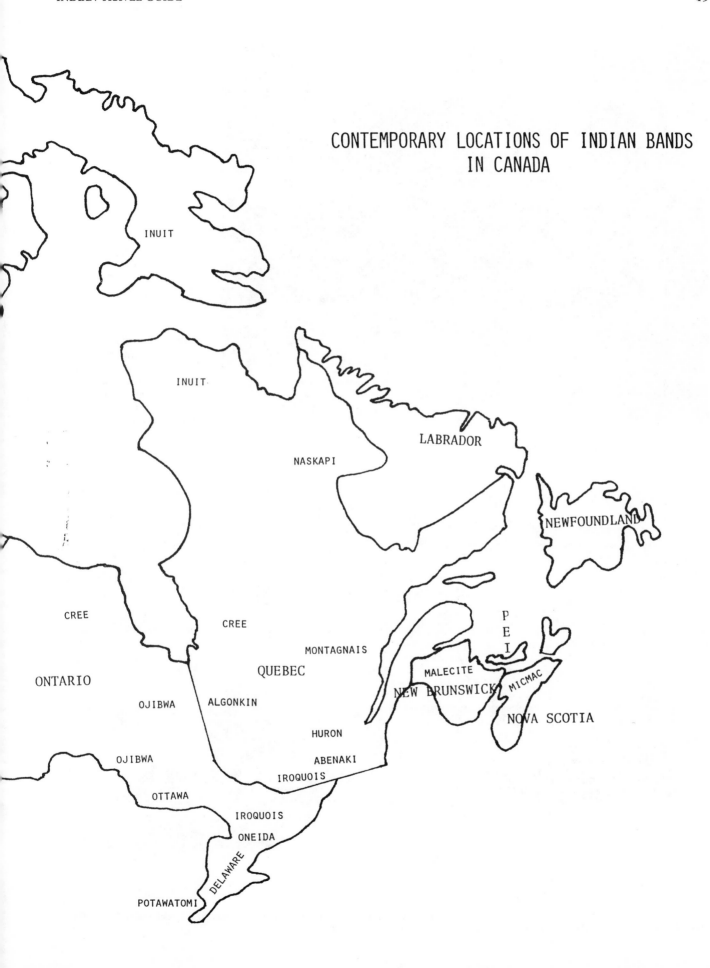

CONTEMPORARY LOCATIONS OF INDIAN BANDS
IN CANADA

Peter Malgokak, stone carver and print maker, of Holman Island, Northwest Territories, at work on a masterpiece. (Dept. of Information, Govt. of Northwest Territories— Tessa Macintosh)

Today the snowmobile is more common among Inuit people than the traditional dog team. Holman Island, Northwest Territories. (Dept. of Information, Govt. of Northwest Territories—Tessa Macintosh)

UNITED STATES

ALABAMA

ALABAMA—FLORENCE
CEREMONIAL INDIAN MOUND & MUSEUM
South Court St
Florence, AL
(205) 766-6742
This is one of the tallest Indian mounds made by the Indians of the advanced Mississippian cultural area. There is a museum with displays.

ALABAMA—MOUNDVILLE
MOUND STATE MONUMENT
Highway 69
Moundville, AL
(205) 371-2572
This well preserved Indian temple mound is enhanced by an excellent replica of the sacred temple that once stood atop the earthen mound. Inside are full sized human figures depicting the original inhabitants of this important archeological site. The village that once stood here may have been the second largest Indian community in the U.S.

ALABAMA—WETUMPKA
FORT TOULOSE PARK & INDIAN MOUND
(205) 567-3002
Three miles west of Wetumpka in historic Creek Indian country. Fort Toulouse Park contains a major Indian mound.

ALASKA

ALASKA—ANCHORAGE
ANCHORAGE HISTORICAL &
FINE ARTS MUSEUM
121 West 7th Ave
Anchorage, AK
(907) 264-4326
Native Alaskan cultural arts and crafts are among the exhibits. Annual ALASKA FESTIVAL OF NATIVE ARTS is held here displaying excellent work.

HERITAGE LIBRARY
National Bank of Alaska
Northern Lights & "C" St
Anchorage, AK
(907) 276-1132
Among the collections are displays of Native clothing and tools. Open weekday afternoons.

ALASKA—BETHEL
YUGTARVID REGIONAL MUSEUM SHOP
P.O. Box 388
Third Ave
Bethel, AK 99559
(907) 543-2098
Eskimo baskets, mats, ivory masks and carvings, dance fans, and much more. Mail order by special request.

ALASKA—CORDOVA
CORDOVA MUSEUM & LIBRARY
Cordova, AK
Among the exhibits are ivory, stone, and basketry artwork, an Aleut bidarka canoe and more.

PALUGVIK, on Hawkins Island across the strait from Cordova, is the historic site of the southern-most extensions of Eskimo territory in Alaska.

ALASKA—FAIRBANKS
UNIVERSITY OF ALASKA MUSEUM
West Ridge area
University of Alaska campus
Fairbanks, AK
(907) 474-7505
Indian and Inuit arts and crafts are exhibited among the collections. "Inuit" is the term for Eskimo people preferred by many Native people. It is pronounced "In-oo-it".

THIYAAT NATIVE ARTS
Fairbanks Native Association
310-1/2 First St
Fairbanks, AK 99701
Athabaskan (Dene) birch bark baskets, Eskimo baskets, mukluks, dolls, carvings, etc., are sold here. During summers, the shop is located at Alaskaland on Airport Road. Mail order.

ALASKA NATIVE ARTS & CRAFTS CENTER OF FAIRBANKS
1603 College Road
Fairbanks, AK 97701
(907) 452-8164
Native American owned and operated business featuring arts and crafts from Indian and Eskimo people of Alaska.

The Chilkat Dancers of southern Alaska offer spectacular Native American dancing. Alaskan Indian Arts presents many Northwest Coast cultural activities at Fort William H Seward in Haines, Alaska. (Alaska Indian Arts)

ALASKA—FORT YUKON
DINJII ZHUU ENJIIT MUSEUM
P.O. Box 42
Fort Yukon, AK
(907) 622-2345
The museum presents Alaskan Athabaskan Indian culture. Indian fish wheels where Native Americans catch a vital part of their food can be seen operating seasonally here. The museum has a gift shop where authentic local Indian items can be purchased.

GWITCHYAA ZHEE NATIVE CORPORATION, Athabaskan Indian owned and operated, has a lodge with restaurant and accommodations for those who wish to visit Fort Yukon. Phone (907) 662-2325.

TOURS OF FORT YUKON
Tours of the cultural and historic points of interest in Fort Yukon are available. Check with the museum or lodge. Fort Yukon can be reached by regularly scheduled air service from Fairbanks.

ALASKA—GLENNALLEN
AHTNA LODGE
South Junction of Richardson & Glenn Hwys
Box 88
Glennallen, AK 99588
(907) 822-3289
The Ahtna Indian people own and operate the new Ahtna Lodge, motel, restaurant, lounge, gift shop, and information center. The Ahtna call themselves the "People of the Copper River" and proudly invite you to stay at their lodge. Permits to fish on Ahtna land can be purchased here.

ALASKA—HAINES
MUSEUM & CULTURAL CENTER
Main St, near Sheldon
Haines, AK
(907) 766-2366
Among the collections is fine Northwest Coast Indian material from the Tlingit people.

FORT WILLIAM H. SEWARD
Port of Chilkoot
Haines, AK
(907) 766-2202
There is much to see at old Fort Seward. Among the attractions are:

ALASKA INDIAN ARTS
Box 271, Old Hospital Building
Fort William H. Seward
Haines, AK 99827
(907) 766-2160
The famous Chilkat Indian dancers perform at Chilkat Center for the Arts from June through October,
on Saturday and Monday evenings. Call for showtimes. Chilkat dancing is beautifully costumed with fine music and dance. Carvers from Alaskan Indian Arts have created a number of very spectacular totem poles well worth seeing. Totem carvings, silverwork and printmaking may be seen here weekdays and by appointment.

CHILKAT INDIAN DANCES OF THE NORTHWEST COAST INDIANS
Chilkat Center for the Arts
P.O. Box 776
Fort William H. Seward
Haines, AK 99827
(907) 766-2366 or 766-2160
Famed for their woven cape-like blankets of unsurpassed beauty, the Chilkat Indian people are a part of the Tlingit Indian Nation of the Northwest Coast. The Chilkat are renowned for their elaborately decorated costumes, carved wood masks, button blankets and other ceremonial regalia. The Chilkat perform high quality Northwest Coast dancing which is among the most spectacular dancing in the world. Performances are offered several times a week during the summer as Tlingit culture is shared with visitors.

NORTHWEST COAST INDIAN VILLAGE OF THE TLINGIT
At Fort William H. Seward
Haines, AK
Indian master carvers create museum quality totem poles, masks, and other objects of wood while visitors watch. There is a Northwest Coast Indian village recreated here, complete with tribal house, storage caches, totems, and other interesting features.

PORT CHILKOOT POTLATCH
Tribal House
Fort William H. Seward
Haines, AK
(907) 766-2000
A salmon bake is held in the tribal house nightly during summer months. This is a popular dining adventure and reservations are recommended. Phone the fort for information.

WELCOME TOTEMS
At the "Y" heading north out of Haines
Haines, AK
Created by the wood carvers of Alaska Indian Arts, each pole symbolically represents cultural beliefs of the Tlingit people. The visitor information center can provide explanations and detailed information about the totem poles.

ALASKA—HOONAH
HOONAH CULTURAL CENTER & MUSEUM
On the hill above town
Hoonah, AK
Hoonah is a Tlingit Indian community where the Native people have donated cultural objects for the museum to display. Open weekdays.

ALASKA—JUNEAU
ALASKA STATE MUSEUM
Whittier St
Juneau, AK
(907) 465-2901
Native Alaskan exhibits are among the displays. Inquire about special events and exhibits. Regularly displayed are fine exhibits on local Aleut, Eskimo, Athabaskan and Northwest Coast Indian cultures.

ALASKA—KAKE
TLINGIT TOTEM POLE
Kake, AK
Kake is a predominantly Tlingit community, home of the Kake band of the tribe. The Tlingit carved the world's largest authentic totem pole (124 feet high) for the 1970 World's Fair in Japan. It is now on display at home in Kake and can be viewed by visitors. Kake holds its Community Arts & Crafts Festival each year in May.

ALASKA—KETCHIKAN
TOTEM HERITAGE CENTER
601 Keermount St
Ketchikan, AK
(907) 225-5900
Haida, Tlingit, and Tsimshian Northwest Coast Indian art is displayed. Educational programs on Indian culture of the region are offered. Check with the Center for programs and special events. Thirty-three old and fine totem poles can be seen here. Guided tours.

SAXMAN TOTEM PARK
South Tongass Highway, 2 1/2 miles south of Ketchikan
Ketchikan, AK
(907) 225-9038
Twenty-two Northwest Coast totem poles are on display. Guided tours. Native American dances and a dinner are offered periodically, Call for dates and times.

TONGASS HISTORICAL SOCIETY MUSEUM
Ketchikan Centennial Building
629 Dock St
Ketchikan, AK
(907) 225-5600
Northwest Coast Alaskan Indian material is displayed among the collections.

ALASKA—KOTZEBUE
Kotzebue is one of the largest Eskimo (Inuit) communities in Alaska. Various tours visit here and the town offers a fascinating introduction to Eskimo life, both traditional and modern. Eskimo foods may be sampled here and traditional dancing occurs periodically.

NUL-LUK-VIK HOTEL
P.O. Box 336
Kotzebue, AK 99752
(907) 442-3331
Eskimo-owned hotel providing a base for exploring Kotzebue and surrounding communities. Modern, open year round. Gift shop with native crafts.

NANA MUSEUM OF THE ARCTIC
Box 49
Kotzebue, AK 99752
(907) 442-3301
Highly praised museum of Eskimo culture with a special two hour presentation on the natural history and Native heritage of Alaska. This museum will orient you to the community and Inuit culture. Check for special events and programs.

Ootukahkuktukvik Museum, 1/2 mile north of the airport also exhibits many fascinating Eskimo cultural objects.

For serious, respectful visitors the cemetery has "spirit houses" built over the graves in honor of loved ones. These structures are beautifully decorated, expressing the affection survivors hold for those passed away. On a lighter note, there are traditional fish drying racks of interest along the waterfront.

Usually the best time to visit Kotzebue is over the Fourth of July and the following week. You will see the Native Games where Eskimo people compete in traditional contests, including seal-hook throwing, muktuk eating, etc. The next week the ARCTIC TRADES FAIR is held with arts and crafts sales, and traditional Native dancing and foods. Be sure to check for exact dates of these events.

Eskimo Olympic trials are held here, usually between Christmas and the New Year. These fascinating events include traditional knuckle hop, highkicking on one foot (you must land on the same foot you left the ground on), finger-pulling contest, and much more. (Eskimo and Indian Olympics are also held in Fairbanks in July.)

Kotzebue is one of the largest Eskimo communities in the world and offers a travel adventure that is unique and exciting. Many travel agencies offer tours here.

ALASKA—METLAKATLA
TSIMSHIAN INDIAN LONGHOUSE
Annette Island
Metlakatla, AK
Actively used for local Tsimshian ceremonies and other events, there are performances by beautifully costumed Tsimshian dancers. Check for dates and times. Native American arts and crafts are displayed and sold here. Very interesting and worthwhile.

DUNCAN COTTAGE MUSEUM
Box 282
Annette Island
Metlakatla, AK 99926
The museum is housed in the former home of Scottish missionary William Duncan who helped found Metlakatla and helped the Tsimshian people develop it into a leading Alaskan community. Native American exhibits among the collections.

ALASKA—NOME
CARRIE MCLAIN MEMORIAL MUSEUM
KEGOAYAH KOZGA LIBRARY
Front St
Nome, AK
(907) 443-5133
Among the exhibits are displays of Eskimo cultures and the Bering Strait land bridge where Native people arrived from Asia.

ALASKA—NORTHWAY
NAABIA NIIGN ARTS & CRAFTS SHOP
Box 476
Milepost 1264.5 Alaskan Highway
Northway, AK 99764
(907) 778-6497 or 778-2297
Athabaskan Indian arts and crafts are sold including fine birch bark baby cradles and other baskets, moccasins, mukluks, gloves, beadwork, and more. The Tanana tribe of Athabaskan-speaking Indian people live in this region.

ALASKA—PRIBILOF ISLANDS
The Aleut native people of the tiny communities of St. Paul and St. George operate a hotel and restaurants in St. Paul. The Pribilof Islands are a famous fur seal breeding area and the islands are popular with naturalists interested in the local plant and animal life. Tours are offered from Anchorage by scheduled air service.

ALASKA—PRINCE OF WALES ISLAND
HAIDA TOTEM POLES
In the community of Hydaburg you will find a fine collection of Haida totem poles. This predominantly Haida Indian community is on the southwestern portion of Prince of Wales Island. More totem poles and an artfully decorated community house may also be seen at Klawock and Craig here on the island. HAIDA WAY LODGE, Box 90, in Craig can assist you (907) 826-3268. This is a Native American owned lodge.

ALASKA—SAVOONGA
SAVOONGA NATIVE STORE
Box 100
Savoonga, AK 99769
Eskimo village owned store offering ivory carvings, sewn skin products, and other arts and crafts. Mail orders please include a stamped, self-addressed envelope.

ALASKA—SITKA
SITKA NATIONAL HISTORIC PARK
Box 738
End of Metlakatla St
Sitka, AK 99835
(907) 747-6281
The park commemorates the 1804 Battle of Sitka between local Tlingit Indian people and Russian and Aleut fur hunters. This major battle was the last significant armed conflict between Europeans and Native Americans in Alaska. Two years earlier the Tlingit's had attacked and destroyed the Russian's Fort Archangel Michael, driving the Russians out of Sitka. But in the 1804 rematch the Europeans permanently returned to the area. There is a visitor center with exhibits and audio-visual presentation.

The SOUTHEAST ALASKA INDIAN CULTURAL CENTER is here and Tlingit artists demonstrate and explain traditional and contemporary Northwest Coast artwork to visitors. A renowned totem pole collection may be seen. Over two dozen Tlingit and Haida totem poles, some over a century old, may be seen.

SHELDON JACKSON COLLEGE & MUSEUM
Sheldon Jackson College campus
Sitka, AK
(907) 747-5228
Named in honor of famed Presbyterian missionary Rev. Sheldon Jackson, the man who suggested bringing reindeer to Alaska as a food source for Native peoples. Rev. Jackson was aided by Captain Michael Healy of the U.S. Revenue Cutter Service (now part

of the U.S. Coast Guard). Captain Healy, known as the "Black Hero of the North", was a black American who led many daring voyages. Both Captain Healy and Rev. Jackson were shocked by the starvation they found among Eskimo people and together determined to aid Native people. The dashing Coast Guard officer and the eloquent Presbyterian clergyman were an unmatched team. Together their work resulted in one of Alaska's most arduous undertakings—bringing herds of reindeer from Siberia to Alaska. Despite great hardship, the mission was accomplished over a period of years and the food supply of Eskimo people was greatly enhanced. The museum will supply more details of this heartwarming saga of the North.

In 1976, NANA Regional Corporation, a Native owned enterprise, again took up reindeer herding to supplement Eskimo food sources.

Visitors to the museum will enjoy the Eskimo and Indian exhibits at the museum along with material dating from the time of Russian ownership of Alaska.

TOTEM SQUARE
On the waterfront across Katlian St
Sitka, Alaska
The park contains a totem pole and petroglyphs.

ALASKA—TOK
Tok is a trading center for Tanana and Ahtna tribes of the Athabaskan language group. Some local Native (Indian) women still make fine birch bark baskets, baby cradles, moccasins, mukluks, etc. which are sold locally. Be sure you get the genuine "Indian Tan" moccasins and mukluks where the moose hide has been tanned in the traditional Indian way. Commercially tanned work is less traditional and less attractive. It also means that your mukluks and moccasins will be worth less in future years than Indian tan ones.

ALASKA—WRANGELL
CHIEF SHAKES ISLAND & BEAR TRIBAL COMMUNITY HOUSE
In Wrangell Harbor, reached by a boardwalk
Wrangell, AK
(907) 874-3505
Chief Shakes was a famous Tlingit leader once featured in *National Geographic* magazine. The Chief Shakes' Community House is a registered Historic Landmark and contains Tlingit art and artifacts, including a Chilkat blanket. Open summers and by appointment. Totem pole carvers sometimes work on Shakes Island and welcome visitors.

WRANGELL MUSEUM
2 blocks from ferry terminal
Wrangell, AK
(907) 874-3770
Good collection of Tlingit Indian tools, blankets, etc. Wrangell Island also offers totem poles (some replicas) and petroglyphs. The petroglyphs are on the beach at the island's north end and are visible only at low tide. Inquire locally for directions.

ARIZONA

ARIZONA—CAMP VERDE
YAVAPAI-APACHE VISITOR CENTER
Take Middle Verde Exit off US Hwy I-17, then 1/4 mile E
Camp Verde, AZ
(602) 567-5276
Exhibits present both traditional and modern life styles of Yavapai and Apache people who live on the Camp Verde Indian Reservation. A film covers interesting facets of Yavapai and Apache life. Camp Verde Apaches began dancing publicly again in recent years and sometimes perform locally. Their Mountain Spirit Dance is excellent. FORT VERDE STATE PARK nearby also has some Native American displays (602) 567-3275.

ARIZONA—CANYON DE CHELLY NATIONAL MONUMENT
Box 588
Chinle, AZ 86503
Monument entrance is 3 miles E of Chinle
(602) 674-5436
Canyon de Chelly is one of the most scenic locations in North America. Surrounded by the Navajo Indian Reservation, the canyon has a long history of occupation by several different Indian peoples. Originally, Basketmaker people lived here in pit houses. They were followed by the ancestors of the modern Hopi and Pueblo. All three of these groups eventually left Canyon de Chelly and today the only native residents are the Navajo. Kit Carson and his heavily armed men uprooted the Navajo and brutally drove them out of the area during the 19th Century. But the Navajo soon returned and today they peacefully farm and raise livestock. Visitors have the opportunity to meet Navajo people since many work as official guides for the National Park Service.

Canyon de Chelly consists of red sandstone walls hundreds of feet high. Many of the sheer rock walls have narrow ledges and built upon them are the ruins of Indian cliff dwellings constructed hundreds of years ago. Along with the scenic natural wonders the canyon holds ancient Indian rock art with fascinating designs.

Two lovely Apache girls with distinctive traditional dresses of their people. (L. Shanks)

All trips into the canyon must be made with an official guide and a reasonable fee is charged. Guides are hired through the Park Service office at the Monument's Visitor Center. Over 60 ruins may be seen and one of the very best, White House Cliff Dwelling, may be entered. Besides campgrounds, there are two motels here, Justin's Thunderbird Motel and Canyon de Chelly Motel. Reservations for both motel and guide service are advised.

Navajo women often come to the visitor center to weave their famous rugs on traditional looms. You will admire their artistic skill as they weave. If you want to photograph them, first ask permission and remember it is customary to make a donation to the Navajo person serving as your model. The visitor center also has a museum and arts and crafts shop.

Besides the great scenery, Canyon de Chelly offers the opportunity to see Navajo culture with people living in their circular hogans, raising their own food, and practicing a respected way of life. If you are looking for a pleasant escape to another world, Canyon de Chelly may be for you.

ARIZONA—CASA GRANDE NATIONAL MONUMENT
Box 518
Coolidge, AZ 85228
(602) 723-3172
The Monument entrance is 1 mile N of Coolidge, just off Hwy 87. Casa Grande is a remarkable ruin built on a flat desert plain in southern Arizona. This unique structure is almost Biblical in appearance and may remind you of something from ancient Babylon. Probably built by the ancestors of today's Pima and Papago, this building stood four stories high and may have been capped by an astronomical observatory. Casa Grande was the intellectual and ceremonial center of a widespread farming culture complete with irrigation systems involving sophisticated canals. The imposing structure remains today, although the Park Service has erected a giant canopy to protect the adobe mud building from further erosion.

You'll find a visitor center here with an excellent collection of Southwestern pottery and other Indian art. The exhibits help you understand Casa Grande, but the best introduction to the ruin is a ranger conducted tour. The site is a brief walk from the parking lot, making this one of the most accessible of the Southwest ruins.

ARIZONA—COLORADO RIVER INDIAN RESERVATION
COLORADO RIVER INDIAN TRIBES MUSEUM
2 miles S of Parker, at Second & Mojave St
(602) 669-9211 ext 213
The Colorado River Indian Reservation is the home of four tribes. The Mojave and Chemehuevi are the original inhabitants of this region while Navajo and Hopi people have moved here in more recent years. The Museum features very important collections of local Indian baskets, ancient and modern arts and crafts, a gift shop, library, and oral history and cultural collections. A special feature of the Museum is the guided tour program which offers tours of both the reservation and the museum. Lectures and classes on Mojave, Chemehuevi, Hopi, and Navajo cultures, crafts, and history are offered periodically. Check with the museum for special events. Closed Sundays.

Nearby, the Colorado River tribes operate a clock factory which produces clocks decorated with artwork from all four groups. Clocks may be purchased here during business hours. Today the Colorado River people also engage in agriculture using the latest farming methods.

ARIZONA—FLAGSTAFF
MUSEUM OF NORTHERN ARIZONA
US Hwy 180, 3 miles N of Flagstaff
(602) 774-5211
The Museum of Northern Arizona offers excellent displays of Southwest Indian cultures. While the Museum is worth a special trip any time, you may want to plan your visit to coincide with either of two wonderful annual events here. The first is the Hopi Crafts Show, usually held over the Fourth of July weekend. Hopi artists come to the museum to demonstrate weaving of baskets and sashes, pottery making, silverwork, and more. Piki bread, the delicious wafer-thin Hopi bread, is made here in the piki house. Be sure and try some. There is also a tremendous display of high quality Hopi kachina dolls, rattles, and other work, nearly all of it offered for sale. The Hopi artists are friendly, well informed people and it is a pleasure to meet and talk with them.

Sometimes during the Fourth of July, Indian dancing is held nearby at the Coconino Center for the Arts located on North Fort Valley Road behind the Pioneers' Historical Museum. Phone the Center at (602) 779-5944 for information. Apache, Walapai, Navajo, Papago and other Southwest tribes often participate.

A pair of handsome elders from the Colorado River tribes—a Mojave lady and Cocopah man at the Malki Museum Fiesta, Morongo, Calif. (R. Shanks)

Around the first of August, the Museum of Northern Arizona stages its other fine annual event. This is the Navajo Crafts Show which is of similar high quality and gives you an opportunity to buy artwork and meet Navajo artists while they work.

For other Flagstaff area Indian events, check with the Chamber of Commerce at (602) 774-4505. Two very rewarding Indian ruins are located near Flagstaff. They are:

WALNUT CANYON NATIONAL MONUMENT
Box 25, Route 1
Flagstaff, AZ
(602) 526-3367
The Monument is just south of Hwy I-40, eight miles east of Flagstaff. Many of the Southwest's cliff dwellings are remote and inaccessible. But Walnut Canyon is quite close to a major highway, has paved (but steep) trails, and allows visitors to enter the ruins. For the casual visitor, Walnut Canyon is one of the most enjoyable archeological sites in the Southwest.

The visitor center overlooks the deep, wooded canyon where the Sinagua Indians once lived. A trail winds down into the canyon to single-story cliff dwellings below. Entering the ruins helps give you an idea of what life was like here in 1200 A.D. The monuments's 7000 foot elevation has a cooler climate with more lush plant life in contrast to ruins located at lower altitudes. Atop the mesa picnicking is allowed among the pinyon pine and juniper trees.

WUPATKI NATIONAL MONUMENT
30 miles N of Flagstaff on Hwy 89, then 14 miles E on park road.
Flagstaff, AZ
(602) 774-7000
Mailing address: Via Tuba Star Route, Flagstaff, AZ 86001
Strangely, Indian life at Wupatki was made possible by the eruption of a volcano. Previously the soil could not sustain agriculture, but in 1064 AD, as if in answer to the people's prayers, nearby Sunset Crater erupted with a huge cinder cloud. The fine ash fluttered to the ground and covered everything. Far from being a disaster, the new layer of ash was a fertile, moisture holding soil perfect for Indian farming. The Sinagua people, ancestors of the modern Hopi, got out their seeds and digging sticks and soon had a city thriving. The result was Wupatki, a ceremonial center of brownish-red sandstone walls complete with sacred amphitheater, ball court, dwellings and a host of suburban towns.

Eventually, the city grew so large that one structure, Tall House, had one hundred rooms. Quite a civilization flourished here until, after about 125 years, the fertile volcanic soil was depleted and the people had to move on. They left dozens of impressive ruins, and many can be explored on self-guided trails.

ARIZONA—GANADO
HUBBELL TRADING POST NATIONAL HISTORIC SITE
Hwy 264, 1 mile W of Ganado
(602) 755-3475
If you've wanted to see an actual old time Indian trading post, this place is for you. The Hubbell Trading Post is still in operation after over a century. It contains a fine collection of Navajo art, including some classic rugs. Navajo women still weave rugs at the visitor center here. Also SEE: NAVAJO INDIAN RESERVATION.

ARIZONA—GLOBE
BESH BA GOWAH RUINS
Jesse Hayes Road
1 1/2 miles S of Globe
Take South Broad St to Ice House Canyon Road to Jesse Hayes Road. Owned by the City of Globe, Besh Ba Gowah is a Salado Pueblo ruin of 200 rooms, numerous ceremonial areas, and smaller surrounding archeological sites. Artifacts from this Indian agricultural center may be seen at the GILA COUNTY HISTORICAL MUSEUM, 1330 N. Broad St, in Globe (602) 425-7385.

ARIZONA—GRAND CANYON
HAVASUPAI INDIAN RESERVATION
Supai, AZ 86435
(602) 448-2121 or 448-2111
Most people are amazed to learn that there is a thriving Indian community at the bottom of the Grand Canyon! Visitors are welcome and tourism is important to the modern Havasupai people. The tribe operates two lodges and several campgrounds. All visits must be arranged through the tribally-owned Havasupai Tourist Enterprise, Supai, AZ.

The single community on the reservation is Supai, a very small town. The tribe lives in a branch of the Grand Canyon called Havasu Canyon. This is a very beautiful area with the world famous cliffs of the Grand Canyon, cool streams of blue-green water, and stunning waterfalls.

Getting there involves a long drive from Peach Springs on the neighboring Hualpai Indian Reservation (SEE: ARIZONA—PEACH SPRINGS). Once at the canyon rim you must leave your vehicle. The only way down into Havasu Canyon is by a steep, eight-mile trail. Most people arrange to pack in using mules or horses which the Havasupai rent for a reasonable fee. This is by far the best way to go because the eight miles back up is unbelievably tough, especially under the hot Arizona sun.

Once in Supai, all visitors must stop at the Havasupai Tribal Office to pay a recreational fee. Supai has a cafe, post office, etc. This is the last place in the United States where the mail still travels by mule train and it is fun to mail letters or post cards from here and get a distinctive postmark.

Dances are held occasionally (SEE: TRIBAL LISTINGS) so check with tourism officials for special events.

This trip is a visit to another world and the Havasupai must regulate the number of visitors the canyon can comfortably hold. Always remember that you are the guest of the Havasupai and be on your best behavior please. All garbage must be hauled out of the canyon to preserve its beauty. This is yet another good reason for renting a pack animal. There is a telephone atop the canyon rim so you can phone the Havasupai when you've arrived at the trail head. Be certain to make prior reservations for your animals, lodgings or campsite. If well planned, this trip can be a wonderful adventure.

ARIZONA—GRAND CANYON NATIONAL PARK
TUSAYAN RUIN & MUSEUM
On East Rim Drive 22 miles E of Grand Canyon Village
South Rim of Grand Canyon, AZ
(602) 638-2411
This modest pueblo ruin has an interesting museum explaining its history. Guided tours are offered by rangers.

ARIZONA—HOPI INDIAN RESERVATION
The Hopi Indian Reservation is one of the great centers of Native American culture. Most Hopi are warm, friendly people and pleasant hosts. Many Hopi are well educated and nearly all speak fluent English. Hopi people seem to have that ability to cope well with modern life but at the same time to be deeply involved in their much admired, rich traditional culture. Most Hopi still live in their timeless villages high atop three mesas in northern Arizona. Their ancient religion is strong and unforgettable. These are people who have learned much of what's important in the world and you can learn much from their culture.

Kachina dances are held when the masked spirits return annually from their home atop the San Francisco Peaks near Flagstaff. Arts and crafts of the highest quality are made here, including kachina dolls, pottery, silverwork, basketry, rattles, sashes, and more.

Before going to Hopi Country there are a few rules to remember. First, alcohol and drugs are not permitted on the reservation. Second, photographs and tape recordings can only be made with the approval of the tribal office. Third, respect all sacred shrines, cultural resources, and the people themselves. Remember that you are a guest. Be courteous, quiet, and when attending ceremonies always act as you would at church for these are sacred rites. Many long lasting friendships have been made between visitors and Hopi people. Maybe you will be lucky enough to build a friendship here, too.

Now, on to your visit. The HOPI CULTURAL CENTER, Box 67, Second Mesa, AZ 86043, (602) 734-2401, is the best base for your visit. The Cultural Center provides a full line of visitor facilities. There is a very good, modern motel built in a Hopi architectural style. There are 33 units but during popular events such as the Snake Dance it can fill up quickly, so make reservations. Next door is the restaurant which features both Hopi and conventional menu items. Be sure and try the delicious Hopi foods as this is probably the only restaurant in the world where they are served. Pancakes of blue corn meal and mutton stews are especially tasty. Piki bread, wafer-thin and delicately flavored, is sold in one of the complex's shops and makes a tasty snack. It is hand made on hot, flat cooking stones by the Hopi women.

Besides fine lodgings and a good restaurant, the Hopi Cultural Center offers several arts and crafts shops, each with good selections of Hopi products. In the very heart of the center is the museum with outstanding examples of Hopi artwork, displays of Hopi history, an exhibit on a Hopi Olympic track star, and much more. Hopi arts and crafts are also sold here as well as in the restaurant. You can easily spend the afternoon looking and shopping while chatting with the Hopi museum staff and shop owners.

The Hopi Silvercraft Cooperative Guild (Box 37, Second Mesa, AZ 86043, (602) 734-2463) is located just west of the Cultural Center and has showrooms offering fine silverwork, and a wide range of other Hopi arts and crafts as well. They sell both retail and wholesale. Traditional Hopi people believe that the mesas here represent the center of the entire universe. This Hopi religious teaching is reflected in the Guild's motto which proudly proclaims its location "At the Center of the Universe." Some of the Guild's members are "song poets" and a booklet of their poetry is also sold here. The Center of the Universe is rich in cultural endeavors.

Montezuma Castle is one of Arizona's most beautiful cliff dwellings. Built for defensive purposes by the Sinagua Indians centuries ago, it is a favorite of visitors. (R. Shanks)

Most Hopi people live in villages built atop three mesas. Arranged roughly east to west, the easternmost is First Mesa, the middle one is Second Mesa, and the westernmost is Third Mesa. Most visitors consider First Mesa the most picturesque, especially the timeless village of Walpi. Second Mesa is the location of the Cultural Center complex along with several other villages. Third Mesa is the site of Oraibi, the oldest of the Hopi villages. There is a trading post with groceries and other supplies between First and Second Mesa on the main road. The Hopi Tribal Office is between Second and Third Mesa.

The best time to visit Hopi communities is when dances are scheduled and the Hopi are expecting guests. Inquire at the Cultural Center as to which villages are dancing and when. Most weekends during summer there will be a dance at one of the towns. The dances are religious performances, not tourist shows, but visitors are courteously welcomed as long as they remember to follow the rules listed earlier. You will see some of the most beautiful costumes and best dancing among North American Indians here. The singing of the men's chorus complements the dancing in an unforgettable presentation. Dancing often lasts all day with periodic breaks of about an hour.

Each Hopi town specializes in various arts and crafts and artists often sell their products from their homes in the villages. Customers are often invited in to see the fine work and make purchases. If you read a few books on Indian art before you go you'll have a good idea of the broad selection of art made in Hopiland.

A trip to the Hopi mesas is a trip to another world. But it is a trip rich in art, music, architecture, religion, history, and human culture. Not to be missed.

ARIZONA—KAIBAB-PAIUTE INDIAN RESERVATION
14 miles W of Freedonia, AZ
Pipe Springs, AZ
(602) 643-7245
The Kaibab-Paiute Indian people own and operate a camper and trailer park for visitors. There is a store and laundromat at the camper park. Pipe Spring National Monument, which preserves a fort from the days of the Indian wars, is located within the reservation. Future plans include a tribal museum of Paiute culture and history. Hopefully, Pipe Spring National Monument will also include Paiute culture in its future programs.

ARIZONA—KINGMAN
MOJAVE MUSEUM OF HISTORY & ARTS
400 W Beal St
Kingman, AZ
(602) 753-3195
This is a fine local museum with an excellent selection of local Indian crafts. Inside, is a reconstructed WALAPAI house plus other Colorado River area Indian displays. A pleasant, refreshing stop as you travel through the desert heat.

ARIZONA—MONTEZUMA CASTLE NATIONAL MONUMENT
Box 68
Clarkdale, AZ
(602) 567-3322
Montezuma Castle National Monument is located about 45 miles south of Flagstaff off Hwy I-17 between Rimrock and Camp Verde. This is probably the most photographed cliff dwelling in all the Southwest. For sheer beauty Montezuma Castle sweeps away the heart of many visitors. Five stories high, framed in massive cream colored cliffs, it is easy to stand among the trees along Beaver Creek and frame these Sinagua homes in a wreath of leaves and the result is a favorite photograph of many a desert vacation. The Indians lived in such a spectacular site not to please future generations of tourists, but for defense against warlike tribes who often raided these peaceful farmers. Montezuma Castle was not only a true high rise apartment, but an impregnable fortress as well. Incidentally, the name Montezuma is entirely fanciful, the famed Aztec leader lived far to the south in Mexico City and had no direct connection to the Sinagua people. There is a visitor center and museum here, self-guided trails, and welcome shade trees. Because of their fragile condition, the cliff dwelling cannot be entered, but a fine view can be seen just below the buildings.

MONTEZUMA WELL is located in a detached portion of Montezuma Castle National Monument. It is just a few miles north of Montezuma Castle and is easily reached. One of the tragedies of this park is that many visitors fail to go here after seeing the Castle. Montezuma Well is just as interesting and in many ways much more fun. The "well" is a natural sink hole, two-hundred feet in diameter, with vertical cliffs indented with cliff dwellings. A good trail leads down the cliff into the well and you will find a different world down here. There is an array of birds, interesting plants (watch out for poison ivy) and good vistas of the ruins. Back at the top yet another trail leads to more ruins and on down to the outlet where water rushes out of the sink and into a creek. It is often cool here with good shade trees. Incidentally, don't miss the pit house ruin along the road about a mile before you reach the well. It is a very ancient form of house worth knowing about.

ARIZONA—NAVAJO INDIAN RESERVATION
NAVAJO NATION
Box 308
Window Rock, AZ 86515
(602) 871-4941
The huge Navajo Reservation occupies most of northeastern Arizona and parts of adjoining states as well. It completely surrounds the Hopi Reservation. This region is a place of tremendous open spaces, red rock mesas, deep canyons, the Painted Desert, flat grasslands, and pinyon and juniper forests. All younger Indian people can speak English, but Navajo and Hopi are still commonly spoken in this part of America. If you feel that you are in a foreign country, just remember this is the First America and perhaps it's time to meet some real Americans.

Appropriately, the Navajo (pronounced NAV-uh-ho) tribe calls itself the "Navajo Nation". It is a nation larger in size and population than some members of the United Nations. The Navajo are the largest Indian group entirely within the United States. Today the Navajo population approaches 200,000 and is growing rapidly. About one in seven Native Americans is a Navajo.

Visiting the Navajo Country is as different as traveling to Europe or the Orient. There are many cultural and natural attractions here, but lodgings in some areas are limited and plans should include reservations.

Within the boundaries of the Navajo Nation are many places worth visiting. Among them are:

WINDOW ROCK, AZ
Window Rock is the capitol of the Navajo Nation and is a good place to begin your visit. The Tribal Council meets here and the Bureau of Indian Affairs has a major office here, too. The NAVAJO NATION ARTS AND CRAFTS ENTERPRISE is east of town at the junction of Hwy 264 and Navajo Hwy 12. Owned by the Navajo, you will find authentic Indian arts and crafts in this store. Besides an exquisite line of Navajo rugs, jewelry and other items, the store also sells fine Hopi and Zuni jewelry. Phone: (602) 871-4095.

Also in the Art and Crafts Building:

THE NAVAJO TRIBAL MUSEUM
State Hwy 264
Window Rock, AZ
Open weekdays, the Navajo Museum presents the history and culture of the Navajo Nation. There are archeological exhibits, displays of traditional culture, arts and crafts, etc. An old time trading post is recreated here. There are special events featuring modern Navajo artists and craftspeople.

MAAZO MAGAZINE, a new publication of Navajo culture, is published here in Window Rock and features writings by Navajo people in fiction, human interest stories, history, current events, etc. Published quarterly at $12.00 a year it is available from Box 1245, Window Rock, AZ 86515.

NAVAJO TRIBAL COUNCIL BUILDING
Box 308
Window Rock, AZ
(602) 871-4941
The Navajo Nation's Tribal Council Headquarters is an architecturally interesting building, especially with the huge arch of Window Rock looming behind it. Inside, the meeting hall is designed to look like the interior of a large hogan, the traditional circular Navajo dwelling. The room is decorated with murals by Navajo artist Gerald Naylor. Tours are available by arrangement when the Council is not in session.

The NAVAJO NATION'S OFFICE OF BROADCAST SERVICES is the public relations branch of the tribe. They are very helpful and knowledgeable. For those wishing to do commercial photography, filming, or other similar activities on the reservation a permit must be purchased from this office.

WINDOW ROCK FAIRGROUNDS
The annual NAVAJO TRIBAL FAIR is held here. This is one of the largest Indian Fairs in the country where the Navajo and their visitors gather late each summer. Check with the Navajo Nation Headquarters for exact dates. You'll see both traditional Navajo dancing and competitive pow-wow dancing. There is a rodeo, horse racing, arts and crafts displays and sales, a Miss Navajo contest, a parade, and food sales. Authentic Navajo mutton stew, fry bread, squash and melons can all be purchased for a unique and very tasty meal. The parade is a highlight and visiting dignitaries participate—actor Robert Redford was one recent participant.

TSE-BINITO NAVAJO TRIBAL ZOO is in TSE-BINITO PARK on the edge of Window Rock. The Zoo has animals representative of those found on the Navajo Nation, including bear, bobcat, mountain lion, sheep, goats, and more.

TSE-BINITO and WINDOW ROCK NAVAJO TRIBAL CAMPGROUNDS
Near Window Rock, AZ

You can camp in these parks operated by the Navajo Nation. Window Rock Park features drinking water, restrooms, and a picnic area. Navajo Tribal Rangers patrol these and other parks and are very helpful about answering questions.

NED A. HATATHLI CENTER MUSEUM
Navajo Community College campus
Navajo Indian Reservation
Tsaile, AZ
(602) 724-3311

The Museum presents and explains Navajo culture, history, and art. On the campus of Navajo Community College, owned by the Navajo Nation. This is an excellent source for information and research on traditional Navajo life. Check for special events.

WINDOW ROCK MOTOR LODGE
Junction of Hwy 264 & Navajo Hwy 12
(Across from the Arts and Crafts Enterprise and Museum)
Window Rock, AZ 86515
(602) 871-4180

For visitors wishing to stay in Window Rock, the Navajo Nation owns and operates the Window Rock Motor Lodge, a pleasant, modern motel.

The Navajo Nation also owns and leases retail stores in its Navajo Nation Shopping Centers located in Window Rock, Tuba City, Chinle, and Kayenta. Here you can purchase groceries, travel items, clothing, etc. Most or all also have restaurants and laundromats for your convenience. There are is an increased number of gas stations now on the reservation thanks to commercial activities of the Navajo Nation. The gas station attendants are often very helpful sources of directions and information during your visit.

MONUMENT VALLEY NAVAJO TRIBAL PARK
North of Kayenta, AZ
(801) 727-3287

Perhaps more than any other place, Monument Valley has come to symbolize the American Southwest. You've probably seen some of those incredible photographs of huge red sandstone mesas soaring above the desert floor for nearly a thousand feet. Well, if you've always dreamed of going to such a place you can now—thanks to the Navajo Nation. The Tribal Council has preserved this area as Monument Valley Navajo Tribal Park. There is a visitor center where tours are arranged with Navajo guides taking you through this scenic wonderland. Call the number listed for information on guided tours and for motel and camping accommodations. Reservations are advised. To reach Monument Valley, take Hwy 163 north from Kayenta, then go four miles off the highway to the visitor center.

NAVAJO NATION VISITOR CENTERS
Cameron, Chinle, and Monument Valley, AZ

These tribally operated visitor centers help orient you to recreational and cultural opportunities on the Navajo Nation. Arts and crafts are sold here. The Visitor Center at Cameron is located at the junction of Hwys 64 and 89 and is a good stopping point for eastbound travelers arriving from the Grand Canyon or Flagstaff. The LITTLE COLORADO RIVER GORGE NAVAJO TRIBAL PARK is along the eastern boundary of Grand Canyon National Park and is worth seeing. Check with the visitor center in Cameron for details.

KINLICHEE NAVAJO TRIBAL PARK
8 miles E of Gando, AZ

Ancient Anasaszi ruins are preserved here. Picnic area. The park boundary is about three miles beyond Cross Canyon Trading Post on an unpaved road which may become impassable in wet weather.

The **SHIPROCK NAVAJO FAIR** in the northeast part of the reservation is held in the community of Shiprock. This small city is the largest community on the Navajo Nation with a population of about 10,000. The community is named for a gigantic rock monolith, a peak steeply rising from the desert floor that is very spectacular. YEI-BE-CHAI CEREMONIES are held at the Shiprock Fair. These are dancers with impressive traditional clothing sometimes including unforgettable buckskin masks. The Yei-be-chai is also called the Night Chant or Night Way ceremony and is commonly used in curing ceremonies. The Shiprock Fair also has a rodeo, Navajo foods, arts and crafts and more. Shiprock is just over the state line in New Mexico on Hwy 666 at Hwy 550. Accommodations are available nearby in Farmington and Aztec, New Mexico. The fair is usually held the first week in October and the Navajo Nation can provide exact dates.

TRADITIONAL DANCES

Many traditional Navajo dances are held periodically all over the reservation. Most are for healing purposes such as curing the sick, ending mental depression, and the like. Visitors are usually allowed at these ceremonies if they are well behaved (no pictures). Most are at night, often beginning around midnight. Inquire at trading posts, visitor centers, or tribal museums.

Navajo people seem to respect people who are quiet, not pushy, and dignified. On the reservation, honor people's right to privacy, do not enter homes unless invited, request permission before taking photographs, and do not disturb archeological sites. Generally, it is a good idea not to be too talkative, loud, or conspicuous. Behave as a respectful guest and you will be comfortable. The Navajo Reservation is a very pleasant, scenic place to visit and if you are a good guest you'll find the Navajo good hosts.

SEE: CANYON DE CHELLY, GANADO, and NAVAJO NATIONAL MONUMENT.

ARIZONA—NAVAJO NATIONAL MONUMENT

Take Hwy 160, NE of Tuba City, AZ; turn off on Hwy 564, before you reach Kayenta.
(602) 672-2366 or 672-2367
Navajo National Monument is operated by the the Park Service, not the Navajo Nation. It consists of scattered Anasazi cliff dwellings dating back to the 13th century. Access is on foot or by horse and the number of visitors allowed at certain ruins is limited.

There is a visitor center here and a Navajo Nation arts and crafts shop. Navajo guides lead tours and may be booked through park headquarters. Horses may be arranged for, too. Betatakin ruin can be visited on a daily ranger led walking tour via a steep 1 1/2 mile trail. Keet Seel, Arizona's largest cliff dwelling, is best visited by horseback as the eight mile trail is a rough one. Navajo guides lead this trip, a real adventure. Be sure to make reservations. Mailing address: c/o Tonalea, AZ 86044. These are fine ruins and a visit here will make you feel a part of the Navajo country.

ARIZONA—PAPAGO INDIAN RESERVATION

SEE: TRIBAL LISTING under Papago

ARIZONA—PEACH SPRINGS

HUALAPAI (WALAPAI) INDIAN RESERVATION
Box 168
Hwy 66
Peach Springs, AZ 86434
(602) 769-2216
Periodic traditional dancing is held—check with the tribal office for dates. One of the most beautiful but least known of American Indian dancing are Hualapai bird dances. The Hualapai women seem to float as they gracefully dance forward, then backward, to the music. The women wear lovely traditional long dresses and beaded collars.

Along with cattle raising and lumbering, the tribe operates HUALAPAI GRAND CANYON OUTFITTERS which offers an exciting river rafting expedition down the lower Grand Canyon that borders the reservation. Contact the tribal office for details.

ARIZONA—PETRIFIED FOREST NATIONAL PARK

Hwy I-40, 25 miles E of Holbrook, AZ
(602) 524-6228
Although more famous for its petrified trees and the Painted Desert, the park does have at least two interesting Indian archeological sites. NEWSPAPER ROCK is easily accessible and contains numerous examples of Indian rock art. PUERCO RUIN consists of an ancient Anasazi pueblo with small houses still remaining. Both sites are marked on maps distributed by rangers as you enter the park.

ARIZONA—PHOENIX
ARIZONA MUSEUM
1002 W Van Buren
Phoenix, AZ
(602) 253-2734
Among the exhibits are Native American displays, including ancient Hohokam Indian material from southern Arizona. Check for special programs.

CANYON RECORDS
4143 North Sixteenth St
Phoenix, AZ
(602) 266-4823
Canyon Records is the largest producer of American Indian records and tapes in the United States. Recordings are available from a very wide range of US, Canadian, and Mexican tribes. They also carry the products of several other Native American recording companies. Mail order catalog available.

If you like Indian music this is the place for you. You can purchase everything from Kiowa gourd dance songs to Creek stomp dance music. Or perhaps your taste runs to Navajo yei-be-chai chants, Spokane stick game songs, or Iroquois false face dances. It's all here and more. The music is memorable and enchanting, sung by people famous in the Indian community. I enjoy it all.

Most of the music is traditional, but contemporary Indian rock, gospel, and chicken scratch groups are all among the titles. Arts and crafts supplies for Indian craftspeople are also sold here. Well worth a visit.

HEARD MUSEUM
22 E Monte Vista Road
Phoenix, AZ
(602) 252-8848
The Heard Museum has a nationally famous collection of Southwestern Indian arts and crafts. The museum regularly features the work of both past and present-day Indian artists. Special exhibits and programs. Audio-visual presentations. Fine collections of kachina dolls, pottery, basketry, and much more.

Indian crafts fair annually in winter. Guided tours by arrangement. Highly recommended.

PUEBLO GRANDE MUSEUM & HOHOKAM INDIAN RUINS
4619 E Washington St
Phoenix, AZ
(602) 275-3452

The Hohokam were important ancient Indian pioneers of the Southwest. Although their communities did not leave impressive ruins like the cliff dwellers, this was also an advanced culture. Pueblo Grande was a town built on the mound platform seen here today. Low walls remain and clay lined irrigation ditches once ten feet deep and thirty feet wide can be seen in the distance. Extensive irrigation systems were a major Hohokam accomplishment. The museum interprets this agricultural community's past. The City of Phoenix owns and operates Pueblo Grande Museum and ruin.

ARIZONA—ROOSEVELT
TONTO NATIONAL MONUMENT
Box 707
Roosevelt, AZ
(602) 467-2241

The monument is located on Highway 88 two miles east of Roosevelt. Salado Indian cliff dwellings are the focus of this rugged desert country park. There have been some impressive archeological finds here including ancient bows and arrows, ceremonial objects, and more. The visitor center interprets such findings. A half-mile trail leads to Lower Ruin, open daily. A visit to Upper Ruins requires advance arrangements with the ranger staff and takes three hours, but it is a rewarding adventure.

ARIZONA—SACATON
GILA RIVER ARTS & CRAFTS MUSEUM
GILA RIVER INDIAN RESERVATION
Hwy I-10, exit freeway at Casa Blanca, Exit 175
Sacaton, AZ
(602) 963-3981

Operated and owned by the Pima and Maricopa Indian people, the Gila River Arts and Crafts Center south of Phoenix is highly recommended. The museum displays and explains Maricopa and Pima cultures from the perspective of the people themselves. The Pima are outstanding basket weavers and the pottery of the Maricopa ranks with the best in the Southwest. Fine Indian arts and crafts are sold in the gift shop with over 30 tribes from the Southwest, California, and Mexico represented. If you are hungry, the restaurant here features Indian food so you can plan a full visit at the arts and crafts complex.

Of special interest is the outdoor museum with reconstructed houses of the PIMA, MARICOPA, PAPAGO, APACHE, and ancient HOHOKAM all on display. These are fascinating and offer good insights into Southwestern Indian cultural history.

Usually during the second weekend in March, the center holds its annual festival. There is traditional Pima dancing, crafts demonstrations, foods, and other activities. Check with the center for exact dates and times. Saint Peter's Mission nearby also sponsors an annual feast day with Pima dancing.

As a special service, Gila River Arts and Crafts Museum will book Indian dance groups (both Pima and others) for special events. Contact them for costs and other details.

ARIZONA—SAN CARLOS
NATIONAL NATIVE AMERICAN CO-OP
Box 5000
San Carlos, AZ 85550
(602) 244-8244 ext 1409

The National Native American Co-op offers a variety of services to Native American people, especially artists and crafts people. Under the direction of Fred Snyder (Colville and Chippewa) and his wife Carole Garcia (Papago), the Co-op has produced a very useful book, the "Native American Directory". Of value both to Indian and non-Indian readers, it lists urban Indian centers, tribal offices, events, health centers, and much more. The Co-op sponsors the American Indian Market the first weekend of the month from October through May. The market includes arts and crafts sales, Indian dancing, and Indian foods, and is held at the Caravan Inn, 3333 E Van Buren in Phoenix. Artists often demonstrate their skills and cameras are usually welcome.

Mr. Snyder hopes eventually to have an Indian owned cultural resort complex and a telephone system for communication among Indian artists and others. For those wishing to know more, contact the Co-op.

ARIZONA—SOMERTON
COCOPAH INDIAN RESERVATIONS
Somerton, AZ
(602) 627-2102

The Cocopah Reservations are south of Somerton, AZ, on county Road 18 and Ave D, 5 miles outside town. This is hot desert country so be sure you have a good map.

The COCOPAH FESTIVITIES DAY is held each year usually in March or April. You'll see traditional Cocopah dancing and singing, including some back and

Apache Mountain Spirit Dancers have distinctive sudden movements, an appearance that commands respect, and beautiful costumes. These dancers are White Mountain Apache high school students from Sherman Institute in Riverside, California. (R. Shanks)

forth dancing, the rabbit dance, and songs danced in circles. There is Indian food for sale including fry bread, beans, and Indian tacos. Arts and crafts are sold with beadwork and fine gourd rattles being two specialties. There is a Miss Cocopah contest and the lucky contestant reigns during Festivities Day. Volleyball, baseball, children's games and other sports activities complete the day's events.

The COCOPAH ELDERLY CENTER on Cedar St on the reservation offers a small gift shop. Beautiful Cocopah ribbonshirts are sold plus beadwork and other arts and crafts, phone 627-2632.

The Cocopah have future plans for a museum at the Yuma Territorial Mall and we wish them well in this project.

Cocopah traditional singers are well known in Indian communities in the Southwest. They often sing at traditional Indian memorial services which are so important in Native American religions in southern California and western-most Arizona. These funeral observances are, of course, private but there are also public Indian events where the Cocopah sing. The lovely music, beautiful ribbon dresses and ribbon shirts, gourd rattles, and graciousness of the Cocopah people will linger in your memory.

ARIZONA—TUBA CITY
SAN JUAN SOUTHERN PAIUTE YINGUP WEAVERS ASSOCIATION
Box 1336
Tuba City, AZ 86045
Living here among the Navajo is a band of Paiute people. The women of the band have made a real effort at preserving and continuing their art of basketry. They have recently received recognition from the National Endowment for the Arts and the Wheelwright Museum of Santa Fe. About 20 Southern San Juan Paiute women make these baskets and they are increasingly being sought by knowledgeable collectors. The baskets are reasonably priced for the many hours of work they require. Mail order available.

ARIZONA—TUCSON
ARIZONA STATE MUSEUM
University of Arizona campus
University Blvd entrance
Tucson, AZ
(602) 626-1604
Among the collections are Southwestern Indian exhibits ranging from ancient archeological finds to present day Native American cultures. Check for special events.

FORT LOWELL COUNTY PARK
End of Craycroft Road
Tucson, AZ
(602) 885-3832 museum, or 885-2680 park
Fort Lowell park contains the Hardy site, an ancient Hohokam village once so large that it covered a quarter square mile. The site was partially excavated by the Arizona State Museum but was later covered to protect it from weathering and vandalism. A pit house floor was reconstructed out of concrete to demonstrate the type of dwelling discovered here. Fort Lowell Museum has exhibits and artifacts from the village.

ARIZONA—TUZIGOOT NATIONAL MONUMENT
Box 68
Clarkdale, AZ
Located 1 1/2 miles N of Clarkdale
(602) 634-5564
Tuzigoot ranks among the most striking of all the Indian ruins in the Southwest. Built atop a ridge overlooking the Verde Valley, this pyramidal pueblo rises to culminate in massive rooms at its summit. A trail allows visitors to walk through the ruins and even to enter the rooms at the very peak. The archeological museum here is particularly well done and is located in a picturesque building. For a better understanding, go to the museum-visitor center both before and after viewing Tuzigoot. Tuzigoot is one of my favorite places and is highly recommended for anyone interested in Southwestern Indian culture and architecture.

ARIZONA—WHITE MOUNTAIN APACHE INDIAN RESERVATION
Box 700
Whiteriver, AZ
(602) 338-4346
The White Mountain Apache Indian Reservation is noted for its scenic mountain splendor. It is popular with the Southwesterners for winter skiing, seasonal hunting and fishing, and cool summer camping. Colorful traditional Mountain Spirit Dancing is frequently performed at Apache events and ranks among the very best of Southwestern dances.

The tribe operates the large and highly rated Sunrise Ski Resort, a year round resort complex, located on the reservation three miles south of McNary, phone (602) 334-2144. It also owns and operates the modern, attractive White Mountain Apache Motel and restaurant at Whiteriver, also on the reservation, phone (602) 338-4927. Sunrise is in the luxury class of accommodations while the motel is for middle-range budgets.

There are many visitor attractions on the White Mountain Reservation including the traditional summer wickiups built at various places including Cebuque (private residences), the ancient Kinishba ruins, Geronimo's Cave, and the tribally owned fish hatchery and lumber mill. Recently, a disastrous fire destroyed the Apache Cultural Center at Fort Apache along with its museum collections. The Apaches are in the process of rebuilding the center and welcome contributions of Apache material for display. Hopefully the new Apache Cultural Museum will be in operation by the time you read this. The center may be contacted at Box 507, Fort Apache, AZ 85926. The lodge, motel or tribal office can all direct you to any of the above visitor attractions.

The annual Apache Tribal Fair is usually held over Labor Day weekend and generally includes Mountain Spirit Dancing. The dances are also properly called Crown Dances and you may hear that term. Use of the outdated and inaccurate term "Devil Dance" for these ceremonies is a name many Apaches resent. The tribal fair includes a parade, rodeo, and other events but the dancing is a highlight for many visitors. Sometimes Mescalero Apaches come from New Mexico and add to the dancing excitement. Sacred girl's puberty rites are still held, often during fair time. These are moving and meaningful coming of age rites for teenage girls and include singing, dancing, running, and prayers. Well behaved visitors are generally welcome. During July and August many dances are held and the tribal office or motels can help you find those that are public. The White Mountain Apache people are kind, friendly hosts and their beautiful homeland is sure to impress you.

ARIZONA—WILCOX
COCHISE VISITOR CENTER & MUSEUM
Junction of Hwy I-10 & Hwy 186
Wilcox, AZ
(602) 384-2272
The center interprets the history of the Apache people and the famous Indian wars of this area. Cochise was a well known chief of the Apache and highly respected for his courage in achieving peace despite much provocation.

ARIZONA—YUMA
QUECHAN INDIAN MUSEUM
Box 1352
Yuma, AZ
(619) 572-0661
The museum is located on the Fort Yuma Indian Reservation off Indian Hill Road across the Colorado River from Yuma, Arizona, in California. Take the old bridge across the river (not the new Interstate highway bridge). It's best to obtain a "Yuma Historic & Cultural Site" brochure from the Chamber of Commerce which includes a guide to historic Yuma with directions included. Contact the Chamber of Commerce at 377 Main, Yuma, AZ 85364, phone (602) 782-2567.

The Quechan or Yuma Indian people have a long and exciting history here at Yuma. They controlled this vital river crossing for centuries and their relations with both the Spanish and the military are recognized in the museum. Highlights are displays of Quechan clay dolls, pottery, bows, arrowheads, cradles, etc.

Fishing permits are sold at the tribal office and there is a bingo enterprise for enthusiasts. The tribal office phone is (619) 572-0213.

ARKANSAS

ARKANSAS—ENGLAND
TOLTEC MOUNDS STATE PARK
Off US 165, 9 miles NW of England, AK
(501) 961-9442
Although not built by Mexican Toltec Indians, these mounds were made by a culture which seems connected to Mexican civilizations. There are temple and burial mounds here along with a museum, an audio-visual presentation, and guided tours. There is also an archeological laboratory on site.

ARKANSAS—FAYETTEVILLE
UNIVERSITY OF ARKANSAS MUSEUM
Hotz Hall on campus
Fayetteville, AK
(501) 575-3555
Native American exhibits among the collections.

ARKANSAS—MURFREESBORO
KA-DO-HA DISCOVERY MOUND BUILDER VILLAGE SITE
Located 2 miles NW of Murfeesboro
(501)285-3736
Excavated Southeastern Indian village with museum displaying material from the site.

ARKANSAS—TEXARKANA
TEXARKANA HISTORICAL MUSEUM
219 State Line Ave
Texarkana, AK
(214) 793-4831
Among the collections are exhibits on the Caddo, an important group of tribes, basically Southeastern in culture famed for their fine pottery. Today, the Caddo live near Hinton, Oklahoma.

White Mountain Apache dancers pause along a desert road. These high school students from Sherman Institute are in the magnificent Mountain Spirit apparel. (R. Shanks)

Opening parade at the American Indian Exposition in Anadarko, Oklahoma. Apache dancers present an impressive sight. Some Oklahoma Apaches are descendants of Geronimo's famous band. (Oklahoma Tourism—Fred Marvel)

ARKANSAS—WILSON
HAMPSON STATE MUSEUM
Hwy 61
Wilson, AK
(501) 655-8622
Exhibits of local archeological finds from a major Indian village excavated nearby.

CALIFORNIA

California has over 200,000 Native American residents, more than any other state. According to the University of California, about half of these are members of tribes native to the state. Native California tribes include the Pomo, Miwok, Maidu, Pit River, Hupa, Karuk, Cahuilla, and others. The other half of California's Indian residents come from other states, especially Oklahoma, Arizona, South Dakota, etc.

California has over 70 Indian reservations, more than any other state. Most are small because they are occupied predominantly by descendants from a single village. Often these villages have been traditional communities for centuries. Most are located at or near their original sites. The homes of the people are contemporary houses, but a few reservations have active ceremonial roundhouses. The large majority of California Indian people live off the reservation because jobs are more plentiful in the cities and suburbs. But many California Indian people return home for cultural events and visits. Check both the California section and the tribal listings.

CALIFORNIA—ALTURAS
MODOC COUNTY MUSEUM
600 South Main St
Alturas, CA
(916) 233-2944
A highlight of visiting this museum is learning about what was probably really the last Indian battle in US frontier history. About 1912, a small band of Paiute people fought it out with local lawmen in a tragic and bloody battle east of here. Remembering, too, that Ishi, the famous "last wild Indian in the United States", lived southwest of Alturas, these two facts combine to make northeastern California the last site of the West's Indian wars. Over two decades after the final Sioux battle at Wounded Knee, South Dakota, California Indians were still struggling for independence.

CALIFORNIA—ARCADIA
HUGO & VICTORIA RIED ADOBE
LOS ANGELES STATE & COUNTY ARBORETUM GROUNDS
301 N. Baldwin
Arcadia, CA
(818) 446-8251
This place takes us to the romantic days of a Spanish ranchero and his beautiful Indian wife. Hugo Ried was one of a number of enlightened Scotsmen who immigrated to America and fell in love with the land of California. His greatest blessing was winning the hand in marriage of Victoria, a lovely Gabrieliño Indian woman. Together they founded and operated Rancho Santa Anita where they rose in prominence and prestige in Mexican California. In later years they became known by the honored titles of Don Hugo and Doña Victoria, evidence of nobility in Spanish territories.

With the advent of the Bear Flag Revolt when the US took California from Mexico, thousands of Anglo immigrants poured into the state. The Gold Rush of 1849 greatly accelerated immigration and attracted much of the worst element of Americans. The local Gabrieliño Indians became virtually enslaved by the gold seekers. Forced to do heavy manual labor day after day, overwork, disease, and alcohol decimated the Indian population.

Hugo Ried was shocked as he saw what was being done to his wife's kinsmen. His voice was one of the few raised on their behalf and his letters to Los Angeles newspapers remain eloquent classics. The service of this white man and his dedication to Native American people should not be forgotten. Hugo and Victoria's adobe home remains, open to visitors today as it was long ago. Perhaps you will visit there and remember, too.

If you wish to read Don Hugo's letters, get *The Indians of Los Angeles County: Hugo Ried's Letters of 1852*, published by the Southwest Museum in Los Angeles in 1968. And what of the Gabrieliño? A few families in the city of San Gabriel, Los Angeles County, proudly remember their Gabrieliño ancestry. A few stone tools remain and fewer baskets.

CALIFORNIA—BAKERSFIELD
KERN COUNTY MUSEUM
3801 Chester St
Bakersfield, CA
(805) 861-2132
Bakersfield is rich in Yokuts Indian heritage and this museum offers an outstanding collection of California Indian artifacts. Especially impressive are the Yokuts baskets, each one a work of art.

CALIFORNIA—BARSTOW
CALICO EARLY MAN ARCHEOLOGICAL SITE
15 miles NE of Barstow via I-15 and Mineola Road
Barstow, CA
(619) 256-3591
One of the oldest sites of human habitation discovered thus far in North America. Dr. Louis Leakey, famed for his archeological work in Africa, believed this site dated back to the distant past. Visitor center and guided tours of excavations.

CALIFORNIA—BERKELEY
ROBERT H. LOWIE MUSEUM OF ANTHROPOLOGY
Kroeber Hall
NW corner of Bancroft Way and College Ave
Berkeley, CA
(415) 642-3681
The University of California at Berkeley led the world in its studies of California Indians for decades. This was no small feat for California Indian territory was generally considered "the most complex ethnographic area in the world" by anthropologists. The researchers have amassed the greatest collection of Indian baskets on the globe. Exquisite work from the Pomo, Maidu, Tubatulabal, Costanoan, Panamint, Kawaiisu, Hupa, Yurok and dozens of others are preserved here. Unfortunately, the museum is underfunded by the State of California and this unparalleled collection is only displayed in small segments on rather rare intervals. This collection is so outstanding that there is a genuine need for a California Indian room where rotating displays present California Indian cultures.

The museum does have a very interesting semi-permanent exhibit on Ishi, the Yahi Indian who was the last Indian in the United States living in a completely aboriginal manner. In this exhibit, you will see many articles made or used by Ishi during his two lonely years as the last living member of a central California Indian tribe.

Lowie Museum also regularly presents outstanding exhibits on people from all over the world, but sadly the current lack of space and low budget results in few dealing with Native Americans. Check the museum gift shop for many interesting items from Central American and other Indian groups.

CALIFORNIA—BISHOP
PAIUTE/SHOSHONE INDIAN CULTURAL MUSEUM
2300 West Line St
Bishop, CA
(609) 873-4478
Built in 1978 on the Bishop Indian Reservation, this Indian owned and operated museum features replicas of local rock art from important sites in the region. There are also interesting Paiute and Shoshone cultural displays. Various museum fund raising activities are held. Contact the museum for special events.

CALIFORNIA—CARMEL
CARMEL MISSION (Mission San Carlos)
3080 Rio Road
Carmel, CA
(408) 624-3600
This beautiful and famous Spanish mission is still active as a church. Father Serra, founder of the missions, is buried here. His library and study remain and may be seen.

All 21 of the California missions were built to serve California Indians and the Costanoan and Esselen tribes were here. A small museum displays Costanoan baskets and stonework along with items from other tribes.

Some anthropologists once erroneously believed that the Costanoan (or Ohlone) Indians were extinct. Recently Ohlone Costanoans to the north have become increasingly well known in the Mission San Jose area. Harry Downie, longtime curator at Carmel Mission, commented to me on the the many visits Costanoan descendants still make to the mission today. He estimated, based on his experiences, that there are probably around 2000 people of part Costanoan ancestry alive today. Not bad for a tribe written off until recently as extinct.

CALIFORNIA—CLEAR LAKE
The Clear Lake region of Lake County is the homeland of the Pomo Indian people. The Pomo created an ecologically sophisticated and deeply religious society here. They were so successful that Clear Lake's environs became one of the most densely populated places in Native America, yet there were no problems of pollution or destruction of resources.

The Pomo lived here for countless centuries and then were abruptly disturbed by Spanish and American invaders. The peaceful, gentle Pomo eventually were almost enslaved by several early settlers and treated brutally. Finally being able to stand it no longer, a group of Pomo men executed two particu-

A Miwok family at the California State Indian Museum's celebration for honoring elders. The family is part of Bill Franklin's Sierra Miwok dance group. (R. Shanks)

larly brutal settlers, Stone and Kelsey, in 1849. The peaceful life resumed for a time, but the US Army was ordered to Lake County to seek revenge for the two deaths.

A large group of innocent Pomo families fled to an island seeking protection from the troops. Unfortunately, the soldiers had brought along whaleboats and they attacked by water. The US Army rowed to the island, then proceeded to slaughter Pomo men, women, and children. Ironically, none of those killed had any connection with the deaths of Stone and Kelsey—the Pomo at the island were from a completely different village. Worse, the Army then proceeded to march into neighboring Mendocino County and kill Indians there who were equally innocent. They were attacked because of the color of their skin alone. None had ever raised a hand against the white intruders.

Today, Lake County residents call the island "Bloody Island" and a plaque may be seen along the west side of Highway 20 about two miles southeast of the town of Upper Lake. The lake has receded here and Bloody Island appears as the wooded hill to the west.

Just beyond Bloody Island is the Robinson Rancheria. In Central California many Indian Reservations still bear the old Spanish name "rancheria", meaning an Indian village in California Spanish. The Robinson Pomo tribe was terminated by the government during the 1950's, but due to the dedicated work of Mrs. Bernadine Tripp and other Pomo leaders a new reservation was established in the early 1980's at this location. Robinson Rancheria is just south of Bloody Island on the east side of Highway 20. Efforts are being made to provide an economic base to allow Robinson Pomo people to return to their home and live again as a community. Plans include new homes and a bingo enterprise.

Southeast of Clearlake Oaks, off Sulphur Bank Drive, the Elem Pomo have a reservation. This is the home of one of the finest Indian dance groups in the state. The Elem Pomo Dancers under the leadership of the Brown family perform the ancient Big Head dance, the Ball Dance, and various shake-head dances. Religious dancing is done here, but public performances are also periodically presented to appreciative audiences.

Just offshore from the Sulphur Bank Rancheria, is Rattlesnake Island. This beautiful oak wooded island is a sacred place to the Elem Pomo. Village sites here date back thousands of years and the Pomo have continued to hold sacred ceremonies on the island. Recently, the island was purchased by an investor and the Pomo restricted in their use of the island. This is a sacred religious site, still used, dating back to before the time of Christ. There is a great need to preserve this island, keep it open to Pomo religious activities, and protect the ecology. Incidentally, there are no rattlesnakes on the island. It was so named to discourage people from trespassing on sacred Indian land.

The Elem Pomo recently built an attractive new tribal office decorated with traditional basketry designs. The lake remains important in Pomo lives and fish and tule reeds are still eaten from the lake. Traditional seaweed and kelp are also a part of some people's diets along with acorn foods and manzanita berry juice.

The Elem Pomo are outstanding dancers and singers and it may be possible to book the dance group for special events. Most California Indian dance groups charge a fee for performances. Tribal Office number is (707) 998-1666.

Along Soda Bay Road between Lakeport and Kelseyville, off Highway 29 is the Big Valley or Mission Rancheria. The Pomo people here continue traditional dances such as the sacred Big Head Dance and various shake-head dances. They have a ceremonial roundhouse here where periodic dances are performed for religious reasons. Some Big Valley people are also wonderful dancers and singers too.

Lake County has several other Pomo Rancherias including Upper Lake, Cache Creek, Scotts's Valley, and Middletown. The latter is not Pomo, but is a Lake Miwok rancheria.

All the Pomo people have a rich, advanced cultural heritage and there is a need for a major Native American cultural center honoring Pomo heritage in either Sonoma, Mendocino, or Lake counties.

Be sure to visit the Lakeport Historical Museum, Main & Third St in Lakeport. They have a fine collection of Pomo baskets. (707) 263-4555.

CALIFORNIA—CRESCENT CITY
DEL NORTE COUNTY HISTORICAL SOCIETY MUSEUM
577 "H" St
Crescent City, CA
(707) 464-3911
Among the collections are some very fine examples of Northwestern California Indian arts and crafts. The Indian collection is particularly strong on local Tolowa and Yurok material. The Tolowa people still seasonally fish for smelt along the beaches north of

here and dry them on driftwood logs. A Tolowa dance group also gives performances occasionally. SEE: CALIFORNIA—REDWOOD NATIONAL PARK.

CALIFORNIA—DESERT HOT SPRINGS
CABOT'S OLD INDIAN PUEBLO MUSEUM
67616 E Desert View Ave
Desert Hot Springs, CA
(619) 329-7610
This museum, built pueblo-style, contains American Indian and Eskimo (Inuit) artifacts. Relics of General Custer's defeat in the Battle of the Little Bighorn are exhibited.

CALIFORNIA—EAST MOJAVE NATIONAL SCENIC AREA
BUREAU OF LAND MANAGEMENT
901 Third St
Needles, CA
The Mojave Desert contains many excellent examples of Indian rock art. There are even gigantic human figures so large that they are visible only from the air! Their purpose remains a mystery today. Other rock art sites are smaller and easily seen. Contact the Bureau of Land Management for directions and information on travel conditions. Be very careful in venturing off well traveled roads in the harsh environment of the Mojave Desert.

CALIFORNIA—EL TORO
AMERICAN ROCK ART RESEARCH ASSOC.
Box 1539
El Toro, CA
The ARARA is an association of professionals and other interested people who are pioneering the study of Native American rock art. Their interests include all types of rock painting, petroglyphs, and the like. The organization has a newsletter "La Pintura", sponsors field trips, and holds a major annual conference. There are various local chapters which meet to discuss rock art and to take field trips to many fascinating sites.

The northern California chapter, The Bay Area Rock Art Association (Mr. Leigh Marymor, editor, 3835 14th Ave, Oakland, CA 94602) is very active taking field trips, holding meetings, and having an occasional newsletter of real value. There are other branches which may be contacted through ARARA at El Toro.

CALIFORNIA—ESCONDIDO
THE INDIAN SHOP
1351 E Valley Parkway
Escondido, CA
(619) 746-5522
California Indian owned shop featuring Southwest Indian art.

CALIFORNIA—EUREKA
CLARKE MEMORIAL MUSEUM
Third and "E" St
Eureka, CA
(707) 443-1947
Outstanding Northwestern California Indian exhibits featuring basketry and other cultural objects. The Yurok, Hupa, and Karuk cultures are particularly well represented here. The museum recently added a large new Indian room. Book shop.

NORTHERN CALIFORNIA INDIAN DEVELOPMENT COUNCIL
241 "F" St
Eureka, CA
(707) 445-8451
The Council serves 16 northwestern California Indian organizations with members from the Hupa, Karuk, Wiyot, Tolowa, Yurok and other tribes. The Council's headquarters has a gift shop and an art gallery offering a good selection of traditional and contemporary arts and crafts from this unique area. Dentalium shell jewelry, wood and bone carvings, basketry, prints and other items are often for sale here. The Council annually produces an attractive calendar with historic photos of Northwestern California Indian people. The calendar may be ordered by mail. Open weekdays.

CALIFORNIA—FOLSOM
PACIFIC WESTERN TRADERS
305 Wool St
Folsom, CA
(916) 985-3851
This is a fine Indian arts and crafts store, a small museum, a book shop, and a cultural center all in one location.

The store has an unusually good selection of traditional California Indian arts and crafts, including many rarely seen items. Work by Native American artists and craftspeople from other regions is also offered. There is a large selection of well chosen Indian books from all over North America. Craft supplies, traditional Pueblo corn meal, ribbonshirts, baskets, carvings, and much more are sold. Good selection of Native American records and tapes.

Pacific Western Traders also sponsors cultural events on Native American subjects. Lectures and demonstrations are presented by both Indian and non-Indian experts. There is a major annual arts and crafts show in the Spring and before Christmas. Recently, the Tache Yokuts dance group performed here and, hopefully, they and other dance groups will return. The store has a mailing list which announces special events. Pacific Western Traders also is usually a good source of information on local Indian events.

The most important traditional food of the central California Indian people was acorn mush. It is still made occasionally by the Miwok, Pomo, Western Mono and other groups. Bitter tannic acid must be removed from the acorn flour by leaching with water before it can be eaten. Later, the acorn meal is boiled in baskets using cooking stones. The hot stones quickly bring the tasty mush to a boil. (R. Shanks)

Ceremonial roundhouse on the Manchester Rancheria (reservation) near Point Arena, California. These buildings are the traditional location of many important central California Indian ceremonies. Both Pt. Reyes National Seashore and Indian Grinding Rock State Park have roundhouses open to the public. (R. Shanks)

CALIFORNIA—FORT ROSS STATE HISTORIC PARK

On Hwy 1, 11 miles N of Jenner
Jenner, CA
(707) 847-3286

Fort Ross was built by Russian settlers in 1812 as an outpost of their Alaskan holdings. Both Russians and Aleuts (Native Americans from the Aleutian Islands) hunted seals and sea otters along the coast and did some farming. The farming was largely practiced near Bodega Bay in Coast Miwok territory. The fort, however, was built to the north in the land of the Kashaya Pomo. There was much contact between the Russians and the Pomo people and even after the Russian departure in 1841, their legacy stayed. To this day, Kashaya Pomo has approximately forty Russian words among its vocabulary.

Besides their influence on the Pomo, the Russians also left their fort behind. Now restored, visitors will see the fortified walls, Russian Orthodox church, commandant's house and more. There are displays of Aleut and Russian artifacts.

The Kashaya Pomo still live nearby, many on the Stewart's Point Indian Reservation. Pomo dance groups have demonstrated their beautiful dances at special events at the fort. Check with the fort for possible upcoming activities. SEE: CALIFORNIA—STEWARTS POINT.

CALIFORNIA—FREMONT

COYOTE HILLS REGIONAL PARK
8000 Paterson Ranch Road
Fremont, CA
(415) 471-4967

To reach the park take Hwy 17 to Route 84, Dumbarton Bridge Exit. Go E on Route 84 to Newark Blvd. Then go left on Paterson Ranch Road to the park entrance, 1 mile ahead. Picnicking and hiking, plus special events.

Coyote Hills Park has a large OHLONE (COSTANOAN) INDIAN VILLAGE site with reconstructed buildings. Tours of the village are offered on Sundays and provide the best way to see the site. The Chochenyo Trail (brochure and map available at the visitor center) takes you to an archeological site and through marsh lands filled with tule reeds. Tules provided the Ohlone with material for boats, houses, baskets, mats and many other useful things. The park gives visitors a good feel for what life was originally like along San Francisco Bay.

The visitor center contains a large tule canoe built by the park staff and volunteers, It actually sails quite well and once made a long journey around San Francisco Bay. Ohlone and Miwok people regularly crossed the bay in such boats, ranking them as daring sailors.

There is a fascinating annual Stone Age Olympics held here featuring ancient Native American implements reproduced for the competition. One unusual event is the atlatl competition where participants throw spears using this ancient tool that pre-dated bows and arrows. The competition is open to all.

Coyote Hills staff is to be congratulated with its creative programs. Incidentally, members of the local Ohlone Indian community have an interest in the park and sometimes participate in programs here. Their help strengthens the fine programs considerably.

CALIFORNIA—HEMET

MAZE STONE COUNTY PARK
Hwy 74, 8 miles NW of Hemet
Hemet, CA
(714) 787-2553

Southern California Indian rock art is found here on a large boulder.

CALIFORNIA—HOOPA VALLEY INDIAN RESERVATION

HUPA TRIBAL MUSEUM & HISTORIC VILLAGES
Box 1245
Hoopa, CA
(916) 625-4110 Museum, or 625-4211 Tribal Office

The museum is located inside the shopping center adjacent to the market in the town of Hoopa on Hwy 96.

The beautiful new Hupa Tribal Museum presents an outstanding display of Hupa, Karuk, and Yurok arts and crafts from the unique cultures of Northwestern California Indian people. The Hupa Museum shows off some of the finest of ceremonial regalia, basketry, wood and antler carvings, and more. Dugout canoes in this area are unique and there is one on display here. If they're not too busy ask a member of the museum staff or a volunteer to explain the human-like body parts of the canoe. A number of Hupa elders are docents at the museum and are very knowledgeable, pleasant people to talk with. Highly informative tours of the museum can be arranged with advance notice.

Hoopa Valley is the location of two traditional Hupa villages which feature reconstructed and historic plank houses. The villages, Takimildin and Madildin, are actual towns the Hupa occupied for centuries. Al-

A traditional northwestern California Indian home. This Hupa home is made of cedar planks and is partially underground for insulation. Lyle Marshall of the Hupa Tribal Museum approaches the round doorway. Two traditional villages are maintained by the Hupa for religious and cultural activities. The Hupa have a fine museum at Hoopa, California, which explains their heritage. (R. Shanks)

A Yurok family house overlooking the mouth of the Klamath River near Requa, California. The Northwestern California Indian people no longer live in such houses but maintain some for cultural and religious reasons. (R. Shanks)

though present day Hupa live in modern houses, the village homes, sweathouse, and ceremonial structures are maintained because of their importance to Hupa cultural and religious life. The houses are semi-subterranean plank houses, built partially above ground and partly below the surface. The sweathouse is similarly constructed. The ceremonial structures are likewise partly below ground, but have no roof. Instead, they are open, encircled with benches creating an amphitheater. Periodically, traditional Hupa dances are held here in the villages and at other sites. Both villages have sacred significance and should be entered only after obtaining permission from the Hupa.

When you enter the valley from the south on Hwy 96, on the right you will notice a historical marker pointing out the site of a now vanished Hupa village across the Trinity River. A little farther along keep watching the far bank of the river and you will see the plank houses of Madildin. These houses are called "xonta" in the Hupa language and feature a low profile and a small, round door. They are unpainted, being allowed to weather in their natural colors. With a good telephoto lens you can take some nice pictures from the highway. Takimildin is north of Hoopa and is not visible from the road. Serious visitors might be able to arrange a visit through the museum staff.

There is a regular round of fine ceremonial dances at Hoopa and also up the Klamath River in Karuk country, especially during odd numbered years. Check with the museum or the Hupa and Karuk tribal offices for dates, locations, and if the particular dance is open to visitors. These dances are religious and must be approached with great respect. Do not take pictures or make tapes without advance arrangements with those ceremonial leaders in charge. If such a privilege is granted, a monetary donation is proper. Occasional public performances outside Northwestern California are done and should not be missed. There is a great need for a Northwestern California Indian Cultural Center in Humboldt County where everyone regularly can come to enjoy this unique and beautiful dancing and singing.

The Hupa Tribe operates the Six Rivers Bingo enterprise in the shopping center at Hoopa and extends a welcome to the public. Phone (916) 625-4242.

CALIFORNIA—INDIAN GRINDING ROCK STATE PARK
Off Hwy 88 on Pine Grove—Volcano Rd
Pine Grove, CA
(209) 296-7488
Set amid forests and oak woodlands, this park helps

preserve Miwok Indian history and culture. For centuries Miwok (MEE-wok) people have come here to a massive low rock of truly amazing proportions. Miwok women have worn hundreds of grinding holes in the bedrock. Called mortars, these depressions were used along with pounding stones called pestles to reduce acorns to flour. A leaching process was used to remove toxic tannic acid from the acorn flour making the meal edible. Acorn meal was made into mush, soup, bread, and other foods. A number of California groups still make it today including the Pomo, Miwok, Monache and others.

In addition to the huge grinding rock with its mortars and rock art, the Miwok people have reconstructed a complete village. You may visit conical bark houses held together by wild grape vines, an acorn storage granary, a handgame house, an Indian football field, and a ceremonial roundhouse. The roundhouse is a magnificent structure, semi-subterranean, with the traditional four center posts of Miwok architecture. Dances are still held here with visitors sitting quietly around the edges. A footdrum made of a board is located opposite the entrance, on the far side of the roundhouse. It is pounded with a pole during dances to help provide a beat for the dancers.

The park is open all year, but the best time to visit is when the Amador Indian Council and the park sponsor CHAW-SE BIG TIME CELEBRATION, usually the last weekend in September. This is one of California's best Indian events and often Pomo, Miwok, and Maidu dancing and singing is done here. Events go on all day and sometimes all night. Usually things start in late morning with group dancing. Around noon there is a deep pit barbecue with beef, beans, salad, and more. Sometimes nutritious acorn soup is served, a real treat. As the afternoon goes along, dancing usually resumes in the roundhouse. Colorful flicker headbands of orange and black feathers flash in time with the singing. The feather dance skirts of the Pomo contrast with the buckskin dance skirts of the Miwok. California Indian dancers often wear no moccasins to keep their feet in close relation to mother earth. The beautiful singing and dancing is unlike any other in North America and is unsurpassed in beauty. Some years the Pomo dance their deeply religious Big Head Dance here, perhaps the most spectacular of California Indian ceremonies. The roundhouse is a sacred place and no pictures or tapes should be made inside. With the exception of the Big Head dance, other dance performers will usually pose for pictures *outside* the dance house. Remember not to stand in the entrance of the dancehouse because it blocks the dancers. Also, never touch the costumes of the dancers because there are religious rules against this.

Besides the dancing, you usually see hand games being played by Miwok, Paiute, and Washo teams. One year a group of Yakima women, all tribal elders, came down from Washington state and outplayed everybody. The guessing game involves one team's holding two sticks or bones, one marked and the other unmarked. The opponents try to guess which hand the marked stick is held in. If they guess right, they are awarded a counting stick. When a team has won all the sticks, they win the game. The contest often goes back and forth and can last all night. All the games are accompanied by beautiful, gentle sounding hand game songs which are a pleasure to sit and listen to.

Arts and crafts are sold during the Big Time Celebration along with fry bread, Indian tacos, and other tasty treats. Often information on Washo and other Indian celebrations is distributed at booths during Chaw-se.

Year round the museum is open with displays and audio-visual presentations on California Indian cultures. Special art shows are occasionally held. There is an active volunteer association, the Chaw-se Indian Grinding Rock Association, that interested persons may join and help out with future activities. Check with the park staff for dates of upcoming events.

CALIFORNIA—JOLON
MISSION SAN ANTONIO DE PADUA
N of Jolon in the Hunter-Leggitt Military Reservation
Jolon, CA
(408) 385-4478
No other mission in California quite achieves the feeling of the old Spanish and Indian days as Jolon does, the most isolated of California missions. As you drive north from Jolon (HOH-lone, rhymes with alone), ignore the military intrusions and focus on the lush oak woodlands which provided the local Salinan Indians with acorns. The processed acorn flour was the most important food in the Salinan diet and it is easy to see how this area once supported a large population of Indian people.

Once past the army fort, the mission is set in a valley beneath the mysterious Santa Lucia Mountains. The mission was built by the Salinans and its museum contains Salinan baskets among the collections. As with all the California missions, visitors are welcome and may tour the church and some of the other buildings. San Antonio mission is a peaceful place worthy of a visit.

CALIFORNIA—KLAMATH
TREES OF MYSTERY & INDIAN MUSEUM
4 miles N of Klamath on Hwy 101
(707) 482-5613
Inside the large gift shop there is an impressive display of Native American arts and crafts. All of it is interesting, but of special significance is local Northwestern California clothing and basketry.

CALIFORNIA—LASSEN VOLCANIC NATIONAL PARK
Mineral, CA 96063
(916) 595-4444
Open summers only, 50 miles E of Redding on Hwy 44.
For many years Lassen Park has employed local Atsugewi Indian people as naturalists and cultural historians. Programs in Lassen Park Indian culture are presented by Atsugewi rangers and include a demonstration in basket weaving. An Atsugewi wickiup covered with pine bark has been reconstructed. This small tribe is also sometimes called the "Hat Creek" people after the nearby stream that is the center of Atsugewi country.

CALIFORNIA—LOMPOC
LOMPOC MUSEUM
200 South "H" St
Lompoc, CA
(805) 736-3888
Lompoc Museum owns a large collection of Chumash archeological specimens and other Native American items.

CALIFORNIA—LOS ANGELES
SOUTHWEST MUSEUM
234 Museum Dr at Marmion Way
Take Pasadena Freeway exit 43
Highland Park area
Los Angeles, CA
(213) 221-2163
This distinguished museum exhibits a large and impressive collection of Native American material from many cultures. Outstanding dioramas of California Indian cultures, Plains Indian exhibit (including tepee), reconstructed Miwok village, and more. Many fine California Indian baskets and Southwest pottery bowls displayed. Exhibits range from the Eastern Woodlands to the Arctic. Special exhibits and programs. Publications. Gift shop with arts and crafts sales.

Be sure to enter through the lower tunnel with its dioramas where Los Angeles' first citizens, the Gabrieliño Indians, are among those portrayed. You then take an old fashioned elevator complete with operator up to the main floor of the museum—a most impressive entrance.

NATURAL HISTORY MUSEUM OF
LOS ANGELES COUNTY
900 Exposition Blvd
Los Angeles, CA
(213) 744-3411
The museum has Native American materials among its collections and sponsors an annual NATIVE AMERICAN FESTIVAL. Well known Indian artists work is displayed and there are traditional dance performances, Indian foods, lectures, films, and more. Call for dates and details.

CALIFORNIA—MARIPOSA
MARIPOSA COUNTY HISTORY CENTER
Hwy 140 at 12th & Jesse St
Mariposa, CA
(209) 996-2924
Among the exhibits is a California Indian village replica.

CALIFORNIA—MISSIONS
There are 21 Spanish missions in California. They stretch from San Diego to Sonoma, north of San Francisco and were built between 1769 and 1823. The missions were the key to Spanish settlement of California. Their purpose was more than converting California Indians to Christianity. Each mission provided an Indian labor force to serve as the basis of economic development. The Indians were carefully trained at the missions and many became highly skilled artisans. In fact, the missions themselves were largely built and decorated by the Indians. The fact that most missions still stand today is a tribute to their Native American builders.

But life at the missions was intolerable for the Indian converts. European diseases, malnutrition, overwork, poor sanitary facilities, crowded living conditions, and suppression of traditional Indian culture and family life all resulted in a high death rate. Native Americans died by the thousands and all of the missions came to have large cemeteries. There were revolts at some missions. Fierce warfare was led by Yokuts, Chumash and Miwok, and widespread infanticide was practiced by women who refused to bring children into such a harsh environment.

Eventually, the Mexican government assumed control of California and terminated the mission system. Surviving mission Indians partly assimilated into other Indian groups or intermarried with Hispanics and Anglos. Contrary to some, the mission tribes did not disappear and thousands of Californians trace their ancestry to various mission groups. In fact, most of the Mission tribes still function today.

Despite all the suffering, the missions remain historic and architecturally beautiful structures to this day. For some Indian families the missions are still places of great meaning and they regularly return to worship. Most missions have very peaceful settings and all welcome visitors. Most have museums with many interesting collections of local Indian materials. Some even have their own Indian Museums as does Mission San Gabriel. Many missions remain active churches and much of the old flavor is still present. The most refreshing and soothing stop a traveler can make is a stop at one of the missions. Most still have a slow pace that remains from an earlier day and leisurely self-guided tours may be taken. Visitors need to remember that worship services, weddings, funerals and the like are still held here and visitors should be respectful of the needs of those worshiping. You will enjoy the architecture, the gardens, the countless relics, and have the opportunity to see rare Indian baskets and other artifacts.

From south to north the missions are:

NAME	LOCATION	MAJOR TRIBES AT THE MISSION
San Diego	San Diego	Diegueño (Ipai-tipai)
San Luis Rey	Oceanside	Luiseño
San Juan Capistrano	San Juan Capistrano	Juaneño
San Gabriel	San Gabriel	Gabrieliño
San Fernando	San Fernando	Gabrieliño
San Buenaventura	Ventura	Chumash
Santa Barbara	Santa Barbara	Chumash
Santa Ynez	Solvang	Chumash
La Purisima	Lompoc	Chumash
San Luis Obispo	San Luis Obispo	Chumash
San Miguel	San Miguel	Salinan
San Antonio	Jolon	Salinan
Soledad	Soledad	Costanoan
Carmel	Carmel	Costanoan
San Juan Bautista	San Juan Bautista	Costanoan

Santa Cruz	Santa Cruz	Costanoan
Santa Clara	Santa Clara	Costanoan
San Jose	Fremont	Ohlone (Costanoan), Yokuts
		Miwok, Wappo, etc.
Dolores	San Francisco	Costanoan and many others
San Rafael	San Rafael	Miwok
Sonoma	Sonoma	Miwok, Wappo, Pomo, Wintun

All of the missions are located on or near Hwy 101, route of the old El Camino Real. Highway signs mark their presence. They are generally open 9-5, although some restrict visitors on Sundays during worship services. Each mission was built a day's walk apart to provide rest stops for travelers. The coolness of the three foot thick walls of these serene sanctuaries makes a stop no less pleasurable today than it was 200 years ago.

Especially recommended are Sonoma, Dolores, San Jose, San Juan Bautista, Carmel, San Antonio, San Miguel, San Luis Obispo, Santa Ynez, Santa Barbara, San Gabriel, and San Diego. Also SEE: CALIFORNIA—CARMEL & JOLON.

CALIFORNIA—MORONGO INDIAN RESERVATION
MALKI MUSEUM
11-795 Fields Road
Morongo Indian Reservation
Banning, CA
(714) 849-7289
To reach the museum take Hwy I-10 east of Banning and take the Fields Road exit.

Owned and administered by the Cahuilla (KUH-wee-uh) Indian people, Malki Museum preserves the cultural heritage of the Cahuilla and Serrano tribes. The museum displays baskets, pottery, ceremonial regalia, historic photographs and more. There is a gift shop with books and arts and crafts. Book catalog available.

Although the museum is a pleasure to visit year round, the most exciting time to come is during the annual Malki Museum Fiesta. This is one of the top Indian events in California and is held over Memorial Day weekend (usually on Saturday; check with the museum). Cahuilla bird singers, Luiseño soloists, Apache mountain spirit dancers, Papago chelkona dancers, and Aztec performers are all typically represented. Sometimes Hopi, Mojave, and Cocopah people come and join in the festivities as well. Some groups are tribal elders while others may be students at Sherman Institute, a Bureau of Indian Affairs high school.

Arts and crafts are sold and you may be lucky enough to acquire a Cahuilla or Cocopah gourd rattle, a Serrano cradle, or a Monache basket. Jewelry, beadwork, and many other items are also offered for sale under the palm-covered ramadas. A delicious deep-pit barbecue is prepared by a Cahuilla master chef and is usually served around noon. A feast of beef, beans, salad and more is sold.

After sundown, the Cahuilla gather to sing bird songs and play "peon" (pay-OWN) handgames. The Cahuilla play their version of handgames in an unusual way. Using a blanket to cover the game bones, the men hold the blanket in their mouths to give their hands freedom to conceal the bones from their opponents. The opposition then guesses which hand holds the marked bone. This ancient game is accompanied by singing and is still popular among southern California tribes. It is pleasant to listen to the songs and watch the competition. One team wins when it gains possession of all the counting sticks by making a long series of correct guesses. The game may go on all night. Often men hold the sticks while women provide the backup singing. The entire day is thoroughly enjoyable. Usually photography is permitted during the day but discouraged at night. Check with those in charge if you wish to take pictures or tape.

CALIFORNIA—NORTH FORK
SIERRA MONO MUSEUM
Intersection of Malum Road (274) & Mammoth Pool Road (225)
North Fork, CA
(209) 877-2115
The museum features the history and culture of the Sierra Mono Indian People. The Western Mono have done a good job of preserving their fine art of basketry and continue to make nutritious acorn mush, the most important California Indian food. The Mono are also sometimes called the Monache.

CALIFORNIA—NOVATO
MARIN MUSEUM OF THE AMERICAN INDIAN
2200 Novato Blvd
Box 864
Novato, CA
(415) 897-4064
California Indian exhibits are presented along with material from other Native American groups. Collec-

The outstanding Coastal Pomo Indian Dancers of Point Arena, California. The Frank family under the leadership of Jesse, Dan and Jackie Frank sing their closing song for the day. Pt. Reyes National Seashore, California. (R. Shanks)

Four Pomo cultural leaders singing traditional Clear Lake Pomo songs at the Robinson Rancheria Land Celebration, Lake County, California. From left, Jim Brown III, Nelson Hopper, Malvina Brown and Raymond Brown. All four have made major contributions to the preservation and appreciation of Pomo culture. (R. Shanks)

Milton "Bun" Lucas, left, a Kashaya Pomo and Coast Miwok, is a well known California Indian cultural historian, singer, teacher, and artist. Mr. Lucas is a National Park Service ranger at Pt. Reyes National Seashore. To the right is Clarence Carillo, one of the most talented and promising young Pomo singers. (R. Shanks)

A lovely member of Bill Franklin's Miwok Dancers performing the women's ribbon dance. She wears a buck cloth dress with Indian shell beads and very old trade beads. Pt. Reyes National Seashore, California. (R. Shanks)

Chumash Indian people reconstructed one of their unique seagoing plank canoes in conjunction with the Santa Barbara Museum of Natural History. In 1976, Chumash men paddled a traditional canoe on the waters of California's Santa Barbara Channel for the first time in over a century. (Santa Barbara Museum of Natural History—Rick Terry, Brooks Institute)

One of the most impressive Native American games is peon (pay-OHN). This traditional game of southern California Indian people is similar to the handgame and stickgame played elsewhere in North America. But instead of hiding the bones in their hands, the Cahuilla tribe uses a blanket held in the players' mouths to add interest to the competition. This game is usually played at night to the accompaniment of haunting songs. The game is unforgettable as the fire reflects on the desert sands. (Malki Museum)

tion of Edward Curtis photographs. Located adjacent to Miwok village site, which may be explored. Special classes, field trips, and children's programs. Annual TRADE FEAST with Indian dancing, arts and crafts, story telling, etc. The outstanding Kashaya Pomo dancers have appeared here. Check for dates.

RANCHO OLOMPALI STATE PARK
US Hwy 101
3 miles N of Novato
(415) 456-1286
Olompali was once one of the largest and most influential of Coast Miwok Villages. After the arrival of the Spanish, Miwok leader Jose Camilo Ynitia was granted Rancho Olompali, his ancestral home. He built an adobe house and administered the rancho. Later, a major battle of the Bear Flag Revolt was fought here when United States citizens invaded Mexican territory and took California from Mexico. Eventually the Coast Miwok population was drastically reduced and survivors intermarried with Pomo and white families.

Today the Miwok village site is preserved, the adobe's walls still stand and visitors may explore this oak woodland park. At present the park is only open a limited number of days. Check for hours.

CALIFORNIA—OAKLAND
OAKLAND MUSEUM
10th & Oak St
Oakland, CA
(415) 834-3401 or 834-2413
Among the exhibits is an outstanding display of California Indian ceremonial regalia, baskets, etc. Of special interest is the rarely seen Big Head costume, most sacred of Central California Indian dance outfits. Note, too, the delicately feathered belt, flicker feather headbands, and Northwestern California moccasin. Special programs and exhibits are regularly presented. Book shop.

INTERTRIBAL FRIENDSHIP HOUSE
523 East 14th St
Oakland, CA
(415) 452-1235
The Intertribal Friendship House is an Indian Center that provides vital services to Native American people and benefits to society in general. The Friendship House is Indian directed and provides many programs of interest to Native Americans. To the general public, the arts and crafts shop here is of special interest. The Friendship House is a good source of information on northern California pow-wows and other celebrations. Check for special events.

CALIFORNIA—PALA
CUPA CULTURAL CENTER
Temecula Road
Pala, CA
(619) 742-3784
The Cupeño Indian people live here on the Pala Indian Reservation. They have an historic mission, a tribal hall administrative center, and the Cupa Cultural Center. The Cupeño celebrate Corpus Christi Day each June and have a Cupa Day every year, too. Contact the Cultural Center or Tribal Hall for more information.

CALIFORNIA—PALM SPRINGS
PALM SPRINGS DESERT MUSEUM
101 Museum Dr
Palm Springs, CA
(619) 325-7186
Among the collections are exhibits relating to the Cahuilla Indians of the Coachella Valley.

PALM CANYON
7 miles S of Palm Springs on the Agua Caliente Indian Reservation. Phone (619) 325-5673.
Visitors may tour this scenic canyon filled with native California fan palm trees for a reasonable fee. Here the Cahuilla people once used the palm fronds as material to make houses, string, sandals and more. SEE: CALIFORNIA—MORONGO INDIAN RESERVATION.

CALIFORNIA—POINT ARENA
COASTAL POMO INDIAN DANCERS OF PT. ARENA
Box 423
Pt. Arena, CA 95468
(707) 882-2218 Contact manager Jackie Frank
There are two Pomo communities near here, the Point Arena and the Manchester Rancherias. Manchester Rancheria is the home of the highly acclaimed Coastal Pomo Indian Dancers, one of North America's best Native American dance groups. Under the direction of the Frank family, the beautiful traditional Pomo singing and dancing of this group has pleased audiences around the state. They do wonderful California Indian traditional dancing and may be booked for public performances. Fees begin at $500 (plus travel expenses)—a very reasonable price for such a fine group.

A very fine Pomo ceremonial roundhouse still stands at Manchester Rancheria awaiting funds for restoration. Hopefully, this beautiful and historic structure will be saved. The Manchester-Point Arena Tribal Office phone number is (707) 882-2788.

Men of the Elem Rancheria of the Pomo Indian people performing the traditional Ball Dance. Participants dance into position in the enclosure accompanied by the leader's singing. Men line up on one side with the women opposite them. As the singing continues, the balls are removed from a pouch and the men and women toss them back and forth. Each person has a partner of the opposite sex and tosses the ball only to them. The men have wooden whistles to accompany the singing. Rattlesnake Island, Clear Lake, California. (R. Shanks)

Indian football is played among some California Indian people. Here a Miwok game is in progress. Note the boy kicking the ball away from the girl (authors' daughter) as she tries to use her hands. Chaw-se Big Time Celebration, Indian Grinding Rock State Park, California. (R. Shanks)

Pomo women and girls playing catch as part of the Ball Dance. No special costumes are needed for this dance, although the balls, pouch, and musical clappers and whistles are especially made. The Ball Dance was once sacred but is now a social dance. The Brown family of Elem (Sulphur Bank) Rancheria deserve credit for preserving this and other Pomo dances. (R. Shanks)

During a Miwok Indian football game, authors' daughter, Torrey, breaks away with the ball heading toward the goal post. The girls' won this game. (R. Shanks)

CALIFORNIA—REDDING
REDDING MUSEUM
Caldwell Park
1911 Rio Dr
Redding, CA
(916) 243-4994
Among the museum collections are northern California Indian displays.

CALIFORNIA—REDLANDS
SAN BERNADINO COUNTY MUSEUM
2024 Orange Tree Lane
Redlands, CA
(714) 825-4825
Among the displays are very good exhibits on Indians of San Bernadino County, the largest county in the United States. Exhibits cover the Mojave, Chemehuevi, Cahuilla, Serrano, and others. Bookstore. Check for special programs.

CALIFORNIA—RIVERSIDE
SHERMAN INDIAN MUSEUM
Sherman Institute
9010 Magnolia Ave
Riverside, CA
(714) 359-9434
Sherman Institute is a Bureau of Indian Affairs high school serving Native American young people from many tribes. The school has an interesting museum with dioramas and collections of American Indian material. The school has several fine Indian dance groups—Apache, Papago, Hopi, etc.—that make periodic public performances. Check for special events.

CALIFORNIA—SACRAMENTO
CALIFORNIA STATE INDIAN MUSEUM
Adjacent to Sutter's Fort
2618 "K" St
Sacramento, CA
(916) 324-0971
The State Indian Museum displays many rarely seen California Indian items including ceremonial regalia, a tule boat, fine baskets, and a great deal more. You will come to appreciate the full richness of the advanced cultures of the California Indians here. Of particular interest are Pomo baskets, including feathered baskets covered with thousands of tiny bird feathers. There are also miniature baskets so small that some are displayed on the head of a pin. These are too small to see the work as you weave and are made by feel, explains Pomo weaver Mabel McKay.

CALIFORNIA—POINT REYES NATIONAL SEASHORE
KULE LOKLO MIWOK INDIAN VILLAGE
(415) 663-1092
The park entrance is 1/2 mile NW of Olema. Trailhead near Bear Valley Visitor Center. Short 1/4 mile hike to the reconstructed village.

National Park Service rangers, the Miwok Archeological Preserve of Marin, and other volunteers have reconstructed a very good Coast Miwok Indian village. Structures include a ceremonial roundhouse, both tule and bark type dwellings, semi-subterranean sweathouse, acorn granary, sun shade, and other structures. An outstanding program features Pomo-Miwok ranger-cultural historians and other Native American staff members. Highly skilled volunteers also help demonstrate many traditional activities. Guided tours and lectures on Pomo and Miwok cultures. Children's programs and school tours.

There is an annual Kule Loklo Celebration which is not to be missed. Held in July or August (check with the ranger in charge of the village for the date), this fine event presents high quality California Indian dancing. Point Arena Pomo, Kashaya Pomo, Miwok, and Maidu dance groups have all danced here at various times. Photos are generally permitted and the colorful dances are magnificent. Among the other activities, acorn mush is served and visitors can sample the most important California native food. Basket weaving, fire making, crafting musical instruments, and many other activities go on. Indian foods and arts and crafts are sold, too. Picnicking. This is one of California's finest Indian events and is highly recommended.

With the inclusion of California Indian people among the ranger staff, Point Reyes National Seashore has improved its program 100 percent. The Strawberry Festival in spring and the Acorn Harvest Festival are Kashaya Pomo and Coast Miwok traditional celebrations at Kule Loklo Village in the Park. Both are outstanding festivals with special blessings, dancing, songs, and eating of Native American foods.

Point Reyes National Seashore is yet another example of the benefit to park and museum programs that deal with Native American subjects by having Indian people on the staff. The results benefit the public, the quality of the park, the non-Indian staff members, and the Indian people. Park staff members Langford "Lanny" Pinola, Esther Pinola, and Milton "Bun" Lucas are all Pomo and Coast Miwok people. They may be contacted for information on the outstanding KASHAYA POMO INDIAN DANCERS, one of the great California dance groups. Mr. Lucas and Mr.

Pinola are noted singers in the Indian community. All three are respected public speakers at community, school and other group events. Mrs. Pinola is recognized for her talks on the role of Native American women. Congratulations to the Point Reyes staff.

There is an annual California Indian Days celebration in the Spring with Pomo and Miwok dancing usually featured. Arts and crafts are sold and Indian foods are available. Outstanding Native American elders are often honored at this time. Check with the museum for the date of this and other programs. A bulletin board announces local Indian events.

UNITED NATIVE AMERICAN EDUCATION CENTER
2100 28th St
Sacramento, CA
(916) 731-5300
Many Indian-oriented special programs and services are offered. The Center has its own Newat Indian dance group which offers classes and presents public performances of Plains style dancing. Check for special events.

CALIFORNIA—SAN DIEGO
MUSEUM OF MAN
Balboa Park, on the California Quadrangle
San Diego, CA
(714) 239-2001
Among the exhibits are Indian displays from North and South America. California Indian exhibits. Check for special programs and exhibits.

CALIFORNIA—SAN FRANCISCO
CALIFORNIA ACADEMY OF SCIENCE
Golden Gate Park
San Francisco, CA
(415) 752-8268
The Academy's Hall of Man is filled with life-size dioramas of many of the world's cultures. Among them are Indian and Eskimo (Inuit) scenes. Especially impressive is a Yurok redwood plank house from Northwestern California, complete with all interior furnishings. Southwestern pottery and Hopi kachina dolls are exhibited. The Hopi kachinas are displayed in a model of a Hopi village as if they were appearing in one of the tribe's ceremonies. This exhibit was prepared by well known Hopi artist Honvantewa (Terrance Talaswaima), director of the Hopi Cultural Center in Arizona. Museum shop, special programs, & magazine. Be sure to see the Ksan totem pole standing in the museum's interior plaza.

M.H. DE YOUNG MEMORIAL MUSEUM
Golden Gate Park
San Francisco, CA
(415) 221-4811
Among the museum's extensive collections are many fine Native American items. Periodically, exhibits are presented on Indian subjects and Native American dancing has been a special event. From time to time, Indian exhibits of unusual quality are scheduled.

AMERICAN INDIAN HISTORICAL SOCIETY
1451 Masonic Ave
San Francisco, CA
(415) 626-5235
The Society publishes a variety of magazines dealing with Native American concerns, history, and children's writing. Established and directed by Native Americans.

CALIFORNIA—SANTA ANA
BOWERS MUSEUM
2002 N Main St
Santa Ana, CA
(714) 972-1900
Among the collections are Native American arts and crafts including California Indian material. Special exhibits.

CALIFORNIA—SANTA BARBARA
SANTA BARBARA MUSEUM OF NATURAL HISTORY
2559 Puesta del Sol Road
Santa Barbara, CA
(805) 682-4711
Outstanding exhibits on the advanced Chumash Indians are presented. A unique system using an antique telephone allows visitors to listen to rare recordings of Chumash songs. A plank canoe used by the Chumash to sail among the Channel Islands is on display. The Chumash and their neighbors were the only tribes in North America to construct plank canoes. Baskets and other local Indian material are also on display. Additional Native American exhibits may be seen nearby in the auditorium. Field trips and special programs, often relating to the Chumash or the Channel Islands are periodically offered. Book store and gift shop. Modern Chumash rock paintings are sold in the gift shop.

PAINTED CAVE
Along Painted Cave Road off San Marcos Pass Road (Hwy 154).
Santa Barbara, CA
This cave has famed Chumash rock art paintings on its walls. The cave is above the road on the left as you head east and is located in a heavily wooded section. The cave entrance is fenced to prevent vandalism but the art is visible from the gate.

Langford "Lanny" Pinola, Chairman of the Kashaya Pomo Tribe and a National Park Service ranger, welcomes everyone to the Pomo Strawberry Festival. Mr. Pinola wears a Pomo shirt decorated with abalone pendants and traditional designs. Point Reyes National Seashore, California. (L. Shanks)

After the flowers have been blessed, Pomo women dancers emerge from the ceremonial roundhouse to begin the dance. The Strawberry Festival celebrates the first fruits of Spring. The women wear flowers and beautiful Pomo dresses. (L. Shanks)

Pomo songs are sung by three singers who keep time with clapper sticks held in their hands. The women dance in front of the singers. The strawberries are arranged in baskets around the singers. (R. Shanks)

After the dancing has concluded, Lanny Pinola's mother blesses the strawberries in the Pomo language. She holds a branch of bay leaves in her right hand. After the blessing, the ceremony is over and everyone joins in eating the strawberries and visiting with one another. The Pomo Strawberry Festival is one of the most beautiful Native American ceremonies. (L. Shanks)

CALIFORNIA—SANTA ROSA
JESSE PETER MEMORIAL MUSEUM
Santa Rosa Junior College campus
1501 Mendocino Ave
Santa Rosa, CA
(707) 527-4479
The museum has California Indian exhibits along with material from a variety of other Native American cultural areas. Along with periodic special exhibits, the museum sponsors an annual multi-cultural celebration at the college's Day Under the Oaks. Usually held in May, the Coastal Pomo Indian Dancers often perform at this event. They are among the finest singers and dancers in all North America. Check with the museum for dates.

CALIFORNIA—STEWARTS POINT
KASHAYA POMO RANCHERIA
Stewarts Point-Skaggs Springs Road at the intersection of Tin Barn Road, about five miles east of Stewarts Point, Sonoma County, CA
(707) 785-2662 Reservation School
The Kashaya (sometimes spelled Kashia) Pomo have done an outstanding job of preserving traditional Pomo culture while at the same time many of their members have become leaders in the broader community. Two Pomo ceremonial roundhouses still stand here, one in use today. The Kashaya Pomo have a dance group that performs in the area and is highly respected. The Kashaya perform the little Big Head dance (different from Big Head dances of the Clear Lake Pomo people) and also have the flicker-feather headbands of the various shake-head dances. The Kashaya Pomo sometimes perform at various public occasions. SEE: CALIFORNIA—POINT REYES.

The roundhouses on the rancheria may be seen from the road but are sacred and should be entered only with permission. The University of California's Lowie Museum in Berkeley has films made at Kashaya of interest to those wanting to learn more about Kashaya traditional life.

The Kashaya Pomo have done an outstanding job of keeping their culture alive. A number of Pomo have written books on their respected culture and others have helped produce films on Kashaya traditional life. Many Pomo have become leaders in the professions of law, education, and medicine.

CALIFORNIA—SUNOL
SUNOL REGIONAL WILDERNESS PARK
Geary Road
Sunol CA
(415) 862-2244
Sunol Park contains a reconstructed Ohlone (Costanoan) Indian village. The village is maintained by volunteers and you may have the pleasure of learning to weave tule mats to cover houses and acorn granaries. Other skills are taught as well. Periodic special events such as the Ohlone Autumn Feast.

CALIFORNIA—UKIAH
LAKE MENDOCINO CULTURAL CENTER
Lake Mendocino Recreational Area
Ukiah, Ca
(707) 462-7581
From Hwy 101, take Calpella exit, N of Ukiah. Go east until you come to a "T", then take a right. Turn left on Maria Dr and proceed over the hill. The Center will be on your right in the Pomo picnic grounds.

The Center displays arts and crafts along with photographs explaining Pomo Indian culture. A video tape may be seen with the Elem Pomo dancing.

The Mendo-Lake Indian Council operates a nice gift shop here with Pomo crafts, books, and the like. The Council also offers classes in traditional Pomo arts such as basketry. There is an amphitheater for talks and cultural demonstrations. Pomo dancing has been held here, too. The building's architecture is inspired by the Pomo ceremonial roundhouse. Open summer months.

THE SUN HOUSE
431 S Main St
Ukiah, CA
(707) 462-3370
This is the picturesque wooden home of one of California's most esteemed artists, Grace Hudson (1865-1937). Mrs. Hudson specialized in accurate, detailed paintings of the handsome Pomo Indian people. Some of her original works hang here amidst her fine collection of Pomo basketry.

CALIFORNIA—VACAVILLE
PEÑA ADOBE and INDIAN MUSEUM
Off Hwy I-80, E of Vacaville at Pena Adobe Road exit
Pena Adobe Park
Vacaville, CA
(707) 446-6785
This small museum displays California Indian artifacts, including two baskets made by the Lake Miwok. Spanish adobe, picnicking, and nature trail.

CALIFORNIA—VENTURA
CHANNEL ISLANDS NATIONAL PARK
1901 Spinnaker Dr (in Ventura Harbor area)
Ventura, CA
(805) 644-8262
There are eight Channel Islands off the coast of southern California, half of them in the National

Park. Indians developed a sophisticated maritime culture on these islands and the adjoining coast. The Chumash, Gabrieliño, and San Nicoleño made plank canoes and trade flourished across these choppy waters. There are many archeological sites on the islands, including soapstone quarries on Santa Catalina where steatite bowls were made. The island Indian population is gone today, with the few survivors assimilated among mainland peoples.

The Park Service's visitor center is designed to introduce the public to these fascinating islands. There are displays along with an interesting video presentation on the Channel Islands. Be sure to note the photos of the plank canoe recently built by modern Chumash people in conjunction with the Santa Barbara Museum of Natural History. (SEE: CALIFORNIA—SANTA BARBARA.) Modern Chumash actually sailed it to the Channel Islands following the ancient trade routes.

On Anacapa Island, closest to the mainland, the Park Service has built a self-guiding nature trail which includes a Chumash shell mound along its route. There is also a tiny museum on Anacapa. Both Anacapa and Santa Barbara Islands have regular boat service while special tours serve Santa Cruz and San Miguel on an irregular basis. To the south and outside the park, Santa Catalina is easily accessible by regular ferry service at Los Angeles harbor. Santa Catalina tour operators take people into the interior on tours and there is a museum at Avalon with Gabrieliño Indian archeological specimens.

All of the Channel Islands are rich in Indian heritage, wildlife, and rare plants. For the adventurous, they offer unparalleled recreational opportunities.

CALIFORNIA—WILLITS
MENDOCINO COUNTY MUSEUM
400 E Commercial St
Willits, CA
(707) 459-2736
The museum contains well presented exhibits of old and new Pomo basketry. Book store with an unusually good selection of local publications. California Indian arts and crafts are offered for sale.

CALIFORNIA—YOSEMITE NATIONAL PARK
INDIAN CULTURAL MUSEUM
Adjacent to the visitor center in Yosemite Village
Yosemite National Park, CA
(209) 372-4454
Miwok Indian people were the park's first inhabitants and some still reside here today. Paiutes from the Owens Valley also came here and the Indian Cultural Museum explains both Miwok and Paiute societies. Besides exhibits, there is a reconstructed MIWOK VILLAGE with conical bark houses. Occasional special events. Within Yosemite Valley, there are archeological sites. Interesting Miwok legends tell of Half Dome and other geologic features. Even the name "Yosemite" is of Miwok origin.

COLORADO

COLORADO—BOULDER
NATIVE AMERICAN RIGHTS FUND
1506 Broadway
Boulder, CO 80302
(303) 447-8760
The Native American Rights Fund (NARF) is a highly respected organization of Indian lawyers and support staff dedicated to important Native American causes. Attorney John Echohawk, a Pawnee, is the director and the staff is comprised of Indian people from California to Maine. The organization's lawyers are members of such tribes as the Chippewa, Cahuilla, Pawnee, Penobscot, Lumbee, Flathead, Ponca, and others.

NARF routinely handles cases which reach the Supreme Court and attorney Arlinda Locklear, a Lumbee, was the first woman Indian attorney to argue before the Supreme Court. The major decisions won with help from NARF include Indian fishing rights in Washington state and restoration to full status for the Menominee tribe of Wisconsin. Many of these decisions had major effects leading to better lives for thousands of Indian people.

NARF depends upon donations and you can request being put on their mailing list. If you are interested in assisting Indian people in their struggle, you may want to support NARF by joining as a contributing member. They fulfill the vital role of bringing high quality legal services to many Indian tribes who previously were unrepresented.

Incidentally, Native American Rights Fund sponsors an annual VISIONS OF THE EARTH ART SHOW at their headquarters in Boulder, CO. Call for dates and details. You will see pleasing traditional and contemporary Indian art.

COLORADO—CORTEZ
EXCALANTE and DOMINGUEZ RUINS
Turn W off Hwy 145 between Dolores and Cortez, on the country road, about 8 miles N of Cortez. Proceed 1 mile W and the ruins are on your right.

These two ruins may be reached by short walks and consist of pueblo house walls and kiva remains. A far reaching view of Mesa Verde country is a highlight of this site. Picnicking.

COLORADO—CORTEZ

INDIAN DANCES are sometimes performed for the public in Cortez City Park adjacent to the Chamber of Commerce office, 808 E Main St, Cortez, phone (303) 565-3414. Contact their office for details and schedule.

COLORADO—DENVER
DENVER ART MUSEUM
100 W 14th Ave Parkway
Denver, CO
(303) 575-2793
Outstanding Native American collections among the exhibits. Contact the museum for special exhibits and programs.

DENVER MUSEUM OF NATURAL HISTORY
2001 Colorado Blvd in City Park
Denver, CO
(303) 370-6363 or 370-6351
Excellent collection of Native American material among the museum's holdings. Check with the museum for special exhibits and programs.

COLORADO—HOVENWEEP NATIONAL MONUMENT
The monument is in Utah and Colorado.
Mailing address: c/o Mesa Verde National Monument, CO 81330
(303) 529-4465 or 529-4475
Hovenweep National Monument is too often overlooked by visitors to its more famous neighbor, Mesa Verde National Park. Despite its isolation and dirt roads that can become impassable in wet weather, Hovenweep is actually one of the Southwest's most fascinating ruins. There are a half dozen major ruins here and many are captivating towers! They may be square, round, oval, or D-shaped when seen from above but altogether they make a highly unusual collection of Anasazi buildings. These unique, tall stone towers are the subject of controversy as to their use. Were they fortresses, prehistoric grain elevators, apartments, or . . . ? Windows are few and the towers seem to have played a defensive role. Some are perched on gigantic tumbled boulders amid arroyos. It's still a mystery today.

Visitors need to first go to Square Tower Group so the ranger can direct you to other sites and provide interpretive brochures. It's a good idea to purchase the trail guide. Also, check with the ranger about weather conditions so you don't get stranded when this country's arid roads suddenly turn to sticky muck during storms. There is a campground with freshwater and toilets, but no fuel or wood for campfires.

Despite the remote nature of the monument, its ruins should not be missed if you are traveling through the high desert. Square Tower ranger station headquarters is located in Utah on a dirt road out of Pleasant View, CO. If you are coming from Utah, take US Hwy 163 to SR 262, south of Blanding, Utah. Headquarters for the monument is 16 miles past Blanding's Trading Post. A good map is essential in this area.

COLORADO—IGNACIO
SOUTHERN UTE TOURIST CENTER
Box 347
Ignacio, CO 81137
(303) 563-4531 lodge, or 563-4522 tribal office
Life on the Southern Ute Reservation centers around Ignacio. Located between the San Juan Mountains and the sandstone cliffs of the high desert, the Ute Indian people have built a major visitor complex. You'll find the new SKY UTE LODGE (Pino Nuche Motel) with swimming pool and other conveniences. In the lobby of the lodge is the SKY UTE GALLERY which sells fine Ute beadwork and other Native American arts and crafts. The Pu-Ra-Sa Restaurant here includes fresh Ute trout and Colorado beef among its menu items. Nearby are the Southern Ute Tribal Offices which provides the visitor with a glimpse of the workings of a progressive Indian tribe. Horse racing at SKY UTE DOWNS and high stakes Indian bingo are regularly scheduled (check for dates). Sky Ute Country Store offers general merchandise and there are also some RV hook-ups and trailer spaces available. Fishing (no Colorado fishing license required) at LAKE CAPOTE is popular with daily bag limits. Camping is available at the lake. Navajo Lake touches the southern edge of the reservation and the state park there has an Indian museum, camping, and boating.

Three annual events highlight the year on the Southern Ute Reservation. The unique BEAR DANCE is usually held in May. This traditional ceremony marks the beginning of spring when the bear ends its hibernation. The sound of the musical rasp reminds you of a bear growling. This is one of the most distinctive of Native American ceremonies and one you'll admire greatly.

The SUN DANCE is generally held in July and is an intensely religious ceremony. Visitors are welcome here, too, but no filming or taping of this religious rite is permitted. Visitors are also asked to dress with appropriate dignity at this and all Indian ceremonies.

Finally, the SOUTHERN UTE FAIR is generally held in September. This fair honors the traditional harvest time. Arts and crafts and Indian foods are among the attractions.

While in Ignacio be sure to see the UTE CHIEF'S MONUMENT commemorating four great leaders of the Ute Nation: Chiefs Ouray, Buckskin Charley, Ignacio, and Severo. Chief Ouray is buried nearby at the Ouray Memorial Cemetery.

The Southern Ute people have gone to considerable effort to open their beautiful reservation to guests and are to be congratulated. The Ute Mountain Ute Reservation is adjacent (SEE: COLORADO—TOWAOC). Mesa Verde, Hovenweep, the Navajo Nation and much more are also close by making Ignacio a highly desirable stop for visitors.

COLORADO—MANITOU SPRINGS
MANITOU CLIFF DWELLINGS MUSEUM
US 24 Bypass
Manitou Springs, CO
(303) 685-5242
Outdoor museum dedicated to the interpretation of Southwest cliff dwelling cultures.

COLORADO—MESA VERDE NATIONAL PARK
MESA VERDE NATIONAL PARK
Box 8
Mesa Verde, CO 81330
(303) 529-4465 or 529-4475
The United Nations recently compiled a list of the world's greatest wonders. The United States was well represented with a number of parks selected, including the Grand Canyon, Yellowstone, and California's Redwoods. Also on this elite list was Mesa Verde National Park, a high tribute to the ancestors of today's Pueblo Indian people. The park is open daily year round, weather permitting. Mesa Verde is a scenic high "table land" topped by a heavy forest of Southwestern trees. Visitors to the park should begin their stay by stopping at Far View Visitor Center for orientation. All cliff dwelling tours are ranger led during the summer because the ruins cannot be randomly visited due to their fragile nature. The rangers are knowledgeable and helpful, and their guide service enriches your stay greatly.

Mesa Verde is easily accessible. For accommodations phone (303) 529-4421 mid-May to mid-October, or (303) 533-7731 the rest of the year. Or you may write to Box 277, Mancos, CO 81328. Many ruins can be visited by car with only short walks over paved walkways to the sites. There are campgrounds and picnic areas. Ranger campfire programs are offered during the evening in summer. Mesa Verde has but one drawback—it is very popular, and like the Grand Canyon or Yosemite, it can be crowded at times. Some ruins and some accommodations are closed in winter.

The crown jewel of the park is Cliff Palace, a huge, elaborate cliff dwelling with towers and kivas. It may be toured on ranger led trips and is open in the summer months. Highly recommended.

Other sites range from ancient pit houses to cliff dwellings to the mysterious Sun Temple. Spruce Tree house is a small city with over 100 rooms and eight kivas. Balcony House is a cliff dwelling that will take your breath away as you climb a very high ladder to its protected location. Many other ruins may be seen. Some are open to visitors while others can only be viewed across the great chasms of deep canyons.

During the summer season only, June through September, Mesa Verde offers a full range of visitor services including motel, restaurants, gas station, store, and laundromat. Towns such as Cortez, Ignacio, Mancos, and Durango offer additional accommodations.

The CHAPIN MESA MUSEUM is open year round and offers archeological exhibits for a full understanding of the Park's original inhabitants. During winter when the visitor center is closed it should be your first stop in the Park.

During recent years an annual Indian arts and crafts show has been held in the Park during June or July. The fair has usually included Southwest Indian dancing from several tribes. Check with the rangers for dates.

It is important to note that when visiting Mesa Verde that all dates and availability of services are subject to change due to seasonal weather conditions. Always check with the the park shortly before making your visit.

It was once the custom at Mesa Verde to include Navajo singers in many of its evening campfire programs. This is no longer done and it is a real loss. Hearing beautiful Navajo chants made the park come alive and improved the visitors' experience substantially. Perhaps this great Mesa Verde tradition can be revived. Also SEE: COLORADO—HOVENWEEP, IGNACIO, & TOWAOC.

Square Tower House is a major cliff dwelling in Mesa Verde National Park. (Colorado Tourism Board)

The Ute Mountain Ute Tribe has created a large park in southwest Colorado on their reservation adjacent to Mesa Verde National Park. This cliff dwelling is just one of the features you may explore on guided tours. (Ute Mountain Tribe—Arthur Cuthair)

Casa Grande Ruins National Monument preserves a major Hohokam Indian community dating back many centuries. This structure was the cultural, religious, and intellectual center of an advanced agricultural community in the Arizona desert. The canopy was built by the Park Service to prevent the caliche soil walls from further erosion. (National Park Service)

Hovenweep National Monument along the Colorado-Utah border preserves ancient Indian towers. Fortress-like in appearance, their exact use is debated, but their functions probably included self-defense and food storage. (National Park Service)

COLORADO—MONTROSE
UTE INDIAN MUSEUM
Hwy 550, 4 miles S of town
Montrose, CO
(303) 249-3098

Much of Colorado was Ute Indian country and two bands of Ute people have large reservations near Mesa Verde National Park. This museum interprets the significant role the Ute people have played in Colorado history.

COLORADO—PLEASANT VIEW
LOWRY PUEBLO RUINS
Located 10 miles W of Pleasant View, CO on a county road off Hwy 666.

One of the least known Southwestern Anasazi pueblo sites, Lowry consists of fine masonry walls and a kiva which still retains its ancient wall paintings. There is a self-guided trail. Brochures are available at the display. Open daily 8 to 6. Picnicking.

COLORADO—TOWAOC
UTE MOUNTAIN TRIBAL PARK
Ute Mountain Indian Reservation
Towaoc, CO 81344
(303) 565-3751 Tribal Office

The Ute Mountain Indian people have recently created their new 125,000 acre Ute Mountain Tribal Park. Much of the park is on the same mesa that Mesa Verde National Park stands upon. In fact, the Ute Mountain Tribal Park offers many of the same high quality attractions found at Mesa Verde. There are spectacular cliff dwellings, ancient Anasazi ruins, beautiful unspoiled country, fascinating rock art sites, and much more.

The Ute Indian people welcome visitors to the park. It is wild, rugged country, not commercialized and visitors are taken on guided full day tours, day hiking tours, overnight camping, and backpacking expeditions. You can join a brief one day trip or even spend a week or more in the primitive back country. Costs, of course, vary with the length and type of trip you take.

All trips are arranged through the tribal office and require knowledgeable Ute guides. The Ute people take you on trips exploring and discovering in their beautiful desert and mountain country.Often the trips are real adventures as new ruins are discovered and ancient artifacts seen for the first time in centuries. It's as if you have the opportunity to visit Mesa Verde as it was a century ago. Contact the tribal office for details, prices, and reservations. Trips generally run from June through September or October, depending on the weather. Trips from one day on up to two weeks may be arranged. Special tours can be accommodated and the Utes have led tours with people arriving at Towaoc by helicopters, mountain bikes, and even covered wagons.

You meet your guide at the tribally owned UTE MOUNTAIN POTTERY FACTORY in Towaoc west of Hwy 160/666, 15 miles SW of Cortez, CO. Tours of the pottery factory are offered and you can buy pottery here, too. For overnight trips, a slide show can be arranged. Camping.

Following your guide in your car you will be led to various points where you can take moderate hikes into the ruins. One trip goes to Mancos Canyon where you climb steep ladders to reach the ruins, much as the ancient cliff dwellers often did.

The Ute Mountain Utes hold their annual UTE BEAR DANCE generally in June. The location is one mile east of the tribal office near Towaoc. The Bear Dance is one of the most distinctive and impressive of Native American dances. The music is accompanied by a musical rasp which produces a sound much like a bear growling. The ceremony is open to the public and is based on an ancient Ute legend which honors the bear's coming out of hibernation. It is a celebration of Spring. Navajo and other Native Americans usually attend, too, and join the Ute people in their important and happy event. SEE: COLORADO—IGNACIO.

CONNECTICUT

CONNECTICUT—NAUGATUCK
EAGLE WING PRESS
Box 579
Naugatuck, CT 06770

This Native American newspaper is an excellent way to keep up with American Indian events. They do an especially good job of covering New England Indian activities. Interesting articles. Write for subscription rates or inquire about the cost of a sample copy.

CONNECTICUT—NORWICH
MOHEGAN INDIAN FORT AND INDIAN CEMETERY
Hwy 32
In Fort Shantock State Park
4 miles S of Norwich, CT

The Algonquian-speaking Mohegan Indians lived in this area and this fort remains from those days. Uncas, famed sachem (chief) of the Mohegans ruled near Norwich. He is remembered for his defeat of the Narragansetts during the Colonial Indian wars. James Fenimore Cooper used Uncas as the basis for his fictional character of the same name in his novel "Last of the Mohicans." The ROYAL MOHEGAN BURIAL GROUND, off Hwy 32 near Sachem and Washington St, has a memorial to Uncas. Incidentally, there are no "last" of the Mohicans as some descendants of the tribe (often spelled Mohegan) still live in Connecticut today.

CONNECTICUT—UNCASVILLE
TANTAQUIDEGEON LODGE INDIAN MUSEUM
1819 Norwich-New London Turnpike
Uncasville, CT
(203) 848-9145
Mohegan and other Native American crafts are displayed here. Eastern woodland LONGHOUSE and WIGWAM have been reconstructed behind the museum. These were the two most typical dwellings of New England Indian people. Mohegan and Pequot people, native to Connecticut, still reside here at Mohegan. The Mohegan and Pequot maintain tribal organizations active to this day.

CONNECTICUT—WASHINGTON
AMERICAN INDIAN ARCHEOLOGICAL INSTITUTE
Junction of Hwy 199 and 47
1 1/2 miles S of Washington, CT
(203) 868-0518
Reconstructed EASTERN WOODLANDS INDIAN VILLAGE with traditional structures and Indian museum. A nature trail introduces visitors to native New England plants used by woodlands Indian groups. Field trips, films, and special events. 12,000 years of Native American history is explained.

DELAWARE

DELAWARE—DOVER
DELAWARE STATE MUSEUM
316 S Governor's Ave
Dover, DE
(302) 736-4266
Native American artifacts pertaining to the state are among the museum holdings.

DELAWARE—SOUTH BOWERS
ISLAND FIELD ARCHEOLOGICAL MUSEUM & RESEARCH CENTER
Hwy 19
S of South Bowers, DE
(302) 335-5395
Eastern Woodlands Indian archeological site from the middle period. Museum displays feature artifacts excavated here. Audio-visual presentation.

DISTRICT OF COLUMBIA

BUREAU OF INDIAN AFFAIRS
US Department of Interior
1951 Constitution Ave NW
Washington, DC 20240
(202) 343-1100
The headquarters of the Bureau of Indian Affairs deals with Indian tribes nationally. The Bureau is often a good source of information on Indian arts and crafts and tourist-oriented facilities. They have many publications of interest relating to Indian and Eskimo people.

The INDIAN CRAFT SHOP, Room 1023, Department of Interior Building on "C" & "E" St between 18th & 19th St, Washington, DC is Indian operated and sells items from many parts of the country. Phone (202) 343-4056.

The INDIAN ARTS AND CRAFTS BOARD, Room 4004, Department of Interior, Washington, DC 20240 annually publishes a "Source Directory of Native American Owned and Operated Arts and Crafts Businesses". This is one helpful way to locate Indian artists and craftspeople if you wish to purchase their work.

The Indian Arts and Crafts Board also can supply you with a "FACT SHEET: Sources of Commercial Reproductions of Works by Contemporary Native American Artists". This publication features silkscreens, lithograph cards, Christmas cards, prints, posters, serigraphs, etc., by Indian artists from many tribes. The Board is very helpful and can supply information on Indian owned museums and cultural centers, too. Phone (202) 343-2773.

Both the Arts and Crafts Board and the Bureau of Indian Affairs can usually help you find out about Indian events in your area as well.

SMITHSONIAN INSTITUTION
NATIONAL MUSEUM OF NATURAL HISTORY
10th St at Constitution Ave NW
Washington, DC
(202) 357-2700
The Smithsonian's world famous collections include a tremendous amount of Native American material, some of it on display. The museum holdings include fine photographic collections relating to Indian and Eskimo people of the US and Canada. Many fine programs, publications, museum shops, and special exhibits. Not to be missed.

The Smithsonian is presently involved in producing the outstanding HANDBOOK OF NORTH AMERICAN

INDIANS series with detailed chapters covering almost every Indian and Inuit group in Canada, the US and northern Mexico. Six volumes of the 20 volume set have been published so far. They are very valuable to anyone interested in the subject. Available from the Smithsonian or the Government Printing Office.

FLORIDA

FLORIDA—CHRISTMAS
FORT CHRISTMAS MUSEUM
Hwy 420
2 miles N of Christmas, FL
(305) 568-4149
Reconstructed fort built originally for the Seminole Indian Wars. Displays explain the attempts to drive the Seminole from their homeland in the Everglades and force them to migrate to Oklahoma. The wars were long and bloody and met with limited success for both sides. Most Seminoles ultimately were driven to Oklahoma, but major segments of the Seminole and the closely allied Miccosukee still own reservations in Florida.

FLORIDA—FORT LAUDERDALE
SEMINOLE INDIAN VILLAGE TOUR & ALLIGATOR WRESTLING
Via JUNGLE QUEEN SIGHTSEEING CRUISE
Bahia Mar Yacht Center
Hwy A1A
Fort Lauderdale, FL
(305) 462-5596
Tourist boat makes a stop at an interesting Seminole Indian village. Alligator wrestling is demonstrated by skilled Seminole athletes.

FLORIDA—FORT WALTON BEACH
INDIAN TEMPLE MOUND MUSEUM
Hwy 98
Fort Walton, FL
(904) 243-6521
Archeological history of northwest Florida is interpreted here. This is an interesting region well worth learning about. The museum publishes a number of books and articles on Florida Indians.

FLORIDA—GAINESVILLE
FLORIDA STATE MUSEUM
Museum Rd and Newell Dr
University of Florida campus
Gainesville, FL
(904) 392-1721
Among the collections are exhibits relating to Florida's Indians. Check for special exhibits and programs.

FLORIDA—MIAMI BEACH
HISTORICAL MUSEUM OF SOUTHERN FLORIDA
Metro-Dade Cultural Center
First St at Flager
Miami Beach, FL
(305) 375-1492
Among the museum's exhibits are two Seminole chickees, traditional Seminole homes, which have been built here for display. Native American history from ancient times to the modern Seminole is covered. Check for special programs.

FLORIDA—MICCOSUKEE INDIAN VILLAGE
25 miles W of Miami on the Tamiami Trail
(Hwy 41)
Box 44021
Miami, FL 33144
(305) 223-8388
The Miccosukee Indian people are closely related to the neighboring Seminole. Their reservation is in the heart of the Everglades and their culture is similar to the Seminole. The Miccosukee are still very traditional in many ways, but have adapted to the modern world through their highly developed tourist program. Visitors will find a wide variety of interesting activities, most pertaining to Miccosukee culture.

The Miccosukee Museum has exhibits, films, photos, and paintings depicting Miccosukee life. There is a village with traditional open-sided Miccosukee "chickees", the distinctive old time houses of the people. Here, you will see traditional cooking, patchwork sewing of colorful Miccosukee clothing, dugout canoes, arts and crafts demonstrations and sales, and an alligator wrestling exhibition.

Across the street from the village you'll find the Miccosukee Restaurant serving both Miccosukee and standard foods. You can try a Miccosukee burger, a specialty of the chef.

Adjacent to the restaurant are the Miccosukee Air Boat rides which takes visitors through the Everglades. This is a real thrill as your guides are experienced Miccosukee fishermen, hunters and froggers who are experts on the Everglades. Many rare and interesting birds and other wildlife are often seen on these trips. A highlight of the trip is a visit to a small, tree-studded island called a "hammock". Here you will tour an actual old time Miccosukee camp. This camp, owned by the Tigertail family, is still used and is an authentic bit of Miccosukee culture. It is quite beautiful here and seeing the "chickee" houses amid the Everglades is unforgettable. Be sure and take the longer air boat ride that includes the island stop.

Lovely Stacey Wasson, a Chickasaw, receives a congratulatory kiss from Chickasaw Nation Governor Overton James. Progressive tribes such as the Chickasaw work hard to give their young people recognition for achievement in many fields. (Chickasaw Nation—Jane Gover)

Seminole Indian people in Florida select a new princess on the Brighton Reservation. (Florida Department of Commerce)

In Florida tourism is a major industry. The Miccosukee Tribe has a major international tourist attraction with a traditional village, arts and crafts sales, and cultural center. Air boat rides are a popular attraction as skilled Miccosukee guides lead visitors through the Florida Everglades. (Miccosukee Tribe and Metro Dade County Dept. of Tourism)

All across the US, Indian owned bingo enterprises are popular forms of recreation. These businesses have created many desperately needed jobs. Profits are reinvested by tribes in other businesses which create additional local jobs. This is the Leech Lake Ojibwa Bingo Place in Minnesota. (Minnesota Chippewa Tribe—Betty Blue)

Tours of the island run about ten minutes of the half hour ride. There is also a nature trail with a boardwalk through the Everglades.

The Miccosukee also allow visitors to drive through their residential and tribal office complex area just west on the small road in front of the village. They do ask, however, that visitors respect their privacy and remain in your car as you pass through.

There are several annual events here, too. Usually the week after Christmas an Indian Arts Festival is held with arts and crafts, dancing, and music from a variety of tribes. The Everglades Music Festival is held generally in mid-July. Indian and non-Indian musicians join together for a cross cultural presentation of a variety of musical styles.

From the beautiful patchwork clothing to the air boat rides to the chickee homes, visitors will find the Miccosukee Reservation varied and exciting. Highly recommended.

FLORIDA—SEMINOLE ARTS AND CRAFTS CENTER
6073 Sterling Rd
Take Hwy 441 W from Hollywood 4 miles past Dania
The Center is located on Sterling Rd near its junction with Hwy 441
(305) 583-2850 or 583-3590, check for hours
This Seminole owned and operated Center offers fine patchwork clothing, baskets, carvings, and more. Check for special Seminole events. Also SEE: TRIBAL LISTINGS section under Seminole.

GEORGIA

GEORGIA—BLAKELY
KOLOMOKI INDIAN MOUNDS STATE PARK
Off Hwy 27
6 miles N of Blakely, GA
(912) 723-5296
Kolomoki is one of the most important groups of Indian mounds in the nation. One mound's interior has been excavated to allow visitors to actually go inside the mound and view its contents. There are seven major mounds here and their culture and history is explained by the park museum. Kolomoki was the home of an advanced Indian society which was part of a network of mound building cultures that spread over most of the South and into the Great Lakes region. Ohio, Illinois, Alabama, Wisconsin, Oklahoma, and West Virginia also have important Indian mounds. SEE: LISTINGS.

GEORGIA—CALHOUN
NEW ECHOTA STATE HISTORIC SITE
Hwy 225
4 miles NE of Calhoun, GA
(404) 629-8151
New Echota was once the capitol of the Cherokee Indian Nation, one of the advanced Five Civilized Tribes. The Native American scholar Sequoyah invented the Cherokee alphabet here. This syllabary made Cherokee the first written Indian language north of Mexico.

A newspaper, the Cherokee *Phoenix*, was published in the language and its office is among the restored buildings. New Echota gives the visitor an understanding of the progress Southern Indians were making before they were brutally driven west. Ignoring both Indian progress and land rights, greedy settlers demanded virtually every acre of land in the South. The tragic forced march west came to be called the "Trail of Tears" because of the heavy of loss of Indian lives. But the Civilized Tribes survived and the *Phoenix* is still published today in Oklahoma.

GEORGIA—CARTERSVILLE
ETOWAH INDIAN MOUNDS HISTORIC SITE
Route 2
6 miles S of Cartersville, GA 30120
(404) 382-2704, closed Mondays & holidays
Etowah Indian Mounds are also among the most important and interesting archeological sites in North America. Visitors begin their tour at the museum which explains life as it existed here centuries ago. Many specimens are displayed, including a pair of white marble sculptures depicting an Etowah man and a woman.

After seeing the museum, tour the mounds and village site. Countless baskets full of earth built the mounds and you can see the borrow pit and moats where the earth was obtained. Defensive moats and a stockade provided double protection against attack and you can see how the town was well defended. You'll also see the six-story high temple mound where the town micco (chief) and priests once conducted rites atop the structure. There are lesser mounds, including a burial mound and another temple mound. Remains of the ceremonial town square or plaza can be seen. There is also a reconstructed stone fish trap visible in the Etowah River during low water. The Etowah Indians were skilled artists and craftspeople and much of their artwork ranks with the best anywhere.

The Etowah people were probably ancestors of such present day people as the Creek or Yuchi, now in Oklahoma. Modern Southeastern tribes in Oklahoma

The most famous Southeastern Indian was Sequoyah, a brilliant Cherokee scholar who invented the Cherokee alphabet and made it the first written Indian language north of Mexico. This statue of Sequoyah is in the National Hall of Fame for Famous American Indians in Anadarko, Oklahoma. Sequoyah's home may be visited near Sallisaw, Oklahoma. (Oklahoma Tourism—Fred Marvel)

Stickball is a popular Southeastern Indian game and is one of the oldest games in the world. It is played at the annual Choctaw Fair near Philadelphia, Mississippi. A player from Bogue Chitto Choctaw Community jumps high in the air for the ball. Players use two sticks in this game which rivals soccer and football as a great sport. (Mississippi Band of Choctaw—Communications Program)

Once the wood is carefully formed, Jonah Sands laces his ball sticks in the traditional manner. (Creek Nation Communications Center— Gary Robinson)

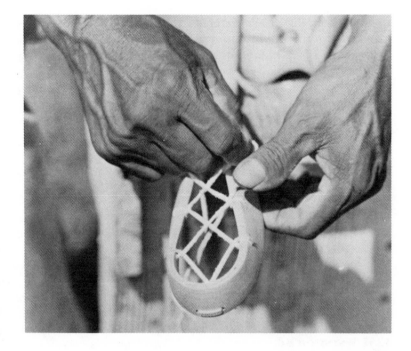

Each pair of ball sticks used in Indian stickball games are hand made. Creek craftsman Jonah Sands bends a ball stick into the proper shape. (Creek Nation Communications Center—Gary Robinson)

A Creek stickball player with a smile of success as he scores a goal at an Oklahoma game. (Creek Nation Communications Center—Gary Robinson)

sometimes arrange their ceremonial grounds quite similarly to Etowah with a rectangular town square and even a small mound at the edge. Green Corn ceremonies and stomp dancers are held at such plazas today and undoubtedly were performed by their mound builders ancestors as well.

GEORGIA—CHATSWORTH
CHEROKEE NATION MEMORIAL & CHIEF VANN HOUSE STATE HISTORIC SITE
Spring Place, Hwy 76
3 miles W of Chatsworth, GA
(404) 695-2598
The Cherokee Memorial is a reminder of the original inhabitants of the South. Chief Vann's house is here, and this historic site dates from the days before the forced removal of most of the Cherokees.

GEORGIA—COLUMBUS
COLUMBUS MUSEUM OF ARTS AND CRAFTS
1251 Wynnton Rd
Columbus, GA
(404) 323-3617
Among the museum's collections is some excellent material relating to the Yuchi Indians who originally inhabited the area. Archeological material from the southeast is displayed. Today the Yuchi live near Kellyville, OK. They have aided and encouraged the museum's efforts to preserve and interpret Yuchi art and culture.

GEORGIA—EATONVILLE
ROCK EAGLE INDIAN MOUND
On the State 4-H Club Center's grounds
7 miles N of Eatonville, GA
(404) 485-2831
There is an Indian mound in the Club's grounds topped by a huge quartz eagle believed to have been used in Native American religious ceremonies. A viewing tower provides a good way to see the site.

GEORGIA—JACKSON
INDIAN SPRINGS STATE PARK & CREEK INDIAN MUSEUM
Hwy 23
4 miles SE of Jackson, GA
This park features a mineral spring used by the Creek Indians and a museum of Creek history. Treaties were once signed here under white pressure giving millions of acres of Indian land to settlers.

The Creek were almost super-human in their efforts to accommodate the settlers and keep the peace. But their non-Indian neighbors offered them no place in the new social order and they were driven to Oklahoma. The Creek have done well in Oklahoma, however, and the Creek Nation is one of the most progressive Indian tribes in the country.

GEORGIA—OCMULGEE NATIONAL MONUMENT
Off Hwy 129N
1 mile E of Macon, GA
(912) 742-0447
Ocmulgee was a major religious center for Southeastern Native Americans. Ocmulgee's Indian mounds are the most impressive features of this 10,000 year old archeological site. At its peak Ocmulgee boasted a populous and important Indian city which had wide influence throughout the area.

There are flat-topped temple mounds here. A restored ceremonial chamber has been built complete with original ceremonial altar, benches, etc. There is a museum plus guided tours, Indian arts and crafts demonstrations, and special programs. Highly recommended. Georgia's Ocmulgee, Etowah, and Kolomoki Indian mounds rank among the great treasures of Native American culture.

Incidentally, when the Creek Indians were driven west from Georgia they named their new capitol in Oklahoma "Okmulgee". It remains the capitol of the Muscogee Creek Nation to this day.

IDAHO

IDAHO—FORT HALL INDIAN RESERVATION
Fort Hall, ID
(208) 238-3700 or 237-0405
The Shoshone and Bannock Indian people hold various summer celebrations here. Shoshone Bannock Indian Day is usually in September and features war dancing, foot races, a cookout, and a horse shoe tournament. Arts and crafts are sold. Sometimes there is a parade, rodeo, and buffalo feast, too. Check with the tribal office for details and dates.

The Fort Hall people are well known for their fine leather work and beadwork. The Fort Hall Indian Museum has exhibits on the Shoshone and Bannock people. Check for current hours. Also SEE: TRIBAL LISTINGS under Shoshone.

IDAHO—LAPWAI
NEZ PERCE INDIAN RESERVATION
Nez Perce Tribal Office
Lapwai, ID
(208) 843-2253
The Nez Perce (NEZ-purse) Indians are the people of famed Chief Joseph. Subject of books and movies, Joseph attempted to lead his band to freedom in Canada. The US Cavalry pursued him hundreds of miles over the Bitteroot Mountains and into northern Mon-

tana. Chief Joseph repeatedly outfought and outmaneuvered the Army until he finally surrendered just forty miles from the Canadian border. Joseph was never allowed to rejoin his people and is buried on the Colville Indian reservation in Washington.

The Nez Perce hold five major annual celebrations. The EPETHES POW-WOW is usually held the first weekend in March in Lapwai. There are championship war dance competitions.

Next is the MAT-AL-YM'A POW-WOW and ROOT FEAST at Kamiah generally occurring on the third weekend in May. This is a Nez Perce Thanksgiving, offering thanks to the Great Spirit for the roots which once formed such an important part of the Nez Perce diet. Dancing is performed.

The third weekend in June the CHIEF JOSEPH AND WARRIORS MEMORIAL POW-WOW is held at Lapwai honoring the famed Nez Perce civil chief and his warriors.

Next comes the LOOKING GLASS POW-WOW in August at Kamiah. Looking Glass was another famed Nez Perce leader. Looking Glass lost his life in the Nez Perce War. There is dancing and singing honoring his memory.

The season generally concludes with the FOUR NATIONS POW-WOW held in October.

The Tribal Office, the Bureau of Indian Affairs, and the Nez Perce National Historic Park should all be able to offer additional information on these events. Watch for fine corn husk bags being sold at arts and crafts booths as these carefully woven bags are a Nez Perce specialty.

IDAHO—MOSCOW
APPALOOSA HORSE CLUB MUSEUM
Hwy 8, Between Moscow and Pullman
Moscow, ID
(208) 882-5578
The Nez Perce Indians developed the famed Appaloosa horse, named in honor of the Palouse Country in eastern Washington. Today the Palouse Country is agricultural land covered by wheat, pea, and lentil crops. But the Appaloosa horse lives on and remains a tribute to Nez Perce horse breeders. The museum recognizes the tribe's key role in the history of horses with exhibits on Nez Perce culture.

IDAHO—NEZ PERCE NATIONAL HISTORICAL PARK
Box 93
Spalding, ID 83551
(208) 843-2261
Honoring the Nez Perce Indian Nation and its major role in the history of the Pacific Northwest states, Nez Perce National Historical Park actually consists of over two dozen interesting sites scattered throughout the area. Each site relates to some aspect of Nez Perce culture or history.

You can write the park for a brochure and map showing the route you take to visit each site. Begin your trip at the visitor center and museum in Spalding. You can visit places such as the rock formation on the Clearwater River called Coyote's fishnet. Coyote is a legendary being, famed among countless western tribes for his power and his trickery. You can see some of his work here. Besides Indian mythology, there are historic places to visit, too. You may want to see the Lolo Trail where Chief Joseph and his band fled while pursued by the US Cavalry. Or you may want to visit one of Lewis and Clark's campsites. Also Reverend Henry Spalding's historic Protestant mission (the town of Spalding is named for him) is here too.

Nez Perce National Historic Park is an exciting concept in national parks. We need more such parks which can preserve and explain historic and cultural sites of other Indian tribes. For more Nez Perce battle sites SEE: MONTANA.

ILLINOIS

ILLINOIS—CAHOKIA MOUNDS STATE HISTORIC SITE
Hwy 40 Business
Between E St Louis & Collinsville
Box 382
Collinsville, IL
(618) 344-5268
Cahokia was once the largest Indian city in the United States and Canada, with a population of over 40,000 people. This highly advanced city included the largest Indian mound north of Mexico—Monks Mound which is 100 feet high. The mounds here are so numerous and so large that the Indian's excavations resulted in vast depressions which formed lakes as they filled with water. A giant palisade wall once surrounded much of the city (part of the wall has been reconstructed). The American Wood-henge, an Indian astronomical observatory using poles, was here too. It was similar in function and design to Stonehenge in England. There are elaborate burials

involving ceremonial practices of the Mississippian tribes. Fine artwork in metal, stone, and pottery has been recovered at Cahokia, too.

There is a visitor center, museum, and gift shop. Special programs and tours. The Cahokia Museum Society has interesting activities and publications relating to this ancient city. The museum is closed November through February.

Be sure and note the annual events here. "Rediscover Cahokia Days" is usually held the second weekend in August. You may be fortunate enough to see the Choctaw Dancers present traditional dances of the type that were once done here. Throughout the year there are various programs ranging from atlatl demonstrations (an ancient type of spear thrower), to pottery and basket classes, to flint knapping (arrowhead making). There are programs for adults and youngsters, including a Kids Day in May.

The United Nations has recognized Cahokia as a World Heritage Site, an elite honor. This is probably the largest archeological site in the US. Over 60 mounds alone are preserved here. With the fine programs, Native American participation, the new museum, and Archeological Field School (open to non-professionals), Cahokia is highly recommended.

ILLINOIS—CHICAGO
FIELD MUSEUM OF NATURAL HISTORY
In Grant Park on Lake Shore Dr
Chicago, IL
(312) 922-9410
A large collection of Native American artifacts from the Eastern Woodlands to the Arctic are housed here. This metropolitan museum also has special exhibits and programs. Newberry Library Center, 60 W Walton, Chicago, also has Native American exhibits among its collections.

ILLINOIS—LEWISTON
DICKSON MOUNDS & MUSEUM
Off Hwy 78
Between Havanna and Lewiston, IL
(309) 547-3721
Another important Indian mound archeological site, Dickson Mounds Museum explains mound builder Indian culture. Guided tours and an audio-visual presentation are available.

ILLINOIS—ROCK ISLAND
BLACK HAWK STATE HISTORIC SITE
Hwy 5
Rock Island, IL
(309) 788-9536
This park honors the memory of Chief Black Hawk

and his Sac & Fox tribe. An Eastern Woodland WIGWAM is reconstructed here. The Hauberg Museum on the grounds has Native American displays among its exhibits. An Indian pow-wow is held annually over Labor Day.

ILLINOIS—SPRINGFIELD
ILLINOIS STATE MUSEUM
Spring & Edward St
Springfield, IL
(217) 782-7386
Native American exhibits are among the collections. Check for special programs and exhibits.

INDIANA

INDIANA—EVANSVILLE
ANGEL MOUNDS STATE MEMORIAL
8215 Pollack St
Evansville, IN
(812) 853-3956
RECONSTRUCTED CEREMONIAL BUILDINGS AND HOUSES highlight this important Mississippian moundbuilder community. Visitor center with audio-visual presentation and displays. The EVANSVILLE MUSEUM OF ARTS & SCIENCES, 411 SE Riverside Dr. also features Native American displays.

INDIANA—INDIANAPOLIS
MUSEUM OF INDIAN HERITAGE
Eagle Creek Park, 6040 DeLong Rd
Indianapolis, IN
(317) 293-4488
Native American displays covering much of North America.

INDIANA—LAFAYETTE
TIPPECANOE BATTLEFIELD STATE MEMORIAL
7 miles N of Lafayette off I-65
(317) 567-2147
The great Shawnee Indian leaders, Tecumseh and his brother the Prophet, attempted to rally the tribes from the Great Lakes to the Deep South in a united effort to stop the settler's encroachment on their lands. They were only partially successful and eventually the numerous, well armed settlers defeated the Shawnee and their allies. A monument marks the site of this battle fought in 1811.

Cahokia was the largest Indian city north of Mexico. The central feature, Monks Mound, is the largest prehistoric earthwork in the US. It is 100 feet high and covers 14 acres. Cahokia Mounds State Historic Site near Collinsville, Illinois preserves this and other archeological treasures. (Cahokia Mounds State Historic Site)

Some parks that preserve the great mounds remember the people who made them and have periodic events with Southeastern Indian dancing. At Rediscover Cahokia Days, Choctaw people have arrived to present traditional dancing and singing. The Choctaw, Creek, Shawnee, Yuchi, Chickasaw, Cherokee and other tribes are among those people whose ancestors' built ancient mounds. (Cahokia Mounds State Historic Site)

Spiro Mounds Archeological State Park preserves one of the archeologically richest mounds in the country. Perhaps made by the ancestors of today's Caddo people, Spiro Mounds has yielded some of the New World's great artwork. (Oklahoma Tourism—Fred Marvel)

IOWA

IOWA—DES MOINES
IOWA STATE HISTORICAL MUSEUM
12th St & Grand Ave
Des Moines, IA
(515) 281-5111
Native American exhibits among the collections.

IOWA—FORT ATKINSON
FORT ATKINSON STATE PRESERVE
Off Hwy 24
About 15 miles SW of Decorah, IA
(319)534-7543
Government fort built to protect the Winnebago Indians from war-like Plains tribes such as the Sioux. Many restored buildings. Museum with Indian exhibits.

IOWA—MARQUETTE
EFFIGY MOUNDS NATIONAL MONUMENT
Hwy 76
North of Marquette, IA
(319) 873-2356
The Indian mounds here are effigies of bird, animal, and other shapes. The mounds are spread for some distance along the river banks, reached by self-guided trails. The museum offers displays and an audiovisual presentations. Guided tours are available during certain hours. Effigy mounds are yet another interesting type of Indian earthwork very different from the temple mounds of the southeast.

Especially interesting are the "Marching Bears", a group of ten mounds each in the shape of a bear. The mounds average about 80 to 100 feet long and about 3 1/2 feet high. They are a remarkable sight when seen from the sky—ten giant bears marching along! They are accompanied by several huge bird-shaped mounds with their wings spread. Strange rectangular mounds follow along behind the bears.

Altogether there are 191 prehistoric Indian mounds in the Monument, 29 in the form of bear and bird effigies. The Indians who made the effigy mounds probably lived here until about 1300 AD when the Iowa tribe displaced or absorbed them. This is a remarkable and interesting archeological site, one of the most important in the nation.

IOWA—IOWA CITY
MUSEUM OF NATURAL HISTORY
McBride Hall, University of Iowa
Jefferson & Capitol St
Iowa City, IA
(319) 353-5893
A MESQUAKIE WIGWAM has been built here and may be seen among other Indian exhibits. The Mesquakie are also known as the Fox and live today near Tama, Iowa. Check with the museum for special exhibits and programs. Also SEE: TRIBAL LISTINGS under Mesquakie.

IOWA—McGREGOR
EFFIGY INDIAN MOUNDS
In the vicinity of McGregor, there are dozens of Indian mounds and earthworks, many in the shape of birds and animals. Inquire locally.

IOWA—MISSOURI VALLEY
HARRISON VALLEY HISTORICAL VILLAGE
Hwy 30
3 1/3 miles E of Missouri Valley, IA
(712) 642-2114
Indian material from local archeological sites is exhibited. Remains of an Indian village exists along St. John's Creek.

KANSAS

KANSAS—BONNER SPRINGS
WYANDOTTE COUNTY MUSEUM
631 N 126th St
Bonner Springs, KS
(913) 721-1078
Among the collections are Wyandot Indian artifacts. The Wyandot were originally from the Great Lakes but lived in Kansas during their long migration to Oklahoma.

KANSAS—COURTLAND
PAWNEE INDIAN VILLAGE SITE
Hwy 266
10 miles NE of Courtland, KS
(913) 361-2255
The Pawnee were among the most advanced of Midwestern Indians. They built big earthcovered lodges, delved into astronomy, farmed large fields, and lived relatively peacefully. This site preserves the floor of one of their lodges along with the artifacts discovered there. Everything has been left in place, just as the Pawnee left it. This is an unusual and interesting archeological site.

Today the Pawnee live in Oklahoma near the town that bears their name. Many have achieved prominence in law, government, and the arts. They hold a high quality pow-wow each July where everyone is welcome. SEE: TRIBAL LISTINGS under Pawnee.

Indians in the eastern half of North America built many mounds and earthworks for ceremonials, burial sites, defense, and as bases for temples. Among the most fascinating are "effigy mounds", those mounds built in the shape of animals. This is an aerial view of the "Marching Bear" mound group at Effigy Mounds National Monument near McGregor, Iowa. There are ten bears, a soaring bird, and two linear mounds. (National Park Service)

112

Most Indian parents encourage their youngsters to learn and cherish the unique culture of their tribe. Michael Brown, age two, comes from a long line of distinguished Pomo dancers and singers and he is off to a good start to follow in his father and grandfathers' footsteps. Clear Lake, California. (R. Shanks)

This youngster takes his dancing quite seriously at the Sac & Fox Pow-wow near Stroud, Oklahoma. (R. Shanks)

A Mesquakie (Fox) boy enjoys the annual pow-wow at Tama, Iowa. (Iowa Development Commission)

KANSAS—HIGHLAND
IOWA AND SAC & FOX INDIAN MISSION MUSEUM
Hwy 36
E of Highland, KS
(913) 442-3304
This is an historic Presbyterian mission built to serve both the Iowa tribe and the Sac & Fox tribe. There are Native American exhibits here..

KANSAS—HORTON
KICKAPOO INDIAN RESERVATION
4 1/2 miles E of the junction of US Hwy 75 and Hwy K-20
7 miles W of Horton, KS
(913) 486-2131
The Kickapoo Indian people hold an annual KICKA-POO POW-WOW usually the third weekend in July, from Friday through Sunday. Both traditional Kickapoo and pow-wow dancing are done. A highlight is traditional Kickapoo Green Corn-type dancing which is a part of this important event. There are also arts and crafts sales including leatherwork, beadwork, wood carvings, jewelry and more. These products are made both by local Kickapoo artists and craftspeople and by those of neighboring tribes who join in the activities.

A special treat is corn soup along with other Indian foods offered for sale. The seeds of this corn soup have been handed down from generation to generation and are carefully planted each year. The corn seeds are in many respects sacred since these are the very type of seeds given to the Kickapoo people long ago by the Creator. The seeds are never sold, but you may enjoy a bowl of delicious soup and taste the bounty of the Kickapoo harvest.

The Kickapoo people have a Bingo enterprise for those visitors wanting a change of pace in their weekend activities.

KANSAS—LARNED
SANTA FE TRAIL MUSEUM & CULTURAL CENTER
Hwy 156
Larned, KS
(316) 285-2054
Although the museum is primarily aimed at explaining pioneer life along the old Santa Fe Trail, Indian culture is part of the story, too. There is a reconstructed WICHITA INDIAN HUNTING LODGE. The Wichita were first visited by Coronado during his explorations of the early 1500's. Coronado pushed as far north as Kansas in search of mythical Indian cities of gold. Instead, he found the Wichita houses which were indeed golden hued, but were made of buffalo grass, not gold. Today the Wichita live near Anadarko, Oklahoma, and have a tribal office there. Also SEE: OKLAHOMA—ANADARKO.

KANSAS—LAWRENCE
MUSEUM OF ANTHROPOLOGY
University of Kansas, Spooner Hall
Lawrence, KS
(913) 864-4245
Native American exhibits.

MUSEUM OF NATURAL HISTORY
University of Kansas, Dyche Hall
Jayhawk & 14th St
Lawrence, KS
(913) 864-4540, weekends only 864-4450
Native American and Eskimo exhibits are among the collections. One section of the museum covers the Eskimo of Greenland, the only country in the world with a predominantly Eskimo population.

Perhaps the most unusual feature of the museum is the presence of "Comanche". This horse (now stuffed) is the famous survivor of General Custer's defeat at the Battle of the Little Big Horn in 1876. "Comanche" was the only living survivor found by relief troops after this Sioux and Cheyenne victory.

KANSAS—SCOTT CITY
LAKE SCOTT STATE PARK
Hwy 95
12 miles N of Scott City, KS
(316) 872-2061
During the disruptive days of the Spanish settlement of New Mexico some Pueblo Indians fled to Kansas seeking a life free of interference. They built a Southwestern pueblo here and its ruins may be visited today.

KANSAS—WICHITA
MID-AMERICA ALL-INDIAN CENTER & MUSEUM
650 N Seneca St
Wichita, KS
(316) 262-5221
The museum has Native American displays. The Center holds its annual MID-AMERICA ALL-INDIAN DAYS featuring Indian dances, arts and crafts. Check for dates.

KENTUCKY

KENTUCKY—WICKLIFFE
WICKLIFFE INDIAN MOUNDS
Hwy 51
1/2 mile N of Wickliffe, KY
(502) 335-3681
Very interesting Mississippian Indian village site excavated so visitors can see the interiors of both temple and burial mounds. Remains of Indian dwellings have also been unearthed for viewing. The contents of mounds and dwellings remain in place so that you can see exactly how they were found.

LOUISIANA

LOUISIANA—BATON ROUGE
INDIAN MOUNDS
Louisiana State University campus
Call campus information for directions
Baton Rouge, LA
(504) 388-5557
Archeological material is also on display in the GEO-SCIENCE MUSEUM in the campus Geology building.

LOUISIANA—MARKSVILLE STATE COMMEMORATIVE AREA
Hwy 5
2 miles E of Marksville, LA
(318) 253-9546
This interesting archeological site overlooks a former channel of the Mississippi River. The hilltop Indian village is surrounded by a defensive earthwork wall and features two burial mounds. There is a museum with exhibits explaining mound builder history and displaying artifacts. Self-guided tours and picnicking.

MAINE

One of the most significant Native American events of recent years was the Maine Indian Settlement Act of 1980. The culmination of an eight year legal struggle resulted in the United States signing the act which compensated the Passamaquoddy Tribe and Penobscot Nation 81 million dollars for the loss of 12 million acres of land.

The Passamaquoddy and Penobscot have invested one-third of their money in economic development and the rest in land acquisition and a trust fund. The tribes are purchasing businesses essential to the benefit of the Indian people and the general economy of the State of Maine. The Passamaquoddy now own a cement company, two radio stations, a blueberry farm, a shopping center, and an arts and crafts store. The Penobscot have an audio cassette manufacturing company, an ice hockey rink, and a lending firm. Both Indians and non-Indians in Maine have benefited from the tribes' business and employment opportunities.

A major goal is to develop programs and services to meet social needs, especially by providing jobs, housing, and alcoholism programs. These problems have not been eliminated yet, but they are being reduced. Education is another area which has seen a great improvement, with over 100 young people now in college. A new health center has also been opened at Peter Dana Point.

The Penobscot Reservation is located on Indian Island at Old Town. The Passamaquoddy Tribe has two reservations, one at Pleasant Point near Perry, and the other at Indian Township near Princeton.

SEE: MAINE listings below and TRIBAL LISTINGS—PASSAMAQUODDY.

MAINE—OLD TOWN
PENOBSCOT INDIAN RESERVATION
Indian Island
Old Town, ME
(207) 827-7776
The Penobscot River is named in honor of the Penobscot Indian people. The Penobscot are a branch of Abenaki and today continue to live on the river at Indian Island just north via a bridge from Old Town. On the island visitors will find the PENOBSCOT MUSEUM along the main street. This museum exhibits fine Penobscot baskets, wood carvings, stone artifacts, beadwork, and more. The museum is open weekdays from noon to four, phone (207) 827-6544. After visiting the museum you will want to visit one or more of the arts and crafts stores on the island that sell Penobscot work. Baskets, moccasins, quill work, beadwork, fish spears, bows, carved canes, war clubs, and other items are found here.

There has been an annual pageant in the summer put on by the Penobscot people, but it is not certain at this time if it will be held again.

The Penobscot people are to be congratulated on keeping so many of their irreplaceable traditional arts and crafts alive.

OLD TOWN MUSEUM
N Fourth St
Old Town, ME
(207) 866-4393
The museum has some very interesting Penobscot items, including a birch bark canoe.

A kicked ball soars closer to the women's goal posts at the Quapaw Indian football game. Enthusiasm and good spirits run high. The ball is made of deer skin and stuffed with hair from a deer tail. The ball is not a toy and is used only for these special games. (R. Shanks)

The Passamaquoddy are the eastern-most Indian tribe in the US. Annually the people celebrate Ceremonial Day and welcome guests to their reservation near Perry, Maine. (Passamaquoddy-Maliseet Bilingual Program—Joseph A. Nicolas)

Quapaw Indian football game, Quapaw, Oklahoma. Indian football uses a round ball and women play against the men. Men can only kick the ball but women can both run with the ball and throw it. To score, you must get the ball through the goal posts of the opposing team. Note the ball flying through the women's goal posts. (R. Shanks)

The Passamaquoddy Ceremonial Day in Perry, Maine, is a fine opportunity to learn about an important New England Indian culture. (Passamaquoddy-Maliseet Bilingual Program—Joseph A. Nicolas)

MAINE—PASSAMAQUODDY INDIAN RESERVATION

The Passamaquoddy people have worked here to continue their important Northeastern Indian culture. Traditional dancing nearly died out, but due to the efforts of Passamaquoddy leader Joseph A Nicholas and others, the dances and music of the tribe continue to live today. Only a few elders remembered tribal traditions in the 1960's when Mr. Nicholas and others began work to preserve these vital traditions.

Today their work has resulted in over 100 Passamaquoddy participating in traditional Eastern Woodlands dancing and singing activities. Around August 1, the Pleasant Point Passamaquoddy hold their annual CEREMONIAL DAY on the reservation between Perry and Eastport, ME. Take Hwy 1 to Perry, and proceed toward Eastport on Hwy 190. The reservation is about two miles from Perry, five miles before Eastport. Phone (207) 853-2551 for information and times.

Ceremonial Day features canoe races, traditional dancing and singing, and a pageant which explains the history of the Algonquin-speaking Passamaquoddy people. There is a chiefs' welcome dance, an official greeting dance, social dances, and a peace pipe ceremonial. The Passamaquoddy people are proud of their heritage and this is an opportunity to share in their fine culture. You may even be fortunate enough to purchase one of the lovely traditional splint and sweet grass baskets that Passamaquoddy weavers still produce.

The Passamaquoddy-Maliseet Bilingual Program (Box 295, Perry, ME 04667, phone (207) 853-4045) has done an outstanding job of developing its own text books in Passamaquoddy and English, teaching traditional culture and history and reinforcing pride in the Passamaquoddy and Maliseet people with their heritage. They have a number of publications available for purchase, including "Chipmunk", a novel of Passamaquoddy history for youngsters.

MASSACHUSETTS

MASSACHUSETTS—ANDOVER
R S PEABODY FOUNDATION ARCHEOLOGICAL MUSEUM
Main St at Phillips
Andover, MA
(617) 475-0248
The museum contains many interesting exhibits relating to American Indian archeology and ethnology.

MASSACHUSETTS—CAMBRIDGE
PEABODY MUSEUM OF ARCHEOLOGY AND ETHNOLOGY
Harvard University campus
24 Oxford St
Cambridge, MA
(617) 495-1910
Outstanding museum collection which spans the world. Among the exhibits are fine Native American displays. Check for special programs and exhibits. One of America's major Indian collections is here.

MASSACHUSETTS—GRAFTON
LONGHOUSE MUSEUM, HASSANAMISCO INDIAN RESERVATION
Grafton, MA
Eastern Woodlands Indian displays relating to the NIPMUC tribe.

MASSACHUSETTS—HARVARD
THE AMERICAN INDIAN MUSEUM
FRUITLANDS MUSEUM group
Old Shirley & Prospect Hill Rd
SW of Harvard, MA
(617) 456-3924
Native American exhibits, crafts, dioramas, gift shop, etc. Check for special programs and exhibits.

MASSACHUSETTS—MASHPEE
MASHPEE TRIBAL MEETING HOUSE
Hwy 28
S of Mashpee, MA
The Old Indian Meeting House stands amid the Mashpee tribal cemetery. The Algonquian Mashpee still retain some of their traditions, including food sources such as cranberry gathering.

MASSACHUSETTS—MARTHA'S VINEYARD
THE WAMPANOAG INDIAN PEOPLE still reside in the Gay Head area and have a distinctive pottery style made from the colorful clay that gives the headland its name. These attractive works of art may be purchased in shops on the island. Local Indian artifacts have been on display on the island and for years there was a Gay Head Indian Museum on Martha's Vineyard. The Wampanoag tribe's address is: RFD, Box 137, Gay Head, MA 02535.

MASSACHUSETTS—SALEM
PIONEER VILLAGE
End of West Ave
Salem, MA
(617) 744-0180
Pioneer Village has reconstructed ALGONQUIAN WIGWAMS among its buildings. These are the traditional bark houses used by many Eastern Woodlands tribes.

MASSACHUSETTS—STOCKBRIDGE
STOCKBRIDGE (MAHICAN) INDIAN CEMETERY
Main St
1 mile W of Stockbridge, MA
The Indian cemetery site is marked today by a monument. The Stockbridge or Mahican Indians were driven west and today live on a reservation in Wisconsin shared with Munsee Delaware. SEE: WISCONSIN—STOCKBRIDGE-MUNSEE.

MICHICAN

MICHIGAN—DETROIT
GREAT LAKES INDIAN MUSEUM
Located at HISTORIC FORT WAYNE MILITARY MUSEUM
6325 W Jefferson
Detroit, MI
(313) 297-9364
Native American displays can be seen here as well as at two other Detroit museums. DETROIT HISTORICAL MUSEUM, Woodward & Kirby Ave, phone 833-1805; and the ANTHROPOLOGY MUSEUM at Wayne State University. The latter has a major Indian collection.

MICHIGAN—FLINT
GENESEE VALLEY INDIAN ASSOCIATION MUSEUM
Genesee Indian Center
124 W First St
Flint, MI
(313) 239-6621
Native American exhibits at an Indian Center.

MICHIGAN—HARBOR SPRINGS
CHIEF BLACKBIRD MUSEUM
MICHIGAN INDIAN FOUNDATION
Hwy 119
Michigan Harbor, MI
(616) 347-0200
Native American displays and craftwork.

MICHIGAN—MACKINAC ISLAND
INDIAN DORMITORY MUSEUM
Old Fort Mackinac
Mackinac Island, MI
(906) 847-3328
Native American displays.

MICHIGAN—NILES
FORT ST. JOSEPH HISTORICAL MUSEUM
5th & Main St
Niles, MI
(616) 683-4702
Sioux Indian collections including historic material relating to Chief Sitting Bull.

MINNESOTA

MINNESOTA—ANNANDALE
MINNESOTA PIONEER PARK
Hwy 55
East of Annandale, MN
(612) 274-8489
Among the exhibits are Plains Indian tepees and other Indian displays.

MINNESOTA—CASS LAKE
LEECH LAKE INDIAN RESERVATION
Box 308
Cass Lake, MN 56633
(218) 335-2207
The Ojibwa Indian people of Leech Lake Reservation have a very active community with many important projects and businesses. For visitors, five annual pow-wows are of particular interest. Pow-wows are usually held over Labor Day, Memorial Day, in Winter, and Spring. Depending on the weather, the singing and dancing are either held at the pow-wow grounds or indoors at the adjacent convention center in Cass Lake. Check with the tribal office for exact dates.

There is also a gift shop with a large selection of birch bark baskets, moccasins, beadwork, paintings, and more. A catalog available for $2.00. They also supply gift shops so if you're a store owner you may want to contact them. The Che-Wa-Kae-Gon Restaurant is here. Gifts, gas, and groceries are also available. Phone (218) 335-2589. There is a bingo enterprise on the reservation and Leech Lake has been a leader in the field.

The Band owns its own construction company and has built such projects as the convention center and community school. They also own and operate an active logging company. Leech Lake Wild Rice is a favorite gourmet item and this company too, is owned and operated by the tribe.

The Leech Lake Ojibwa have made many fine accomplishments. When you visit the area, be sure to check for events at the convention center. A wide range of events are held there including a dinner theater, square dance conventions, and even boxing matches.

The White Earth Treaty Celebration Pow-wow is held annually in White Earth, Minnesota. This is an Ojibwa event and dancers present a fine appearance along side the arbor. The White Earth Ojibwa combine appreciation of the traditional culture with active pursuit of progressive tribally owned businesses. (White Earth Tribal Council)

Ojibwa craftsman George Bryan works a catlinite stone into a ceremonial pipe. Sioux Indian Museum, Rapid City, South Dakota. (Indian Arts & Crafts Board, US Dept. of Interior)

The convention center can also be rented for group activities.

MINNESOTA—FOND DU LAC INDIAN RESERVATION
FOND DU LAC OJIBWA BAND
105 University Rd
Cloquet, MN 55720
(218) 879-1251
The annual FOND DU LAC POW-WOW is usually held in July and is sponsored by the tribe. There is traditional dancing, arts and crafts, and other activities.

Wild rice harvesting is usually done in September. Wild rice is traditionally the most important food of the Ojibwa people and still is an important part of many people's diet. Many Ojibwa gather the wild rice by canoe in the old time manner. Some people continue to hand parch it in the ancient way which results in an especially tasty product. The Fond Du Lac Tribal Office can advise you where you may view the wild rice harvest.

The Fond du Lac Ojibwa people, one of the six Bands of the Minnesota Chippewa, have many important activities on their reservation. The Band owns and operates a construction company as well as a company which manufactures wood furnaces and other steel products. There is also a bingo enterprise being built in Duluth in cooperation with the City of Duluth.

Also of importance is the Band owned and operated Mash-Ka-Wisen chemical-dependency clinic which serves those in need of health care from alcohol or drug problems. Mash-Ka-Wisen, means ''Be strong enough to accept help'' and is a very meaningful Ojibwa saying. The clinic is Indian owned and staffed and is a source of pride for its effective work.

The Fond Du Lac people have many admirable programs and businesses working for the benefit of the Band. Members take pride in both their progress and continuation of Ojibwa traditions.

MINNESOTA—DULUTH
NI-MI-WIN
Spirit Mountain Ski Facility
Duluth, MN
(218) 897-1251, Fond Du Lac Tribal Office
NI-MI-WIN is a major Ojibwa cultural event and is usually held the third weekend in August. The event's name means ''Everybody come and dance'', and is sponsored by the non-profit Ojibwa cultural organization, Ni-Mi-Win, Inc. Its goal is to bring the dozens of Ojibwa (Chippewa) bands together from Canada, the Great Lakes and the northern Plains. It

also serves to educate both non-Indians and Indians about Ojibwa culture and everyone is welcome. Spirit Mountain is a historic meeting place for the Ojibwa and its choice for this event is appropriate.

There are many activities of great interest. Guest speakers include Indian spiritual and cultural leaders, historians, and anthropologists. There are demonstrations by Ojibwa artists and craftspeople of leatherwork, birch bark and black ash basket making, and more. Often there are about 50 booths with arts and crafts people demonstrating, explaining, and selling their beautiful products.

Both traditional Ojibwa food and standard contemporary foods are sold. You can try venison, wild rice, and fry bread for a delicious Native American meal. Wild rice processing is sometimes demonstrated and it's a chance to see how the most important Ojibwa food is properly prepared.

There are games to watch, too. The traditional moccasin game, an ancient Woodlands guessing game is often demonstrated and is not to be missed. There are usually canoe races and running competitions as well.

There is fine Ojibwa dancing and singing to see and hear. Many traditional Ojibwa songs are sung along with some inter-tribal ones as well. Sioux and Cree people sometimes join the Ojibwa in the dancing, too.

The Ojibwa call themselves the Anishinabeg, the Original People, and Ni-Mi-Win certainly carries on the good spirit of the original people.

MINNESOTA—GRAND PORTAGE INDIAN RESERVATION
GRAND PORTAGE TRIBAL OFFICE
Box 428
Grand Portage, MN 55605
(218) 475-2279 or 475-2277
The Ojibwa Indian people of Grand Portage live in the beautiful and historic northeastern tip of Minnesota. This was a center for fur trading activities of the French and Indian trappers and hunters. These adventurous early days of the fur trade are still remembered by the Ojibwa people. Much of the flavor and tradition of those early days remain at Grand Portage. Even the name dates back to the famous fur trade days when the Grand Portage trail was necessary to bypass falls and rapids along the main canoe route. The trail is still here and you may hike its 8 1/2 mile length. The trail begins at GRAND PORTAGE NATIONAL MONUMENT where the old trading post and stockade have been partially reconstructed. The

monument phone number is (218) 728-1237. The Monument has periodic special programs involving Ojibwa Indian and fur trade activities.

The Ojibwa people of Grand Portage hold their annual RENDEZVOUS DAYS usually the second weekend in August. The name honors the fact that the Ojibwa and fur traders met at this spot for many years to conduct their trading. For their present day Rendezvous Days celebration the Ojibwa people have fine traditional singing and dancing. There are wonderful foods available including such traditions as moose stew, wild rice soup, corn, and more. Also sold are modern moose burgers and herring fish burgers. Ojibwa women still make fine beadwork and it is generally sold here, too.

Although Rendezvous Days is a highlight of the whole year, the Grand Portage Ojibwa people have provided visitor attractions to appeal to people all year round. The reservation surrounds the National Monument and there are excellent visitor facilities. The Ojibwa people own the GRAND PORTAGE LODGE & CONFERENCE CENTER, on Hwy 61 in Grand Portage, phone (218) 475-2401. The modern lodge features such attractions as an indoor pool, sauna, tennis, a game room and lawn games. The RESTAURANT is decorated with Ojibwa art work and specializes in fresh Lake Superior fish and Indian foods along with standard menu items. There is a marina with boat rentals, also owned by the Grand Portage Indian Band. A cabin is available for day use by hikers near Fort Charlotte on the Pigeon River. At Crawford House in the National Monument, Ojibwa women demonstrate and sell beadwork. During the winter season, the Band maintains about 70 miles of cross country ski trails for its guests. Isle Royal National Park is served by ferry service from Grand Portage.

The Grand Portage Ojibwa people have additional accomplishments besides the visitor facilities. The Band owns its own construction company, logging operation, commercial fishing company, community arts center, and even operates its own elementary school. The Grand Portage Ojibwa have accomplished much and are rightfully proud of both their achievements and traditional culture.

MINNESOTA—INTERNATIONAL FALLS
GRAND MOUND INTERPRETIVE CENTER
Hwy 11
15 miles W of International Falls, MN
(218) 279-3332
Very large Indian burial mound may be visited here. Museum exhibits explain the function and history of the mound and its builders. Audio-visual program.

MINNESOTA—JEFFERS
JEFFERS PETROGLYPHS
Hwy 10
7 miles NE of Jeffers, MN
(507) 877-3647
Indian rock art on attractive red stone can be seen here.

MINNESOTA—MILLE LACS INDIAN RESERVATION
MILLE LACS INDIAN MUSEUM
Star Route, Box 195
Onamia, MN 56359
(612) 532-3632 Museum, 532-4181 Tribal office
Mille Lacs Indian Museum is located twelve miles north of Onamia on US Hwy 169. The museum features a fine collection of Ojibwa and Dakota artifacts including clothing, food, medicine, hunting and other exhibits. The Four Seasons Room has life size dioramas of Ojibwa traditional life as it was in each of the four seasons. Artwork, including paintings, is also exhibited. The Mille Lacs people hold their Open House annually, generally in mid-August. This event includes both traditional pow-wow dancing, Ojibwa moccasin games, and the construction of an old time Ojibwa wigwam. Wigwams are now very rare in the Ojibwa country and it is a real treat to see one. It is built with a basswood sapling frame and covered with bark. Traditional cultural foods of the Ojibwa are also served including wild rice, corn on the cob, syrups, fry bread, fish, and brown sugar—all original Native American foods.

There is a bingo enterprise for those interested in the game. The Mille Lacs people also own and operate an electrical bench assembly plant here.

MINNESOTA—MINNEAPOLIS
MINNEAPOLIS AMERICAN INDIAN CENTER MUSEUM
1530 E Franklin Ave
Minneapolis, MN
(612) 871-4555
This busy urban Indian center includes a museum with Native American displays. Most Indian people in Minneapolis are Ojibwa, but other tribes are represented here too.

MINNESOTA—NETT LAKE
BOIS FORT INDIAN RESERVATION
Nett Lake, MN 55772
(218) 757-3261
The Bois Fort Ojibwa hold an annual pow-wow, usually the first weekend in June. It features traditional Ojibwa dancing and singing and people come great distances to attend. Of special interest are the traditional Indian dish or bone games, an ancient and en-

joyable game played by the Ojibwa. It's necessary to speak Ojibwa to play, but the games are very enjoyable to watch. Ojibwa foods are served including bannock (Woodlands Indian bread) and wild rice. Arts and crafts are exhibited and sold, including beadwork, paintings (watercolors are a specialty), and wood carvings (beautiful duck decoys are produced). There is a princess contest and pow-wow competition dancing. In English, the Bois Fort Pow-wow is called "Moon of the Bursting Buds" in honor of the ripening wild rice crop. Contact the Bois Fort Tribal Office for exact dates and times of this popular pow-wow.

Wild rice was the most important food of the Ojibwa people for many centuries. Nowhere in the world does it grow better than Nett Lake and other lakes of this region. The Bois Fort Indian people still harvest wild rice, both for home use and for commercial production. Marketed under the brand name, BOIS FORT WILD RICE, this gourmet quality food is in high demand. Bois Fort executive director Dave Villebrun explains that this is natural Lake Rice, grown naturally and without fertilizer in Minnesota's scenic lakes. Growing the slow, natural way, lake rice is of high quality. The lake wild rice provides fine grains, retains moisture, cooks fast, and results in an unusually fine product. Additionally, it is often hand parched in the old Indian way which adds to the quality of each grain. Bois Fort Wild Rice is a prestige brand. (For wholesale purchases, contact the Tribal Office's executive director.)

MINNESOTA—NEW ULM
BROWN COUNTY HISTORICAL MUSEUM
Center & Broadway St
New Ulm, MN
(507) 354-2016
Among the presentations are Native American exhibits. Of particular interest are displays relating to the Great Sioux Uprising of 1862. The eastern Sioux retaliated against settlers' encroachments and drove large numbers from their lands. This was a major, although temporary, victory for the Sioux. Both the uprising and subsequent events resulted in tragedy and hardship for Sioux and settlers alike.

MINNESOTA—PIPESTONE
One of the great Native American sites in the US, Pipestone is where Midwestern Indians obtained the red stone used to carve peace pipes. This unique stone is called catlinite and can be worked into elaborate, high quality carvings. Indian pipe makers still come here today to quarry the fine red stone for their pipes. Some of these are made for sale and may be purchased locally. The carvings on many are of such high quality they are really small sculptures.

PIPESTONE NATIONAL MONUMENT
Off Hwy 75
Outside of Pipestone, MN
(507) 825-5463
The monument preserves the actual Catlinite quarries where Indian people have come for centuries to obtain their sacred stone. During the summer visitors can often see pipes being made as Indian artists work here. There is an interpretive center, audio-visual presentations, and trails through the quarries. Also here:

THE UPPER MIDWEST INDIAN CULTURAL CENTER, is located by the Monument's visitor center. The Cultural Center has special events and offers Catlinite pipes and other Indian art for sale. The Pipestone Shrine Association has a mail order catalog ($1.00) for those interested in buying a pipe. Write: Pipestone Shrine Association, Box 727, Pipestone, MN 56164. Two fine Chippewa pipe makers are Dan and Ed Needham who operate the Chippewa Indian Craft Shop, Red Lake Indian Reservation, Goodridge, MN 56725, phone (612) 378-4210 or 378-4322. They also have a catalog ($1.00) for mail order.

MINNESOTA—ST. PAUL
INDIAN MOUNDS PARK
Earl St & Mounds Blvd
St. Paul, MN
(612) 292-7400
Located in Dayton's Bluff section, the park preserves six Indian mounds. Picnicking.

MINNESOTA—WALKER
MUSEUM OF NATURAL HISTORY & INDIAN ARTS AND CRAFTS
Leech Lake Chamber of Commerce Building
Hwy 200
Walker, MN
(218) 547-1313
Indian exhibits here in Ojibwa country.

MINNESOTA—WHITE EARTH
WHITE EARTH OJIBWA INDIAN RESERVATION
Box 418
White Earth, MN 56591
(218) 983-3285
The WHITE EARTH TREATY CELEBRATION POW-WOW is held annually, usually in June. The pow-wow grounds are east of US Hwy 59 at White Earth. Ojibwa dancing, arts and crafts, Indian foods, and a softball tournament are highlights. The Senior Citizens Arts and Crafts Fair in the gym offers both traditional Ojibwa arts and crafts and contemporary products as well.

The lovely White Earth country offers fine lakes, fish-

Lake of the Woods Ojibwa Cultural Centre in Kanora, Ontario, preserves and revives the history and culture of the Ojibwa Indian people. Researcher Dorothy Favel, Ojibwa (at left), and Center director Maria Seymore, a Cree, model traditional jingle dresses. (Lake of the Woods Cultural Centre)

Minnesota, Wisconsin and Ontario have many Ojibwa cultural events. Ni-Mi-Win, an Ojibwa cultural gathering in Duluth, Minnesota, features traditional dancing and a variety of enjoyable and educational activities. (Fond du Lac Tribal Office — David Danz)

Ojibwa dancer at Ni-Mi-Win, a major event in Duluth, Minnesota sponsored by the Ojibwa people. (Fond du Lac Tribal Office—David Danz)

Ninety-one year old Jim Garner of the Pearl River Choctaw Community in Mississippi has taught important traditions to younger Choctaw people. Such elders are true cultural historians. (Mississippi Band of Choctaw Indians—Communications Program)

The late Micmac Chief Peter Wilmont of Wagamatcook Reserve, Cape Breton, Nova Scotia. Chief Wilmont wears a Woodlands style Glengarry cap and clothing with traditional Micmac designs. Elders represent the source of the Indian people's cultural heritage. (Micmac Association of Cultural Studies—Peter J Christmas)

ing, camping, and hunting. Visitors need to contact the tribal conservation office for required permits, and to familiarize themselves with tribal regulations.

Pinehurst Resort at Nayatahwaush is owned and operated by an Ojibwa businessman and offers cabins, trailer lots, a lake and restaurant. Phone (218) 935-5745. The reservation also has a bingo enterprise which travelers may want to visit.

The White Earth Ojibwa people have a number of other important tribally owned businesses. The White Earth Garment Manufacturing Company produces sports team uniforms, hospital and nursing uniforms and gowns, sportswear and the like. They welcome group purchases and can do custom work for group orders.

The tribal saw mill produces Ojibwa Forest Products and there is also the Ojibwa Building Supply Company. High quality kiln dried firewood is sold under the brand name of Indian Wood. Potential customers for any of these products can contact the tribal office.

The White Earth Ojibwa people have a senior citizens housing program which adds to their list of impressive accomplishments and activities.

MISSISSIPPI

MISSISSIPPI—CHOCTAW INDIAN RESERVATION
Route 7, Box 21
Philadelphia, MS 39350
(601) 656-5251
The Tribal Headquarters are located at Pearl River Community, off Hwy 16, 5 miles W of Philadelphia, MS.

The history of the Choctaw Indian people in Mississippi reaches back many thousands of years. Descendants of the famed mound builders, Choctaw religious history traces the tribe's origin to the great Nanih Waiya mound (now a part of a state park near Preston, MS). The Choctaw people came from this mound, and after a long period of wandering, settled in their present home. For many centuries a highly developed culture evolved until disrupted by the arrival of Europeans. Eventually most of the Choctaw were driven west to Oklahoma where a majority of the Choctaw Nation lives today. SEE: OKLAHOMA—DURANT and TUSKAHOMA.

But the Mississippi Band of Choctaw Indians, despite tremendous opposition and hardship, managed to remain in their homeland. Health and economic conditions were so severe that it wasn't until an Indian agency and hospital were established by the Federal government in 1930 that the population began to increase. Today over 4000 Choctaw people live in seven communities scattered around Philadelphia, MS.

Although the population began increasing in 1930, areas such as education lagged much longer. As late as 1950, few Mississippi Choctaws had more than two years of education. Even into the 1960's almost no Choctaws here had completed high school. Jobs were scarce and times hard. But then an amazing transformation occurred. Following the Civil Rights movement and with outstanding new tribal leadership, life began to change in exciting ways.

A new high school was built, a health center opened, a housing construction program implemented, and human services projects begun. Businesses were attracted to the reservation, often from major corporations. Today Choctaw Greetings Enterprise has become the third largest greeting card production company in the world and Chahta Enterprises is a major supplier of parts for General Motors. Significantly, they had the lowest rejection rate of any supplier for GM. Choctaw Electrics supplies Chrysler in yet another joint venture business enterprise. Health standards are rising steadily and over 60 Choctaws have graduated from college while 150 more are currently enrolled.

Through these developments the Choctaw people have been a leader in preserving their culture. Most Choctaw people are bilingual in English and Choctaw. Traditional ribbon dresses and shirts are often worn, especially on festive occasions. Traditional Choctaw dancing is popular, arts and crafts (including beautiful cane baskets) are maintained, and the traditional stickball game is regularly played.

If you would like to see these and other traditional activities the CHOCTAW ANNUAL FAIR in mid-July is a fine opportunity. Traditional Choctaw dancing with women in the beautiful long ribbon dresses and men wearing traditional shirts and hats is one highlight. Stickball games are played with the competitive vigor for which Choctaw players have been famed for centuries. Arts and crafts are displayed and sold, too. There are exhibits, food booths, entertainment, some Plains pow-wow dancing, and much more. Often 20,000 people attend. Check with the Choctaw Tribal Offices for exact dates.

Visitors will also want to see the CHOCTAW MUSEUM OF THE SOUTHERN INDIAN here. It features historic items, arts and crafts exhibits, clothing displays, and information on famous tribal leaders. Basketry, beadwork, and other items are sold here.

Choctaw dancers in Mississippi perform traditional dances that honor nature and animals. They also perform social dances. These dancers are wearing traditional Southeastern Indian clothing. (Mississippi Band of Choctaw—Communications Program)

Many Southeastern Indian events are accompanied by delicious traditional foods. Mabel Jackson prepares hominy the old fashioned way, outdoors in a big iron pot over an open fire. This is a Choctaw celebration in Mississippi. (Mississippi Band of Choctaw Indians—Communications Program)

One of the greatest art forms of Southeastern Indian women is cane basketry. Susan Denson, a Mississippi Choctaw, works at this ancient art. Cane baskets are the finest and most traditional of Southeastern arts. (Mississippi Band of Choctaw Indians—Communications Program)

Chief Philip Martin and the Choctaw people can certainly be proud of what they have achieved in just two decades.

MISSISSIPPI—GREENVILLE
WINTERVILLE MOUNDS STATE PARK & MUSEUM
Hwy 1
5 miles N of Greenville, MS
(601) 334-4684
Several Indian mounds may be visited here. A museum explains the culture of the Native Americans who built these interesting structures.

MISSISSIPPI—NATCHEZ
Site of THE GRAND VILLAGE OF THE NATCHEZ INDIANS
400 Jefferson Davis Blvd
Natchez, MS
(601) 446-6502
The Natchez Indians had their great village here in the city that bears the tribes's name. Explorers and others marveled at the Natchez's culture, but at an early date the French attacked the Indians and destroyed their society. Survivors fled and joined the Creek and Cherokee Nations.

Today, you can see a reconstructed NATCHEZ INDIAN HOUSE, mounds, and displays of artifacts. There are interpretive trails through the village area. This is one of the most historic archeological sites in the country.

Contrary to many sources, the Natchez are not extinct. Descendants are found today among the Creek and Cherokee in Oklahoma and some of the old ceremonialism still survives there.

EMERALD MOUND
Off Natchez Trace Pkwy
11 miles NE of Natchez, MS
Another interesting Indian archeological site is found here. This is a temple mound where elaborate ceremonies were held.

MISSISSIPPI—SAUCIER
JP MUSEUM OF INDIAN ARTIFACTS
Hwy 49
Saucier, MS
(601) 832-3584
Native American exhibits, including archeological material, are displayed.

MISSISSIPPI—TUPELO
CHICKASAW INDIAN VILLAGE SITE
Between Hwy 6 and 78
NW of Tupelo, MS
This is the archeological site of a palisaded (walled)

Chickasaw village. There are displays, an audio-visual presentation, and self-guided trails. Today the Chickasaw live in Oklahoma. SEE: TRIBAL LISTINGS under Chickasaw.

MISSOURI

MISSOURI—COLUMBIA
MUSEUM OF ANTHROPOLOGY
University of Missouri, Swallow Hall
Columbia, MO
(314) 822-3764
Native American displays including collections of Mississippian area pre-Columbia material. Museum gift shop.

MONTANA

MONTANA—BIG HOLE NATIONAL BATTLEFIELD
Box 237
22 miles SW of Anaconda near Wisdom, MT 59761
(406) 689-3155
After settlers took northeastern Oregon's Wallowa Valley from the relatively peaceful Nez Perce tribe, the Indians were forced onto a reservation in Idaho. Chief Joseph and a portion of the Nez Perce subsequently attempted to flee to Canada where they hoped for a kinder policy toward Indian people. The US Army was ordered to stop them and a series of battles were fought across Idaho and Montana, the Nez Perce defeating the Army at White Bird Canyon, Idaho (now part of Nez Perce National Historic Park, SEE: IDAHO—SPALDING). The troops persisted, however, and many Nez Perce men, women, and children were either shot or died from harsh wartime conditions. Here at Big Hole National Battlefield, the Army attacked the Nez Perce. The Indian families escaped but were ultimately defeated just 50 miles from the Canadian border. There is a visitor center and museum at Big Hole Battlefield and a self-guided trail. Also SEE: Montana—CHINOOK.

MONTANA—BOX ELDER
ROCKY BOY INDIAN RESERVATION
Chippewa-Cree Business Office
Rocky Boy Route
Box Elder MT
(406) 395-4478
Located 15 miles S of US Hwy 2 on State Hwy 234 near Havre. The tribes here offer fine fishing and camping. Check with the tribal office because you need both a state license and a tribal permit to fish. Camping and trailer hookups. The tribe will also conduct group tours by prior arrangement. TEPEES

for rent for camping. Rocky Boy Indian Days, usually the first weekend in August, offers enjoyable traditional dances and other festivities. Check with the tribal office for details on all of the above. There is also the Bear Paw Ski bowl for winter skiing.

MONTANA—BROWNING
MUSEUM OF THE PLAINS INDIAN
Northern Plains Indian Crafts Association
Box E
Browning, MT
(406) 338-2230
Located on US Hwy 89 in Browning, near Glacier National Park. Open daily summers, and weekdays only the rest of the year. This is a wonderful stop for visitors to Montana because of traditional and contemporary Plains Indian arts exhibits and crafts, murals, dioramas, an audio-visual presentation, and special exhibits by leading Indian artists. Besides being an active museum, the crafts shop sells fine moccasins, hair roaches, basketry, beadwork, Indian tanned hides, and much more with an ever changing variety. There are periodic Blackfeet Indian ceremonies on the nearby Blackfeet Reservation and you can check at the museum or the Tribal Office for information, (406) 388-7276.

Be sure to also visit the BLACKFEET CRAFTS ASSOCIATION SHOP 32 miles north on Hwy 89 in St. Mary, for more arts and crafts. Check with the Museum or Tribal Office for current hours.

MONTANA—CHINOOK
CHIEF JOSEPH BATTLEGROUND OF THE BEAR'S PAW STATE MONUMENT
16 miles S of US Hwy 2 on MT Hwy Sec 240
Near Chinook, MT
This was the place where Chief Joseph and his Nez Perce people finally surrendered after being pursued across Idaho and Montana by the US Cavalry in 1877. These were years of great suffering for Indian and non-Indians alike. Custer had been defeated by the Sioux and Cheyenne at the Battle of the Little Bighorn the previous year and the Nez Perce had smashed the US Army at White Bird Canyon, Idaho the following year. But despite these famous victories, the suffering of the Indian people became greater. Loss of land, constant warfare, loss of food resources, and disease all made life harsh. Yet the Plains Indian wars raged on until 1890 when the Army slaughtered a band of Sioux families at Wounded Knee, South Dakota.

Fighting actually continued longer in northeastern California and northwestern Nevada when a group of Paiutes fought a battle as late as 1912. SEE: CALIFORNIA—ALTURAS. Some Apache families, descendants of warring bands in Arizona, actually lived a renegade life in the mountains of Sonoma, Mexico until the 1950's. The struggle continues today in courtrooms and some of the best young lawyers in the nation are Native Americans—ask the Supreme Court, where a number of cases have recently been won by Indian attorneys.

SEE: IDAHO—SPALDING and MONTANA—BIG HOLE for more Nez Perce history.

MONTANA—CUSTER BATTLEFIELD NATIONAL MONUMENT
2 miles SE of Crow Agency on I-Hwy 90, exit 510
Crow Agency, MT 59022
(406) 638-2622
It was here on June 25, 1876 that the Sioux and Cheyenne Nations defeated General George Armstrong Custer and the US Army's Seventh Cavalry. The most famous (but not the only) Native American victory in US history was fought with the result that all of the troops immediately under Custer's command lost their lives.

The visitor center and museum offer exhibits and a good explanation of how the battle progressed. The monument is open daily with guided tours available. You will see the actual sites where the troopers fell and where the Sioux and Northern Cheyenne camped. Custer had a bloody past in his treatment of Indian people, having lead the slaughter of Southern Cheyenne families in Oklahoma eight years earlier (SEE: OKLAHOMA—CHEYENNE). Custer's leadership was replaced by the more humane policies of General Crook, best known for his efforts with the Apache in Arizona.

Incidentally, the Little Bighorn country where Custer and his men died is still Indian Country to this day. The immediate area is owned by the Crow Tribe who served as scouts for Custer and helped fight on the side of the US troops here. Each year the Crow sponsor one of the most famous pow-wows and Indian encampments in America, the highly rated CROW FAIR at Crow Agency in August. Contact the monument or the Crow Tribal Office in Crow Agency for dates and details, phone (406) 638-2601. You'll see tepees, traditional dancing, and have the opportunity to sample Indian foods and purchase artwork and crafts. Best of all you'll meet the Plains Indian people.

For those interested in Plains Indian art, Crow arts and crafts can also be purchased at the visitor center.

The Northern Cheyenne live nearby at Lame Deer. Be sure to note the NORTHERN CHEYENNE ARTS AND CRAFTS ASSOCIATION, US Hwy 212 at State Hwy

A Blackfeet chief presents a proud figure as he rides in a Montana Indian celebration. (Montana Dept. of Commerce)

The Sun Dance is among the most important religious events of the Plains Indian people. This deeply meaningful ceremony is being conducted at Pine Ridge, South Dakota by Sioux men. (Dept. of Highways, State of South Dakota)

The flattened hair roach is a distinctive style of the Crow Nation. The Crow sponsor Crow Fair annually in Montana, one of the largest Indian events on the northern Plains. (Montana Dept. of Commerce)

315 in Lame Deer, MT 59043. Check with the Northern Cheyenne Tribal Office for current hours, (406) 477-6284. Moccasins, buckskin, beadwork, jewelry and other items are sold. The tribal office can inform you of dances or other Cheyenne events open to the public.

NORTHERN PLAINS CRAFTS ASSOCIATION, 2822 First Ave, Billings, MT, (406) 338-5661, is a good source of Plains Indian arts and crafts direct from an Indian crafts cooperative.

MONTANA—EKALAKA
MEDICINE ROCKS STATE PARK
11 miles N on Hwy 7 between Baker and Ekalaka
Ekalaka, MT
This park preserves a ceremonial site consisting of huge rock formations used by Plains Indians. In traditional Plains Indian thought, many objects had power in themselves which could bring about healing or influence events. Hence the term "medicine", since the objects with their spiritual power were often used to cure people.

MONTANA—FLATHEAD INDIAN RESERVATION
SEE: TRIBAL LISTING under FLATHEAD

MONTANA—HAVRE
H. EARL CLACK MEMORIAL MUSEUM
US Hwy 2 at Hill County Fairgrounds
Harve, MT
This museum features the archeological findings of a buffalo jump site where Plains Indians once stampeded buffalo off a cliff to harvest them. Tours of an archeological site may be arranged.

MONTANA—LAME DEER
NORTHERN CHEYENNE TRIBAL MUSEUM
Lame Deer, MT
(406) 477-6284
Presents the history and culture of the Cheyenne Indian people.

MONTANA—PRYOR
CHIEF PLENTY COUPS STATE MONUMENT
3 miles SW of Pryor, MT
Museum relates history of Crow Chief Plenty Coups, a distinguished leader.

NEBRASKA

NEBRASKA—BANCROFT
GRAVE OF SUZETTE LA FLESCHE TIBBLES
Mrs. Tibbles was an Omaha Indian woman who campaigned nationally for Indian Rights. She wrote and lectured advocating fair treatment for Native Americans, helping to bring about positive changes in the law. Daughter of an Omaha chief, she died in 1903 and is buried in the town cemetery.

NEBRASKA—CRAWFORD
FORT ROBINSON STATE PARK & MUSEUM
Hwy 20
3 miles W of Crawford, NE
(308) 665-2660 park, 665-2852 museum
Fort Robinson was built during the Plains Indian wars of the 1870's. It was most famous as the site where Sioux Chief Crazy Horse was killed while under guard. Crazy Horse is famous for his defeat of General Custer at the Little Bighorn in Montana. The chief's life was one of high drama and is a saga in itself. The museum and fort offer insights into both the US Cavalry and the Indian people during the Plains wars.

CRAZY HORSE MUSEUM
Crawford City Park
At the end of W Main St
Crawford, NE
(308) 665-1462
The museum recalls Chief Crazy Horse and pioneer life with exhibits pertaining to American Indians and the settlers.

NEBRASKA—LINCOLN
NEBRASKA STATE HISTORICAL SOCIETY MUSEUM
15th & "P" St
Lincoln, NE
(402) 471-4754
Native American exhibits are among the displays. Check for special programs.

UNIVERSITY OF NEBRASKA STATE MUSEUM
Morril Hall, University of Nebraska
14th & "U" St
Lincoln, NE
(402) 472-2642
Native American displays are among the exhibits.

NEVADA

For Nevada also see TRIBAL LISTINGS under Paiute, Shoshone, and Washo.

NEVADA—AUSTIN
HICKSON PETROGLYPH RECREATION SITE
Hwy 50, 24 miles E of town
Austin, NV
(702) 635-5181
Nevada Indian rock art is preserved here. Near the

The drum is the center of most Plains Indian music. Newat Singers at Cal Expo, Sacramento, California. (L. Shanks)

old Pony Express Trail. Camping and picnicking, but no water.

NEVADA—CARSON CITY
NEVADA STATE MUSEUM
North Carson & Robinson St
Carson City, NV
(702) 885-4810
Among collections are many exhibits relating to the Paiute and Washo Indians of Nevada. There is a life-sized exhibit of a traditional Nevada Indian camp complete in all details. Interesting exhibits of clothing and other items made of tule reeds and sagebrush. Baskets woven by the famed Washo artist Dot-So-La-Lee are here. These are considered to be among the finest baskets in the world. Archeological displays and bookshop. Very interesting museum.

NEVADA—FALLON
CHURCHILL COUNTY MUSEUM
1050 S Maine St
Fallon, NV
(702) 423-3677
The museum exhibits cultural items from the Paiute and other Nevada tribes. An outstanding museum project in cooperation with local Paiute Indian artists and craftspeople is to encourage the revival of making duck decoys and other products of traditional tule reeds. This is an ancient art form once widespread in Nevada, California, and Oregon but now is very rarely practiced. The Smithsonian Institute's recent film, "Tule Technology: Northern Paiute Uses of Marsh Resources in Western Nevada", was filmed near here. A particularly worthwhile exhibit at the museum is the reconstructed Paiute tule house. The museum also offers field trips monthly to rock art and archeological sites.

NEVADA—OVERTON
LOST CITY MUSEUM OF ANTHROPOLOGY
Hwy 169, E of town
Overton, NV
(702) 397-2193
Restoration of Pueblo Grande de Nevada ancient archeological ruin. The museum displays material excavated from this and other sites as well as more recently made Native American arts and crafts. Few realize that pueblo-style architecture extended into Nevada. Also, the Southern Paiute Indians east of here were agriculturalists. Both are evidence of southern Nevada's close ties to the Southwest.

NEVADA—PYRAMID LAKE INDIAN RESERVATION
Box 256
Nixon, NV
(702) 476-0140 Tribal Office
Pyramid Lake Paiute people own this beautiful desert lake with its many scenic geological features. The pyramid-like islands give it its name. The lake is well known for offering some of the finest fishing in Nevada. Fishing permits must be purchased from the Paiute and are available at the Tribal Enterprise Office in Sutcliffe, Pyramid Lake Store in Nixon, and at Abe and Sue's Store in Nixon. Large trout live in the lake and are popular with sports fishermen.

The Paiute people wage a constant struggle against those who would divert the Truckee River, the lake's only source of water. Lowered lake levels would destroy the fishery as well as the scenic wonders of the basin. The rare cui-ui fish is found in the lake and is still a part of the Paiute diet. It is caught seasonally at the point were the Truckee River enters the lake. Because of limited numbers of cui-ui, only Paiutes are allowed to fish for them.

Camping and boating are recreational attractions. The old Indian Trail running along the east side of the Truckee between Nixon and Wadsworth can still be seen in places today. A few women continue to make the magnificent traditional baby cradles. These are woven baskets with a leather covering so finely decorated that the cradles are true art forms. These are sold occasionally at pow-wows and some young Paiute mothers still use them.

NEVADA—RENO
EARTH WINDOW INDIAN ART AND CRAFTS
RENO/SPARKS INDIAN COLONY MALL
2001 E Second St (One block W of MGM Grand Hotel)
Reno, NV
(702) 329-2573
Owned and operated by the Paiute and Washo people of the Reno/Sparks Indian colony, this shopping center has a good variety of businesses including the arts and crafts shop.

NEVADA STATE HISTORICAL SOCIETY MUSEUM
1650 N Virginia St
Reno, NV
(702) 798-0190
This museum includes exhibits on the Nevada Indians among its presentations. Gift shop.

NEVADA—STEWART
STEWART INDIAN SCHOOL MUSEUM
5366 Snyder Ave (3 miles S of Carson City, off Hwy 395)
Stewart, NV
(702) 882-1808
Recently restored by its graduates, this former Indian school has tree shaded grounds and stone buildings on a very lovely campus. The museum interprets Nevada Native American culture, has a collection of Edward Curtis photographs, and explains life at an Indian boarding school. There is a Museum Trading Post here offering arts and crafts for sale.

NEW JERSEY

NEW JERSEY—CAPE MAY COURT HOUSE
HISTORICAL MUSEUM
Hwy 9
N of Cape May Court House, NJ
(609) 465-3535
Among the museum collections are local Native American artifacts. New Jersey is the traditional homeland of the Delaware Indians. SEE: TRIBAL LISTINGS under Delaware.

NEW JERSEY—TRENTON
NEW JERSEY STATE MUSEUM
W State St
Trenton, NJ
The Main Museum contains American Indian exhibits.

NEW MEXICO

The New Mexico section of this book is organized in a slightly different manner than the other states. It begins with the Pueblo Indian Cultural Center and continues through all the modern Indian pueblo communities. Following that is the conventional section with an alphabetical listing of all other Native American cultural attractions in the state. There are many pueblo towns that grouping them together emphasizes their shared cultural heritage.

The first listing, the Indian Pueblo Cultural Center in Albuquerque, is the best place to begin a visit to New Mexican pueblos. They will help orient you and can answer any questions. Your visit here and your reading the descriptions in this book will help you choose which pueblos to see. BE SURE TO CHECK THE TRIBAL LISTING SECTION UNDER PUEBLO FOR DANCES AND OTHER SPECIAL EVENTS. Always check with the Cultural Center or the Pueblo office to be certain of dates before making a long journey.

At most pueblos you will need to stop at the governor's office to pay a fee for photographing or touring. The governor's office routinely deals with visitors and will orient you about your stay. What can and cannot be photographed varies by pueblo and it is important to inquire about local rules. The Pueblos may limit visiting to certain hours of the day, often normal business hours. The best times to visit are during ceremonials, but many pueblos have visitor centers and crafts cooperatives that are exciting any time. Some of the pueblos are unusually interesting, built high atop rugged mesas or with architecturally pleasing styles. By remembering that you are a guest and by being on your best behavior you will gain the most from your visit. Most of the pueblos produce museum quality arts and crafts in all price ranges. The opportunity to purchase such work directly from the Native American artists is a special appeal of a visit here.

The more books you read before you go, the more you will appreciate all that you see. The Pueblo Indians are pleasant, dignified people with an unexcelled cultural heritage.

NEW MEXICO—ALBUQUERQUE
INDIAN PUEBLO CULTURAL CENTER
2401—12th St
Albuquerque, NM 87102
(505) 843-7270
Located conveniently close to I-40 in the city of Albuquerque, the Indian Pueblo Cultural Center is one of the nation's top Native American attractions. Stop by the Center before visiting New Mexico's many pueblos to learn about the people's cultures and to orient yourself. It is owned and operated by the Pueblos, and you will be very impressed by all that is here. The Center is built in a giant D-shape with a round plaza in the middle, the architecture being inspired by an ancient Pueblo Bonito. You walk underground, much as entering a semi-subterranean kiva, to see separate exhibits depicting art and culture at each of the state's 19 pueblos. When you have completed this self-guided tour you will find that you have made a circle around the building. There is an arts and crafts store with authentic Pueblo work of high quality. More choices await you at individual pueblos.

An outstanding feature of the Cultural Center is the restaurant which serves both Pueblo and Southwestern food. It is immaculate, with good service, and the food is among the best in the Southwest. Breakfast and lunch are regularly served, check about dinner.

Pueblo traditional dancing and craft demonstrations

are held many weekends during the summer. Check for special events and for restaurant hours. Fourth of July weekend usually features dancing and an Indian market with crafts and food.

Don't miss the ANNUAL ARTS AND CRAFTS FAIR here with Pueblo Dance performances of artistic merit plus competitive arts and crafts shows. Check for dates. The Indian Pueblo Cultural Center is highly recommended, one of the finest Native American experiences in the US.

TODAY'S INDIAN PUEBLOS

ACOMA PUEBLO
Box 309
Pueblo of Acoma, NM
(505) 552-6606
Reached by driving W from Albuquerque on I-40 to the Acoma Indian Reservation, then S on Hwy 23. Acoma pueblo is one of the most spectacular towns in the world. Often called "Sky City", this Native American community is located high atop Acoma Mesa, a massive flat-topped mountain. If you only have time to visit a few pueblos, Acoma should be among them. Acoma people function both in their traditional culture and in the larger society. Besides farming many work in nearby cities and several dozen are college students or graduates. The pueblo has a visitor center at the base of the mesa where guests register and pay a reasonable fee for a tour and additional fees for photography or painting privileges. Renowned Acoma arts and crafts are sold here and the center is a good place to orient yourself. Periodic ceremonial dancing is performed for religious purposes, some of which is open to the public. A few days each year the pueblo is closed to visitors while important sacred rites are conducted. Otherwise, guests are welcome.

COCHITI PUEBLO
Box 70
Cochiti Pueblo, NM
(505) 465-2244
Located N of Albuquerque on the Cochiti Indian Reservation. Cochiti is noted for its fine drums, pottery (including storyteller figures), and jewelry. The pueblo has an annual Corn Dance which also serves as a homecoming and is well attended by Indians and Anglos alike. No photographing is allowed here, but visitors are welcome.

ISLETA PUEBLO
Box 317
Isleta Pueblo, NM
(505) 869-3111
16 miles S of Albuquerque on I-25
Isleta pueblo is a large, progressive community of about 3000 people. Visitors must check in at the governor's office to pay a recreation fee. There is camping, picnicking, fishing, arts and crafts. Jewelry and pottery are made here, but most Isletans work at urban jobs nearby. Ceremonial dances are held periodically and are well worth attending. Check with the governor's office for rules concerning photography.

JEMEZ PUEBLO
Box 78
Jemez Pueblo, NM
(505) 834-7359
N of Albuquerque via I-25, then NW on Hwy 44, and finally N on Hwy 4.
Jemez people are active in both strengthening their traditional culture and in participating in the outside society. Ceremonial dances remain important and pottery and other crafts are made. But Jemez citizens are now often employed in urban jobs and commute to nearby cities. The pueblo has produced many people active in community affairs such as school boards, local government, and the like. Check with the pueblo office for dance dates and photography rules.

LAGUNA PUEBLO
Box 194
Laguna, NM
(505) 552-6654
Laguna Pueblo is located just off I-40 on the Laguna Indian Reservation between Albuquerque and Grants. There is a vista point on the freeway where you can pull off and get a good view of the pueblo. The pueblo is open during daylight hours and photographs are allowed after paying a fee at the pueblo office. Laguna is a very progressive Indian community and pools its resources to provide its young people with full college scholarships. Laguna is probably the wealthiest and most modern of New Mexico's pueblos. Laguna's traditional culture is also preserved and there are periodic ceremonial dances.

NAMBE PUEBLO
Route 1, Box 117
Santa Fe, NM
(505) 455-7692
25 miles N of Santa Fe off Hwys 84 & 285 at Nambe.
Nambe is a pueblo which is well integrated into the

New Mexico's Pueblos are renowned for their sacred ceremonials with impressive costumes. This is an important San Juan Pueblo dance. (New Mexico Economic Development and Tourism Dept)

This San Ildefonso Pueblo dance is a prayer for rain and a good harvest, and has deep religious significance. Note the traditional Pueblo homes. (New Mexico Economic Development and Tourism Dept)

local community life. Its young people almost always complete high school and many go on to further their education and training. There is still occasional traditional dancing, but almost no crafts, as people choose to work at less traditional occupations. The church here is architecturally interesting, being shaped like an arrowhead when seen from the sky.

PICURIS PUEBLO
Box 228
Penasco, NM
(505) 587-2519
7 miles NW of Penasco off Hwy 75

In recent decades there has been an increase in ceremonial dancing at Picuris and fine dancing is done here. Some nice undecorated micaceous pottery is made here. Many men are among the courageous fire fighters that work for the US Forest Service.

POJOAQUE PUEBLO
Route 1, Box 71
Santa Fe, NM
(505) 455-2278
16 miles N of Santa Fe at US Hwy 285 and SR 4

Pojoaque is blessed with an excellent location for commercial enterprises, and the pueblo owns and is landlord for Pojoaque Pueblo plaza shopping center, La Mesita Restaurant, and numerous other businesses.

Concurrent with its business ventures, Pojoaque people make pottery, jewelry, and other crafts. Check in at the pueblo-style community center to contact arts and crafts people. More a business center than a traditional pueblo in some ways, Pojoaque is justly proud of its progress. Scholarships are provided for Pojoaque young people seeking higher education.

SAN FELIPE PUEBLO
Box A
Algondones, NM
(505) 867-3381

San Felipe is located on the San Felipe Indian Reservation approximately halfway between Albuquerque and Santa Fe. Although some jewelry is made here, few crafts are made for sale. Check with the pueblo governor's office for dates of ceremonial dances and community rules for visitors.

SAN ILDEFONSO PUEBLO
Rt 5, Box 315
Santa Fe, NM
(505) 455-2273
22 miles NW of Santa Fe

San Ildefonso is not one of the larger pueblos, but it is one of the best known. Famous potters and artists live here and this was the home of the late Maria Mar-

tinez, perhaps the best known of New Mexico's potters. Beautiful dances are conducted and visitors are welcome during daylight hours. There is a fee for photography or painting privileges.

SAN JUAN PUEBLO
Box 1099
San Juan Pueblo, NM 87566
4 miles NE of Espanola, NM
(505) 852-4400

San Juan is a very interesting pueblo. The people have organized and built the Oke Oweenge Crafts Cooperative, a beautiful building where San Juan's arts and crafts are sold and where visitors can often see lovely red pottery, beadwork, embroidery, and other arts being made. There is fine traditional dancing and singing. The pueblo is open daylight hours and charges a fee to photography or sketch. The Eight Northern Pueblos Indian Council has its headquarters here. For those interested in Pueblo or Hopi cooking, long time merchant Peter Casados store is here. He offers excellent Pueblo blue corn flour, chilis, spices, and more. Mr. Casados has a catalog providing mail order services (Box 852).

The Northern Pueblo Indian Artists Guild (Box 1079) offers mail order service for pueblo crafts ranging from drums to traditional clothing.

The ANNUAL AMERICAN INDIAN ARTIST AND CRAFTSMAN SHOW sponsored by the Eight Northern Indian Pueblos Council is a major event featuring high quality art by talented Pueblo people. Check for dates.

SANDIA PUEBLO
Box 608
Bernalillo, NM
(505) 867-2876
Off US Hwy 85, 2 1/2 miles S of Bernalillo, NM

Sandia is a modern, progressive community with little unemployment and many young people are enrolled in higher education. Sandians once made excellent willow baskets and pottery but seldom do so today.

SANTA ANA PUEBLO
Box 37
Bernalillo, NM
(505) 867-3301
Located NW of Bernalillo, NM, off Hwy 44

As with the other pueblos, Santa Ana's life today is a blend of cultures. Although many Santa Ana people are employed off the reservation, most return for the colorful religious ceremonies held at the pueblo.

SANTA CLARA PUEBLO
Box 580
Espanola, NM
(505) 753-7326

Santa Clara is famous for its magnificent pottery, but its artists produce other fine work as well. Many beautiful ceremonial dances are performed including the festival at the ancient Puye cliff dwelling the last weekend in July. The public is invited to the Puye Festival and for a reasonable fee visitors can take photographs, eat fine Santa Clara foods, purchase artwork, and meet the Santa Clara people. Santa Clara Canyon, also on the reservation, offers picnicking, camping, and fishing. Many Santa Clarans are employed in off-reservation jobs and the pueblo has progressively developed its economic resources and tourism potential. Santa Clara demonstrates the winning combination of preserving tradition while adopting the best of the larger society.

SANTA DOMINGO PUEBLO
Santo Domingo Pueblo, NM
(505) 465-2240
Located 35 miles SW of Santa Fe

Santo Domingo is a very conservative pueblo noted particularly for its huge, spectacular Corn Dance each August 4th. Fine turquoise jewelry is made here. Most men are engaged in traditional farming. Religious practices are central to the life of the community.

TAOS PUEBLO
Box 1846
Taos, NM
(505) 758-8626

Taos pueblo is located 2 1/2 miles N of the plaza in the town of Taos. This is the five-story high pueblo so often pictured in books and magazines. It is truly a beautiful structure and may be photographed for a reasonable fee. There are many ceremonies here during the year and many are open to visitors. The pueblo is open weekdays 9-5 and 9-3 weekends and holidays. As is true at some other pueblos, pictures may not be taken during dances. There is an information center to orient tourists. Arts and crafts are sold here. Remember, every pueblo is made up of private homes and they can only be entered by invitation. This is a famous, historic community which retains its unique character making it well worth a visit.

TESUQUE PUEBLO
Santa Fe, NM
(505) 982-9415
9 miles N of Santa Fe

Tesuque has produced some interesting pottery and other crafts and has annual ceremonial dances. Farming remains important here. Tesuque has outstanding eagle dancers.

ZIA PUEBLO
San Ysidoro, NM
(505) 867-3304
Off SR 44, NW of Bernalillo, NM

This pueblo stands atop a mesa overlooking the Jemez River. The Zia people are fine dancers, make beautiful orange-on-white pottery, and continue many traditions. Some well known artists are Zians and the New Mexico State symbol is a Zia sun symbol.

ZUNI PUEBLO
Box 339
Zuni, NM
(505) 782-4481

Zuni is reached by either taking Hwy 53 from Grants, NM or Hwy 32 from Gallup then continuing W on 53. Zuni is a large, famous, and friendly pueblo highly recommended to visitors. Rich in history and art, Zuni may well be the best known of the pueblos. This is one of the mythical "Seven Cities of Cibola" which Coronado believed to be filled with gold. Coronado was wrong for there was no gold at Zuni, but there were, and are, riches in art and culture. Zuni Craftsmen Cooperative Association, Box 426, Zuni, NM 87327, has a mail order catalog ($2.00) offering silver and turquoise jewelry. Located on State Hwy 53 at the pueblo, a very good selection of Zuni work may also be purchased in the gift shop here.

In November or December the Zuni hold their spectacular Shalako dances. Giant kachina-like figures ten feet tall dance and race during sacred ceremonies. Visitors are welcome at these dances of the masked gods, but need to be highly respectful. Other dances are listed in the TRIBAL LISTING section.

ZUNI INDIAN RESERVATION
HAWIKUH PUEBLO RUINS
12 miles S of Zuni Pueblo

Another visitor attraction at Zuni is Hawikuh ruins. Permission to visit this historic site must be obtained from the Zuni Tribal Office and requires a Zuni guide. Hawikuh was an active pueblo when visited in 1539 by black explorer Esteban and Spanish priest Fray Marcos. A conflict developed and Esteban was killed. Fray Marcos retreated to Mexico and the following year Coronado returned and attacked Hawikuh. The pueblo continued, with increased Spanish influence, for over a century. It was abandoned after the famous Pueblo Revolt of 1680 when the Indians drove the Spanish out of New Mexico. Now Hawikuh is in ruins but it is a very historic site to visit, one of

Mesa Verde National Park's best known cliff dwelling is the Cliff Palace. You can descend the mesa and tour this ancient Indian community in Colorado. (Colorado Tourism Board)

Pueblo Bonito is a gigantic New Mexico ruin with over 800 rooms. Part of Chaco Culture National Historic Park, this city represents one of the most elaborate developments of Native American architecture and culture. (New Mexico Economic Development and Tourism Dept.)

An interior view of Mesa Verde's Cliff Palace showing an inhabitants' perspective beneath the looming cliffs. (Colorado Tourism Board)

Montezuma Well cliff dwellings overlook a beautiful lake within a natural sink hole below the desert floor. They are a part of Montezuma Castle National Monument in Arizona. (R. Shanks)

the famed Seven Cities of Cibola the Spanish mistakenly believed was filled with gold.

Zuni guides can also lead you to the Village of the Great Kivas, also on the reservation. The site is named for two large kivas whose remains are here. Rock art paintings can be viewed. These were made by Zuni people in the early Twentieth Century.

More recent Zuni art can be seen in the mission church at the pueblo. There is a tribal campground, stores, restaurants, and gas stations at Zuni. Don't miss the pueblo's arts and crafts shop.

NEW MEXICO—OTHER ATTRACTIONS

NEW MEXICO—ABIQUIU DAM
N of Espanola, NM, off Hwy 96 between the dam & Hwy 84
Operated by the US Army Corps of Engineers, this is a centuries old Navajo site with the archeological remains of hogans and animal pens. There is a campground and picnic area here and exhibits at the dam's offices.

NEW MEXICO—ALBUQUERQUE
In addition to the INDIAN PUEBLO CULTURAL CENTER, perhaps Albuquerque's top visitor attraction (see listing at the head of the section on New Mexico's Pueblo Indians), there are other excellent attractions as well. Among them:

ALBUQUERQUE MUSEUM
2000 Mountain Rd NW
Albuquerque, NM
(505) 766-7392
History of the various ethnic groups of the Rio Grande Valley.

INDIAN ARTS AND CRAFTS ASSOCIATION
4215 Lead SE
Albuquerque, NM 87108
(505) 265-9149
The Indian Arts and Crafts Association is comprised of stores which have pledged honest representation of Indian goods and proper business activities. The goal is to guide the buyer to stores where genuine Indian and Eskimo arts and crafts are offered for sale. The Association offers a membership directory and buyers guide for about three dollars. It is a handy way to locate many excellent arts and crafts dealers. They also sell several informational booklets to guide you in buying authentic Indian arts and crafts. Write for details.

MAXWELL MUSEUM OF ANTHROPOLOGY
Redondo Dr at Ash St
(505) 277-4404
Changing exhibits on Southwest Indian cultures.

BIEN MUIR INDIAN MARKET CENTER
I-25 off exit 234 at Tramway Dr
Box 10367
Albuquerque, NM
(505) 821-5400
Large selection of Hopi, Navajo, and Pueblo Indian work. Well known throughout the Southwest.

INDIAN PETROGLYPHS STATE PARK
SR 448, exit Atrisco Dr
Rock art, rock shelters, and grinding sites are among massive boulders. Picnic area. Loop drive with stops along the route for hikes to nearby petroglyphs. Closed Tuesdays and Wednesdays.

NEW MEXICO STATE FAIR
Box 8546
State Fairgrounds on San Pedro Dr, between Lomas & Central Blvd
The State Fair is usually held in late summer and generally has Indian dancing along with an Indian Village. Native American agricultural products are also displayed. New Mexico Indians plus Aztecs often dance here. The NEW MEXICO ARTS AND CRAFTS FAIR is usually held here the last weekend in June. Other events such as Indian rodeos, pow-wows and ceremonial dance contests occur periodically. Check for dates.

NEW MEXICO—AZTEC RUINS NATIONAL MONUMENT
Off US Hwy 550
Aztec, NM
(505) 334-6174
Despite its name, these ruins were made not by Mexico's Aztecs but by local Anasazi Indians. This ruin is one of the best preserved and most interesting in the Southwest. The Great Kiva offers visitors an opportunity to see a reconstructed pueblo-type ceremonial chamber that is one of the high points in Native American architecture. The west wing of the ruin is also particularly well preserved, with even ceilings left intact. Museum. Highly recommended.

NEW MEXICO—BANDELIER NATIONAL MONUMENT
12 miles SE of Los Alamos, NM, via Hwy 40 to Pojoaque. Then proceed W on Hwy 4 for 24 more miles.
(505) 672-3861
Cliff dwellings, cave dwellings, and even a circular village may all be visited here. Interesting huge cliffs

surround the sites. Visitor center, guided tours, campfire programs, hiking, trails, and more are. provided for visitors. Picnicking and camping. Check for special events.

NEW MEXICO—CHACO CULTURE NATIONAL HISTORICAL PARK (PUEBLO BONITO)

SR 4, Box 6500
Bloomfield, NM
(505) 786-5384

This is one of the great archeological sites in North America. Reaching it requires travel over dirt roads which may become impassable in wet weather. Towing trailers is not recommended. The park is located on SR 57 reached from the north off Hwy 44, SE of Bloomfield. From the south, turn off I-40 at Thoreau on SR 57. Both routes involve many miles of dirt roads.

Despite the roads (which the State of New Mexico should improve), once at Chaco Canyon the visitor will be well rewarded. In the monument are nearly a dozen large pueblo ruins and hundreds of smaller remains. There are roadways 30 feet wide along which logs for construction undoubtedly were rolled. An ancient astronomical observatory site here was used to time ceremonies and agricultural activities. But the crown jewel is Pueblo Bonito, a huge D-shaped city full of ceremonial kivas and 800 dwelling rooms. Walls are spectacularly high.

A visitor center, guided tours, campfire talks, and self-guided trails are provided. Permits are needed to visit certain sites. Freshwater is available only at the visitor center. This great site is highly recommended, but visitors should consult with park staff before their trip as facilities are limited and weather conditions can be harsh.

NEW MEXICO—CORONADO STATE MONUMENT

State Hwy 44
2 miles NW of Bernalillo, NM
(505) 867-5351

There were once many more Pueblo villages in New Mexico than remain today. This is the ruin of a Tiwa village called Kuaua which was visited by the famed explorer Coronado in 1540. Rarely seen murals from the ceremonial kiva are on display. The kiva may be visited via a ladder through the smoke hole, the traditional means of entry. The kiva is square, not round like many of these ceremonial chambers. The visitor center has a museum to orient the traveler. Stop here first, for the pueblo has over 1000 excavated rooms. This great site was built by the ancestors of the Isleta and Sandia pueblo people.

NEW MEXICO—DULCE
JICARILLA APACHE TRIBAL MUSEUM
JICARILLA APACHE INDIAN RESERVATION
Box 507
Dulce, NM
(505) 759-3242 or 759-3362

The Jicalla Apache Arts and Crafts Industry is a tribally sponsored effort aimed at reviving Jicarilla arts and crafts, including basketry, buckskin tanning, leatherwork, beadwork, etc. There are crafts on display in the Jicarilla Museum. The gift shop sells fine Jicarilla work. Mail order. Both are open Monday through Friday. Check with the museum or tribal office for ceremonial dances and fiestas.

NEW MEXICO—EL MORRO NATIONAL MONUMENT

Hwy 53, 43 miles SW of Grants, NM
(505) 783-5132
Mailing address: Ramah, NM 87321

You can make an interesting loop trip from I-40 visiting both El Morro and Zuni Pueblo off Hwy 53 at Grants and ending up via Hwy 32 back at I-40 at Gallup. Eastbound travelers simply reverse the direction by beginning at Gallup. Note that Zuni Pueblo is 11 miles west of the junction of Hwy 53 and 32. The Ramah Navajo Reservation is also along this route.

El Morro features a variety of attractions: scenic, historic, and archeological. El Morro is a mesa over 1200 feet high with an ancient Zuni village near the top. At Inscription Rock there are Indian petroglyphs, Spanish conquistador's inscriptions, and the carved names of early pioneers. Visitor center, self-guided trails, picnicking and camping. Ranger led campfire programs are held Friday and Saturday evenings.

NEW MEXICO—GALLUP
INTER-TRIBAL INDIAN CEREMONIALS ASSOCIATION
Box 1
Church Rock, NM 87311
(505) 863-3896 or 722-2228

The Ceremonials are held at Red Rock State Park, just off Hwy I-40, 6 miles E of Gallup. Held annually in August.

Established in 1922, this is one of the best known of America's Indian events with dancing by many tribes, arts and craft sales, demonstrations, a big parade with many Indian participants, an Indian rodeo with 500 competitors, games, a foot race, and more. Such tribes as the Navajo, Pueblo, Hopi, Quechan, Apache, Pima, Comanche, Kwakiutl, Kiowa, Crow, Pawnee and others have appeared here through the years. Zuni Pueblo has been represented every year since

1922. Southwestern and Plains dancing is most common, but groups from as far as the Northwest Coast have performed. Hoop dances, buffalo and deer dances, Navajo chants, pow-wow drum groups, and more continue for four days. Photography is allowed and the Sunday afternoon program and daily dances in the plazas provide especially good opportunities. The arts and crafts show offers a broad range of items including a great number for sale. Everyone soon works up an appetite watching all the exciting activities and Indian foods are offered for sale. You can try Pueblo chili stew, Zuni oven bread and meat pies or Navajo tacos and fry bread. Tickets for this popular event generally go on sale in April and continue thereafter. Highly recommended.

RED ROCK STATE PARK (address above) has the RED ROCK MUSEUM with Navajo, Zuni, and Hopi exhibits. There is a gift shop with Southwestern Indian arts and crafts. Heritage Canyon in the park has recreated an Indian village, Spanish rancho, and a frontier town. Phone (505) 722-5564 or 722-6196.

NEW MEXICO—MESCALERO
MESCALERO APACHE INDIAN RESERVATION
Box 176
Mescalero, NM
(505) 671-4495
The scenic Mescalero Apache reservation is in the heart of south central New Mexico's finest recreation area. The Apache people have taken advantage of their great location by building "New Mexico's premier resort", the four star rated INN OF THE MOUNTAIN GODS (Box 269, Mescalero/Ruidoso, NM 88340, phone (800) 545-9011 or (505) 257-5141). There you will find tennis courts, swimming pool, boat and bicycle rentals, whirlpool, saunas, and more. During winter, the Apache owned Sierra Blanca Ski Resort is very popular. Apache arts and crafts are sold at the Inn of the Mountain Gods.

One of the southwest's finest Indian events is held here annually over July 4th. This is the Apache girl's ceremony which honors young women coming of age. There are beautiful religious ceremonies, spectacular Mountain Spirit Dancing, a rodeo, and other festivities. Three Apache tribes live here: the Mescalero, the Chiricahua, and the remnants of the Lipan. Cattle raising is an important economic activity along with tourism.

The MESCALERO APACHE CULTURAL CENTER MUSEUM presents interesting exhibits worth seeing.

NEW MEXICO—PECOS
PECOS NATIONAL MONUMENT
Drawer 11
Pecos, NM 87552
(505) 757-6414
Pecos was a historic Pueblo village built too far from the protective Rio Grande Valley. The pueblo served as a middle-man for trade between the agricultural pueblo people to the west and the wandering Plains tribes from the east. This trading position worked well until the horse transformed Plains Indian life and warfare increased. Ultimately, the pueblo was destroyed and its few survivors fled to Jemez pueblo in 1838. Today visitors may tour the ruins of the pueblo and its mission churches the Spaniards built. There is a visitor center and self-guided trails. Interestingly, one Pecos Indian ceremony may still be seen today. Each August 2nd, the Jemez pueblo people perform the old Pecos Bull Dance, taught to them long ago by the 17 survivors of Pecos Pueblo.

NEW MEXICO—PORTALES
PALEO-INDIAN INSTITUTE MUSEUM
EASTERN NEW MEXICO UNIVERSITY
1400 Second St
Portales, NM
(505) 562-2303
Exhibits from Early Man archeological sites nearby dating back to the Stone Age. At BLACKWATER DRAW MUSEUM, Hwy 70 seven miles NE of Portales, there is also an archeological site and museum which may be visited. Phone (505) 562-2202. New Mexico has yielded some of the earliest archeological finds in North America, including famous sites at Sandia Cave, Clovis, and Folsom.

NEW MEXICO—SALINAS NATIONAL MONUMENT
Box 496
Mountainair, NM 87036
(505) 847-2585
Salinas National Monument is composed of three separate locations each with the ruins of a pueblo and mission church. These Indian communities suffered from exposed positions east of the Rio Grande Valley making them vulnerable to attacks by the Apache. The arrival of the Spaniards made times even more difficult and disease and drought struck. The end result was that all the Salinas villages were abandoned after heavy loss of life and the survivors fled to the Rio Grande Valley pueblos and to El Paso. All three major ruins are in the vicinity of Mountainair: ABO is 11 miles SW of Mountainair via Hwy 60 and 513; GRAN QUIVIRA is 26 miles SE of Mountainair on Hwy 14; and QUARAI is 8 miles N off Hwy 14. Each is well worth visiting and all have visitor centers and self-guided trails.

NEW MEXICO—SALMON RUINS

US Hwy 64
2 1/2 miles W of Bloomfield, NM
(505) 632-2013

Built in the Eleventh Century, this C-shaped pueblo features a tower kiva and large multi-story dwellings. The San Juan County Archeological Research Center is located here with a museum and library. Audio-visual presentation.

NEW MEXICO—SANTA FE

There are many opportunities to see Native American art in Santa Fe. Among them are:

INSTITUTE OF AMERICAN INDIAN ARTS MUSEUM

1300 Cerrillos Rd
Santa Fe, NM
(505) 988-6281

Contemporary and traditional Southwest Indian arts are displayed. Native Americans take a very active role here which helps make this a high quality museum. The museum shop has a fine selection of Southwest Indian work. Check for special events.

UNIVERSITY OF NEW MEXICO MUSEUMS
LABORATORY OF ANTHROPOLOGY
Camino Lejo off Old Santa Fe Trail
Santa Fe, NM
(505) 827-6460

Open weekdays. Southwest Indian collections, including much archeological material.

MUSEUM OF FINE ARTS
Near Palace of the Governors across
Lincoln Ave
Santa Fe, NM

Modern Native American art displayed.

PALACE OF THE GOVERNORS
North side of the Plaza
Santa Fe, NM

Local Indian artists sell their wares here in the portal. Exhibits inside relating to Southwest Indian cultures.

WHEELWRIGHT MUSEUM
704 Camino Lejo
Santa Fe, NM (505) 982-4636

Outstanding Southwest Indian collections, with an emphasis on the Navajo. Fine special exhibitions.

ALSO IN SANTA FE: The NORTHERN PUEBLO INDIAN ARTISTS GUILD holds arts and crafts shows in April and December at DeVargas Mall. For details, phone (505) 852-4283; or write Box 1079, San Juan Pueblo, NM 87566. The INDIAN MARKET is held mid-August at the Plaza with excellent and varied Indian dancing and crafts sales. Check with the Santa Fe Chamber of Commerce, 200 W Marcy St, Santa Fe, NM 87501, (505) 983-7317 for details. These and other fine arts events are not to be missed.

NEW MEXICO—SILVER CITY
GILA CLIFF DWELLINGS NATIONAL MONUMENT

End of Hwy 15 approximately 44 miles N of Silver City, NM. Or take Hwy 35 and 61 via Mimbres E of Silver City for easier driving or if pulling a trailer. These roads intersect Hwy 15 mid-way to the monument.
(505) 534-9461

Ancient Mogollon Indians built cliff dwellings in caves here. Stop by the visitor center for orientation and then drive to the trail. The trail is a one mile loop and has some fairly steep sections. The cliff dwellings can be entered and you'll gain a good insight into these early pueblo peoples. Weekend programs are offered by the ranger staff. The GILA VISITOR CENTER has exhibits, an audio-visual presentation, and trail guidebooks.

NEW MEXICO—TAOS
MILLICENT ROGERS MUSEUM

Hwy 3, 4 miles N
Taos, NM
(505) 758-2462

American Indian arts with emphasis on Taos area.

NEW MEXICO—THREE RIVERS
THREE RIVERS PETROGLYPH SITE

5 miles E from Three Rivers Intersection, 30 miles N of Alamogordo, NM
(505) 523-5571

Rock art petroglyphs by the thousands are located here. Although some are difficult to comprehend, others are quite interesting and attractive. Done 500 to 1000 years ago by ancient Mogollon Indians, there is a display area for visitors as well as trails through the rock art.

NEW YORK

NEW YORK—AUBURN
CAYUGA MUSEUM OF HISTORY AND ART

203 Genesee St
Auburn, NY
(315) 253-8051

Native American art can be seen among the exhibits.

Oneida craftsman Dick Chrisjohn's work is exhibited in museums on two continents. Among his best work are wooden war clubs and gus-to-weh headdresses. (Assoc. for the Advancement of Native North American Arts and Crafts)

Seneca craftsman Milton Lay of Cattaraugus Reservation in New York state works lovingly on a horn rattle. Iroquoian people are leaders among North American Indian people in preserving traditional arts and crafts. (Assoc. for the Advancement of Native North American Arts and Crafts)

This beautiful Iroquois dress was made by Mohawk seamstress and designer Georgia Thomas and is worn by her daughter. Complete with scalloped beaded trim, this is a traditional style dress of the Iroquois people. (Assoc. for the Advancement of Native North American Arts and Crafts)

Lacrosse is a Native American game invented by the Iroquois. Mohawk craftswoman Esther Mitchell laces a lacrosse stick. (Assoc. for the Advancement of Native North American Arts and Crafts)

Oneida craftsman and athlete Albert Porter holds snowsnakes he handcrafted. Snowsnakes are thrown along a track dug in the snow in this Iroquois contest. This is a great winter sport that deserves more recognition. (Assoc. for the Advancement of Native North American Arts and Crafts)

IROQUOIS INDIAN VILLAGE
Emerson Park
Owasco Lake
2 1/2 miles S of Auburn, NY
(315) 253-5611
An Iroquois Indian village has been reconstructed here. The longhouses of the Iroquois are very interesting bark-covered houses well worth seeing. Museum.

NEW YORK—BASOM
TONAWANDA SENECA INDIAN RESERVATION
7027 Meadville Rd
Basom, NY
(716) 542-4244
Each year the Seneca people hold their annual FIELD DAY, usually the first Sunday in August. There are arts and crafts sales, including wood carving, jewelry, beadwork etc. Some tasty Iroquois foods are offered, including corn soup and fry bread. Both traditional Seneca and western pow-wow dancing are done. Seneca music is very beautiful and pleasing to listen to and the mixture with western pow-wow music gives the fair a nice variety. Traditional Iroquois la crosse is played and visitors will get to see an exhibition game. Fire ball is also played. It is a game similar to regular soccer, except that the ball is actually on fire. Both games are exciting and interesting to watch.

On Meadville and Bloomingdale roads there are arts and crafts stores run by Seneca people that offer a selection of Iroquois work for sale.

NEW YORK—BINGHAMPTON
ROBERSON CENTER FOR ARTS & SCIENCES
30 Front St
Binghampton, NY
(607) 772-0660
A special feature here is that an Eastern Woodlands IROQUOIS LONGHOUSE has been reconstructed. Check for special events.

NEW YORK—BUFFALO
HISTORICAL SOCIETY OF TONAWANDAS
113 Main St
Buffalo, NY
(716) 694-7406
Among the collections are Iroquois Indian exhibits, research material, and photographs.

NEW YORK—FONDA
MOHAWK-CAUGHNAWAGA MUSEUM & SHRINE
Hwy 5
1/2 mile W of Fonda, NY
(518) 853-3678
The museum exhibits North & South American Indian material. You will also see an IROQUOIS INDIAN VILLAGE ARCHEOLOGICAL SITE fully excavated to show the layout of the community. An audio-visual presentation explains the history of the village. Also here is the NATIONAL SHRINE OF BLESSED KATERI TEKAKWITHA, a Mohawk Indian girl, who is in the process of being declared a saint by the Catholic Church. Her potential sainthood is a matter of great significance and pride to Native American Catholics all across North America. Picnic grounds and nature trail. Annual Indian Festival, check for details.

NEW YORK—HOGANSBURG
AKWESASNE MUSEUM
St Regis Mohawk Indian Reservation
Route 37
Hogansburg, NY
(518) 358-2240
Mohawk Indian culture, history, and arts and crafts are featured at this Native American owned and operated museum. Sweetgrass Gift Shop. Akwesasne Library is here with its collections on the Mohawk. The reservation extends into Canada and includes nearby Cornwall Island. Be sure to SEE: QUEBEC—ST REGIS.

NEW YORK—IRVING
SENECA SPORTS ARENA & IROQUOIS LACROSSE GAMES
Hwy 5
Box 207
Irving, NY 14081
(716) 549-0888
Lacrosse is a game invented by the Eastern Woodlands Indian people and the Seneca excel at it. Games are held here from May through September. There is an Iroquois lacrosse league involving teams from New York and Canada. Check for schedule.

NEW YORK—NEDROW
ONONDAGA NATION
Box 152
Nedrow, NY 13120
(315) 469-3738
The Onondaga originally lived at the center of the Six Nations of the Iroquois and occupied a prestigious position. Today many Onondaga still live in their New York homeland. Some arts and crafts are made and sold here and the important annual Green Corn ceremony is maintained.

Of special interest is the annual fair sponsored by the Onondaga Volunteer Fire Department as a fund raiser. Usually held in August, the fair is open to all and features traditional Onondaga foods such as Indian bread, corn soup, and parched corn. There is Iroquois dancing, craft sales, and a box lacrosse game with outstanding players. Check with the Onondaga Nation office for dates and details.

NEW YORK—NEW YORK CITY

New York City was originally owned by the Delaware Indian Nation. Although some Delaware people still live in New Jersey, Pennsylvania, and adjoining states, most of the tribe was driven west to Oklahoma, Wisconsin, and Ontario. The Delaware often call themselves the Lenni Lenape or simply the Lenape (La-NAW-pay). Also SEE: TRIBAL LISTINGS—DELAWARE and IROQUOIS.

New York City has several outstanding museums with impressive Native American collections. Among them are:

AMERICAN MUSEUM OF NATURAL HISTORY
Central Park West at 79th St
New York, NY
(212) 873-1300
Fine Indian collections among the displays. Many rare items owned. Check for special programs and exhibits.

BROOKLYN MUSEUM
Washington Ave & Eastern Pkwy
Brooklyn, NY
(718) 638-5000
Collections span the world with a Native American section among them. Check for special events.

MUSEUM OF THE AMERICAN INDIAN—THE HEYE FOUNDATION
Broadway at 155th St
New York City, NY
(212) 283-2420
One of the largest and finest collections of American Indian material in the world. Because it is not in the best location in New York City, the Heye Foundation has been discussing relocating the museum. Wherever it goes, the museum offers the opportunity to see a fabulous collection of Native American art and artifacts. Check for special programs.

AMERICAN INDIAN COMMUNITY HOUSE AND GALLERY
842 Broadway, Second Floor; 116 Mercer St (Gallery)
New York City, NY
(212) 598-0100 or 219-8931 gallery
Native American exhibits at an Indian operated gallery. Indian center.

NEW YORK—NIAGRA FALLS
THE TURTLE—NATIVE AMERICAN CENTER FOR THE LIVING ARTS
25 Rainbow Hall
Niagra Falls, NY 14303
(716) 284-2427
The Turtle features an American Indian museum, art gallery and craft shop. Local IROQUOIS INDIAN DANCING is performed here regularly during the summer, often on a daily basis. Check for times. Guided tours are offered by prior arrangement. There is a speakers' bureau and classes led by Native Americans. MUSEUM OF HOUDENOSAUNEE HERITAGE here features life-size Iroquois dioramas. Very worthwhile Iroquois operated museum.

NEW YORK—ONCHIOTA
SIX NATIONS INDIAN MUSEUM
N of Saranac Lake between Hwy 3 and 192
Onchiota, NY
(518) 891-0769
An Iroquois run museum featuring ancient and modern Indian methods of storing food, lectures on Iroquois culture and history, a council ground, etc. Located in the Adirondack Mountains. Open June through early September and by appointment until the end of October.

NEW YORK—ROCHESTER
ROCHESTER MUSEUM
657 East Ave
Rochester, NY
(716) 945-1738
The museum includes anthropology exhibits with an emphasis on local Indian cultures.

NEW YORK—SALAMANCA
SENECA IROQUOIS NATIONAL MUSEUM
Broad St Extension
Salamanca, NY
(716) 945-1738
This fine museum is owned and operated by the Seneca Indian Nation. Located on the Allegany Indian Reservation, both ancient and modern art is exhibited. Museum collections exceed 300,000 items. Carved wooden false face masks, woven corn husk masks, corn husk dolls, baskets, and horn rattles, are among the traditional Seneca arts and crafts offered

for sale in the museum shop. The museum has especially impressive displays of wampum belts, clothing, masks, games, and the like. Not to be missed.

SENECA INDIAN RESERVATION GROUP TOURS
ALLEGANY INDIAN RESERVATION
Tribal Public Relations Office
Box 231
Salamanca, NY
(716) 945-1738
Tours of this important Iroquois Indian Reservation where the Seneca Nation lives today. Includes (by request only) an All Indian Foods Dinner.

SENECA NATION LIBRARY
Box 231
Salamanca, NY 14779
(716) 945-3157
Library collection devoted to the history and culture of the Seneca Nation. Tribally owned. There is also a branch at Cattaraugus Reservation, Irving, NY (716) 532-9449.

AMERICAN INDIAN CRAFTS
719 Broad St
Salamanca, NY
(716) 945-1225
Seneca arts and crafts are offered for sale, including beadwork, cornhusk work, etc. Seneca artists and craftspeople demonstrate traditional and contemporary work and offer lessons. Check for a schedule of these activities.

NEW YORK—SCHOHARIE
SCHOHARIE MUSEUM OF THE IROQUOIS INDIAN
Box 158
Schoharie, NY 12157
(518) 295-8553 or 234-2276
The museum is located in the William Bagley Museum of the Old Stone Fort complex just off Hwy 30 N of Schoharie. Open May 1 through October.

The Schoharie Museum presents Iroquois Indian culture, both in ancient times and as it exists today. Exhibits include archeological displays of the Owasco culture and the later Iroquoian tribes. Other exhibits present the Iroquois nations as they appeared in historic times with interpretations of a wide variety of subjects including the role of famed Iroquois religious leader Handsome Lake.

Along with these interesting displays, visitors will also find a museum shop selling traditional Iroquois arts and crafts as well as contemporary work. Educational programs for both adults and school children

are available. There is a research library with a large photographic collection of Iroquois subjects.

The annual IROQUOIS INDIAN FESTIVAL is held over Labor Day weekend at State University of New York in Cobleskill. Visitors will see authentic traditional Iroquois dancing, and sample Iroquoian foods such as corn soup, corn bread, etc. In addition, Iroquois artists exhibit and sell a wide range of work. Iroquois games are played, films and slide shows offered, and lectures are available. A high point is seeing beautiful traditional Iroquois costumes worn by the Native American dancers and singers. Call the museum for details and exact location. The museum and the Iroquois people are both to be congratulated on offering this fine event.

Nearby, there is a Kateri Indian Festival in Fonda, and the Mountain Eagle Indian Festival in Hunter. The museum can provide information on these events also.

The museum has an outstanding book available, *Iroquois Arts*, produced by the Association for the Advancement of Native North American Arts and Crafts. This largely Iroquois association has produced a guide to hundreds of Iroquois artists and craftspeople with illustrations of them and their work. Descriptions of each person's accomplishments, artistic interests, and often philosophies are presented along with photographs of the people and their work. This book is a must for anyone interested in Native Americans. The book may be ordered by mail from the museum.

NEW YORK—SOUTHAMPTON
SOUTHAMPTON HISTORICAL MUSEUM
17 Meeting House Lane
Southampton, NY
(516) 283-2494 or 283-0605
Shinnecock Indian artifacts are displayed. SEE: TRIBAL LISTINGS—SHINNECOCK.

NORTH CAROLINA

NORTH CAROLINA—CHEROKEE
CHEROKEE INDIAN RESERVATION
Hwy 441 at Drama Rd
Cherokee, NC
(800) 438-1601, (704) 497-9195
Cherokee is highly recommended for anyone interested in Southern Indian culture and the Cherokee Nation.

The Eastern Cherokee have created a most impressive presentation of their traditional culture and history. Among the major points of interest here are:

OCONOLUFTEE INDIAN VILLAGE
(704) 479-2315

This is a reconstructed traditional Cherokee village actually built by the tribe. Knowledgeable Cherokee guides lead visitors through the village explaining many fascinating sights. You will see the Council House which is seven-sided with one side for each of the seven Cherokee clans. Inside there is the sacred fire, so important in Southern Indian religion, plus traditional carved masks and ceremonial objects. Cherokee people take time in the Council House to explain ancient ceremonials and religious beliefs.

Traditional Cherokee arts and crafts are demonstrated during the tour by Indian artists. You will see beautiful river cane baskets of museum quality, including the renowned "double weave" style. Fine finger-woven sashes, pottery and other arts are often demonstrated. Dugout canoe construction using the old time fire and axe method may be seen. Corn is pounded into meal using the interesting traditional kenuchi stump mortar and wooden pestle. A real surprise for many visitors is the blowgun demonstration. The Cherokee were among the Southern tribes which made this weapon. Used only for hunting, the blowgun shoots thistle tufted darts with surprising accuracy. The village has dwellings dating from both precontact and pioneer days. The whole experience is truly living history and should not be missed.

QUALLA ARTS AND CRAFTS STORE

Qualla Arts and Crafts is one of the most highly respected Indian cooperatives in the country. They are made up entirely of Cherokee artists and you will see some fine work here. Finger woven sashes, exquisite river cane baskets, blowguns and darts, and carved masks are among the best items offered for sale. Mail order available at Box 277, Cherokee, NC 28719, phone (704) 497-3103.

MUSEUM OF THE CHEROKEE

The museum interprets the history of the Cherokee Nation using six mini-theaters and various audio-visual and other displays. The Cherokee people's lives from ancient to modern times are covered. (704) 497-3481.

CHEROKEE VISITOR CENTER

Located on Main St, this is a good place to begin your visit, and it will help orient you to the various attractions here. (704) 479-9195.

CHEROKEE BOTANICAL GARDEN

The garden has nature trails featuring plants used by the Cherokee in many ways, including medicinally.

"UNTO THESE HILLS" OUTDOOR DRAMA
Mountainside Theater in Cherokee
(704) 497-2111

"Unto These Hills" is an entertaining and historic drama of the Cherokee's people story, featuring primarily Cherokee actors and actresses. The play dramatizes the period from the arrival of DeSoto in 1540 through the forced march to Oklahoma on the Trail of Tears. This is an exciting way to learn some Native American history. Presented nightly except Sunday during the summers. Call for show times.

FOR MORE CHEROKEE NATION ACTIVITIES, SEE: OKLAHOMA—TAHLEQUAH.

NORTH CAROLINA—MOUNT GILEAD
TOWN CREEK INDIAN MOUND STATE HISTORIC SITE & RECONSTRUCTED VILLAGE
Between Hwy 73 & 731
8 miles SE of Mount Gilead, NC
(919) 439-6802

This is the site of an important Southeastern Indian cultural and religious center. The village here has been partially reconstructed with two temples, a mortuary building, and a palisade wall. Town Creek offers an excellent opportunity to learn about an ancient Southeastern Indian community. There is also a visitor center with exhibits and an audio-visual presentation. Not to be missed.

NORTH CAROLINA—ROANOKE ISLAND
ROANOKE INDIAN VILLAGE
Hwy 64
1/2 mile NW of Fort Raleigh
Roanoke island, NC
(919) 473-2463

Roanoke Indian village is a reconstructed Sixteenth Century Indian village of coastal North Carolina. It is surrounded by a stake fence, and has wattle huts and a dancing circle. Traditional Native American activities such as flaking arrowheads and tanning hides are demonstrated. There is a campfire program evenings where dancing and songs are taught to visitors. A campground is adjacent.

NORTH CAROLINA—ROBESON COUNTY

Robeson County is the home of tens of thousands of Lumbee Indian people. Descended from various North Carolina tribes, the Lumbee in part trace their ancestry to the Croatan tribe. The Croatan captured and absorbed the English colonists from Roanoke Island Colony into their ranks. Thus, many Lumbee people trace their roots both to Native American groups and to early English settlers. To this day, many Lumbee Indian people have the same last names as over twenty of the colonists. For those interested in the history of Lumbee culture, the following play will be of interest:

Eva Wolfe, an Eastern Cherokee, works on a double woven river cane basket that is marketed through Qualla Indian Arts and Crafts of Cherokee, North Carolina. It is hoped that younger women will follow the lead of such artists and continue cane basketry. (Indian Arts and Crafts Board, US Dept. of Interior)

STRIKE AT THE WIND
Lakeside Amphitheater
Hwy 1354
4 miles NW of Pembroke, NC
(919) 521-3112 or 521-2489
STRIKE AT THE WIND, an outdoor drama, presents the history of the Lumbee Indian's struggle for US citizenship during the Civil War. Lumbee leader Henry Berry Lowrie's heroic life is particularly interesting since he led a dramatic struggle for Lumbee rights and dignity. Both entertaining and educational, the play runs mid-summer, several nights a week. Call for dates, reservations, and hours.

NORTH DAKOTA

NORTH DAKOTA—MANDAN
MANDAN INDIAN EARTH-COVERED LODGES
Fort Abraham Lincoln State Park
Hwy 1805, 5 miles S of Mandan, ND
(701) 663-9571
Magnificent reconstructed Mandan Indian earth-covered lodges (houses) situated on the actual site of a Mandan village. The setting overlooks the Missouri River and is quite impressive. Earth-covered lodges were as important to many Plains tribes as the more famous tepees. The Mandan, Hidatsa, Pawnee, and other tribes lived in dwellings of this type.

The museum here has displays of pioneer and Indian life. Fort Abraham Lincoln played a major role in the history of the Old West. From this fort General George Armstrong Custer and his Seventh Cavalry set out for their disastrous defeat by the Sioux and Cheyenne at Little Bighorn, Montana, in 1876.

NORTH DAKOTA—FORT BERTHOLD INDIAN RESERVATION
THREE AFFILIATED TRIBES MUSEUM
Right after the Lake Sakakawea bridge on
Hwy 23
6 miles W of New Town, ND 98763
(701) 627-4477 museum, 627-4781 tribal office
The Fort Berthold Indian Reservation is the home of the three affiliated tribes—the Arikara, Hidatsa, and Mandan. These three Plains tribes had highly developed farming cultures on the Upper Missouri. The three peoples' heritage is presented largely through the gracious generosity of Helen Gough, an Arikara, who left her oil money to the tribes for a museum and for college scholarships. Both benefit the people to this day and you will see a sculpture of Helen Gough on display.

The museum exhibits buckskin clothing, Native American farming tools, traditional Indian foods, paintings, old maps, cannonballs from Plains battles,

and more. There is a portrait hall of fame honoring tribal council members of the past and present.

The museum arts and crafts shop is very good, offering moccasins, beadwork, star quilts, shawls, pow-wow princess crowns, men's staffs, etc. All are made by the tribes of the Fort Berthold Reservation. The museum holds an annual Grand Opening Day, usually in May with a luncheon and other activities. There is a memorial long distance run in memory of tribal members who have died. This run has spiritual importance as well as helping the people remember the tragic loss of loved ones.

The museum is highly recommended, and is open weekdays year round and daily during the summer. It's a good idea to call for hours before making a long trip.

There are many recreational activities available on the reservation. The Four Bears Motor Lodge is tribally owned and offers accommodations to visitors. Their lodge and museum are all located in or near the tribal office complex. Motel phone is (701) 627-3737.

There are usually five major pow-wows each year at Fort Berthold Reservation. The White Shield Pow-wow is generally held the second weekend in July; the Mandaree Pow-wow is usually held the third weekend in July; the Little Shell Pow-wow is normally held the second weekend in August at the Pow-wow grounds adjacent to the tribal complex; the Twin Buttes pow-wow is generally held the last weekend in August; and finally there is a Santee Pow-wow which is unscheduled at this writing. By calling the museum or tribal office you can confirm dates and locations. The various drum groups at Fort Berthold are highly respected singers of top quality Plains music.

OHIO

Ohio has an outstanding collection of spectacular Indian mounds and other earthworks built by advanced Native American cultures. Major Indian mounds and ancient town sites are among the listings found below. Mounds come in a variety of shapes and sizes. Some were used to support ceremonial temples or as burial chambers. Many are rich in archeological findings.

Great Serpent Mound near Locust Grove, Ohio, is nearly a quarter mile long and represents one of the most impressive of the effigy mounds. Effigy mounds are found most frequently in Iowa, Wisconsin, and neighboring states. (Ohio Historical Society)

OHIO—BAINBRIDGE
SEIP MOUND STATE MEMORIAL
Hwy 50
3 miles E of Bainbridge, OH
(614) 466-1500
Huge central mound with smaller mounds and other types of earthwork nearby. The visitor's facility explains Mound Builder culture with exhibits.

OHIO—BROWNSVILLE
FLINT RIDGE STATE MEMORIAL & MUSEUM
Hwy 668
2 miles from Brownsville, OH
(614) 787-2476
Eastern Woodland Indians quarried flint here for their arrowheads and other uses. A trail leads through the pit areas where the flint quarrying occurred. A museum provides displays explaining the use of Flint Ridge.

OHIO—CHILLICOTHE
MOUND CITY GROUP NATIONAL MONUMENT
Hwy 104
3 miles N of Chillicothe, OH
(614) 774-1125
Mound City was an important Hopewell mound builder Indian community. Nearly two dozen mounds are surrounded by an earthwork wall. The Park Service has done restoration and provides displays in the visitor center. An observation platform and self-guided trails allow you to gain a good view of the prehistoric community and its structures. Check for special programs.

You'll see interesting sites such as Mound of the Pipes, Death Mask Mound, Mica Grave Mound and the Charnal House. The visitor center and a taped message help rangers explain this large Indian cemetery's purpose and meaning.

OHIO—COALTON
LEO PETROGLYPH STATE MEMORIAL
Off Hwy 28
4 miles from Coalton, OH
(614) 466-1500
Many interesting Indian rock art petroglyphs may be seen here.

OHIO—COLUMBUS
OLENTANGY INDIAN CAVERNS
1779 Home Road
8 miles NW of Columbus, OH
(614) 548-7917
These caves were once occupied by Wyandot Indians and a museum displays related material. OHIO FRONTIER LAND is also here and includes reconstructed Indian homes. You can see an Eastern Wood-

lands longhouse and a wigwam along with a Plains tepee.

OHIO—LEBANON
FORT ANCIENT STATE MEMORIAL & MUSEUM
Hwy 350
7 miles SE of Lebanon, OH
(513) 932-4421
Fort Ancient is a very important Indian archeological site. It was originally a major Indian metropolis built by the Hopewell culture. Villages, mounds and cemeteries were all surrounded by a great wall enclosing 100 acres of the community. The earthwork wall remains today along with burial mounds, village remains and gravestones. This highly significant site is well worth seeing. The museum is open summers and fall. Exhibits feature artifacts from Fort Ancient and explain life here.

OHIO—LOCUST GROVE
SERPENT MOUND STATE MEMORIAL & MUSEUM
Hwy 73
4 miles NW of Locust Grove, OH
(513) 587-2796
Serpent Mound is one of the most famous archeological sites in North America. This amazing Indian mound is built in the shape of a giant snake nearly a quarter of a mile long! One of the great achievements of prehistoric Native Americans, the flowing lines of Serpent Mound lend an artistic beauty to it. A viewing tower and museum help the visitor understand this remarkable mound builder site.

This is one of the few effigy mounds in Ohio, and is the largest serpent mound in the country. It was built of stones and lumps of clay, then covered using basket loads of earth. No burials are in the mound, but one large and several small conical mounds south of the Serpent contain burials and artifacts. The entire complex was built by Adena Indian people at least 1200 years ago. Serpent Mound is of great interest and should not be missed. The mound is open Memorial Day through Labor Day, Wednesday through Sunday and weekends only from Labor Day through October. Call for hours: (614) 466-1500.

OHIO—MARIETTA
MOUND CEMETERY
Marietta, OH
(614) 373-5178
A contemporary cemetery was built around this fine example of an American Indian burial mound. The prehistoric mound is 30 feet high.

Southeastern Indians used blowguns for hunting, never for war. A Cherokee guide at Tsa-La-Gi demonstrates the amazing accuracy of a blowgun. Blowguns are still made from river cane by Eastern Cherokees. (R. Shanks)

The most common traditional dance of Southeastern Indians is the Stomp Dance. Featuring beautiful singing by the men and accompanied by the artistry of women "shell shakers", stomp dancing is among the most distinctive of Native American dances. Stomp dances would have been a common sight among the town squares and temple mounds of the mound builders. Here, members of the Greenleaf Ceremonial Ground, Creek Nation, Oklahoma, participate in a stomp dance around the sacred fire. Two of the four brush arbors at the edge of the square can be seen. They are a type of Southeastern ceremonial structure dating from ancient times. (Creek Nation Communications Center—Gary Robinson)

Close-up of a stomp dance at Tallahassee Ceremonial Ground in the Creek Nation of Oklahoma. As the dancers circle the fire, some move their arms and briefly bow toward it in respect. Stomp dances may be joyful social occasions or deeply meaningful religious events depending on the purpose of the dances. (Creek Nation Communications Center—Gary Robinson)

Every stomp dance must have its' shell shaker women to accompany the men's singing. Terrapin (turtle) leg rattles are strapped to each leg and worn during the stomp dance. The resulting sound is very beautiful and skilled shell shakers are highly respected. Here, Christine Henneha straps on her terrapin shell shakers in preparation for the Creek women's ribbon dance at the annual Green Corn Ceremony. (Creek Nation Communications Center—Gary Robinson)

OHIO—MIAMISBURG
MIAMISBURG MOUND STATE MEMORIAL
Hwy 725
Outside of Miamisburg, OH
(614) 466-1500
Located one mile from town, Miamisburg Mound is the largest conical Indian mound in the state. Impressive amounts of earth were moved by hand to build this imposing structure.

OHIO—NEWARK
NEWARK EARTHWORKS & OHIO INDIAN ART MUSEUM
Exit I-70 in Licking County, OH, then take Hwy 79, 14 miles N toward Newark. MOUND BUILDERS EARTHWORKS and the OHIO INDIAN ART MUSEUM are located along Hwy 79 in the SW edge of Newark.
(614) 344-1920 museum, or 345-8224 visitors bureau
Newark earthworks is a giant Hopewell Indian center created over 1500 years ago. A huge earthwork wall surrounded major Indian mounds in what was once an important Indian religious, agricultural, and social center. The wall reached 14 feet in height and 1/2 mile in diameter. Although some portions have been destroyed, important sections are preserved at OCTAGON MOUND and MOUND BUILDERS sites. Octagon Earthworks enclosed 50 acres and is joined by parallel walls of yet another large earthwork. The GREAT CIRCLE EARTHWORKS enclosed 26 acres of a thriving community at Mound Builders State Memorial. High quality arts and crafts have been uncovered here, created by the early Hopewell culture. The museum can explain the form and function of this fascinating ancient community and give you a glimpse of the fine art produced here. This was a great cultural center with all its defensive earthworks once covering four square miles.

It is best to begin at the museum for orientation to the three major sites. Check for museum hours and days open. OCTAGON MOUND is off Parkview St, while WRIGHT EARTHWORKS is at James and Waldo St.

OHIO—SINKING SPRING
FORT HILL STATE MEMORIAL & MUSEUM
Off Hwy 41
3 miles N of Sinking Spring, OH
(513) 588-2360
Fort Hill is a massive mound builder earthwork wall up to 20 feet high and reaching 1 1/2 miles in length. The significance and history of this major site is explained at FORT HILL STATE MEMORIAL MUSEUM here.

OKLAHOMA

Oklahoma is now home to more Eastern Woodlands, Southeastern, and Plains Indian tribes than any other state. If you are Native American, chances are you have relatives here. For all people seeking to regain the heritage of the First People of the eastern half of the United States, Oklahoma is the place to go. The list of famous tribes now living here (and usually maintaining tribal headquarters as well) is impressive. It includes the Cherokee, Creek, Choctaw, Chickasaw, Seminole, Pawnee, Shawnee, Delaware, Seneca-Cayuga, Yuchi, Osage, Sac & Fox, Kiowa, Apache, Comanche, Potawatomi, Modoc, Wyandot, Wichita, Kaw, Caddo, Tonkawa, Ottawa, Quapaw, Peoria (Illinois), Iowa, Otoe, Missouri, Alabama, Arapaho, Cheyenne, Natchez, Kickapoo, Ponca, Miami, and others. While many of these tribes have branches in other states such as the Seminole in Florida and the Apache in Arizona and New Mexico, Oklahoma offers a visitor the opportunity to attend a greater variety of Indian cultural events than is found in any other state.

During the summer almost every weekend has pow-wows, stomp dances, art exhibits, ceremonial rites, historical festivals, tribal reunions, or other special occasions presented by Oklahoma Native Americans. Most are open to the public and Oklahoma Indian people are unsurpassed in their warmth, good humor, and friendliness. If you are from the East or South and you've always wondered what happened to the Indian people of your area, chances are their descendants are here. The opportunities to meet Indian people are numerous and you will be impressed. Oklahoma Indian people are often leaders in medicine, education, law, art, business, and many other fields. At the same time many work hard to preserve the rich cultural heritage of their Indian nations. Be sure to check the TRIBAL LISTINGS section for additional Oklahoma Indian events.

OKLAHOMA—ADA
CHICKASAW NATION HEADQUARTERS
Box 1548
Arlington & Mississippi St
Ada, OK 74820
(405) 436-2603
The Chickasaw Nation is one of the Five Civilized Tribes that was relocated to Oklahoma from the South during the early Nineteenth Century. The headquarters of this modern and progressive Native American people are located here. Visitors may view a number of historic displays and pictures in the tribal headquarters building.

From the earliest days travelers commented on how much Indian people love their children. That love is still strong today. It's easy to see why with youngsters such as Misty Dawn Powell, a Potawatomi, dressed up for a pow-wow. (Pat Sulcer—Citizen Band Potawatomi Tribe of Oklahoma)

The links between the ancient mound builders and contemporary Indian people are many. Compare the similarity of the face painting of this young man with those shown in the mural. (Oklahoma Tourism—Fred Marvel at the American Indian Exposition in Anadarko, OK)

Museums have been established at many major Indian mounds to explain the cultures that flourished there. This mural is at Spiro Mounds Archeological State Park near Spiro, Oklahoma. (Oklahoma Tourism—Fred Marvel)

Nettie Standing, a Kiowa, is both manager of the Oklahoma Indian Arts and Crafts Cooperative and a noted craftswoman. The Cooperative is located in the Southern Plains Indian Museum in Anadarko, Oklahoma. (Indian Arts and Crafts Board, US Dept. of Interior)

Interior shot of the Choctaw Museum showing traditional clothing, cane basketry, and early photos. The museum presents both early day and contemporary Choctaw life in Mississippi. A gift shop offers Choctaw arts for sale, including rare cane baskets. (Mississippi Band of Choctaw Indians—Communications Program)

Of special interest is the CHICKASAW NATION AN-NUAL DAY held the first Saturday in October, usually at Byng School five miles north of Ada. At this event, the governor of the Chickasaw Nation gives his annual address, tribal awards are presented, gospel and country music is sung, a Chickasaw princess is selected, and a lunch (sometimes including buffalo) is served. A highlight is the opportunity to see booths representing most of the 34 programs operated by the Chickasaw Nation.

The Chickasaw have moved away from many of their traditional ways, but the warmth and intelligence of this great Indian nation has never changed. If future plans go as expected, the Chickasaw will benefit from both the old way and the new. There is a tribal museum proposal and plans to open a trading post with traditional and contemporary Native American products for sale.

The Chickasaw Nation is one of the most progressive Native American groups in the country and continues to benefit from far-sighted leadership. Governor Overton James, Chief of the Chickasaw, has extended a welcome for the public to visit the Chickasaw Nation headquarters during normal working hours.

CHICKASAW ENTERPRISES in Ada is a Chickasaw Nation business which produces high quality cabinets, chests, and other fine woodwork items. Contact the tribal headquarters for more information on their products. SEE: OKLAHOMA—SULFUR and TISHOMINGO.

OKLAHOMA—ANADARKO

The community of Anadarko has Caddo, Wichita, Apache, Delaware, Kiowa, Comanche, Cheyenne, Arapaho, Kiowa-Apache, and other tribes living in or near here. Visiting Anadarko is a must for anyone seriously interested in Native American culture. The area has many places worthy of a visit. For details, contact the Chamber of Commerce at Box 366, Anadarko, OK 73005, phone (405) 247-6652.

There are many tribal dances and other public Indian events in or near Anadarko during the year. The Chamber of Commerce, Indian City, the Southern Plains Museum, and the Anadarko Office of the Bureau of Indian Affairs should be able to advise you about many of these activities. Be sure to SEE: TRIBAL LISTING section under Comanche, Caddo, Kiowa, Wichita, and Cheyenne. Also SEE: OKLAHOMA—CARNEGIE.

INDIAN CITY—USA
Hwy 8
3 miles E of Anadarko, OK
(405) 247-5661
Built under the supervision of the University of Oklahoma in consultation with tribal elders, INDIAN CITY—USA presents well run tours led by articulate Indian tour guides. Visitors are led through eight reconstructed Indian villages, each made of authentic materials and traditional styles. You will see huge Wichita buffalo grass lodges, intriguing Pawnee earth-covered lodges, Kiowa tepees surrounded by a winter fence, an Apache brush shelter, Southeastern-style Caddo homes as well as a Navajo hogan, and a Pueblo-style dwelling. Seeing Wichita grass lodges are worth the price of admission alone, but every step of the tour from a Plains burial scaffold to the inter-tribal dances at tour's end is fascinating. There is a museum, gift shop, and snack bar here as well. Check for various annual Indian events here. One of the top Indian attractions in the nation. Highly recommended.

AMERICAN INDIAN EXPOSITION
Box 705
Anadarko, OK 73005
(405) 247-6651 or 247-6053
The American Indian Exposition is one of the greatest Native American gatherings in North America. Indian owned and operated, the Exposition has a history of over 50 years of Indian fairs. Thirteen tribes form the board of this non-profit organization and the current president is Myles Stevenson, a Wichita. Mr. Stevenson is an enthusiastic supporter of the Exposition and just talking to him makes you want to attend. The Exposition draws thousands of Indian and non-Indian people. Everyone is welcome to six days and nights of Native American culture and fun. The Exposition opens (and later closes) with a parade through downtown Anadarko. Often it is 1 1/2 hours long with proud Indian people in traditional clothing.

A high point of the entire week is the PAGEANT, often held the first night. Here, traditional tribal dances and songs are presented. Among those usually seen are the WICHITA horn dance, the FORT SILL APACHE mountain spirit dance, the CADDO bell and bear dances, the KIOWA-APACHE Blackfeet dance, the KIOWA war dance, the COMANCHE tewee dance plus other fine dances presented by the PAWNEE, PONCA, DELAWARE, CHEYENNE, ARAPAHO, IOWA, and the APACHE Tribe of Oklahoma. Seeing all these traditional dances and hearing such fine old time Indian music makes the Pageant alone worth the trip.

But there is much more. Each of the participating tribes operates its own food booths serving traditional Indian food as well as standard food. There are arts and crafts exhibits, sales, and demonstrations. Powwow type dancing contests are held, Indian archery competition using hand-made bows is a highlight, and there is a world championship war dance contest. A carnival, horse racing, greyhound racing, and the like also go on during the week. All in all there are five full nights of Indian dancing. Camping is available, but make reservations early if you want a motel.

From the Pageant to the presentation of the outstanding Indian of the Year award, you will be impressed with western Oklahoma's great contribution to Indian cultural activities. Highly recommended.

OKLAHOMA—ANADARKO
SOUTHERN PLAINS INDIAN MUSEUM AND CRAFTS CENTER
Hwy 62
E side of Anadarko, OK
(405) 247-6221
Operated by Native American people in conjunction with the US Department of Interior, this combination museum and arts and crafts store is the sales outlet of the Plains oriented Oklahoma Indian Arts & Crafts Cooperative. There is a large gift shop with some fine contemporary and traditional Native American products. You're guaranteed authenticity here and this is a great place to shop for Plains work. (For Eastern Woodlands and Southern tribes' work eastern Oklahoma provides the best selections.) Periodic special exhibits of important Indian artists are presented, and are of very high quality. There is an annual tepee display outside the exhibit hall where you'll see some of the most artistically decorated tepees in the country—check for dates.

NATIONAL HALL OF FAME FOR FAMOUS AMERICAN INDIANS
Hwy 62
E side of Anadarko, OK
(405) 247-6651
The Hall of Fame is actually an outdoor collection of statues of about two dozen prominent Native American men and women. A tour through the park and visitor center is an enjoyable lesson in the important role Indian people played in America. Among those represented here are Osceola (Seminole), Chief Joseph (Nez Perce), Will Rogers (Cherokee), Sacajawea (Shoshone), Hiawatha (the real Mohawk statesman—not Longfellow's imaginary character), Vice-President of the United States Charles Curtis (Kaw), Pocahontas (Virginia Algonquian), General Clarence Tinker (Osage), Roberta Campbell Lawson (Delaware), and many more.

WICHITA TRIBAL CULTURAL CENTER
Hwy 281
1 mile N of Anadarko, OK
(405) 247-2425, Open weekdays only
The Wichita Tribe has a museum in their cultural center displaying interesting material from their rich history. The Wichita are one of the most interesting of the Plains tribes and learning about their history and culture is very rewarding.

The WICHITA ANNUAL DANCE is held usually in August at Anadarko and, along with standard inter-tribal songs, includes some fine traditional Wichita music too.

OKLAHOMA—BARTLESVILLE
WOOLAROC MUSEUM & WILDLIFE REFUGE
Hwy 123
10 miles SW of Bartlesville, OK
(918) 336-0307
The Woolaroc Museum explains the cultural development of New World people. Artifacts, paintings, sculpture, etc., comprise exhibits ranging from prehistoric times to the present day. Among the displays are those relating to North and South American Indians. These include everything from Southwestern pottery to South American shrunken heads (North American Indians did not shrink the heads of war victims.)Among the artwork, many famous painters are represented.

The museum is surrounded by a wild game refuge where longhorn cattle, buffalo, elk, etc. roam among woodlands and prairie. (Visitors must remain in their cars while traversing the refuge as some animals are dangerous.) The National Y-Indian Guide Center is also located on a portion of the grounds. The multi-media production "Arrows Skyward" reflects the culture and achievement of American Indian people and is presented by the Center. Nearby is an interesting nature trail.

OKLAHOMA—CARNEGIE
KIOWA TRIBAL MUSEUM
1/4 mile W of the four way stop (Hwy 9 & Hwy 58) on Hwy 9. Located in the center of the Tribal Office complex.
Carnegie, OK
(405) 654-2300 ask for museum staff
The Kiowa Tribe operates a very interesting museum at their headquarters. Highlights include ten murals commissioned by the tribe depicting the history of the Kiowa from legendary times to today. Traditional Kiowa clothing and other material are displayed, on loan from local families. Often you will see items that were used by the grandparents of modern Kiowa people. Contemporary art by Native Americans is

These youngsters can see Kiowa history illustrated in a series of vivid murals at the Kiowa Tribal Museum in Carnegie, Oklahoma. (Kiowa Tribal Museum)

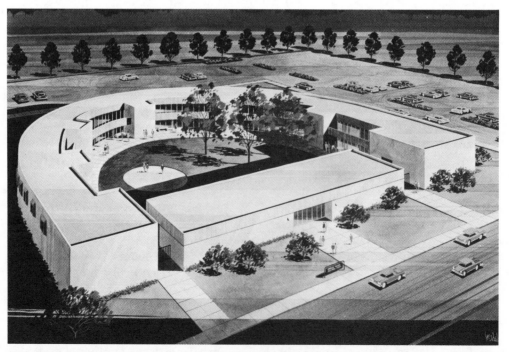

The Indian Pueblo Cultural Center is built in the D-shape of New Mexico's ancient Pueblo Bonito. This modern Cultural Center is in Albuquerque and is a good place to begin a visit to the Southwest. It is owned by the Pueblo Indian people. (Indian Pueblo Cultural Center)

also on display. The Kiowa Tribal Museum is open weekdays only.

The museum has an annual fund raiser in the fall. The event includes traditional Kiowa dancing along with a pow-wow. A special feature is a traditional Kiowa meal with fry bread, hominy, berry pudding, meat, and more—a real treat!

During the annual Kiowa Gourd Society Dances over the Fourth of July, the museum usually has a contemporary Kiowa arts and crafts show. Pulitzer Prize-winning author N. Scott Momaday is a Kiowa and has written of his joy in participating in the Gourd Dances here. All these events are exciting and enjoyable, and when it comes to putting on Plains Indian events the Kiowa are among the best in the country.

OKLAHOMA—CHEYENNE
BATTLE OF THE WASHITA HISTORIC SITE
Hwy 47A
2 miles W of Cheyenne, OK
(405) 497-3929
More properly termed the "Massacre of the Southern Cheyenne" in the opinion of many historians, in 1868 General George Armstrong Custer and his US Army troops attacked the Cheyenne here. The southern Cheyenne felt safe after signing a peace treaty with the American government, but Custer attacked the sleeping camp. Chief Black Kettle, a peace-loving man, was slaughtered along with his men, women, and children. This incident is the inspiration for the bumper stickers you occasionally see on Native American owned automobiles proclaiming that "Custer had it Coming!" Custer, of course, was defeated by the Northern Cheyenne and Sioux in Montana eight years later.

BLACK KETTLE MUSEUM
Hwy 47 and US Hwy 283
Near Cheyenne, OK
(405) 497-3929
Items from the actual conflict are displayed here along with a diorama which explains the course of the tragic "Battle of the Washita". The museum helps serve as a memorial to those who lost their lives here. Today, surviving Southern Cheyenne still live in western Oklahoma, descendants of those fortunate enough to escape the massacre.

OKLAHOMA—DURANT
CHOCTAW NATION TRIBAL HEADQUARTERS
16th & Locust St
Drawer 1210
Durant, OK 74701
(405) 924-8280
This is the administrative center of the Choctaw Na-

tion. Numerous vital programs and projects are administered here, ranging from agriculture and housing to nutrition and senior citizen projects. This historic building was originally a College and the third floor is the site of the THREE VALLEY MUSEUM. The museum preserves the area's history. Museum phone number is (405) 920-1907. For other Choctaw activities, SEE: OKLAHOMA—TUSKAHOMA.

OKLAHOMA—HEAVENER
PETER CONSER HOME
Hwy 59
4 miles W of Heavener, OK
(918) 652-2493
During the days prior to statehood, Oklahoma was called Indian Territory. The region was actually governed by independent Native American nations with sophisticated governments complete with capitol buildings. To handle law enforcement, Indian policemen, called "light-horsemen", were trained and authorized to keep order. Peter Conser was an officer in the Choctaw Nation's light-horsemen and his restored home may be visited here. Exhibits.

OKLAHOMA—LAWTON
FORT SILL MILITARY RESERVATION & MUSEUM
Hwy 277
4 miles N of Lawton, OK
(405) 351-5123
Historic Fort Sill remains an active military base to this day. However, visitors are welcome to tour the fort's many historic places. The best place to begin a visit is at the FORT SILL MUSEUM, on base, with its introduction to the history of the army post. Among the exhibits are Plains Indian tepees and other Native American material.

After the Apache Indian Wars in the Southwest in 1886, the famed Chiricahua Apache Chief Geronimo was imprisoned here. You can still see the guardhouse where Geronimo and some of his warriors lived. Geronimo spent his final years at Fort Sill, became a member of the Presbyterian Church, and is buried on Chief's Knoll in the Old Post Cemetery.

Although most Chiricahua Apache remained in New Mexico on the Mescalero Reservation (SEE: NEW MEXICO—MESCALERO) where most live today, many of the descendants of Geronimo's band chose to stay in Oklahoma. These great-grand children of Geronimo's people still live northeast of Lawton.

While visiting Fort Sill, you can also see William Tecumseh Sherman's home. Called Sherman House today, it is the old commandant quarters. It was here that fierce Kiowa warriors almost killed General

Sherman during the wild days of the Old West. The Fort Sill Museum provides a self-guided tour and audio-visual presentation to orient visitors to these and other interesting sights.

THE WICHITA MOUNTAINS NATIONAL WILDLIFE REFUGE, 15 miles W of Lawton, offers a rare opportunity to see buffalo in their natural setting on the Southern Plains. Buffalo were the major source of food for most Plains Indian tribes and a major spiritual being in traditional religion here. Settlers hunted the buffalo to near extinction and many Plains Indians thought they would never see the sacred animals again. Eventually, the Wichita Mountains refuge was created and a small herd of buffalo was brought by train to Lawton to restock the refuge. Indian elders gathered at the station to watch the buffalo's arrival. Seeing the sacred buffalo once again was so moving to the old Plains warriors that many wept openly as the animals arrived. Phone (405) 429-3222.

OKLAHOMA—MIAMI
INTER-TRIBAL COUNCIL OFFICES and GIFT SHOP
Located just behind the Welcome Center off west-bound Hwy I-44, Miami, OK. The Inter-Tribal Council complex may be reached by exiting at Miami on Steven Owens Blvd, then take the access road on the 1400 block parallel to the freeway.
(918) 542-4486
Northeastern Oklahoma has many Eastern Woodlands Indian tribes now living here. The Inter-Tribal Council is made up of representatives of the Eastern Shawnee, Seneca-Cayuga (Iroquois), Peoria (Illinois), Ottawa, Miami, Wyandot, Quapaw, and Modoc tribes (the Modoc are westerners, coming originally from California and Oregon). The friendly, progressive Native American people of Ottawa County still take time out from their busy daily lives to make a few high quality arts and crafts. These arts and crafts are often for sale at the Inter-Tribal Council Building.

Several major Native American events are held annually in or near Miami, OK. INDIAN HERITAGE DAYS, sponsored by the Inter-Tribal Council, is held annually under the leadership of the eight tribes listed above plus the Cherokee. Usually held in late May, the exact date can be obtained by calling the Miami Chamber of Commerce at (918) 542-4481. Parades, Indian dancing, traditional costumes, Indian foods, canoe races, Indian football, and stomp dancing highlight this outstanding weekend event. Highly recommended.

The architecturally interesting Seneca-Cayuga Tribal Office with huge wampum belt figures molded into the upper walls is near the Inter-Tribal Council Offices. The Miami Tribe maintains their office a short distance away, too.

Between the Inter-Tribal Council Building and the Oklahoma Welcome Center is a monument with the seals of each of the eight Miami area tribes displayed. It is an attractive and interesting tribute to Native Americans of this area.

The OTTAWA COUNTY MUSEUM in Miami also has displays pertaining to local Indian heritage among their collections.

Also of interest are two very enjoyable pow-wows: the Quapaw pow-wow in July and the Ottawa pow-wow in late summer. The Inter-Tribal Council or the Chamber of Commerce can provide the dates for both. SEE: TRIBAL LISTINGS under QUAPAW and OTTAWA.

OKLAHOMA—MUSKOGEE
FIVE CIVILIZED TRIBES MUSEUM
Atop Agency Hill on Honor Heights Dr
Muskogee, OK
(918) 683-1701
This museum exhibits two floors of displays relating to the Five Civilized Tribes—the Creek, Cherokee, Choctaw, Chickasaw and Seminole. So called because of their ability to successfully adopt European methods of government, education, and agriculture these five Indian Nations became leaders in Oklahoma. Their achievements are all the more remarkable because they had to endure the pain of the tragic Trail of Tears. Settlers drove these advanced peoples out of the South. A long march with a high death rate eventually brought the Five Civilized Tribes to Oklahoma where they carved out a new life for themselves. Today their tribal members are state leaders in many fields.

The museum preserves both traditional Indian culture and relics of the pioneer period when the five tribes lived similarly to their non-Indian neighbors.

The ANNUAL FIVE CIVILIZED TRIBES ART SHOW is a highly respected competitive exhibition of paintings and sculpture by artists of the Seminole, Creek, Choctaw, Cherokee, and Chickasaw tribes. Many of the competing artists are of regional or national stature.

Special exhibits are presented, such as a recent one featuring contemporary women artists of the five tribes.

There is a gift shop here too. The museum is housed in the historic Indian Agency building overlooking Muskogee. Check for special exhibits.

The Cherokee National Historical Society's reconstructed village of Tsa-La-Gi allows visitors to see many fascinating traditional Cherokee activities. Peggy Sweeney, a Yuchi, explains how dugout canoes are made using fire. Tablequab, Oklahoma. (R. Shanks)

The tepee is the most famous of Plains Indian dwellings, but was just one of several important house styles. These are fine examples of tepees decorated with Plains artwork. They are part of the annual tepee display at the Southern Plains Indian Museum in Anadarko, Oklahoma. (R. Shanks)

The Pawnee of Oklahoma have a contemporary ceremonial lodge where indoor dancing, meetings, and other events are held. Similar buildings are found among other tribes as far north as Minnesota and the Dakotas. The Pawnee Homecoming is one of the country's most popular pow-wows. Pawnee, Oklahoma. (R. Shanks)

Three major types of houses were built by Plains Indian tribes. All three styles can be seen today at Indian City in Anadarko, Oklahoma. These are the spectacular grass lodges of the Wichita tribe. Lodges like these were described by Coronado during his explorations of Kansas in the 1500's. (R. Shanks)

The earthlodge was another common Plains dwelling. This is a Pawnee lodge at Indian City in Anadarko. Similar homes were found from Oklahoma to North Dakota. (R. Shanks)

BACONE COLLEGE'S ATALOA LODGE MUSEUM
Bacone College campus
Muskogee, Ok
(918) 683-4581
Bacone College is noted for having educated many prominent Oklahoma Indian graduates. The museum here presents exhibits of Native American materials from across the country.

BUREAU OF INDIAN AFFAIRS
Federal Building, 125 S Main St
Muskogee, OK
(918) 687-2296
The Muskogee BIA office can be a good source of information on eastern Oklahoma's many Indian tribes. Through the years this has been one of the Agency's most helpful offices.

FORT GIBSON STOCKADE
Hwy 62
6 miles NE of Muskogee, OK
(918) 478-3282
Fort Gibson was a prominent place in Indian Territory during the days when the Five Civilized Tribes governed Oklahoma. A major purpose of the fort was to protect the Five Civilized Tribes from the Osage Indians, the original inhabitants of northeastern Oklahoma. Sam Houston, in whose honor the Texas city is named, once lived in this area. His Cherokee Indian wife, Talihina, is buried nearby at the Fort Gibson National Cemetery.

OKLAHOMA—OKLAHOMA CITY
OKLAHOMA CITY NATIVE AMERICAN INDIAN CENTER
2830 South Robinson
Oklahoma City, OK
(405) 232-2512
This respected Indian Center is a good source of information on upcoming Indian events in the state. Also, many services are provided here for Native American people.

KIRKPATRICK CENTER'S AMERICAN INDIAN GALLERY
2100 NE 52nd St
Oklahoma City, OK
(405) 427-5461
This museum complex reserves a special gallery for Native American exhibits. Check for special events and exhibits.

NATIONAL COWBOY HALL OF FAME
1700-NE 63rd St, off Hwy I-44
Oklahoma City, OK
(405) 478-2250
Although largely aimed at presenting the history of the cowboy, this impressive center includes Native American exhibits as well. Actor John Wayne's famous collection of Hopi Indian kachina dolls is exhibited as well as J.E. Fraser's moving sculpture "End of the Trail".

OKLAHOMA—OKMULGEE
CREEK NATION TRIBAL CAPITOL COMPLEX
Hwy 75 at Loop 56
N of Okmulgee, OK
(918) 756-8700
Okmulgee is the historic capitol of the Creek Indian Nation, one of the most progressive tribes in the Untied States. The Creek (also called the Muscogee) have a large tribal office complex here with many services administered by Creek officials serving the Indian people. There is a large, attractive auditorium here whose design was architecturally inspired by the Creek council houses of old. The chiefs and other officials of the Five Civilized Tribes still meet here periodically and council meetings are generally open to the public. Discussions are very contemporary and concerns are likely to focus on such issues as voter registration drives, health programs, or commercial development. Listening to one of these meetings is a good education on current Indian concerns and goals.

There is a very good GIFT SHOP located in the Creek Nation complex with a fine selection of Muscogee Creek arts and crafts. The communications office also has video tapes and other resources of interest to researchers and educators.

CREEK COUNCIL HOUSE MUSEUM
112 W Sixth in the Town Square
Okmulgee, OK
(918) 756-2324
This is the historic Creek Capital Building dating from the days when the Creek Nation governed this portion of Oklahoma. It is a charming old structure, one of the most historic in the entire state. Many distinguished leaders of the Muscogee Indian people once met here to make laws much as Congress does today. Paintings of some of those leaders are exhibited and you may tour the rooms where a great nation once ruled.

The museum also displays traditional Creek items such as ballsticks and other ethnographic specimens. Material from the pioneer period of the tribe's history is also here. There is a GIFT SHOP with excellent Creek arts and crafts for sale.

Each year the Creek Council House Museum sponsors a WILD ONION FESTIVAL. The event celebrates the ripening of edible types of wild onions (not all types can be eaten). Held during Spring when the on-

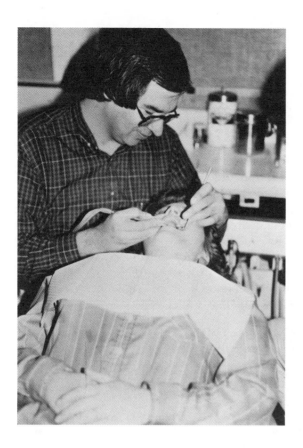

Indian people have long suffered from inadequate medical and dental care. In response to this need, the Creek Nation of Oklahoma has worked hard and effectively to create its own medical and dental programs. The tribe owns its own hospital and medical offices. Over 50,000 patient visits a year are serviced annually. Here, a Native American dentist performs oral surgery. (Creek Nation Communications Center—Gary Robinson)

Not only healing the sick, but preventing illness as well is a major goal of the Creek Nation's Health Clinics. Heart disease is the number one cause of death among Native Americans and 37% of the Indian people die before the age of forty-five. Blood pressure checks such as this practiced by a Creek Nation nurse can alert patients to problems and help reduce heart attacks. (Creek Nation Communications Center—Gary Robinson)

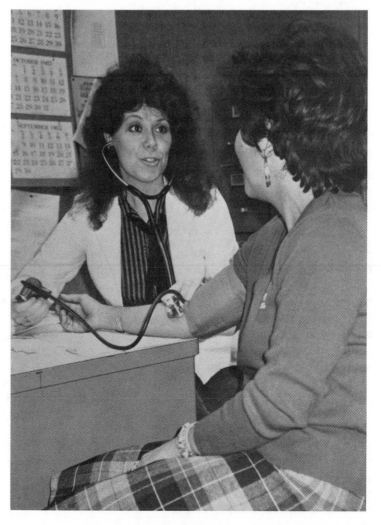

ions are ready, you need to call the museum for exact days. In recent years the festival has been held in the Methodist Church with menus printed in Creek, Yuchi, and English. Many different Creek and Yuchi Indian foods are offered during this unusual opportunity to sample Native American cooking.

The MUSCOGEE CREEK FESTIVAL is also held in Okmulgee and includes an Indian Olympics, rodeo, soft ball games, arts and crafts sales, etc. Best of all, there are usually stomp dances late in the evening. Fascinating and beautiful, stomp dances include ancient dances and songs of the Creek, Yuchi, and neighboring tribes. Check for dates and location.

An ANNUAL CHRISTMAS EXHIBIT at the museum in December honors Creek Masters, who are outstanding artists of the Muscogee Indian Nation. Check with the Council House Museum for the dates of these and other events.

OKLAHOMA—PAWHUSKA
OSAGE MUSEUM
Grandview Ave
Box 178
Pawhuska, OK
(918) 287-2495
This is the Osage Tribal museum on Agency Hill with displays of this important tribe, the original inhabitants of the state of Oklahoma. There are costumes, Osage artwork and craft products. Finger woven sashes are an Osage specialty. The Osage put on some fine pow-wows and you can check with the museum or with the tribal office for dates.

OKLAHOMA—PAWNEE
PAWNEE TRIBAL OFFICES, INDIAN AGENCY & ROUNDHOUSE CEREMONIAL BUILDING
E of town on the main street
Pawnee, OK
(918) 762-3624
This pretty little town is the headquarters of the famed Pawnee Indians. The Pawnee were Plains Indians who lived in earth-covered lodges, farmed the land, and were much more peaceful was usual on the High Plains. The historic Pawnee Agency has a number of beautiful old buildings, including the tribal offices. There is also a convenience store here operated by the Pawnee. Most interesting is the ceremonial roundhouse about 1/2 mile beyond the tribal headquarters (take the right fork in the road). Tradiional ceremonies, meetings, etc., are held here.

The annual Pawnee homecoming is usually held here, during the Fourth of July and is one of the best pow-wows in the nation. Just meeting the fine people of the Pawnee Nation makes it worth attending. SEE: TRIBAL LISTINGS—PAWNEE.

PAWNEE BILL MUSEUM, Hwy 64, has Native American exhibits and a park, 762-2513.

OKLAHOMA—PONCA CITY
THE INDIAN MUSEUM OF THE PONCA CITY CULTURAL CENTER
1000 E Grand Ave
Ponca City, OK
(405) 762-6123
The museum, housed in the cultural center, includes both archeological and historic Native American displays from nearly a dozen tribes. Emphasis is on five local Indian tribes: the Ponca, Tonkawa, Kaw, Otoe, and Osage. This community is the home of the Ponca tribe, and an annual Ponca Indian Pow-wow is usually held in August. Check with the tribal office, Chamber of Commerce or museum for exact dates. SEE: TRIBAL LISTING under PONCA.

OKLAHOMA—POTEAU
KERR MUSEUM
6 miles SW of Poteau, OK on US Hwy 271,
then 1 mile E
(918) 647-8221
Excellent southeastern Oklahoma Native American collections from Spiro Mound, Oklahoma's outstanding mound builder site. Also features exhibits on the Choctaw people.

SPIRO MOUNDS ARCHEOLOGICAL STATE PARK
US Hwy 59, 15 miles NE of Poteau, OK
(918) 962-2062
Nationally important archeological site consisting of at least nine Indian mounds and a village site. Many exquisite embossed copper artifacts have been discovered here. A RECONSTRUCTED MOUND BUILDER HOUSE can be seen here, too. The Interpretive Center displays some of the high quality artifacts from Spiro's mounds.

OKLAHOMA—SALLISAW
HOME OF SEQUOYAH, Creator of the Cherokee Written Language
SR 101, 11 miles NE of Sallisaw, OK
(918) 775-2413
Cherokee Indian scholar Sequoyah lived here after his people were driven west on the Trail of Tears from their native land in the Southeast. This brilliant man created an alphabet for the Cherokee language and it became the first written Native American language. California's redwood trees, the world's largest, are named "Sequoia" in his honor. Many Cherokee people still live in this region, and thousands are fluent in the language.

OKLAHOMA—SHAWNEE
CITIZEN BAND POTAWATOMI TRIBE
Route 5, Box 151
S Beard St
Shawnee, OK
(405) 275-3121
The Citizen Band branch of the Potawatomi Tribe is very active in several areas. They have an excellent senior citizen program for Potawatomi elders which ranges from a meals program to teaching nearly forgotten traditional arts and crafts.

The Potawatomi hold an annual POTAWATOMI POW-WOW, usually during the last weekend in June. Held at the tribal complex in Shawnee, both pow-wow and traditional northern Potawatomi dancing is presented. Often one or more drums from the northern branches of the Potawatomi attend and add to the singing and dancing. Recently, five bands of Potawatomi met together and a new unity among the widespread groups of the Potawatomi seems to be developing.

The Potawatomi Tribe owns and operates the FIRE LAKE GOLF COURSE near the tribal office complex on South Beard St in Shawnee. This public golf course is popular with area golfers and is yet another example of Native American business progress.

The POTAWATOMI INDIAN NATION MUSEUM AND ARCHIVES exhibits material relating to the history and culture of the Potawatomi people. The Potawatomi have developed a good working relationship with historians and other scholars who have generously shared their work with the tribe. At the same time the Potawatomi have been very active in gathering oral histories and other data to insure that the history of the Citizen Band Potawatomi is preserved. A book, "Grandfather Tell Me a Story", has recently been published by the Band and contains oral history accounts from tribal elders. The museum also has a gift shop with Potawatomi and other Native American arts and crafts offered for sale.

Traditionally, the Citizen Band of Potawatomi are called the "Keepers of the Fire" and this motto adorns the tribal seal. Tribal members believe that the fire is burning brightly today and that they are "one of the tribes at the forefront of economic progress in the white man's world". Education, business enterprise and agricultural progress are all being emphasized. But at the same time, the tribe is proud that "a traditional spiritual leader from the Kansas Prairie Band Potawatomi Reservation has begun teaching the Citizen Band the old ways" once again.

MABEE-GERRER MUSEUM
ST. GREGORY COLLEGE campus
1 mile E of Hwy 177 on MacArthur St; turn left onto the campus, go as far as you can, then turn left.
Shawnee, OK
(405) 273-9999
This art museum holds its annual American Indian Exhibit each May, June, and July.

OKLAHOMA—STROUD
SAC & FOX TRIBAL MUSEUM AND PARK
Hwy 99, 5 miles S of Stroud, OK
(918) 968-3526 or (405) 275-4270
The Sac & Fox Tribe of Oklahoma has built a beautiful facility for welcoming visitors to their land. There is an Art & Cultural Center building with an interesting museum containing displays of Sac and Fox history. Also here is a memorial and exhibit featuring the Sac & Fox tribe's most famous member, Olympic champion Jim Thorpe. Voted the greatest athlete in American history by the nation's sports writers, Jim Thorpe won both the Decathlon and Pentathlon in the 1912 Olympics. Some of his medals are on display and the current chief of the tribe is a member of the Thorpe family. Black Hawk and Keokuk are two famous Sac & Fox leaders honored here as well. The highly respected anthropologist Dr. William Jones, Ph.D who worked for a number of famous museums and universities is also proudly remembered as yet another Sac & Fox son.

North of the Culture Center is the tribe's attractive RV Park where a store offers arts and crafts along with groceries. The stores' architecture is modeled after an old time Sac & Fox summer lodge. If you are lucky you may find a traditional Sac & Fox ribbonshirt for sale along with other items. You can camp in the modern campground with swimming pool, showers, and recreational facilities, one of the nicest campgrounds around.

In early July the Sac & Fox hold their annual pow-wow. From the earliest days explorers commented on how outstanding the Sac & Fox were in their rich costumes, hair roaches, etc. The Sac & Fox have lost none of their glamour and the annual pow-wow is one of the great sights in Native America. Call the tribal office for exact dates.

OKLAHOMA—STILLWATER
OKLAHOMA STATE UNIVERSITY MUSEUM
(405) 624-6260
MUSEUM OF NATURAL & CULTURAL HISTORY and the ART GALLERY are on campus while the SHEERER CULTURAL AND HERITAGE CENTER is downtown. Check these for permanent or changing Native American exhibits.

Caddo Indians lived on the edge of the Southeastern cultural area. Their traditional houses are similar to those used by tribes in the South. Indian City, Anadarko, Oklahoma. (R. Shanks)

The Iroquois Longhouse religion continues today. Present day longhouses are of modern design and are used for religious ceremonies. The buildings are contemporary but the rites are ancient and sacred. Seneca-Cayuga longhouse, Turkey Ford, Oklahoma. (R. Shanks)

This Caddo House at Indian City shows another typical southeastern home. Warm weather allowed a number of Southern tribes to live in open-sided houses similar to this one. (R. Shanks)

Interior of a contemporary longhouse showing benches along the sides. Most longhouses are enclosed, but this Seneca-Cayuga longhouse in Oklahoma is open. Many Iroquois people have deep affection and respect for their longhouses and ceremonial grounds. (R. Shanks)

OKLAHOMA—SULPHUR
CHICKASAW MOTOR INN & ARTESIAN RESTAURANT
W First & Muskogee
Sulphur, OK
(405) 622-2156
Both the restaurant and motor inn are owned by the Chickasaw Indian Nation. Both have received recommendations from various travel guides and the Artesian Restaurant was praised in *Oklahoma Today* magazine for its food. Nearby is the CHICKASAW NATIONAL RECREATION AREA noted for its mineral springs and natural areas. These springs were once used by the Chickasaw and other Indian groups. Guided tours are available summers. The recreation area is located five miles south of Sulphur, off Hwy 7. For more listings on the Chickasaw Nation, SEE: OKLAHOMA—ADA and TISHOMINGO.

OKLAHOMA—TAHLEQUAH
Tahlequah is the historic Capitol of the Cherokee Nation dating from the heartbreaking days of the Trail of Tears when the tribe was moved west. The old capitol building still stands as well as the nation's supreme court building, all reminders that the Cherokees once ruled much of northeastern Oklahoma from their headquarters. Today the Indian Nation's offices administer health, educational, vocational, managerial, arts and crafts, and other programs for many thousands of Cherokee people. Tourism is a major tribal industry and the Cherokee operate one of the finest tribally owned complexes in North America. The visitor can literally spend days here enjoying Cherokee culture and history.

CHEROKEE HERITAGE CENTER: TSA-LA-GI
3 miles S of Tahlequah on Hwy 62, then 1 mile E
(918) 456-6007
COMPLETE RECONSTRUCTED CHEROKEE VILLAGE INSIDE TRADITIONAL TIMBER PALISADE. College students from the Cherokee, Yuchi or other tribes lead visitors on a guided tour of this unsurpassed recreation of an ancient Cherokee town. There are so many interesting sights that even the well trained guides can't point them all out! You'll see modern Cherokee people dressed traditionally while performing such old time crafts as weaving, basket making, canoe building, etc. There is a blow gun demonstration. You'll see the ceremonial council house (where the seven clans of the Cherokee met), dwellings, dugout canoe, storage buildings for agricultural crops, the sacred fire with four large logs, a ball pole with a fish symbol atop it, and much more. The guides graciously answer questions and are well versed in the culture. Occasionally traditional dances are held. The annual Cherokee National Holiday is usually held the first week in September and includes traditional activities.

CHEROKEE NATIONAL MUSEUM
On the same grounds as the village
(918) 456-6007
Outstanding displays of current artwork from Native American artists, with many unforgettable paintings. This is a true Native American art museum displaying many talented painters' products. Other displays relate to Cherokee history and culture. Some traditional crafts are sold here as well. A great place for anyone who appreciates vibrant, living art.

On the same grounds you will find a replica of a pioneer-type community typical of the way the Cherokee later lived after they abandoned their traditional villages. There is also a small zoo with animals significant to the Cherokee. Trees and shrubs chosen for landscaping were those used by the Cherokee. The remains of the old seminary for Cherokee girls is marked by picturesque pillars and may be seen here. The Ross family cemetery may be visited nearby, too. John Ross was perhaps the most famous of many well known Cherokee leaders.

TRAIL OF TEARS OUTDOOR DRAMA
On the grounds at Tsa-la-gi
(918) 456-6007
This very enjoyable play combines drama and music to recount the story of the Cherokee's being driven out of the South, and their new life in Oklahoma. Performed by a professional cast which includes Cherokee actors and actresses, it is highly recommended. Evening plays are performed outdoors in a lovely amphitheater with air conditioning.

TSA-LA-GI LODGE
Hwy 62, 4 miles S of Tahlequah, OK
(918) 456-0511
This is a fine, modern motel operated by the Cherokee Nation. Air conditioned rooms, an arrowhead-shaped swimming pool, and an excellent restaurant. It is a good choice to stay here when visiting the Cherokee Nation in Tahlequah. There is also a large gift shop with Cherokee arts and crafts. (Note: the lodge is not on the same site as the other attractions, but is a short drive away.)

CHEROKEE NATIONAL HISTORICAL SOCIETY
TSA-LA-GI
Box 515
Tahlequah, OK 74464
(918) 456-6007
This educational and historical society owns and operates Tsa-La-Gi, including the ancient Cherokee village, the museum, theater, etc. They also have the Cherokee National Archives and Library and can help researchers arrange interviews, locate materials, and so on. The achievements of the society are impressive as the listings under Tahlequah indicate.

NORTHEASTERN OKLAHOMA STATE UNIVERSITY is also located in Tahlequah, and visitors may check for special events or exhibits related to Native American people.

OKLAHOMA—TISHOMINGO
CHICKASAW COUNCIL HOUSE AND MUSEUM
Court House Square
Tishomingo, OK
(405) 371-3351
In the days when the Five Civilized Tribes ruled much of Oklahoma, each had its own capital with a council house and various other buildings. The Chickasaw Council house has displays depicting the Indian Nation's history both in the South and in Oklahoma. (The Cherokee capital is in Tahlequah, the Creek in Okmulgee, the Chickasaw here in Tishomingo, the Choctaw in Tuskahoma, and the Seminole in Wewoka. All can be seen today.)

OKLAHOMA—TULSA
GILCREASE INSTITUTE OF AMERICAN HISTORY AND ART
1400 N 25th W Ave
Tulsa, OK
(918) 582-3122
The Gilcrease has one of the US's major collections of Native American material with displays here relating to this subject. Book store and gift shop. Special programs, contact the museum for details. Thomas Gilcrease, the oilman who founded the institute, was of Creek descent.

PHILBROOK ART CENTER
2727 S Rockford Rd
Tulsa, OK
(918) 749-7941
Native American art is displayed among the collections at this noted museum. Contact the museum for special exhibits and programs.

OKLAHOMA—TUSKAHOMA
CHOCTAW COUNCIL HOUSE AND MUSEUM
Council House grounds
Tuskahoma, OK
(918) 569-4465
This is the historic capitol building of the Choctaw Nation, one of the Five Civilized Tribes. The building is now a museum and may be toured. The history of the Choctaw people, both as a Native American tribe and as some of Oklahoma's earliest settlers is recounted here.

Inside the museum is a gift shop. Of particular interest are authentic traditional Choctaw women's dresses and men's shirts offered for sale. The men's shirts have the traditional diamond pattern representative of Choctaw shirts. There is also a selection of hats, tee shirts, carpet mats, and more, with the Choctaw Nation seal on them. A selection of Chickasaw beadwork is available, too.

On the same grounds is the modern CHOCTAW NATION TRIBAL COUNCIL BUILDING. The tribal Council meets here usually the second Saturday of each month to discuss contemporary Choctaw issues. Interested visitors are welcome to attend the meetings which normally begin at 10 am. Sometimes Choctaw church or arts and crafts groups operate a food concession during the break. The Council may be contacted in the administrative headquarters in Durant, OK, at (405) 924-8280.

Each year the CHOCTAW NATION OF OKLAHOMA LABOR DAY FESTIVITIES are held in Tuskahoma. Usually running Friday through Monday, there are games and sports, a princess contest, tours of the Tribal Council House, contemporary music entertainment, and traditional Indian dancing. A highlight is the Stickball Exhibition, a major traditional game for which the Choctaw are famous. This is a very interesting and truly Choctaw event from the people's rich heritage. Church services are held on Sunday and the four day get together concludes with a dinner on Monday. Tanchi Labona, a Choctaw favorite, is among the dinner items. The Choctaw Nation graciously welcomes the public to their annual festivities.

The Choctaw Nation Parade is usually held on Saturday in nearby Talihina, OK. Some of the Choctaw women still wear the beautiful, old time dresses, a tribal tradition. Also SEE: OKLAHOMA—DURANT and MISSISSIPPI—CHOCTAW.

OKLAHOMA—WEWOKA
SEMINOLE NATION MUSEUM
1 mile SE of junction of US 270 and SR 56
Wewoka, OK
(405) 257-5580
Most Seminoles today live in Oklahoma, not Florida, as the bulk of the Seminole Nation moved west over the infamous Trail of Tears. This is the old capital of the Seminole Nation (the capital building still stands) and many of the people live near here today. The museum contains a SEMINOLE HOUSE, the type still seen in Florida. Exhibits explain the culture and history of the Seminoles. An unusually good craft shop and art gallery features traditional and modern Seminole work, including fine patchwork clothing done in the old Seminole way. Many other rarely seen treasures of the tribe's artisans are sold here. SEE: TRIBAL LISTINGS—SEMINOLE

Dip net fishing for salmon on the Columbia River at Celilo Falls, Oregon. This historic place was a great fishing and trading center of Plateau Indian people. Lewis and Clark visited here on their 1804-1806 expedition. Tragically, an ill planned dam project inundated Celilo Falls in 1957, destroying this historic and economically vital place. Other fishing sites remain on the Columbia and its' tributaries and dip net fishing continues as an important economic and cultural resource for Indian people. (Oregon Historical Society)

Commercial fisheries is a major industry for Pacific Northwest Indian nations. Nineteen tribes in Washington state now operate hatcheries to rebuild North America's salmon population. Indian tribes are leaders in the field of fisheries management. Skookum Creek Fish Hatchery. (Northwest Indian Fisheries Commission—Steve Robinson)

OREGON

OREGON—CHILOQUIN
KLAMATH TRIBAL OFFICE
Box 436
Chiloquin, OR 97624
(503) 783-2218

The Klamath Tribe (including Klamath, Modoc and Paiute) is active in southern Oregon, and its people participate in several major events. The CHIEF SCHONCHIN DAYS POW-WOW is usually held over Memorial Day weekend at the fairgrounds in Klamath Falls, Oregon. There is dancing, an all Indian rodeo, a parade and other activities. This is southern Oregon's largest pow-wow.

In March, the Klamath All Indian Basketball Tournament is held at the Big Gym in Chiloquin. For over three decades this has been a world championship Indian basketball tournament and Native American teams from all over the US participate. There is generally a pow-wow held in the gym along with the tournament.

For many years lovely Klamath tule baskets and other crafts were sold at Chiloquin. The Klamath Tribe is working to restore the art and hopes to eventually construct a museum and gift shop along Hwy 97 so visitors can again appreciate the rich and unique culture of the Klamath people. SEE: OREGON—FORT KLAMATH and KLAMATH FALLS.

OREGON—COOS BAY
NATIVE AMERICAN RESEARCH CENTER MUSEUM
COOS, LOWER UMPQUA, & SIUSLAW TRIBAL HALL
E Michigan Rd
Empire area of Coos Bay, OR
(503) 269-1611 or 269-0568

The three coastal tribes of Southwestern Oregon (Coos, Lower Umpqua, and Siuslaw) waged a long struggle to recover some of their tribal homelands. Today a tribal hall and museum stand on tribal land, beautifully painted with Northwest Coast Indian designs by Native American artists Paul Trinidad and Doug Stutzman. The museum emphasizes the culture of the three tribes both in photographs and historic arts and crafts. The tribes also have negotiated an agreement with the Coast Guard allowing them to once again use their ancient cemetery at Cape Arago Lighthouse. Check with the tribal office for special programs or events.

OREGON—CORVALLIS
HORNER MUSEUM, Oregon State University
Gill Coliseum
Corvallis, OR
(503) 754-2951

Native American exhibits with emphasis on the Pacific Northwest. Changing exhibits and special programs.

OREGON—EUGENE
MUSEUM OF NATURAL HISTORY, University of Oregon
The campus is bounded by Franklin, Alder, Moss, and 11th & 18th Ave
Eugene, OR
(503) 686-3024

This is the state archeology museum and the collection includes Oregon basketry, Northwest Coast materials, archeological specimens from eastern Oregon, and other Native American material. Open afternoons, closed Sunday and Monday.

OREGON—FLORENCE
INDIAN FOREST
Hwy 101, 4 miles N of town
Florence, OR
(503) 997-3677

Reconstructed Native American dwellings from different regions of the country in a forested setting with deer and buffalo. Rare Siuslaw dugout canoe on display. Gift shop and self-guided tours. Open daily.

OREGON—FORT KLAMATH
FORT KLAMATH HISTORIC FRONTIER POST
Hwy 62
Fort Klamath, OR
(503) 882-2501

The fort was built to protect Oregon settlers from the Indians, but much of the time the US Army spent protecting Indians from the settlers. Although the Modoc waged the famous Modoc War in 1873 under Chief Captain Jack, most southern Oregon and northern California Indian wars consisted of the settlers attacking peaceful Indians. Fort Klamath dates from this period and there are historical displays pertaining to Indian and pioneer life.

Until the late 1950's the large Klamath Indian Reservation, home of both Klamath and Modoc people, was just east of here. Under an unwise government termination policy, the timber-rich reservation was dissolved and many local Indian people were left homeless. (SEE: TRIBAL LISTINGS—KLAMATH)

To the south, beautiful Klamath Lake may be visited. Here, the Klamath people once gathered wocas (water lily) seeds which still may be seen in certain parts of the lake. The seeds were pounded into a nutritious meal and eaten in a variety of tasty ways. The seeds were gathered in dugout canoes of a distinctive style. Local people say the canoes were kept under water to prevent them from splitting, and to this day occasionally one will pop up to the surface and be found.

Plans are under way to display Klamath and Pit River dugout canoes at Collier State Park nearby in Klamath Agency, phone (503) 783-2471.

Today many Klamath people live around Chiloquin, and Modoc people at Sprague River. Both communities are east of Fort Klamath. A number of Modocs also still live near Miami, Oklahoma, where they were taken after the Modoc War. SEE: OREGON—CHILOQUIN.

OREGON—KLAMATH FALLS
KLAMATH COUNTY MUSEUM
1451 Main St
Klamath Falls, OR
(503) 882-2501, ext 208
Highly recommended for anyone interested in the unique cultures of the Klamath and Modoc peoples. Interpretive dioramas, a model of a Klamath earthlodge, and other interesting displays. Covers the Modoc Indian War of 1872 when the small Modoc tribe held off the US Army at Lava Beds in northern California. SEE: CALIFORNIA—LAVA BEDS NATIONAL MONUMENT.

FAVELL MUSEUM OF WESTERN ART AND INDIAN ARTIFACTS
125 Main St
Klamath Falls, OR
(503) 882-9996
Wide variety of Native American exhibits with emphasis on western tribes.

OREGON—NORTH BEND
COOS COUNTY HISTORICAL SOCIETY MUSEUM
Simpson Park, Hwy 101
North Bend, OR
(503) 756-6320
Located just north of Coos Bay, the Coos County Museum has an outstanding collection of rare coastal Oregon Indian baskets seldom seen outside the area. Photo archives.

OREGON—PENDLETON
UMATILLA INDIAN RESERVATION
ARTS AND CRAFT SHOP OF MISSION MARKET
Box 638
Pendleton, OR 97801
(503) 276-8772 or 276-3165
Mission Market is owned and operated by the tribes

of the Umatilla Indian Reservation and has an arts and crafts shop at the store. (Take I-84 SE to the Mission Interchange and turn N on Hwy 80N to the Market.) Beadwork, moccasins, cradleboards, traditional clothing, etc., are sold. The Umatilla, Walla Walla, and Cayuse tribes all share the reservation. There is a traditional ceremonial longhouse, community center, and tribally owned medical clinic. Check with the tribal office for occasional celebrations. Many local Indians participate in the famous Pendleton Round-up each year. Write the Round-up at Box 609, Pendleton, OR 97801 for information.

PENDLETON WOOLEN MILLS
1307 SE Court Place
Pendleton, OR
(503) 276-6911
The famous Pendleton Indian blankets are still made here and remain popular as gifts during "give aways" at pow-wows. Tours of the mill are available during certain hours weekdays.

OREGON—PORTLAND
OREGON HISTORICAL SOCIETY CENTER
1230 SW Park Ave
Portland, OR
(503) 222-1741
Native American exhibits on Oregon Indians. Changing exhibits and special programs. Bookshop.

PORTLAND ART MUSEUM
1219 SW Park Ave
Portland, OR
(503) 226-2811
Northwest Coast Indian exhibits and Middle American Art from Mexico and Guatemala are among the exhibits. Special programs.

OREGON—THE DALLES
CELILO PARK INDIAN FISHING GROUNDS SITE
Off I-84, E of The Dalles
The Dalles, OR
(503) 298-8732, The Dalles Dam office can direct you to the park.
The Dalles was once the location of the great Indian fishery at Celilo Falls. Here fishermen gathered from surrounding tribes to fish with nets when the salmon were running. This was a vital, sacred fishing ground for Pacific Northwest Native Americans—one of the most important to Indian people in all North America. I recall seeing the south bank of the Columbia River covered with small, temporary homes as Indian fishermen were busy working all over the hillside. In the ancestral manner, Indian fishermen caught salmon with dip nets from platforms suspended over the water on stilts. It was a sight always to be remembered. Then, in the 1950's under the Eisenhower ad-

ministration, a series of dams were begun. Eventually, Celilo Falls was inundated beneath reservoir waters in 1967.

Besides the economic importance to the Indian people, Celilo Falls was a very historic place. Lewis and Clark visited here and immigrants along the Oregon Trail floated their wagons downstream from here on rafts. Modern engineers say the falls could have been saved by relocating the dam a short distance away, but that Celilo was an annoyance to riverboat traffic and was really destroyed as a navigational hazard. As a boy, this was my first awakening to the loss Indian people confront when their economic and cultural resources are threatened.

Today some Indian dip net fishing continues along the Deschutes and Columbia Rivers. Traditional board platforms are still built out over the rushing waters where men use dip nets to catch migrating salmon. Salmon have long been the most important food of Pacific Northwest Indians and remain vital, especially along the coast where commercial salmon fishing sustains whole communities.

One reminder of the great fishing days at Celilo Falls is the Indian community just off Hwy I-84, 13 miles E of The Dalles. This is Celilo, nestled against the volcanic bluffs of the Columbia River gorge. When the falls were destroyed most Indian people returned to nearby reservations, but a few chose to remain. Life has not been easy here, but the local people with the help of the Yakima, Umatilla, and Warm Springs tribes along with the the Bureau of Indian Affairs are working to strengthen their community. A ceremonial longhouse and tribal office are here.

OREGON—WALLOWA VALLEY
OLD JOSEPH MONUMENT
N end of Wallowa Lake
Joseph, OR
The beautiful Wallowa Valley was the original homeland of the Nez Perce Indians. Removal from their homeland here and reservation confinement brought about the Nez Perce War in 1877. Today most Nez Perce live in Idaho. The monument reminds us of the great leaders of the Nez Perce and the tribe's struggle to keep their valley. Old Joseph was the father of famed Chief Joseph.

OREGON—WARM SPRINGS INDIAN RESERVATION
KAH-NEE-HAH Lodge and Resort
Box K
Warm Springs, OR 97761
(503) 553-1112 or (800) 831-0100
The Confederated Tribes of the Warm Springs Reser-

vation invite visitors to stay at their elegant, new lodge and to learn about their cultures. Highly rated in travel guides, Kah-Nee-Tah is an outstanding resort lodge with swimming pools, hot springs, tennis courts, saunas, and more.

On Sunday, May through October, traditional Warm Springs Indian dancing is held. Special tribal celebrations occur at various times during the year. Check with the tribal office or lodge for dates. For those who enjoy camping, TEPEES may be rented, providing an exciting and authentic stay among Plateau-Great Basin Indian people.

The major tribes of Warm Springs Reservation are the Wasco, Warm Springs, and Paiute. The Warm Springs tribe is made up of four bands: The Tygh, Tenino, Wyam, and John Day groups. Some arts and crafts are still made. SEE: TRIBAL LISTINGS under WARM SPRINGS.

PENNSYLVANIA

PENNSYLVANIA—ALLENTOWN
LENNI LENAPE HISTORICAL SOCIETY
RD 2, Box 9
Fish Hatchery Rd
Allentown, PA 18103
(215) 797-2121 or 434-6819
The Lenni Lenape (la-NAW-pay) or Delaware Indians were the original people of much of New York, New Jersey, Pennsylvania, and Delaware. Best known as the Delaware, many tribal members prefer the name Lenni Lenape.

While most Lenape live in Ontario, Oklahoma, or Wisconsin today, some remain in their traditional homeland. The Lenni Lenape Historical Society was organized to serve those living in the east (as well as members of other tribes, too). The Society is educational, historical, and cultural in its activities and purposes. There is a museum with bows, arrows, war clubs, metal work and other items, some quite old. Classes and a library help youngsters in their school work and with research into the culture. Education is strongly supported and a variety of publications produced.

The Lenni Lenape Historical Society sponsors several annual events of interest. In May a traditional corn planting is held. September 23 is Native American Day in Pennsylvania and it is celebrated on that date or the preceding Sunday with traditional dancing, stories, food, and ceremonies. A major goal of the Society is to establish a national Native American Day and support is encouraged in this admirable goal. In

Lake of the Woods Cultural Centre provides outdoor education experiences for young people where ancient Indian skills are learned. (Lake of the Woods Cultural Centre)

The Lenni Lanape Historical Society of Allentown, Pennsylvania, carries on cultural activities of the Delaware and other Eastern Woodlands Native American people. President and founder Carla Messinger, a Delaware, is shown with her daughters. (Lenni Lenape Historical Society)

October on the third Sunday, a traditional Indian Thanksgiving is held. An audio-visual presentation is shown at some events to help explain Native American heritage. There are other activities, including the old time roasting of ears of corn, usually in August. Members come from other tribes besides Delaware, and you may meet Mohawks, Senecas, and others at the events.

PENNSYLVANIA—CARLISLE
CARLISLE INDIAN SCHOOL
Carlisle Barracks
Hwy 11
1 mile N of Carlisle, PA
(717) 245-3611
Carlisle was once the most famous Indian school in America. Its football teams were famous for beating top college teams of the day. Jim Thorpe (Sac & Fox) began his famous sports career here, leading Carlisle's team to repeated victories. Jim Thorpe went on to become an Olympic gold medal winner and professional athlete. In the 1950's US sports writers voted Mr. Thorpe the greatest athlete in American history. Recently accorded full recognition by the International Olympic Committee, Jim Thorpe was one of a number of US Olympians who were Native Americans.

CUMBERLAND COUNTY HISTORICAL MUSEUM
21 N Pitt St
Carlisle, PA
The museum exhibits include displays relating to Carlisle Indian School and Jim Thorpe. Also SEE: OKLAHOMA—STROUD.

PENNSYLVANIA—JIM THORPE
JIM THORPE MEMORIAL
Hwy 903
1/2 mile E of Jim Thorpe, PA
This Pennsylvania community changed its name at the time of Jim Thorpe's death in the 1950's to honor this great Indian athlete. Thorpe's widow had made a plea for a suitable memorial to the Olympian and now has a community named in his honor.

PENNSYLVANIA—PITTSBURG
MUSEUM OF NATURAL HISTORY
Carnegie Institute
4400 Forbes Ave
Pittsburg, PA
(412) 622-3289
Native American exhibits are among the collections. Audio-visual presentations. Guided tours weekends.

RHODE ISLAND
RHODE ISLAND—BRISTOL
HAFFENREFFER MUSEUM OF ANTHROPOLOGY
Near the junction of Metacom & Tower Rd
Bristol, RI
(401) 253-8388
Contains North and South American Indian items among its exhibits.

RHODE ISLAND—EXETER
TOMAQUAG INDIAN MEMORIAL MUSEUM
Summit Rd
Exeter, RI
(401) 539-7795
This Narragansett Indian museum interprets New England Native American culture and history.

RHODE ISLAND—PROVIDENCE
ROGER WILLIAMS PARK MUSEUM OF NATURAL HISTORY
Elmwood Ave
Providence, RI
(401) 785-9450
Indian and Eskimo exhibits are among the displays here.

SOUTH CAROLINA
SOUTH CAROLINA—BEAUFORT
BEAUFORT MUSEUM
713 Craven St
Beaufort, SC
(803) 525-7471
Local Native American artifacts are among the exhibits.

SOUTH CAROLINA—CHARLESTON
CHARLESTON MUSEUM
360 Meeting St
Charleston, SC
(803) 722-2996
Native American exhibits are among the collections.

SOUTH CAROLINA—ROCK HILL
Catawba Indian people still live in this area and a few continue to make pottery. Inquire locally. SEE: TRIBAL LISTINGS—CATAWBA.

A Sioux youngster expresses the joy of traditional dancing at this South Dakota pow-wow. (South Dakota Division of Tourism)

The Plains Indian tepee has become the most famous tent in the world. Tribes gather annually for encampments and tepee villages once again rise on the Great Plains each summer. Green River Rendezvous, Wind River Mountains, Wyoming. (Wyoming Travel Commission)

SOUTH DAKOTA

SOUTH DAKOTA—CUSTER
CRAZY HOUSE MEMORIAL
Off US 16, 5 miles N of Custer, SD
(605) 673-4681
Massive stone sculpture of Chief Crazy Horse, famed Dakota war chief, who was one of the leaders when the Sioux defeated the US Army under General Custer. When finished, the statue will be over 500 feet high. Crazy Horse's descendants helped sculptor Borglum select this site. There is also an Indian museum here.

SOUTH DAKOTA—EAGLE BUTTE
CHEYENNE RIVER SIOUX INDIAN RESERVATION
HV Johnston Cultural Center
Box 590
Eagle Butte, SD 57625
(605) 964-2542
The Cheyenne River Sioux Reservation is the home of Sioux, not Cheyenne people. The Cultural Center here is a community center, and performs many important services for the local Indian people.

Cheyenne River Sioux have much to be proud of with the programs for their people. Particularly impressive is their toy distribution program for youngsters held shortly before Christmas. With snow drifts often 12 or 14 feet high and temperatures far below freezing, they make their way to Sioux youngsters' bringing Christmas gifts. The Sioux people understand the true meaning of Christmas.

The Cultural Center is a good source of information on pow-wows held here annually. There is a pow-wow sponsored by the Cultural Center, held anytime between April and September. There is also a reservation-wide pow-wow, the Cheyenne River Sioux Pow-wow usually held over Labor Day weekend. There is Sioux dancing, a buffalo feast, and a rodeo. The Cheyenne River Sioux raise both buffalo and beef cattle.

Sioux arts and crafts are sold in the Cultural Center, including fine pow-wow costumes and beadwork. The Cultural Center is usually open weekdays, call for current hours. Currently, there is a weekly bingo enterprise with games held each Friday. For time, dates, and prizes call the Cultural Center.

SOUTH DAKOTA—LOWER BRULE SIOUX INDIAN RESERVATION
SE of Pierre
Lower Brule, SD 57548
(605) 473-5561
The Sioux Indian people hold their Lower Brule Sioux Tribal Annual Pow-wow usually the second weekend in August. The pow-wow and fair runs Friday through Sunday each year. The tribal office can provide more information and exact dates.

The tribe's Wildlife Management Office oversees a herd of buffalo and elk. Guided tours of the herds may be arranged through the office. Check for costs and details. Hunting and fishing permits may be obtained through the wildlife management office, too.

SOUTH DAKOTA—MITCHELL
MANDAN INDIAN VILLAGE SITE
Indian Village Rd
1 mile N of Mitchell, SD
(605) 996-5473
Archeological excavation may be seen here on guided tours of the remains of a Mandan village. There is a visitor center with displays and an audio-visual presentation. Early travelers were quite impressed with the Mandan people, but tragically most of the tribe was wiped out by a smallpox epidemic early in the 19th Century. The survivors live among the Arikara and Hidatsa today in North Dakota.

SOUTH DAKOTA—MOBRIDGE
GRAVE OF CHIEF SITTING BULL
10 miles SW of Mobridge, SD
Sitting Bull was the famed Sioux leader and statesman. He guided the Sioux through their long and difficult troubles with the US government and greedy settlers. There is also a memorial here to Sacajawea (also spelled Sakakawea), the Shoshone woman who fearlessly guided Lewis and Clark in 1805 to the Pacific Ocean at the mouth of the Columbia River. KLIEN MUSEUM, US 12, near Mobridge, displays Sioux cultural items, (605) 845-7243. Sioux arts and crafts are sold at the museum.

SOUTH DAKOTA—PINE RIDGE
Pine Ridge is a Sioux Indian community and is the administrative center of the large Pine Ridge Indian Reservation. There are pow-wows and art shows nearby. The Oglala Sioux Tribal Office is here, phone (605) 867-5821.

The tragic Wounded Knee massacre occurred 25 miles north of Pine Ridge in 1890, last of the Plains Indian conflicts. A monument marks the mass grave of Sioux families killed by the US Cavalry.

SOUTH DAKOTA—RAPID CITY
SIOUX INDIAN MUSEUM
West Blvd (US Hwy 90)
Between Main & St. Joseph St in Halley Park
Rapid City, SD
(605) 348-0557

The Sioux Indian Museum presents the history and culture of the Sioux tribes. A highlight is an annual exhibition series with exhibits of work by top Native American artists and crafts people from many tribes. Demonstrations are periodically scheduled featuring Indian artists working at the museum.

The TIPI SHOP (Box 1542, Rapid City, SD 57709, (605) 343-8128) at the museum sells moccasins, Indian dance accessories, beadwork, basketry, jewelry and other products made by the Sioux and neighboring tribes. The Tipi Shop is especially noted for carrying porcupine quillwork, a rare art form unique to North American Indians. Quillwork pre-dated the introduction of European trade beads and is perhaps the most beautiful of Plains artwork. The Sioux excel at quillwork and the Tipi Shop is one of the few places where you can find this rare art for sale. Mail order.

TENNESSEE

TENNESSEE—MEMPHIS
CHUCALISSA INDIAN MUSEUM AND MOUNDBUILDER VILLAGE
Adjacent to Fuller Park on Mitchell Rd
9 1/2 miles SW of Memphis, TN
(901) 785-3160

Operated by the Department of Anthropology of Memphis State University, Chucalissa is the actual site of an ancient Mississippian culture Indian community. Atop the main mound, a chief's house has been reconstructed. Surrounding the mound are nine dwellings and the plaza. There are archeological exhibits, a fine museum, audio-visual presentations, a lecture schedule, and other activities. Not to be missed.

TEXAS

TEXAS—DEL RIO
SEMINOLE CANYON STATE HISTORICAL PARK
US Hwy 90
8 miles W of Comstock, TX
(512) 272-4464

Very old Indian pictographs are found here and may be seen on hour long guided tours mid-day. The visitor center has displays of artifacts and models showing what life was like here for early Indian families.

TEXAS—EAGLE PASS
KICKAPOO INDIAN COMMUNITY
Near the International Bridge
Eagle Pass, TX

The Kickapoo are an Eastern Woodlands people speaking an Algonquian language. Originally from the Great Lakes area, the Kickapoo divided into three major groups. Two settled in Kansas and Oklahoma where they made major adjustments to non-Indian society. A third group, however, refused to make more than the minimum necessary changes in their traditional way of life and kept moving away from Euro-American encroachment. Eventually, these Kickapoo fled to Mexico where they have been living until recently. They still build and live in traditional Woodlands wigwams and fully practice their ancient religion.

A few years ago the Kickapoo, now impoverished, left Mexico and moved to the border town of Eagle Pass. Church groups in the US have acquired land for a reservation and the tribe may be moving to a location six miles outside of Eagle Pass along the Rio Grande. Seeing the Kickapoo village is a rare opportunity to see a functioning Eastern Woodlands Indian village. However, it is important to note that the Kickapoo are very shy and prefer to be left alone. They do not yet appreciate either photographers or visitors. If you want to look at the wigwams, just do so from a distance and respect the people's privacy. Give them time and hopefully we can build friendship and trust between the Eagle Pass Kickapoo and non-Kickapoo people. SEE: KANSAS—HORTON.

TEXAS—EL PASO'S SUBURB OF YSLETA
TIGUA INDIAN RESERVATION
Take I-10, 12 miles S to Exit 32 (Ave of the Americas), then 2 1/2 miles S on Zaragosa Rd. Turn on Alameda Rd one block E to 122 S Old Pueblo Rd, Ysleta
(915) 859-3916 or 895-7913

This portion of Texas and adjoining New Mexico has a long history. By the 16th Century, Spaniards had begun colonizing the Rio Grande Valley north of here. The Europeans arrived just 47 years after Columbus first touched the new world. The Europeans soon dominated the native Indians, a situation which was a particular hardship on the agricultural Pueblo people of New Mexico. In 1680, the Pueblo Indians revolted and drove the Spanish back to Mexico. (This was nearly a century before George Washington led a similar revolt against European domination, and for many of the same reasons.)

It was many years before the Spanish dared return to the Rio Grande. During these difficult times one group of Pueblo people left their ancient homelands

Alabama and Coushatta Indian people near Livingston, Texas, perform the Basket Dance using traditional cane baskets. These girls wear lovely traditional dresses representative of the Alabama and Coushatta tribes. (Alabama and Coushatta Tribe)

and moved south to El Paso. These are the Tigua (TEE-wah) Pueblo people and for over three hundred years they have remained here, little known and forgotten for much of that time. But today the Tigua people have a new flowering of their culture and they are eager to share their rich heritage with others. Visitors are welcome to the reservation, the ARTS AND CRAFTS CENTER, the MUSEUM, and the TRIBAL RESTAURANT. You will also see the ceremonial kiva where religious rites are held, adobe ovens for baking bread, and daily (except Wednesday) public INDIAN DANCES. Ysleta mission may be visited here, too. The reservation is closed on some major holidays. Well worth a visit.

HUECO TANKS STATE HISTORICAL PARK
32 miles NE of El Paso, TX
(915) 859-4100
Indian rock art is preserved in this area, and the park contains over 2000 pictographs. Some Tigua Pueblo Indians are among the park staff.

TEXAS—HARLINGEN
RIO GRANDE VALLEY MUSEUM
Boxwood & Raintree St
Harlingen, TX
(512) 423-3979
The original inhabitants of much of south Texas were the Coahuiltecan and Karakawa Indians, groups who seem to have faded away long ago. This museum offers exhibits on these past cultures of the First Texans.

TEXAS—HOUSTON
MUSEUM OF FINE ARTS
Montrose & South Main
Houston, TX
(713) 526-1361
There are Southwest Indian exhibits including Pueblo and Hopi work among the displays. Also in Houston is the MUSEUM OF ART OF THE AMERICAN WEST, 1221 McKinney St, (713) 650-3933, with artwork on Native American subjects.

TEXAS—LIVINGSTON
ALABAMA-COUSHATTA INDIAN RESERVATION
Route 3, Box 640
Livingston, TX 77351
Take Hwy 190, 17 miles E from Livingston, TX
(409) 563-4391, (800) 392-4794 from some areas
The Alabama gave the state their name but along with the Coushatta were driven west to Texas. Both tribes' original homeland was in Alabama where they were members of the Creek Confederacy. Today, the Alabama (sometimes spelled Alabamu) and Coushatta live primarily in Texas and Oklahoma, with a few Coushattas also living near Kinder, Louisiana. Over

500 members of the tribes now live near Livingston, Texas, on the Alabama-Coushatta Reservation. Another large group live nearby in off-reservation communities.

The Alabama-Coushatta Indian Reservation welcomes visitors and offers an outstanding number of visitor attractions placing it among the most popular places to tour in the state. The Alabama-Coushatta Nation benefits from its unique location amid the scenic Big Thicket Wilderness, a beautiful natural area with fascinating plant and animal life. The Alabama and Coushatta people have planned well to make your visit to their reservation and the surrounding country a pleasant one.

The two tribes present their culture and history to the public in a variety of effective ways. There is a RECONSTRUCTED INDIAN VILLAGE, the MUSEUM OF ALABAMA AND COUSHATTA CULTURE AND HISTORY, and both traditional and introduced Indian dancing. The dancing is generally held on weekends and often includes the traditional and beautiful girl's basket dance and the Green Corn Thanksgiving Dance. Other dances often done include the buffalo, snake, round, and friendship dances. Another dance is the boys or men's hoop dance, an introduced dance, but one that the Alabama-Coushatta excel at. One young man among the tribe is considered to be one of the greatest hoop dancers in America—an incredible feat of coordination and agility where hoops are passed over arms and legs and body while dancing to the music. By the time the dance is over, the hoops have passed from head to foot, all in time to the dance steps. (Dance groups may also be booked for special events or schools in your Texas community. Contact the tribe for costs and details.) Photographs are welcomed during the dances.

GUIDED TOURS OF THE BIG THICKET WILDERNESS are offered by the people who know it best, the Alabama and Coushatta. You can camp, canoe, swim, and fish at the recreational facilities owned and operated by the Indian people. For campers, there is a grocery store, camper hookups, laundromat, and showers. Lake Tombigbee is beautiful, and forms the center piece of the camping area.

A real treat is to meet the Alabama and Coushatta people and learn of their culture. Treat them with respect and dignity and they will respond by telling you of their unique way of life. You may learn about ball sticks, gourd rattles, the meaning of dances, and much more. You may also be told of the times of hardship and poverty of the people and how the recreational facilities have created new jobs and promise for the future.

Among the new facilities is the award winning INN OF THE TWELVE CLANS restaurant, an arts and crafts shop (Alabama and Coushatta river cane baskets are rare treasures), the Indian Chief Railroad, Indian Country and Big Thicket Tours, the tribal council house, and the tribal dance square (a fascinating traditional feature).

The outdoor drama, "BEYOND THE SUNDOWN", is presented most nights except Sunday in the very comfortable 1600 seat outdoor amphitheater. This is a pageant which recounts the dramatic story of Indian history in Texas during the 1836 Texas fight for independence from Mexico. For tickets and reservations call (409) 563-4777.

Some facilities are open all year, but during the winter months, things partially close down. "Beyond the Sundown" normally runs from mid-June through August.

The entire Alabama and Coushatta Nation's recreation area is highly enjoyable and offers a great array of activities for the whole family. Highly recommended.

TEXAS—SAN ANTONIO
SAN ANTONIO MUSEUM OF ART
200 W Jones Ave
San Antonio, TX
(512) 226-5544
Collections include a good emphasis on Indian art of both North and South America.

TEXAS—TEXARKANA
TEXARKANA HISTORICAL MUSEUM
219 State Line Ave
Texarkana, TX
(214) 793-4831
Museum includes exhibits on the Caddo Indians, the original inhabitants of this region. The sophisticated Caddo were Southeastern people known for their fine black pottery. Today the Caddo live in Oklahoma near Binger.

UTAH

UTAH—BLANDING
UTAH NAVAJO MUSEUM
Broken Arrow Center
Box 827
Blanding, UT
Navajo Nation exhibits.

EDGE OF THE CEDARS STATE HISTORICAL MONUMENT
North St, off Hwy 191
Blanding, UT
(801) 678-2238
A highlight of this Anasazi ruin is the reconstructed kiva (ceremonial room). There are ruins of other kivas and dwellings of pueblo-style architecture. Easily reached with an interesting museum and Indian arts and crafts shop. This is a nice place for a picnic and walk through the ancient community. Open daily.

WESTWATER CLIFF DWELLING
S of Blanding, UT, take Hwy 163, 1 1/2 miles then turn right at the sign "Scenic View—2" and proceed 2 miles to the ruin.
There is a trail from the parking lot to the ruin. Vandals have seriously damaged the site and there is no visitor center or ranger here.

MULE CANYON RUINS
At the rest stop on Hwy 95
Between Blanding and Natural Bridges National Monument, 30 miles W of Blanding.
This is a small pueblo with dwellings, kivas, and a tower.

UTAH—BLUFF
SAND ISLAND PETROGLYPHS
2 miles SE of Bluff, UT on Hwy 163
This is a large, easily reached rock art site with dozens of petroglyphs including animals, abstract designs, etc. To prevent vandalism, it is fenced.

UTAH—BOULDER
ANASAZI INDIAN VILLAGE STATE PARK
Hwy 12, 2 miles N of Boulder and 28 miles N of Escalante
Boulder, UT
(801) 355-7308
This ancient Anasazi Indian village has been partly excavated and includes restored buildings. A visit here gives insight into a 900 year old community located on the edge of the Puebloan cultures. There is a museum, visitor center, and a picnic area. Open daily.

UTAH—FORT DUCHESNE
UINTAH AND OURAY UTE INDIAN RESERVATION
Box 190
Fort Duchesne, UT 84026
(801) 722-4992 or 722-5141
The Ute tribe is engaged in developing its large reservation, and business facilities are increasing. Hunting and fishing opportunities exist here and are being developed. A museum is being established. Contact the Ute Tribal Office for details.

A number of annual events on the Uintah and Ouray reservation will be of special interest to visitors. The Ute Bear Dance is held in April or May in several communities here. Pow-wows are held usually over the Fourth of July and in the fall. Sun Dances are normally held in July and August. These events range from social to sacred in meaning and it's a good idea to check with the tribal office for dates, locations, and rules regarding photography. An annual basketball tournament is also a highlight.

UTAH—HOVENWEEP NATIONAL MONUMENT
SEE: COLORADO—HOVENWEEP

UTAH—MOAB
CANYONLANDS NATIONAL PARK
446 S Main St
Moab, UT 854532
(801) 259-7167
Although not well known for its archeological resources, Canyonlands is rich in impressive rock art paintings done in colorful spiritual designs. Horse Canyon, Salt Canyon, The Maze, and Ruins Park all have a variety of attractions including cliff dwellings, rock art, and granaries. Roadside Ruin is a well preserved ancient storage granary used to store crops. Most of the park's Indian art work can be reached only by hiking trails or off road vehicles over rough "roads". This is arid country so plan any trip off the main roads very carefully and be certain to consult the park ranger staff. The rock art is particularly rewarding and it alone would more than justify a visit.

UTAH—MONUMENT VALLEY NAVAJO TRIBAL PARK
Navajo guides are available at Gouldings with four wheel drive vehicles for half day and full day tours. Contact Gouldings Lodge, (801) 727-3231, Box 1-A, Monument Valley, UT 84536. Reservations for both tours and lodging are required. A store and arts and crafts shop are here, too. This is the magnificent red mesa country so beloved by Hollywood film-makers and seen on countless calendars. SEE: ARIZONA— NAVAJO RESERVATION for more details.

UTAH—MONTICELLO
NEWSPAPER ROCK STATE PARK
27 miles NW of Monticello, UT, off Hwy 163 on the N side of Hwy 211, 12 miles W of the turn off.
The San Juan Travel Council can supply more information, 88 N Main St, Monticello, UT 84535, (801) 587-2833.
There is more than one "Newspaper Rock" in the Southwest, each being named for the bountiful display of rock art scattered about the boulder's surface.

Never a newspaper, of course, such rocks include a variety of figures: animals, spirits, abstract designs, etc. Picnic area.

VERMONT

VERMONT—PITTSFORD
NEW ENGLAND MAPLE MUSEUM
US Hwy 7
N of Pittsford, VT
(802) 483-9414
Maple sugaring was invented by Eastern Woodlands Indians and the museum includes Native American origins in describing the history of maple syrup.

VIRGINIA

VIRGINIA—FRONT ROYAL
THUNDERBIRD MUSEUM AND ARCHEOLOGICAL PARK
On CR 737, 8 miles SW of Front Royal, VA
(703) 635-7337
Excavations of 3000 year old Native American archeological sites are in progress and may be seen. Audio-visual presentation, self-guided tour, gift shop, museum.

VIRGINIA—HAMPTON
KECOUGHTAN INDIAN VILLAGE
US Hwy 258 at 418 W Mercury Blvd
Hampton, VA
(804) 727-6248
Reconstructed Virginia Algonquian Indian village with guided tours and the SYMS-EATON MUSEUM next door. Native American displays.

VIRGINIA—JAMESTOWN FESTIVAL PARK
INDIAN VILLAGE
Next to Jamestown Island, VA
(804) 229-1607
Virginia Algonquian Indian village reconstructed and featuring traditional Native American activities. Guided tours of homes, chief's house, temple, etc. Created near Jamestown to celebrate the 350th anniversary of the founding of the first permanent English colony in the US.

VIRGINIA—KING WILLIAM
PAMUNKEY CULTURAL CENTER MUSEUM
Box 217-AA
King William, VA
Culture and history of the Pamunkey Indian people is presented here.

VIRGINIA—MATTAPONI INDIAN MUSEUM

MATTAPONI INDIAN RESERVATION
13 miles W of West Point on Hwy 30
King William County
RFD 1, Box 667
West Point, VA 23181
(804) 769-2229, call for current hours, usually open daily.

The Mattaponi are one of the tribes of the famous Powhatan Indian Confederacy. The reservation is located today where famous chiefs Powhatan (father of Pocahontas) and Opechaneough visited. The Mattaponi still own a necklace believed to have been worn by Pocahontas, famous for her rescue of Captain John Smith. Also owned is a tomahawk used by Chief Opechaneough during battles in 1622 and 1644. These are displayed at times in the museum.

Chief Opechaneough is not as well known as Powhatan and Pocahontas, but he remains a tribal hero. Present day tribal leaders take pride in telling others of his deeds. Even as an old and infirm man he was carried on a litter to battle so that he could inspire his people by his presence.

Such inspirational leadership has continued and Chief O.T. Custalow, who led the Mattaponi until his death in 1969, was a dedicated Christian who was a great writer and speaker. Today others of the Custalow family still serve as chiefs of the Mattaponi.

Farming, fishing, hunting, and trapping are still practiced and the Baptist Church is a center of social activities.

Some traditional arts and crafts are maintained today, including pottery made from native clay found on the banks of the Mattaponi River. The best of the pottery is made in the old Indian coiling method with traditional incised designs. Beadwork, miniature items, etc., are also made and are sold by the museum.

Special programs for groups may be arranged with the museum director, Mr. Norman T Custalow.

Occasionally traditional dances are still done including a princess dance, round dance, snake dance, peace dance, and war dance, but these are generally done for private enjoyment rather than public performances.

WASHINGTON

WASHINGTON—CASHMERE

CHELAN COUNTY HISTORICAL MUSEUM
E edge of town
Cashmere, WA
(509) 782-3230

Large collection of Columbia River area Indian material displayed. The atlatl exhibit explains the use of this type of spear-thrower which predates the use of bows and arrows.

WASHINGTON—COLVILLE INDIAN RESERVATION

Pow-wows, rodeos, and other events are held annually at Nespelium and Omak—check with the tribal office or the Omak Chamber of Commerce (509) 826-1880, for dates and activities. Chief Joseph, famous leader of the Nez Perce, is buried near Nespelium.

FORT OKANOGAN STATE PARK, just off the reservation near Brewster has an interpretive center explaining the fur trade which was so important in the early days of Indian-white interaction in the Northwest. There are also Native American exhibits here. The park is open summers only, (509) 689-2798.

WASHINGTON—ILWACO

LEWIS & CLARK INTERPRETIVE CENTER
Fort Canby State Park
3 miles SW of town at Cape Disappointment
Ilwaco, WA
(206) 642-3029

The mouth of the Columbia River was once a great Indian trading area dominated by the Chinook tribe. The Chinook were skilled businessmen and controlled trade with both Indians and whites. Their language formed much of the basis for the widespread Chinook trade jargon of the day, which was named after them. The Chinook people have a tribal office nearby in the town of Chinook and sponsor an annual salmon bake. Chief Concomly, famed leader of the Chinook, is buried in the Ilwaco cemetery. The Lewis & Clark Interpretive Center makes note of Indian contributions to the success of Lewis & Clark in this area.

WASHINGTON—LUMMI INDIAN RESERVATION

Lummi Business Council
2616 Kwina Rd
Bellingham, WA
(206) 734-8180

The Lummi Reservation is located about 5 miles NW of Bellingham near Marietta, WA.

Cedar wood carvings are a Northwest Coast specialty. At Tillicum Village visitors can meet carvers and learn more about their artwork. (Tillicum Village, Seattle, Washington)

The Lummi sponsor their annual LUMMI STOMMISH, a Native American water carnival. Held annually in June, Lummi Stommish is a major event in the Pacific Northwest. There are war canoe races using dugout canoes with teams from both the Lummi people and neighboring Indian nations. There is traditional Indian dancing, a salmon bake, arts and crafts sales, carnival rides and more.

The Lummi have achieved national recognition for their creative business activities. The Lummi are a coastal people and the water has long been a way of life. The Lummi Aquaculture Project has led to a tribally owned and operated fish hatchery, shellfish hatchery and other enterprises. The tribe raises and markets salmon, oysters, and trout. The extensive aquaculture (sea and lake farming) has been featured in national magazines for its innovative techniques. The Lummi people have also established retail stores, a restaurant, a herring fishery, fireworks outlets, a construction company, and sand and gravel companies. The tribal leadership and the Lummi people have made major achievements in Washington state.

WASHINGTON—NEAH BAY
MAKAH CULTURAL CENTER & MUSEUM
E side of Hwy 112 as you enter town
Neah Bay, WA
(206) 645-2711
Neah Bay is an important stop for anyone interested in Northwest Coast Indian culture. The Makah Nation recently built a museum to house the greatest archeological finds in the entire Pacific Northwest. About 500 years ago a Makah village nearby at Cape Alva, was buried in a huge mud slide. The sudden burial preserved over 50,000 artifacts, among them many items previously unknown. Washington State University and the Makah people worked together to carefully excavate the site and the tribe built the cultural center to display the magnificent findings. Open daily summers, closed Monday and Tuesday other seasons.

Along with ancient and modern Makah artwork and other material culture, there is an excellent gift shop featuring Makah woodcarvings of high quality. Other Makah shops in or near Neah Bay also sell carvings and baskets; among them is distinguished tribal elder Isabelle Ives who operates Indian Isabelle's Shop.

Annually in late August the Makah people sponsor one of the Northwest Coast's finest Native American events. This is MAKAH DAYS. Usually lasting three days, the celebration includes fine Makah dancing, sales of arts and crafts, and much more. Contact the culture center for dates and details. Highly recommended.

WASHINGTON—OLYMPIA
NORTHWEST INDIAN FISHERIES COMMISSION (NIFC)
6730 Martin Way East
Olympia, WA 98503
(206) 438-1180
In 1974, Washington state Indian tribes regained their right to half the commercial fish catch in the state. As a result, fishing continues to be a major economic and cultural resource of the Indian people. Well planned fisheries management has been typical of the Northwest Coast Indian nations for centuries. This continues today with tribal hatcheries, aquaculture (farming of the sea), restocking, stream improvement, and progressive commercial fishing practices.

The Commission represents 19 western Washington tribes and helps coordinate and develop sound fisheries policy. The public information and education branch can provide speakers and materials for community groups and schools. The Commission can also provide information assisting you in visiting some of the more interesting fisheries projects such as tribal fish hatcheries.

All of the following tribes operate hatcheries in western Washington: Lummi, Nooksack, Upper Skagit and Sauk-Suiattle, Swinomish, Stillaguamish, Tulalip, Suquamish, Jamestown Klallam, Port Gamble Klallam, Muckleshoot, Puyallup, Nisqually, Squaxin Island, Skokomish, Elwha, Quinault, Makah, Hoh, and Quileute. Many Indian nations also have other interesting fisheries projects under way and the NIFC's publications can help you learn about them. SEE: INTRODUCTION—FISHERIES section.

WASHINGTON—PASCO
SACAJAWEA STATE PARK
3 miles SE on Hwy 12
Pasco, WA
(509) 545-2361
Situated at the confluence of the Columbia and Snake Rivers, this museum, visitor center, and park stresses the historic role the young Shoshone Indian woman, Sacajawea, played in leading explorers Lewis and Clark across the continent. There is a display of local Columbia River area archeological specimens and interpretive exhibits. Open summers Wednesday through Sunday.

A Nootka chef prepares salmon the traditional Northwest Coast Indian style. You may enjoy such a meal at Tillicum Village near Seattle, Washington. (Tillicum Village)

Indian canoe racing is a popular and thrilling sport along the rivers of Washington's Olympic Peninsula. An outboard motor powers this Quinault canoe, but some tribes still prefer traditional paddles. (R. Shanks)

Elaborately carved wooden masks, often with ingenious moving parts, are characteristic of Northwest Coast Indian dancing. Inside Tillicum Village's longhouse, a masked dancer presents an unforgettable appearance beside the fire. At left a woman dances wearing a fine Chilkat blanket. (Tillicum Village)

Northwest Coast singers using hand drums at a ceremony in Washington state. Unique and beautiful singing is characteristic of the Northwest Coast Indian nations. (Northwest Indian Fisheries Commission— Steve Robinson)

WASHINGTON—QUINAULT INDIAN RESERVATION

Quinault Nation
Box 198
Taholah, WA 98587
(206) 276-8211

The Quinault Indian people live on their heavily forested reservation in Washington's Olympic Peninsula. Their principle town is Taholah, located at the mouth of the Quinault River. There is a tribally operated cannery producing Quinault Brand canned salmon as well as an architecturally interesting circular tribal administration building.

Fourth of July weekend the Quinault generally hold their annual CHIEF TAHOLAH DAYS. Highlights of the event usually include a salmon bake using the traditional Northwest Coast Indian method of fileting the salmon down its back and removing the bones. The salmon is opened butterfly-style and baked on an open fire while mounted on cedar sticks. This slow, careful method of cooking produces the best salmon anywhere and many Northwest Coast tribes still prepare the fish this way. If you're lucky enough to be in Taholah on Chief Taholah Days it's often offered for sale.

Chief Taholah Days usually features Indian canoe races using Northwest Coast style canoes, but powering the boats with outboard motors. The Quinault, Hoh, and Quileute compete in an exciting race that begins at high tide at Taholah's waterfront and goes for miles up the Quinault River. It's a fast, dangerous sport as the one-man canoes dodge rocks and snags along the way. The canoe racers spend quite a while warming up at the river mouth and you can easily watch them from the water's edge. Much of the race is along the Quinault River with no access roads, but they return in half an hour and charge toward the finish line. There is often a foot race, tee shirt sales, and a few arts and crafts available. Check with the Quinault Nation Office for details.

It is a pleasure to see the canoes with their animal head prows once again pulled up on the beach at Taholah. The Quinault people are friendly and it is a pleasant, relaxed celebration, although fire crackers are often in abundance since fireworks sales are a minor industry on the reservation. The beaches on the reservation are closed to the public to protect the marine life, but you can walk down to the area where the canoes are launched and see the boats up close. Chief Taholah Days is an enjoyable event and the Quinault people deserve praise for it.

WASHINGTON—SEATTLE
TILLICUM VILLAGE

Blake Island Marine State Park
Seattle, WA
(206) 392-5700

Boats leave regularly from Pier 56 at the foot of Seneca St in Seattle. Call for departure times.

Your visit to forested Blake Island begins with an interesting boat ride across Elliott Bay, Seattle's harbor. Upon arriving at the island you'll be greeted by Tillicum Village's friendly Indian staff. Dressed in traditional Northwest Coast clothing, the people look regal in their carved wooden headdresses and 19th century button blankets. The guides seem to enjoy posing and this is a good opportunity to take some fine photographs. Moments later you will be served a delicious Indian version of clam chowder, much appreciated after the boat ride.

After this royal welcome you enter the huge Northwest Coast longhouse with its highly decorated exterior walls. These designs are still found on Northwest Coast community halls and tribal offices and they date from ancient times. There are totem poles and other wood carvings both in front and back of the longhouse.

Inside the longhouse you'll find a restaurant, carvers' work area, and gift shop. A Nootka chef masterfully cooks your salmon dinner in traditional Northwest Coast Indian style before your eyes. The entire fish has been fileted down its back and is cooked upright on split cedar sticks. Local Indian chefs have been cooking salmon like this for thousands of years and have it down to an art.

You soon move along to a buffet where you'll receive a full dinner including generous portions of salmon. You are then escorted into the longhouse for dinner and Native American dancing. While you eat, excellent Northwest Coast dancers present traditional music and dance in unforgettable masked costumes representing animal spirits. The beaks of some of the bird masks are several feet long and clack as the mouths open and close. Pictures are allowed and for best results bring a flash and ask your waitress to seat you close to the stage.

After dinner you can roam the island before returning to the mainland. Be sure to take time to talk with the carvers as they create masks and other ceremonial objects. Many of these pieces are offered for sale and they are truly art objects. Miniature Nootka canoes are offered at a reasonable price. The carvers are usually quite happy to explain their art and its' significance. Most of Tillicum's staff are Native

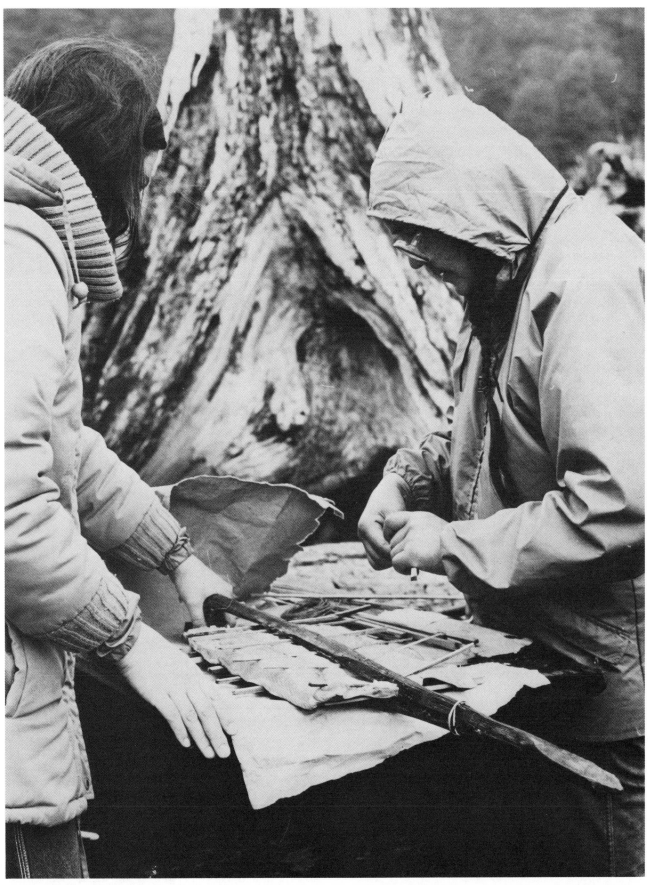

Quinault women prepare a huge salmon filet on cedar sticks. Salmon is the most important food of the Northwest Coast Indian nations. Chief Taholah Days, Taholah, Washington. (R. Shanks)

Americans and everyone is friendly and helpful. The hardest part about visiting this beautiful island is leaving this unique Indian setting—you'll want to stay on. Just plan another visit, the masks and dances change regularly and you'll see new presentations as well as repeats of old favorites. Tillicum Village offers one of Native America's top cultural experiences and is highly recommended.

WASHINGTON—SEATTLE
DAYBREAK STAR ARTS CENTER
United Indians of All Tribes Foundation
Discovery Park, W Government Way at 36th Ave
Box 99253
Seattle, WA 98199
(206) 285-4425
Daybreak Star Arts Center is Native American owned and operated. Located in Seattle's beautiful Discovery Park, the Center is in an attractive building designed in four wings. The design honors the four seasons, the four directions, and the four races of human beings. The Center is open weekdays and includes an art gallery exhibiting high quality work by Indian artists. The Artists-in-Action program allows visitors to watch Indian artists paint, carve, and sculpt in the studio. Adjoining the museum exhibit area is a sales office featuring the artists' work. The Center is proud of its major art collection.

One of the most exciting achievements is the INDIAN DINNER THEATER. This is located in the heart of the Center and is decorated with natural wood complemented by Native American painting and wood carvings. Authentic Indian entertainment and cuisine is available to the public Friday evenings. Northwest Coast Indian dancing and singing is presented with Tlingit dancers wearing stunning button blankets and carved headdresses. A fashion show is also presented. A traditional smoked salmon dinner appropriately accompanies the evening's entertainment. Call for reservations and hours.

An INDIAN ART MART is held at the Center on certain Saturdays each month. Native American craftspeople and artists offer their work for sale. A salmon lunch is served at noon. Call for dates and lunch prices.

Another project of the Center is the DAYBREAK STAR INDIAN READER. This monthly 24 page publication is aimed at Native American youngsters in grades four through six. Many non-Indian people also subscribe as the publication provides an Indian perspective on historic and contemporary events. For subscription and other information contact the Center.

The Center also offers professional printing services with its DAYBREAK STAR PRINTING COMPANY, (206) 343-3111.

The Center can also guide Native Americans to a wide range of Indian operated education and employment centers, family counseling programs, head start and youth services, and the like. The United Indians of All Tribes have an impressive cultural, entertainment, and social service program of interest to both Indian and non-Indian people.

AMERICAN INDIAN TOUR & TRAVEL AGENCY
Box 3195
607 First Ave
Seattle, WA 98114
(206) 285-4425
Native American travel agency offering tours to Indian Reservations and Indian owned resorts. Serves the Northwest Coast, Plains, Southwest and other regions. A variety of packaged tours are available. Also books visitors for the Daybreak Arts Center salmon dinners and Northwest Coast Indian dances at Discovery Park in Seattle.

SACRED CIRCLE GALLERY OF AMERICAN INDIAN ART
607 First Ave
Seattle, WA
(206) 223-0072
An enterprise of the United Indians of All Tribes Foundation, the gallery exhibits and sells highly collectable Native American art. At the same address in Pioneer Square is the AMERICAN INDIAN WORLD TRADE CENTER, (206) 621-0425, which coordinates domestic and export sales of goods and materials produced by Pacific Northwest Indian tribes. A wide range of products are offered including wood products, clothing, canned salmon, aluminum cases, and more.

PACIFIC SCIENCE CENTER & KWAKIUTL INDIAN FAMILY HOUSE
Seattle Center near the Space Needle
305 Harrison St
Seattle, WA
(206) 625-9333
Using portions of an original Kwakiutl Indian family house from British Columbia, Sea Monster House has been reconstructed inside the Science Center. Both inside and outside Sea Monster House are magnificent Northwest Coast traditional carvings and paintings. Inside Sea Monster House there are periodic craft demonstrations and occasional special programs.

Along side the family house is a video presentation of the Hamatsa Dance and other films of Indian culture. The Hamatsa is a very important traditional dance of the Northwest Coast tribes and is still done at a few locations.

SEATTLE ART MUSEUM
Volunteer Park
E Galer & 15th Ave E
Seattle, WA
(206) 447-4670
Among its collections are Native American material including pre-Columbian work.

WASHINGTON—SPOKANE
MUSEUM OF NATIVE AMERICAN CULTURES
E 200 Cataldo St
Spokane, WA
(509) 326-4550
Spokane has one of the finest Native American museums in the country in this tepee-shaped five story building. Many displays of a wide range of Indian cultures are offered here. Bookstore and gift shop. Highly recommended.

EASTERN WASHINGTON STATE HISTORICAL SOCIETY
CHENEY COWLES MEMORIAL MUSEUM
W 2316 First Ave
Spokane, WA
(509) 456-3931
Collections include a large and worthwhile section of Native American articles.

WASHINGTON—SUQUAMISH
SUQUAMISH MUSEUM
Hwy 305, 2 miles S of town, W end of Agate Pass Bridge
Box 498
Suquamish, WA 98392
(206) 598-3311
The Suquamish Museum is an outstanding cultural facility owned and operated by the Suquamish Indian people. The city of Seattle is named in honor of Suquamish leader Chief Seattle. A major exhibit, The Eyes of Chief Seattle, is featured here after its showing on the European continent. Fascinating photographs, artifacts, and quotations explain the history and culture of the Suquamish as seen through the eyes of both Chief Seattle and other elders. Particularly significant is a display with the only known portrait of Chief Seattle and a quote from him that he expected to see his people vanish during the epidemics that were sweeping Indian communities during the last century. Next to the picture and the quote is a photograph of happy, healthy Suquamish youngsters of today. The tribe's miraculous comeback from an 80 percent loss of population is evidenced in these young Native Americans. Today the tribe is growing in population.

The museum also exhibits finely woven baskets, dugout canoe, tools and fishing equipment. The audio-visual narrative "Come Forth Laughing" is not to be missed. Spanning a century of tribal history, the presentation is truly a Native American approach to history. Tribal elders explain Suquamish history and life as they have experienced it. Using their own words, they bring the visitor through history and up to modern day Suquamish life. At the end of the presentation, pictures of the narrators appear along with their quotes so the audience will feel as if they have met the tribal narrators. The museum grounds also offers a nature trail, a beach walk, and nearby points of interest.

Annually CHIEF SEATTLE DAYS is generally held the third weekend in August, Friday through Sunday. Visitors are welcome and will see such Northwest Coast Indian highlights as the naming of the year's Suquamish princess, a traditional salmon bake, and dugout canoe races with men's, women's and coed teams. Lummi, Makah, Quileute, Klallam, and various Canadian bands all compete in the Suquamish canoe races. Some canoes are quite large with 11 person crews. Traditional Suquamish and other Northwest Coast dances are presented and are a real treat to watch. Plains-style dancing is also often done.

Chief Seattle's former home, OLD MAN HOUSE, partially reconstructed, is nearby. This is believed to have been the largest Indian longhouse in the Pacific Northwest, some 500 to 600 feet in length and 50 to 65 feet wide. During winter most of the Suquamish tribe lived here and winter dancing and singing remain traditions today. Chief Seattle's grave may be reverently visited here, providing yet another link to this great Native American leader.

The Suquamish people have much to be proud of in their care and presentation of a living culture. Visitors to the museum will also want to see the gift shop and be aware that a beautiful exhibit catalog "The Eyes of Chief Seattle", can be purchased.

WASHINGTON—VANTAGE
WANAPUM DAM TOUR CENTER
5 miles S of I-90, exit 137 on Hwy 243
Vantage, WA
(509) 754-3541
This area is the home of the tiny Wanapum Indian tribe whose members still live here. The Tour Center includes exhibits on local Indian culture among its displays.

GINGKO PETRIFIED FOREST STATE PARK
I-90, exit 136
Vantage, WA
(509) 856-2700
Columbia River Indian rock art can be seen along the interpretive trail near the visitor center.

WASHINGTON—WALLA WALLA
WHITMAN MISSION NATIONAL HISTORIC SITE
8 miles W of Walla Walla off Hwy 12
Walla Walla, WA
(509) 525-6360
Established by Presbyterian missionaries Marcus and Narcissa Whitman in 1836, the Whitman's provided religious and medical instruction for local Indians and a vitally important stopping point for the Pacific Northwest's early travelers. Eventually the immigrants inadvertently introduced diseases to the Indians and the Whitman's were blamed. In 1847, one group of long suffering Cayuse Indians consequently attacked the innocent Whitmans and killed them and others at the mission. The mission was then burned to the ground.

Today archeological work is progressing at the site and the locations of the buildings can be seen. There is a visitor center and museum. Weekends during the summer various traditional Native American arts and crafts are demonstrated, including weaving of tule mats and corn husk bags. Call for schedule.

WASHINGTON—WELLPINIT
SPOKANE INDIAN RESERVATION
Box 385
Wellpinit, WA 99040
(509) 258-4581
The Spokane Indian people hold the annual Spokane Labor Day Celebration at Wellpinit each year. Visitors will see war dance competition, food booths (stew and fry bread are specialties), arts and crafts exhibits and sales, and other activities. The highlight is the traditional STICK GAME competition where each tribe sings its own songs and competes in these age old Indian guessing games. Usually other tribes join the Spokane for the stick games, and Coeur D'Alene, Kalispel and other stick game teams also sing their beautiful songs as well. Games can go on for many hours and are scenes Lewis and Clark or Chief Joseph would recognize. Spokane stick games were the first I ever saw as a youngster and I have loved the game and its songs ever since.

The Spokane Community Center has an arts and crafts sales shop and a small museum of Spokane history and culture upstairs. Check with the tribal office for hours and also for other special events.

WASHINGTON—YAKIMA INDIAN RESERVATION
YAKIMA NATION CULTURAL CENTER
Box 151
Fort Road
Toppenish, WA 98948
(509) 865-2800
The Yakima Indian Nation has created a magnificent new cultural center with a broad range of attractions for visitors. The center preserves the distinctive culture of this important Plateau region Indian tribe. You will come away with a new understanding and appreciation of Yakima cultural heritage.

The center includes a MUSEUM with dioramas explaining the natural environment of central Washington, traditional methods of living in that world by fishing, gathering, and hunting; the importance of tule marshes; Celilo Falls history as an unparalleled fishing center, and more. You'll see a "time ball", a Native American women's calendar of events of her life. A Yakima earth lodge has been reconstructed here, too.

The museum has a full size Yakima winter lodge made of tule reed mats and a village with tule tepees, all traditional Yakima homes. These lodges are a rare treat to see.

There is a gift shop with beadwork, silverwork and other fine Yakima arts and crafts. Products of other tribes are offered, too. The center also houses a library with materials of interest to researchers, including films on the Yakima Nation.

The HERITAGE INN RESTAURANT offers standard American food plus authentic Yakima specialties. Among the delicious Native American items you can order are: fresh salmon, fry bread, lukmein (Yakima fish chowder), and huckleberry pie (some items are available seasonally).

If you are staying in the area, the Yakima owned HERITAGE THEATER offers a choice of feature films from Hollywood.

The Yakima host a variety of major Native American events annually. The YAKIMA NATION SUMMER ENCAMPMENT and the TOPPENISH POW-WOW are both usually held over the Fourth of July weekend. The Cultural Center can help orient you to these events and you will learn more about the Yakima people. The encampment includes impressive tepees (remember these are private), ceremonies (some on horseback), and more. The Yakima are among the best stick game players in the West and this traditional Indian guessing game is a pleasure to watch. The

The striking new Yakima Nation Cultural Center in Washington State contains exciting exhibits of Plateau Indian life. (Yakima Nation Cultural Center)

pow-wow offers more good music, dancing, and contests. Arts and crafts are sold. Remember: the encampment is in White Swan while the Toppenish pow-wow is in Toppenish. Among a number of other worthwhile events, is the Yakima Pow-wow usually held in September. The Cultural Center can provide dates as they are set. The Yakima Nation is to be congratulated on its fine cultural programs and the Yakima Cultural Center is highly recommended.

FORT SIMCOE STATE PARK is 28 miles W via Hwy 220, (509) 874-2372. The fort helped keep peace in the Yakima Valley during frontier days by protecting Indian treaty lands and military roads. Original buildings have been restored.

WEST VIRGINIA

WEST VIRGINIA—MOUNDSVILLE
GRAVE CREEK INDIAN MOUND and DELF NORONA MUSEUM
801 Jefferson Ave
Moundsville, WV
(304) 843-1410
Grave Creek Mound was built over 2000 years ago by the Adena Indian culture. Grave Creek Mound is 69 feet high and is reputed to be the largest conical mound ever built by the Adena. It was originally surrounded by a moat about 40 feet wide and five feet deep.

This is an important and fascinating mound, once the heart of a Native American religious center. The Delf Norona Museum exhibits material from the mound, explains Adena culture and offers an audio-visual presentation on the Adena. There is a gift shop and lunch is served in the museum's West Virginia Dining Room.

WISCONSIN

WISCONSIN—BAYFIELD
BUFFALO ARTS CENTER
RED CLIFF CULTURAL INSTITUTE
RED CLIFF INDIAN RESERVATION
Box 51
Hwy 13, 3 miles N of Bayfield, WI
(715) 779-5858
The Buffalo Arts Center presents the history and culture of the Lake Superior Chippewa (Ojibwa) people. The architecturally impressive center is located in a beautiful setting on the shores of Lake Superior. The museum has both permanent displays and frequent special exhibits making visitors want to return time and again. Owned and operated by the Red Cliff

Chippewa, the Center is developing exhibits in consultation with the Smithsonian Institution.

Permanent exhibits feature traditional Chippewa outfits displayed on full size figures centering around the sacred drum. Another section will show the seasonal activities of traditional Lake Superior Chippewa life—wild ricing, maple sugaring, birch bark canoe building, snow shoe construction, and similar activities. Historical exhibits will cover the influence of the Catholic Church (with family Bibles of the Chippewa people displayed), the Treaty of 1854, and more recent events.

There are usually five or six special exhibits and demonstrations each year. Both local and nationally known Native American and Canadian artists are featured. Crafts demonstrations vary from stone pipe making to birch bark canoe construction. In the winter, art classes are often held. The Red Cliff Festival of the Arts is in July.

The Buffalo Arts Center is normally open May through September. There is a museum shop with a good selection of beadwork, birch bark baskets, posters, cards, and more.

The annual RED CLIFF POW-WOW is in August or September. Check with the Center for exact dates.

The Red Cliff Chippewa people have much to be proud of in their fine Center.

EFFIGY MOUNDS IN ANIMAL FORMS
DEVIL'S LAKE STATE PARK
SR 123, near Baraboo, WI
(608) 356-8301
Wisconsin is rich in distinctive Indian mounds in the shape of animals. Lynx, bear, eagle, etc., are some of the mound shapes found here. Wisconsin's effigy mounds are very different from the temple and burial mounds seen elsewhere.

WISCONSIN—BELOIT
LOGAN MUSEUM OF ANTHROPOLOGY
Beloit College, Bushnell St
Beloit, WE
(608) 365-3391
Includes Native American displays.

WISCONSIN—COOPER CULTURE MOUND STATE PARK
South of Oconto, WI
Indian mounds are preserved in this state park.

Snow covers the 69 foot high Grave Creek Mound near Moundsville, West Virginia. This is the largest conical mound built by the Adena Indian culture. The Delf Norona Museum here offers exhibits. (Delf Norona Museum)

Mound City Group National Monument near Chillicothe, Ohio, has fine examples of conical burial mounds. (National Park Service)

Winnebago dancers in the Stand Rock Ceremonials at Wisconsin Dells, Wisconsin. (Wisconsin Dells Visitor & Convention Bureau)

WISCONSIN—EGG HARBOR
CHIEF OSHKOSH INDIAN MUSEUM
SR 42
Egg Harbor, WI
(414) 743-4456
Exhibits of the life of the famous Menominee leader Chief Oshkosh, including some of his possessions.

WISCONSIN—FORT ATKINSON
PANTHER INTAGLIO
1236 Riverside Dr
Fort Atkinson, WI
This is a figure of a panther dug into the ground rather than built up as a mound. Yet another fascinating Native American religious shrine.

Also in Fort Atkinson, the HOARD HISTORICAL MUSEUM has native American exhibits, at 407 Merchants Ave, (414) 563-4521.

WISCONSIN—HAYWARD
LAC COURTE OREILLES OJIBWA RESERVATION
Hayward, WI
(715) 634-8934
The Lac Courte Oreilles Ojibwa Indian people hold their annual Honor the Earth Pow-wow here usually in July. Historyland, on Hwy 27, has an Ojibwa Indian museum open summers.

WISCONSIN—LAC DU FLAMBEAU
INDIAN BOWL CHIPPEWA INDIAN DANCES
Main St
Lac du Flambeau, WI
For information contact: Chamber of Commerce, Box 158, Lac du Flambeau, WI 54536, (715) 588-3346.
The INDIAN BOWL features Chippewa (Ojibwa) Indian dancing during July and August on Tuesday and Thursday evenings at 8:30. The Indian Bowl is located on the lakeshore amidst the Lac du Flambeau Indian Reservation. Some well known Chippewa drummers and singers often perform here.

The PUBLIC LIBRARY and MUSEUM CULTURAL CENTER here have interesting Chippewa Indian exhibits.

There is also an annual BEAR RIVER POW-WOW held usually in July on the pow-wow grounds. The location is on Old Indian Village Road, 2 miles outside town. For dates and further information, contact the Chamber of Commerce.

WISCONSIN—LAKE MILLS
AZTALAN STATE PARK
County Trunk Road B
3 miles E of Lake Mills, WI
From I-94, use Exit 259, S onto Hwy 89 into Lake Mills, then E of County B.
(414) 648-5116 or 648-5792
Aztalan is a famous Native American archeological park preserving the remains of Wisconsin's largest archeological site. Occupied during the 12th and 13th centuries, Aztalan was a Middle Mississippian mound builder village surrounded by a stockade 12 to 19 feet high and complete with defensive watch towers. Inside was a village of thatched roof houses, mounds, and ceremonial buildings. The truncated pyramidal mounds were once crowned with temples. These mound building Indians were farmers, fishermen, and hunters. Today, the mounds remain, portions of the stockade have been rebuilt, impressive artifacts excavated, and general restoration work done. Nearby is the Lake Mills-Aztalan Historical Museum and park. A 30 foot high observation tower provides a splendid view of the mounds and valley. This is one of the most important archeological sites in the country and well worth visiting.

WISCONSIN—MADISON
WISCONSIN STATE HISTORICAL SOCIETY MUSEUM
816 State St
Madison, WI
(608) 262-9606
Native American displays relating to Wisconsin history are presented.

WISCONSIN—MENOMINEE INDIAN RESERVATION
MENOMINEE INDIAN TRIBE OF WISCONSIN
Chairmen's Office
Box 397
Keshena, WI 54135
(715) 756-3917
The Menominee Indian tribe was terminated as an officially recognized Indian tribe by the Federal Government in 1961. The Termination policy was an ill conceived attempt by the government to end services to certain Indian tribes, to force these tribes to assimilate into non-Indian society, and to open Indian lands up to economic exploitation by non-Indian business interests. Leadership was taken out of Menominee hands and the results were disastrous. Tribal lands were sold off, the tribal hospital closed, unemployment soared, poverty and health problems increased, and social disorganization followed. By the time the program was well under way, Indian leaders, Congressmen, and even the President were all calling the Termination Program a disaster.

Some Menominee never gave up and the Restoration Committee, under the leadership of Ada Deer, worked for years to reinstate the tribe and restore Indian control. Fortunately, they finally succeeded and in 1973 new legislation was signed into law restoring the Menominee Tribe and much of its lands. Under Menominee leadership there is now a new health clinic, education programs, housing construction projects, a tribal judiciary system, and wildlife management programs. The tribal lumber company has reopened. The Menominee are justly proud of the amazing comeback they have achieved. It is a pleasure to include this listing.

For visitors to the Menominee Reservation there is the annual MENOMINEE POW-WOW, usually held in July. The MENOMINEE LOGGING CAMP MUSEUM, 1/2 mile north of Keshena at the junction of Hwy 47 and Hwy VV, offers one of the best logging museum's in the country with old time buildings. For current hours, call (715) 799-3757. MENOMINEE TRIBAL RAFTING offers river rafting opportunities at reasonable prices. You can rent rafts and make one of the runs offered down the beautiful Wolf River through Smokey Falls. For information or reservations, contact Menominee Tribal Rafting at (715) 799-3359.

WISCONSIN—MILWAUKEE
MILWAUKEE PUBLIC MUSEUM
800 W Wells St
Milwaukee, WI
(414) 278-2700
This distinguished museum offers Native American displays.

WISCONSIN—ODANAH
BAD RIVER LIVING HISTORY CENTER (Under construction at press time)
Bad River Ojibwa Indian Reservation
14 miles E of Ashland on US Hwy 2
Box 39
Odanah, WI 54861
(715) 682-4212
The center will be built of logs and will feature the culture, arts, crafts and history of the Bad River Ojibwa people. The traditional MANOMIN (Wild Rice) CELEBRATION is held usually the weekend before Labor Day. Visitors are warmly received with a feast, Ojibwa dancing and singing, and other activities.

WISCONSIN—ONEIDA
ONEIDA NATION MUSEUM
Box 365
On Road "EE", west of Hwy "E" between Oneida and Freedom
Oneida, WI 54155
(414) 869-2768
The Oneida Indians are an Iroquoian tribe originally from New York. In the 1820's these "People of the Standing Stone" moved west and became some of Wisconsin's first settlers. Today they live on a reservation near Green Bay and the tribe has established the Oneida Nation Museum to preserve the treasure of Oneida culture.

The museum features an outdoor stockaded Oneida village with longhouses and other exhibits reconstructed by the Oneida people. Demonstrations in the village include corn grinding, tomahawk throwing, Indian games and other seasonal activities.

Inside the new museum you will see excellent exhibits with Oneida moccasins, clothing, basketry, gustoweh feathered hats, porcupine quill, moose hair and birch bark artwork. Life-size dioramas. The role of Oneida women and their high status in the tribe is explained.

There is a hands-on exhibit where youngsters and others can use actual Native American crafts products, ceremonial items, and clothing. Tours aimed at both adults and school children may be arranged in advance.

The museum has an herb garden nearby which preserves medicinal herbs used by the Oneida. You can picnic in the stockaded village after touring the museum and grounds. Teachers will be pleased to learn that the museum has a traveling exhibit available to schools. The Oneida are to be congratulated on their fine museum program.

The Oneida Nation has a traditional Iroquoian dance group which performs periodically and continues this rich dance form. There is an annual pow-wow over Fourth of July with Plains-type dancing (not traditional with the Oneida), arts and crafts, visiting tribal groups, and horse races. The Aztec dancers from Mexico are among the groups seen here in recent years.

WISCONSIN—PRAIRIE DU CHIEN
WYALUSING STATE PARK
County Road "C"
12 miles S of Prairie de Chien, WI
(608) 996-2261
Contains Indian mounds of Sentinel Ridge high above the Mississippi River.

WISCONSIN—SHEBOYGAN
SHEBOYGAN INDIAN MOUND PARK
South 9th St, S of Panther Ave
Sheboygan, WI
Sheboygan Indian Mound Park preserves fine effigy mounds built over 1000 years ago by Native Americans. The mounds are called effigies because most

Oneida men constructing longhouses for the village at the Oneida Nation Museum in Wisconsin. (Oneida Nation Museum)

Oneida longhouse at the Oneida Nation Museum in Wisconsin. The longhouse is the traditional dwelling of the Iroquois, Huron and other Eastern Woodlands tribes. (Oneida Nation Museum)

are formed in the shape of animals, especially panthers, deer and fawns. Other mounds are conical, oval, and linear in shape. Effigy mounds are found predominately in the southern part of Wisconsin, and adjacent areas in Iowa, Minnesota, and Illinois. They are very different in appearance and function from the mounds made by Indian people in Georgia, Alabama and much of Ohio.

Visitors leave the parking area for a self-guided tour through the effigy mounds. Another trail leads to three conical mounds. A nature trail identifies natives plants of the park. Originally there were 34 mounds, but by the time the dedicated people of the Sheboygan area Garden Clubs succeeded in their efforts to preserve their unique treasures, just 18 mounds remained. Those having questions about the park should contact the City of Sheboygan.

WISCONSIN—STOCKBRIDGE-MUNSEE INDIAN RESERVATION

The STOCKBRIDGE-MUNSEE RESERVATION offers a variety of interesting and worthwhile cultural and recreational opportunities. The reservation is west of Green Bay, via Hwy 29 through Shawano, west to Bowler. Turn off Hwy 29 on County Trunk Road J to Bowler. Then take County Trunk Road A, 3 miles to Mohheconnuck Road. Proceed 2 miles N on Mohheconnuck to the log building.

STOCKBRIDGE-MUNSEE HISTORICAL LIBRARY AND MUSEUM
Route 1, Box 300
Bowler, WI 54416
(715) 793-4270
Open weekdays, the combination library and museum preserves the history of the Stockbridge and Munsee people. (The Stockbridge are also called the Mahican. The Munsee are a branch of the Delaware people.) Once inside you get the feeling of the warm, home-like atmosphere of a traditional wigwam. There are books and historical materials relating to the history of these two important Algonquian-speaking nations. Baskets, some quite old, are displayed, along with actual and reproduced stone tools and other artifacts.

The future plans for the museum call for exhibits tracing the Stockbridge-Munsee heritage from the days before Columbus, through the fur trade, missionization, the move west from New England and New York to Wisconsin, on to the days of life as Native American pioneers, and concluding with the life of the people today. It is hoped that funds will become available to reconstruct an actual Stockbridge-Munsee village as it existed in the east before the tribe migrated to Wisconsin. The library welcomes

donations to help make these goals a reality. Contact the library staff or the tribal planning office if you can help.

Annually the museum-library holds a fund raiser and auction on tribal election day, the second Saturday in October. Hot cider and fry bread are served.

The annual STOCKBRIDGE-MUNSEE POW-WOW is held during the summer, usually either in June or August. Call the tribal office at (715) 793-4111 for exact dates. Potawatomi, Menominee, Chippewa, and Winnebago dancers and drums all join the Stockbridge-Munsee people for the event. The pow-wow is held two miles north of the library on Mohheconnuck Road in the vicinity of the tribal campground and picnic area. (Camping is available along the Red River.) The Stockbridge-Munsee have lost all their dances through the centuries of missionization, but young people are learning pow-wow dancing as a partial replacement. It is a pleasant pow-wow with dancers of many tribes competing in the tribal dance bowl arena with its arbor in the center. Traditional hull corn soup can be sampled here along with other Native American foods.

For those who enjoy the game, the tribe operates a bingo enterprise. Check for days and times.

The Stockbridge-Munsee have excellent future plans for their library and museum and it is hoped that the dream of a reconstructed traditional village will become a reality. As tribal planner Molly Shawano so beautifully said, "I was in a reconstructed Iroquois village once and it felt as if I was home again." Perhaps the future Stockbridge-Munsee traditional village will once again make this fine Indian nation's people feel "home again".

WISCONSIN—WEST BEND
LIZARD MOUND STATE PARK
County Road "A"
4 miles N of West Bend, WI
(414) 644-5248
Fascinating collection of effigy mounds in the shape of birds, animals, and other forms. Self-guided tour.

WISCONSIN—WISCONSIN DELLS
STAND ROCK INDIAN CEREMONIALS
Produced by Neesh-la Indian Development Corporation
Box 560
Wisconsin Dells, WI 53965
(608) 254-2538 or (800) 22-DELLS
The Stand Rock Ceremonials are presented nightly at 8:45 from mid-June through Labor Day, four miles north of Wisconsin Dells on Stand Rock Road. You

may also travel to the ceremony by boat, and tickets are sold by Dells Boats Co, Olsen Boat Line, and Riverview Boat Line. Boats leave about an hour before the show.

The dancers and performers are primarily local Winnebago Indian people, the original inhabitants of The Dells. You'll see dancing, hear Native American music, and see the history pageant. Special appearances are also sometimes made by Aztec dancers from Mexico, Zuni dancers from New Mexico, and Choctaws from the south.

WYOMING

WYOMING—CHEYENNE
WYOMING STATE MUSEUM
Barrett Building
23rd & Central
Cheyenne, WY
(307) 777-7510
Contains excellent material relating to Wyoming Indian cultures. Changing exhibits. Open daily.

WYOMING—CODY
PLAINS INDIAN MUSEUM
BUFFALO BILL HISTORICAL CENTER
720 Sheridan Ave
Cody, WY
(307) 587-4771
Extensive western and Indian collections in four museums. One museum specializes in Native Americans of the Plains, with paintings, photographs, clothing, weaponry, quill and beadwork. Some items once belonged to famous Plains Indian leaders. Special exhibits periodically. Gift shop. Open daily.

WYOMING—GRAND TETON NATIONAL PARK
LAUBIN ANCIENT INDIAN DANCES
Jackson Lake Lodge, 5 miles N of Moran
Box 240
Moran, WY
(307) 543-2855
Reginald and Gladys Laubin are well known professional dancers and authors who have worked closely with a number of Plains Indian groups (especially the Sioux and Crow) to learn and present traditional Native American dances. The Laubins are non-Indians, but generally their fellow dancers are Native Americans. They have won much acclaim for their work. The Laubin's books, THE INDIAN TIPI and INDIAN DANCES OF NORTH AMERICA are extremely useful for anyone interested in Plains Indian cultures. Performances are held Friday at the lodge. Check for exact schedule.

WYOMING—RIVERTON
RIVERTON MUSEUM
700 E Park Ave
Riverton, WY
(307) 856-2665
Presents among its collections Arapahoe and Shoshone displays from the adjacent Wind River Reservation.

WYOMING—SHERIDAN
PLAINS INDIAN BATTLEFIELDS SELF-GUIDED TOUR
Contact Chamber of Commerce, Box 707
Hwy 90 at Fifth St
Sheridan, WY 82801
(307) 672-2485
A number of local sites are of interest to those fascinated by the Plains Indian Wars. Contact the Chamber of Commerce for tour guides of the battlefields. Sioux Chief Red Cloud's defeat of the US Army occurred 20 miles south of here at FETTERMAN MASSACRE MONUMENT, named in honor of the commanding officer. Too often in the Old West when the whitemen won the conflict was called a "battle", but when the Indians won it was termed a "massacre", thus explaining the monuments label.

WYOMING—WIND RIVER INDIAN RESERVATION
The large Wind River Reservation is shared by the Arapahoe and Shoshone tribes and each has a distinct culture, language, ceremonies, and tribal organization. At least two famous citizens of the West are buried here. Sacajawea, the Shoshone Indian woman who led Lewis and Clark's expedition across the Rocky Mountains and down the Columbia River to the Pacific Ocean is buried near Fort Washakie. Also buried here is Chief Washakie, the great Shoshone leader who played a prominent role in Wyoming history. St. Michael's Mission in nearby Ethete has a collection of Arapahoe arts and crafts. The Northern Arapahoe are developing an ARAPAHOE CULTURAL MUSEUM in Ethete, which explains the tribe's history and culture.

A number of pow-wows, Sun dances, and other events are held annually. There is a Tribal Information Office in the government complex in Fort Washakie. For dates and events check with the Tribal Office at (307) 255-8265.

One of the greatest sights I experienced as a youngster was coming over a hill near Lander and seeing a huge encampment of Shoshone and Arapahoe tepees gathered for a summer celebration. Such encampments are still held today and are as impressive as ever. Native Americans gather at a pow-wow or other

A Wyoming Plains Indian dancer presents a fine appearance as he prepares for a Shoshone or Arapaho pow-wow. (Wyoming Travel Commission)

A handsome young man in a Wyoming Indian celebration. The two major Indian nations in Wyoming are the Arapaho and Shoshone. Most young Indians share their elders' pride in their heritage. (Wyoming Travel Commission)

The Shoshone and Arapaho Indian people of Wyoming care about their traditional cultures and work effectively to keep them alive. (Wyoming Travel Commission)

events from long distances and many families own te-pees for camping. It is an old Plains and Plateau cus-tom, a time for fellowship, dancing and fun. Some-times sacred ceremonies are also conducted.

WYOMING—THERMOPOLIS
GATHERING OF THE WATERS PAGEANT
Chamber of Commerce

Hot Springs State Park Building
Hwy 20
Thermopolis, WY
(307) 864-2636
Shoshone and Arapahoe Indian people join in the pageant commemorating the Indian heritage of the hot springs. Indian dances, parade, and buffalo barbecue.

Northwest Coast Indian people often wore elaborately carved headdresses such as this one. This young man also wears a traditional button blanket and painted skirt. He works on the staff of Seattle's Tillicum Village. (R. Shanks)

The Haida Nation village at University of British Columbia's Anthropology Museum. Northwest Coast Indian villages were often built facing the sea or a river. Magnificent wood carvings reached artistic greatness in totem poles and "longhouses" such as these. (R. Shanks)

CANADA

ALBERTA

ALBERTA—CALGARY
CALGARY STAMPEDE, an annual event the second week in July, includes Indian dancing. Phone (403) 261-0101.

GLENBOW-ALBERTA INSTITUTE
9th Ave at First St SE (Part of Convention Centre)
Calgary, Alberta
(403) 264-8300
Indian and Eskimo exhibits are among the collections.

NICKLE ARTS MUSEUM
University of Calgary campus
Calgary, Alberta
(403) 284-7234
Exhibits include Indian archeological displays.

ALBERTA—EDMONTON
PROVINCIAL MUSEUM AND ARCHIVES
12845—102nd Ave
Edmonton, Alberta
(403) 427-1730
The museum has an anthropological gallery. Periodic demonstrations and films pertaining to Indian people.

STRATHCONA ARCHEOLOGICAL CENTRE
Off Hwy 16A on 17th St
Edmonton, Alberta
(403) 427-9487
This is a 5000 year old Indian archeological site. Interpretive centre.

NORTHERN IMAGES
West Edmonton Mall
Box 241
8770—170th St
Edmonton, Alberta T5T 3J7
(403) 487-8992
Inuit and Dene Indian soapstone sculptures, clothing, crafts, prints, and more. Native owned. Mail order catalog.

ALBERTA—FORT MacLEOD
HEAD-SMASHED-IN BUFFALO JUMP
18 km W of Fort MacLeod on Spring Point Rd
(403) 553-2030
Here Plains Indians drove buffalo over cliffs to harvest the animals for food, clothing, tepee coverings, etc. Fort MacLeod Museum, in the town of Fort Mac-Leod should be able to provide additional information, phone (403) 553-2500.

ALBERTA—HIGH RIVER
OLD WOMAN'S BUFFALO JUMP
Another buffalo jump, this one is located in the vicinity of High River. Inquire locally for directions.

ALBERTA—MILK RIVER
WRITING-ON-STONE PROVINCIAL PARK
Near Junction of Hwys 501 and 878
42 km SE of Milk River, Alberta
(403) 647-2364
Plains Indian rock art. Guided tours, extensive education program, interesting archeological sites.

BRITISH COLUMBIA

BRITISH COLUMBIA—ALERT BAY
U'MISTA CULTURAL CENTRE
Box 253
Alert Bay, BC VON 1AO
(604) 974-5403
Alert Bay is reached by ferryboat service from Port McNeill, BC. Alert Bay is a community of the Nimkish Indian people and the cultural centre is located here.

During the 1920's the Canadian government took much of the Nimkish and Kwakiutl Indian people's art away from them and displayed it in government and private museums. Recently, portions of these items have been returned to the Indian people. The Kwakiutl Museum (SEE: BRITISH COLUMBIA—QUADRA ISLAND) has about one-third of the collection and the U'Mista Cultural Centre has about the same percentage. The remainder has yet to be returned.

The U'Mista Cultural Centre is built like a Northwest Coast Big House with a main gallery and three smaller display galleries. The main gallery holds the Potlatch Collection of Northwest art, including fine carvings, woodwork, etc. Of the smaller galleries, one holds the work of a famous early Northwest Coast artist, while another houses contemporary artists work including basketry, masks, carvings, and more. The third gallery serves as a classroom and contains a traveling exhibit, photographs, a display explaining the traditional origin of the Nimkish, and other material.

The Cultural Centre sponsors button blanket-making classes (these are beautiful Northwest Coast capes made of red and black wool and are generally decorated with high quality buttons arranged in traditional designs), dance and singing classes, a teacher training program, and a video program.

Two award winning films are shown by prior arrangement to visitors. "Box of Treasure" is about cultural survival and the other film is on the ill advised potlatch prohibition of the early Twentieth Century.

For large tour groups, special Nimkish traditional dance groups will perform high quality Northwest Coast dancing. Contact the Centre for details and costs.

Visitors to Alert Bay will see the cultural centre, the Big House, and the traditional cemetery with its fine totem poles. It is very important that visitors do not enter the cemetery, but view the totem poles from the outside. Be sure to call the cultural centre to check on hours before making the trip to Alert Bay.

BRITISH COLUMBIA—CAMPBELL RIVER
CAMPBELL RIVER MUSEUM
1235 Island Hwy
Campbell River, BC
(604) 287-3103
Coast Salish, Kwakiutl, and Nootka artwork is among the collections. Indian gift shop with Northwest Coast Indian art.

BRITISH COLUMBIA—HAZELTON
'KSAN INDIAN VILLAGE
Hwy 16 to New Hazelton, then 5 1/2 km NW via Hwy 62 to Hazelton, BC
(604) 842-5544
This is a colorful traditional Gitksan Indian village which welcomes visitors to its many attractions. The Gitksan (a branch of the Tsimshian tribe) are famous for their high quality wood carvings that are featured in museums world wide. Northwest Coast tribal houses such as Fireweed House, Frog House, Feast House, and Wolf House may be seen. There is a Treasure Room and Exhibition Centre with Museum containing rare Gitksan art work. You can see the Carving Shed where totem poles as well as other wood carvings are made. There is also the 'Ksan Shop and a workshop for crafts people. These buildings are fine Northwest Coast old style Indian buildings. There are guided tours of the buildings, artists' areas, museum, and a gift shop.

Traditional Northwest coast dancing is presented many evenings during July and August in the Wolf House at 'Ksan Village. Check for times and special events.

KISPIOX is another of the Tsimshian tribes's communities and is located north of 'Ksan and features a group of totem poles on display.

KITSEGUECLA Indian community, along Hwy 16, SW

of Hazelton just beyond Skeena Crossing, has more totem poles still standing in their original locations.

GITWANGAK Indian Reserve and community is located on Hwy 37 west of the town of Kitwanga, toward Prince Rupert from Hazelton. There are totem poles here, too.

KITWANCOOL, Hwy 37, N of Kitwanga, is the fifth of the Gitksan Indian towns in the area and it has many very old totem poles of high quality. The well known Hole-in-the-Ice totem pole is here.

The town of Hazelton has a Hand of History Tour guide of local points of interest. There is a campground adjacent to 'Ksan village with showers, trailer hookups, etc. Phone (604) 842-5940.

The many villages of the Tsimshian tribe plus the great appeal of 'Ksan makes this an interesting area to visit. Also SEE: BRITISH COLUMBIA—NEW AIYANSH, for another of the area's Indian communities.

BRITISH COLUMBIA—KELOWNA
KELOWNA CENTENNIAL MUSEUM
470 Queensway Ave
Kelowna, BC
(604) 763-2417
Among the collections is an interesting display of earth-covered semi-subterranean Indian houses and other Native Canadian exhibits.

BRITISH COLUMBIA—KOOTENAY NATIONAL PARK
Radium Hot Springs, BC
(604) 347-9615
INDIAN ROCK ART of animals is found on ledges in the Sinclair Canyon area (southwestern portion of the park). Inquire at the park for directions. In Marble Canyon, trails lead to yellow ocher gathered by the Blackfeet and other tribes as pigment for body paint, tepee decoration, etc.

BRITISH COLUMBIA—NANAIMO
NANAIMO MUSEUM
100 Cameron St
Nanaimo, BC
(604) 753-1812
Collections include cultural items from the Cowichan and other Coast Salish people. The Nanaimo Band of Cowichan sometimes hold dugout canoe races locally. The much admired Cowichan sweaters, among the world's highest quality sweaters, are made here and are sold locally. The sweaters are typically of delicate tones of grey and off white and are made by the Cowichan and neighboring bands.

BRITISH COLUMBIA—NEW AIYANSH
NEW AIYANSH INDIAN VILLAGE
(604) 633-2215
New Aiyansh is in the vicinity of Terrace, BC, accessible only over potentially dangerous logging roads where logging trucks have the right of way. However, this active Indian community does feature both an attractive tribal council building and traditional totem poles.

BRITISH COLUMBIA—PORT ALBERNI
ALBERNI VALLEY MUSEUM
Echo Recreation Centre
4255 Wallace St
Port Alberni, BC
(604) 723-2181
Northwest Coast Indian items are among the collections. Nootka Indians sometimes hold fine dance performances in the area.

BRITISH COLUMBIA—PRINCE RUPERT
MUSEUM OF NORTHERN BRITISH COLUMBIA
First Ave & McBride
Prince Rupert, BC
(604) 624-3207
Collections include Northwest Coast Indian art. Of special interest is a carvers' shed where Northwest Coast Indian artists work at wood carvings.

BRITISH COLUMBIA—QUADRA ISLAND
KWAKIUTL MUSEUM
Box 8
Quathiaski Cove, BC VOP INP
(604) 285-3733
The museum is located 3.6 miles S of the ferry terminal on Green Rd in the Cape Mudge area. Quadra Island is reached by ferry service from Campbell River, Vancouver Island.

The Museum features the great Kwakiutl potlatch collection recently restored to its original owners, the Kwakiutl Nation. The Kwakiutl Indian people's museum presents cedar masks and large numbers of other beautiful artwork. The collection was originally confiscated by the Canadian government during the 1920's in an ill advised attempt to suppress the Kwakiutl from giving away gifts to their friends and relatives as a part of their religion. The people were given the choice of giving up their priceless artwork and ceremonies or going to jail. They chose to give up their artwork and the collections were shipped off to various museums. Recently, the Kwakiutl were successful in getting part of the collection returned to them and it is now on display here and at Alert Bay.

Besides exhibits of Kwakiutl arts and crafts, the museum offers a variety of interesting programs. Guided tours are available and an attempt is made to have traditional Kwakiutl foods on hand for visitors to try. If you are lucky you may sample salmon, seaweed, or olachen oil, the latter derived from candlefish. Persons desiring group tours can often arrange for these treats to be available in advance.

Traveling exhibits are available for institutions and special children's programs are offered. Especially popular features are the exact replicas of ancient petroglyphs at the museum where visitors may make rubbings to take home and frame. (Making petroglyph rubbings is illegal because it can injure the ancient rock art, but the Kwakiutl people have made reproductions, so you can make a rubbing without hurting the original).

In summer, tours of the ancient village site and actual petroglyphs (1/2 mile from the museum) are offered by appointment.

The Museum's cultural exchange program is imaginative and very worthwhile. Recently a group of Ainu people, the original native Caucasian settlers of Japan, visited the Kwakiutl and it was an exciting experience learning of the similarities between the two cultures.

A gift shop is in the museum with fine traditional carved masks, decorated bent wood boxes, jewelry, paintings, books, and much more. There are plans to have a totem pole raising with traditional dancing and a salmon barbecue soon.

Besides the spectacular collection of Northwest Coast Indian art and the exciting special programs offered, beautiful totem poles are displayed here on the Reserve. Traditional dancing is occasionally done on the island. Check with the museum for dates of special events.

BRITISH COLUMBIA— QUEEN CHARLOTTE ISLANDS
HAIDA NATION TOTEM POLES and HISTORIC VILLAGES
These remote and heavily forested islands boast fascinating abandoned villages where Haida Indian totem poles and other ancient wood carvings may be seen. As archeological relics, they rival the artwork of Middle America, but are perishable because they are made of wood rather than stone as in Mexico and Guatemala. The Haida people want to see these works of art protected. Therefore, before visiting old villages you need to obtain permission from the two Haida Band offices. The Masset Haida Band Office's phone number is (604) 626-3337, and the Skidegate Haida Band Office's phone number is (604) 559-4496.

Haida culture flourishes today and there are contemporary attractions, too. The CHARLES EDENSHAW MEMORIAL LONGHOUSE at Masset is a good example of a present day Northwest coast longhouse and features magnificent painted wall carvings with traditional Haida designs. About 30 Haida carvers produce work of high quality, including such well known artists as Robert Davidson and Bill Reid. Totem poles are again being made on Queen Charlotte Island after 80 years of dormancy. There is a new pride in Haida art and dance, and beautiful dances are occasionally performed for guests. Check with the tribal offices for dates.

Both air and ferry services to the islands are available from Prince Rupert and Vancouver, British Columbia.

BRITISH COLUMBIA—TERRACE
INDIAN MUSEUM and CRAFT CENTRE
**Junction of the Kalum River and Hwy 16,
W of Terrace, BC**
Tsimshian owned and operated business and museum. Authentic local Tsimshian Indian wood carvings, totem poles, leather work, and more are sold here. Museum exhibits relating to Northwest Coast Indian culture.

BRITISH COLUMBIA—VANCOUVER
ANTHROPOLOGY MUSEUM
**University of British Columbia campus
Vancouver, BC
(604) 228-5087**
As you enter this museum it becomes more impressive with each step you take. First, you pass through a gift shop with items pertaining to Northwest Coast Indian culture. Then upon entering the display areas you see large cedar carvings of animals and spirits. Wandering further, the visitor encounters rows of Indian and Eskimo exhibits containing countless baskets, carvings, and decorated clothing. As if this were not enough, notice that the cabinet drawers open. Each drawer is glass-topped allowing visitors to actually look through the museum's storage drawers and see even more Native Canadian art. If you tire of this, there is yet a greater treat in store ahead. The museum ceiling soars high to hold totem poles indoors. Then you come face to face with a gigantic wall of glass. Look through it and outside you'll see a Northwest Coast Haida Indian village. There are three handsome cedar plank houses facing a collection of elaborate totem poles. Best of all, you can walk around the museum to the rear and stroll through the village. The Northwest Coast Indian houses alone make a trip to the Museum worthwhile. When you add in the totem poles, vast displays, gift shop, creative architecture, and forested setting, the result is one of the world's finest museum experiences.

Check also for special programs and events. Highly recommended.

BRITISH COLUMBIA—VICTORIA
PROVINCIAL MUSEUM
**601 Belleville St
Victoria, BC
(604) 387-3701**
This highly acclaimed museum contains well presented exhibits pertaining to Northwest Coast Indian life. You'll sit in a room where the lights darken as carved cedar masks appear one after another in a dramatic presentation. There is a full sized interior of a Northwest Coast house with many interesting details. A cave is accurately recreated with sacred spiritual offerings shown in the traditional Indian manner. Quite unusual is a full sized earth covered lodge, the type used by Indians in the interior of British Columbia and elsewhere in North America. There is an excellent gift shop.

Be sure to go outside the Museum to the corner of Belleville and Douglas Streets to THUNDERBIRD PARK, (604) 387-3504. Here you'll see a spectacularly painted Northwest Coast house with full color animal designs on the walls. The house is surrounded by many totem poles and large animal carvings. Some were done by famed Nootka carver Mungo Martin. Here too, is a carver's house where Indian artists often work during summer months so you can see a totem pole being created. Highly recommended.

LABRADOR

LABRADOR—GOOSE BAY
HERITAGE & CULTURE CENTRE
**Goose Bay, Labrador
(709) 896-2872**
The Centre displays local Native Canadian cultures. There is an annual LABRADOR HERITAGE FESTIVAL usually held in July.

MANITOBA

MANITOBA—CHURCHILL
CHURCHILL ESKIMO MUSEUM
**In town near the mission
Churchill, Manitoba**
Inuit (Eskimo) arts and crafts are displayed.

MANITOBA—FALCON LAKE
WHITESHELL PROVINCIAL PARK
**Trans-Canada Hwy
Near Falcon Lake, Manitoba**
Ojibwa Indian rock art is found in the park at Ban-

nock Point, including animal and bird effigies. Inquire at the park for directions.

MANITOBA—WINNIPEG
MANITOBA INDIAN CULTURAL EDUCATION CENTRE
199 Sutherland Ave
Winnipeg, Manitoba
(204) 942-0228
The Centre works to promote awareness and understanding of Indian cultures among both Indian and non-Indian people. Services are provided for Cree, Ojibwa, Chipewyan, and Sioux nations. Many services are offered for Indian bands including a library, library training, graphic arts services and publication production assistance, audio-visual program development, research, and cultural workshop planning and organization. For schools and others there are presentations, displays and workshops. Assistance is given both in buying and selling arts and crafts. Open to the public weekdays.

NEW BRUNSWICK

NEW BRUNSWICK—REXTON
RICHIBUCTO RIVER MUSEUM
Hwy 11
Rexton, New Brunswick
(506) 523-9460
Among the collections are exhibits on local Micmac Indians.

NEW BRUNSWICK—ST. JOHN
NEW BRUNSWICK MUSEUM
277 Douglas St
Saint John, New Brunswick
(506) 693-1196
Collections pertaining to Eastern Woodlands Indians. Also in St. John is the OLD CITY MARKET, near King Square between Germain and Charlotte Street, where Micmac Indian baskets are often for sale. The Micmac people are the First Canadians of this region.

NEWFOUNDLAND

NEWFOUNDLAND—PORT AU CHOIX NATIONAL HISTORIC PARK
Box 70
St. Lunaire-Griquet, Newfoundland
(709) 623-2608
Archeological excavations of 4000 year old Maritime Archaic Indian culture sites. A visitor center shows the work and the history of these early people who used the sea as their major source of food.

NEWFOUNDLAND—SAINT JOHN'S
NEWFOUNDLAND MUSEUM
Duckworth St
Saint John's, Newfoundland
(709) 737-2460
Indian displays are among the exhibits.

NEWFOUNDLAND—TWILLINGATE
TWILLINGATE MUSEUM
Off Hwy 340
Twillingate, Newfoundland
(709) 884-2825
Ancient Maritime Archaic Indian culture exhibits are among the collections.

NORTHWEST TERRITORIES

Among the provinces and states of Canada and the US, only one has a population which is predominately Native North American—the Northwest Territories. Most people here are Indian, Inuit (Eskimo), or Metis. Many of the Native people are teachers, government workers, artists, skilled workers and the like, but others lead traditional lives of hunting, fishing, and trapping. This is a frontier in many areas and it is possible to enjoy adventures long gone elsewhere. Begin by contacting: TRAVELARCTIC, Government of the Northwest Territories, Yellowknife, NWT, Canada Z1A 2L9, phone (403) 873-7200. Under the leadership of Mr. Tagak Curley, a Native Canadian, this organization has the expertise and publications necessary to help orient you to the Far North. Their magazine, "Northwest Territories Explorers' Guide" is invaluable. You'll find listings for the Eskimo owned Arctic Co-operatives, hotels in Inuit communities, annual events including Dene (Athabaskan) Indian drum dances at Rae-Edzo and Fort Simpson, museums in Inuit and Dene communities, and much more. You'll learn that Canada North Outfitting, Box 1230, Watertown, Ontario L0R 1H0, phone (416) 689-7925, has package tours ranging from Inuit Art Tours to Inuit Camping Experiences where you join Cape Dorset Eskimo families for ten days of travel while hunting and fishing across the Arctic. TRAVELARCTIC can also teach you about Inukshooks and Etigaseemautes, ancient Eskimo rock cairns that often look like people from a distance. (Some cairns were used as navigational aids by travelers coming in from a frozen sea to a featureless winter coast.)

Northwest Territories is rich in Dene and Inuit arts and crafts. Dene Indian clothing, leatherwork, moose hair tufting, and other products rank with the best in North America. Eskimo arts and crafts are also of extremely high quality and their art is exhibited in the world's great museums.

A beautiful woman of the North, Beeima, a Cape Dorset Inuit model wearing a handcrafted necklace. (Dept. of Information, Govt. of Northwest Territories—Tessa Macintosh)

Plan your trip carefully knowing that reservations are essential and that weather conditions can be harsh. For the adventuresome, the Northwest Territories offers unbeatable travel opportunities and a fabulous introduction to Indian and Eskimo cultures of the North.

Note: at some of the Far North hotels, rooms on occasion may be shared by different parties. To avoid this, be sure to make arrangements with the management.

NORTHWEST TERRITORIES— CAPE DORSET
WEST BAFFIN ESKIMO CO-OP PRODUCER DIVISION
Cape Dorset, Northwest Territories ZOA OCO
(819) 987-8944
Cape Dorset is the home of many famed Eskimo artists and their products include carvings, sculptures, prints, etc. They also have a show room and sales office in Toronto.

NORTHWEST TERRITORIES— ESKIMO POINT
INUIT CULTURAL INSTITUTE
Eskimo Point, Northwest Territories XOC OGO
(819) 857-2085
The Inuit Cultural Institute has been a leader in Inuit social and cultural activities. Traditional Eskimo dancing is done here periodically. Local outfitters lead tours. Historic sites and trails are attractions, and the Institute offers orientation courses for visitors. The cultural and academic achievements of the Institute, particularly in linguistics, are well known in the North. Eskimo Point is an Inuit community with a population of over 1000. The Keewatin Summer Games are held here generally in August. They include fascinating Eskimo competitions.

NORTHWEST TERRITORIES— FORT LIARD
ACHO-DENE NATIVE CRAFTS
General Delivery
Fort Liard, Northwest Territories XOG OAO
(403) 770-4161
The Slavey (SLAY-vee) Athabaskan Indian people call themselves the Dene (da-NAY), as do most related tribes in the Northwest Territories. The Slavey make very beautiful quill decorated birch bark baskets, often with floral or animal designs. Their crafts shop is generally open weekday afternoons.

NORTHWEST TERRITORIES— FORT McPHERSON
CHIEF JULIUS SCHOOL
Fort McPherson, Northwest Territories
Exhibits in the schoolhouse feature photographs on the history of this Kutchin (Loucheaux) Indian community. Some traditional Kutchin arts and crafts are still made here. Inquire at the school.

ARCTIC RED RIVER is also a Kutchin Indian community, located east of Fort McPherson. Historic Hudson Bay Trading Posts may be seen here.

NORTHWEST TERRITORIES— FORT PROVIDENCE
Slavey Indian people make moose hair embroidery and porcupine quill birch bark baskets in attractive styles. Check locally for craftspeople offering items for sale. In August, MACKENZIE DAYS is held with traditional games, canoe races, and a carnival. For details write the Settlement Council, Fort Providence, NWT, Canada XOE OLO.

NORTHWEST TERRITORIES— FORT SIMPSON
FORT SIMPSON HANDICRAFTS
NATS Enelu Society
Box 60
Fort Simpson, Northwest Territories XOE ONO
(403) 695-2497
Beadwork, quillwork, moose and caribou hair tufting, embroidery, birch bark baskets and other arts and crafts are produced. Wholesale and retail sales. The Dene Indian people of Fort Simpson are mostly members of the Slavey tribe.

There is an annual Beaver Tail Jamboree usually in March that includes traditional Dene drum dancing. Write the Village Office for details.

NORTHWEST TERRITORIES— FORT SMITH
NORTHERN LIFE MUSEUM and NATIONAL EXHIBITION CENTRE
King St
Fort Smith, Northwest Territories
(403) 872-2859
Athabaskan Indian and Inuit (Eskimo) arts and crafts are among the collections.

THEBACHA CRAFT GUILD
Fort Smith, Northwest Territories
Traditional Athabaskan Indian crafts are made here by the Dene Indian people. This is the region of the Athabaskan-speaking Chipewyan Indian people.

NORTHWEST TERRITORIES—HOLMAN
Annual KINGALIK JAMBOREE with Inuit Arctic crafts, contests, seal skinning, bannock making, and races exhibiting many traditional Eskimo skills. Usually held in June. HOLMAN HISTORICAL SOCIETY offers exhibits. Check with the Hamlet Office, phone (403) 392-3511. ARCTIC CHAR INN and dining room is owned by the Holman Eskimo Co-operative, phone (403) 396-3501.

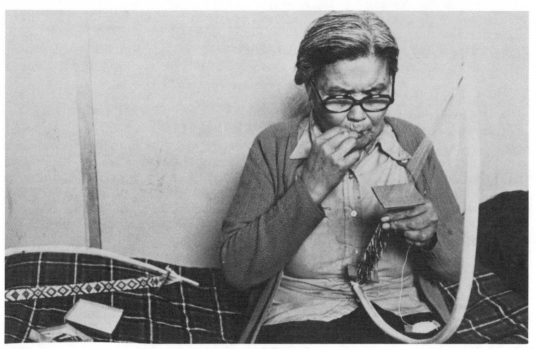

One of the oldest and finest arts of subarctic Indian people is quillwork. Dene' Indian artist Margaret Sabourin is takes dyed porcupine quills and weaves them on a traditional bow loom. Fort Providence, Northwest Territories. (Dept. of Information, Govt. of Northwest Territories—Tessa Macintosh)

Dene' Indian women tanning moose hide in the traditional manner at Yellowknife, Northwest Territories. The hide is used to produce exquisite clothing decorated with moose hairtufting or beadwork. (Dept. of Information, Govt. of Northwest Territories—Tessa Macintosh)

Mary Ann Rabesca models a Dene' Indian stroud jacket and mukluks appropriate for spring. Exquisite, handmade traditional Indian clothing adapted for modern wear is a specialty of Dene' Indian women in Northwest Territories and the Yukon. Note the floral beadwork designs. (Dept. of Information, Govt. of Northwest Territories—Tessa Macintosh)

NORTHWEST TERRITORIES—INUVIK
NORTHERN GAMES ASSOCIATION
Box 1184
Inuvik, Northwest Territories XOE OTO
The Northern Games consist of traditional Athabaskan Indian and Eskimo (Inuit) competitions in sports and survival skills. One portion is the Good Woman Contest where Inuit women race to perform other tasks vital to Inuit life. People come from all across the Arctic for these unique and interesting events. You'll see bannock, a traditional Indian food of the North, being made and crafts offered for sale.

The famous blanket toss is done with contestants hurled high in the air. The games are held in summer and the site may be at Inuvik or other Far North communities. Write for dates and details.

IGLOO CHURCH
Inuvik, Northwest Territories
This much photographed Christian Church is shaped much like an igloo. Inside, the stations of the cross are presented in an Inuit style. Open to visitors.

Aklavik, Tuktoyatuk, and other Eskimo communities may be reached by charter airplanes out of Inuvik.

NORTHWEST TERRITORIES—LAC LA MARTRE
Old trading post community. Dogrib Indian people have a small hotel. Arts and crafts sales. For information contact the Settlement Office at (403) 573-3401.

NORTHWEST TERRITORIES—PELLY BAY
Annual KITIMEOT NORTHERN GAMES, usually in July. Good Woman contest where Inuit women compete at traditional Eskimo skills. Bannock making, seal skinning, and tea making. Phone (403) 769-7281. PELLY BAY HOTEL and dining room are Inuit owned, phone (403) 769-7212 or 769-6231.

NORTHWEST TERRITORIES—RAE-EDZO
DOGRIB (DENE) NATIVE CRAFTS SHOP
Rae, Northwest Territories
The Dogrib Indian tribe of the Athabaskan-speaking Dene people have a crafts store offering Dogrib arts and crafts. Contact the Hamlet office (403) 392-6500 or 392-6561 for information on annual events such as the Winter Carnival (March) and Happy Days (August) which usually include traditional Dene Indian drum dances.

NORTHWEST TERRITORIES—TUKTOYATUK
Annual BELUGA JAMBOREE, usually in April, features traditional Inuit games, drum dances, and more. Contact Hamlet Office, Tuktoyaktuk, NWT, Canada

XOE 1CO. For accommodations, phone HOTEL TUK INN at (403) 977-2381.

NORTHWEST TERRITORIES—YELLOWKNIFE
PRINCE OF WALES NORTHERN HERITAGE CENTRE
Government of the Northwest Territories
Yellowknife, Northwest Territories X1A 2L9
(403) 873-7551
The Heritage Centre is an impressive museum located on a beautiful lake-shore. Exhibit galleries present the history and cultures of the Inuit (Eskimo) and Dene (Athabaskan Indian) peoples. You'll see a large mooseskin boat, ancient carvings, natural history displays, and exhibits. There are often demonstrations of traditional Native Canadian skills such as hide tanning.

The centre has extensive archives including thousands of photographs. One of the Heritage Centre's major goals is to assist Native and non-Native people across the North in preserving their local history.

There are special exhibits, audio-visual presentations, classes and archeological projects. A visit to the Heritage Centre is a must for anyone wanting to orient themselves to the North.

ARCTIC CO-OPERATIVES LTD
Box 2039
Yellowknife, Northwest Territories X1A 2P5
(403) 873-3481
Wholesale and retail Native arts and crafts from the Northwest Territories. Owned by 35 member co-operatives across the North.

NOVA SCOTIA

NOVA SCOTIA—SYDNEY
MICMAC ASSOCIATION OF CULTURAL STUDIES
Box 961
Sydney, Nova Scotia B1P 6J4
(902) 539-8037
The Micmac Association of Cultural Studies is a cultural and educational organization which serves the needs of the Micmac Indian people. Nearly 12,000 Micmac live in Nova Scotia, New Brunswick, Quebec and Prince Edward Island. They are one of the largest and most important Indian nations in eastern North America.

The Association is active in promoting understanding and appreciation of Micmac culture. Executive Director Peter Christmas and his staff have produced excellent publications and assisted other Micmacs with their work. Among these is Micmac poet Rita Joe whose book, "Poems of Rita Joe" will nourish your understanding of contemporary Indian thought. Mr. Christmas' book, "Wejkwapniaq", is a very good introduction to Micmac life. The Association also helped develop programs for young people and others aiding in the advancement of Micmac cultural understanding.

The Mik'maq Theatre group presents historic and cultural performances relating to Micmac heritage.

Recently the Micmac people celebrated the 375th anniversary of their conversion to Christianity with an event called the Membertou Signtasimgeoeim at Port Royal National Historic Site, Port Royal, Nova Scotia. Cultural activities were held at the reconstructed Micmac Cultural Village, phone (902) 532-5197. Grand Chief Membertou, who was baptized in 1610, was honored along with early clergymen.

To this day the Micmac people have a grand chief. Mr. Donald Marshall, Sr., is now Grand Chief of the Micmac Nation and his key objectives are "the promotion of Micmac unity and the concept of Christianity among the Micmac people".

For more information on Micmac cultural activities, contact the Association. Also SEE: PRINCE EDWARD ISLAND—CHARLOTTETOWN for an interesting reconstructed Micmac village and art centre.

ONTARIO

ONTARIO—BRANTFORD and THE GRAND RIVER INDIAN RESERVE OF THE IROQUOIS

For those unfamiliar with the history of this important Eastern Woodlands Indian group, the Six Nations or Iroquois is a confederation of six tribes. Centuries ago, the Cayuga, Mohawk, Oneida, Onondaga, Seneca, and Tuscarora united to become a great Indian republic. So politically sophisticated was, and is, the league that many historians believe that the Founding Fathers of the United States copied some of the Iroquois concepts when creating the American constitution. The original home of the Six Nations of the Iroquois Indian people is New York and Ontario. But during the American Revolution many Iroquois remained loyal to the British. After the American victory under George Washington, loyalist Iroquois settled in Canada. Today many thousands of Iroquois people live near Brantford on the Six Nations' Grand River Indian Reserve. The people represent all six tribes of the Iroquois confederacy but the Mohawk and Cayuga are by far the largest tribes. There are

also several hundred Delaware among an Iroquoian population of about 10,000.

Six Nations is a major center of Eastern Woodlands Indian culture and there is much to see here and in nearby Brantford. Arts and crafts of high quality flourish on the reserve. Unique "false face" masks of wood and "husk face" masks of corn shucks are made. These represent spirits and they have unforgettable, other-world appearances. Traditional "gustoweh", Iroquois men's feathered hats, are also produced and are among the most beautiful of all Native American art. Finger woven sashes, pottery, traditional clothing, soapstone carvings, musical instruments, and much more are made. These are sold at IROQRAFTS, RR 7P, Ohsweken, Ontario, Canada NOA IMO. Phone (416) 765-4206. This is one of North America's best sources of Indian arts and crafts and is owned by Iroquois people. Mail order catalog ($2.00) offers an outstanding selection of Eastern Woodlands Indian products from the Six Nations and other tribes as well. IROQRAFTS is located 2 miles SW of Caledonia, Ontario (near Brantford) off Hwy 6. Open seven days a week from 9 to 6. Be sure to visit the Iroqrafts Store on the Reserve at Ohsweken.

There are also other good Iroquois-owned stores on the Reserve offering Iroquois and other Indian arts and crafts.

Also on the Reserve is CHIEFSWOOD, home of the highly respected Iroquois poet Pauline Johnson. This popular attraction is 13 miles south of Brantford, not far from Iroqrafts. Phone (519) 759-1329.

In nearby Brantford is the ROYAL INDIAN CHAPEL where Joseph Brant is buried. The city of Brantford is named in honor of this great Iroquois leader. The Chapel is on Mohawk St. Many Iroquois are Christians and the MOHAWK CHAPEL is the oldest Protestant Church in Ontario. BRANT COUNTY MUSEUM, 57 Charlotte St, Brantford, displays local Indian artifacts. Phone (517) 752-2483.

For information on Iroquois events and tours of the Reserve, see the Woodland Indian Cultural Centre (next listing). For Iroquois or other Eastern Woodlands Indian places to visit SEE: ONTARIO and NEW YORK listings.

Several "longhouses" are in use as religious centers for those Iroquois who practice the traditional tribal religion. Ancient Iroquois religious ceremonies are still held using false face and husk face masks. These modern-style buildings are closed to the public.

SEE: TRIBAL LISTINGS—IROQUOIS for more information.

Iroquoian longhouses, mortars and pestles, and work areas can be seen inside the palisade wall at Ska-Nah-Doht Indian Village near Mount Brydges, Ontario, Canada. (Ska-Nah-Doht: Lower Thames Valley Conservation Authority)

Interior of a reconstructed Huron longhouse showing the fires used by individual families and dried food hanging from the rafters. People slept on shelf-like bunks along the walls. Sainte-Marie among the Hurons at Midland, Ontario. (Sainte-Marie among the Hurons)

WOODLAND INDIAN CULTURAL EDUCATION CENTRE
184 Mohawk St
Box 1506
Brantford, Ontario N3T 5V6
(519) 759-2650

This major Indian cultural center is located on land owned by the Iroquois of Grand River Reserve. The Centre itself is jointly operated and administered by six Indian bands, including Iroquois, Delaware, and Mississauga people. The Centre preserves Eastern Woodlands Indian cultures in a variety of effective ways.

The MUSEUM tells the story of Woodlands Indians from prehistoric times to the present. There are archeological exhibits of the Middle Woodland Period, wampum displays, carved wood items in a "Spirit of the Woods" display, a full size longhouse interior, birch bark baskets, false face masks, medicine man mural, stone carvings, etc. Exhibits also cover contact with Europeans, cultural maintenance, and the present active longhouse religion. A Canadian Indian Hall of Fame is here, too.

Research material is offered from sociological to archeological data and researchers ranging from graduate students to police officials come here to learn and understand Woodland Indian cultural perspectives.

Other programs include preservation and teaching of Woodlands Indian languages, traveling exhibits (some have gone as far as Japan and Holland), school programs, guided tours (make requests well in advance), teacher education programs, and more. Inquire about TOURS OF THE GRAND RIVER RESERVE.

There are regular changing special exhibits of high quality contemporary North American Indian art, so repeat visits are rewarding. There is an arts and crafts fair and film festival, too.

The annual SIX NATIONS INDIAN PAGEANT held usually in August is a special occasion popular with Six Nations Reserve visitors. This excellent historic pageant tells the story of the Iroquois and includes some traditional Six Nations dancing as well. Seeing Iroquois dancing is a wonderful treat. There is also an annual Grand River Pow-wow and other events. Check with the Centre for dates.

A highlight is the annual SNOWSNAKE TOURNAMENT. Snowsnakes are beautifully finished wooden poles, much like javelins made for this traditional Iroquois game. Long ditches, often up to a mile in length, are dug in the snow and prepared for the tournament. The snowsnakes are hurled along the track and often travel at 75 miles per hour. Players compete for distance and the snowsnakes travel for amazing distances as they speed through the snow. The snowsnake tournament is usually held in late January or early February and is one of the most interesting Native North American sports. Often lasting two days, other events sometimes are held in conjunction with the tournament. Not to be missed.

The Woodland Indian Cultural Centre is one of North America's best and is highly recommended.

ONTARIO—CURVE LAKE INDIAN RESERVE
WHETUNG OJIBWA CRAFT CENTRE & ART GALLERY
Curve Lake Indian Reserve
Curve Lake, Ontario KOL 1RO
(705) 657-3661

Curve Lake Reserve is N of Peterborough, Ontario, via Hwy 28 & 507. Turn left off Hwy 507 between Selwyn and Buckhorn.

This is the home of Mississauga people of the Ojibwa Indian Nation. The Centre is a handsome log building featuring local arts and crafts along with Indian and non-Indian products from across the continent. Quill work, moose hide products, stonework, snowshoes and modern paintings by Native Canadian artists are among the items sold.

A special feature is the Tea Room, open weekends during the summer. Here you can sample Indian corn soup and fry bread along with your tea.

ONTARIO—DELAWARE
SKA-NAH-DOHT INDIAN VILLAGE
Longwoods Road Conservation Area
Hwy 2, SE of Hwy 402; take Mr Brydges/Delaware Interchange exit 86; 25 miles W of London, Ontario
Mailing address: Ska-Nah-Doht Indian Village; Lower Thames Valley Conservation Authority; RR 1, Mount Brydges, Ontario NOL 1WO
(519) 264-2457 or 264-2420

"Ska-Nah-Doht" is from the Oneida Indian language and means "Village Stands Again." This is a descriptive name for an Iroquoian village does in fact stand here again. This is an outstanding reconstruction of a palisaded village of the Glen Meyer culture, of early Iroquoian farmers, gatherers, and hunters. The whole village is accurately represented and is exciting to visit.

You enter through the high palisade wall that encircles the village. Once inside you'll see Iroquois bark covered longhouses, where 40 to 50 people lived. The longhouses alone are reason enough for a visit but there is much more. You'll see distinctive East-

From the earliest explorers to visitors today, everyone has been impressed with the regal appearance of Sac & Fox traditional clothing. Note the hair roaches atop the men's heads, ribbonshirts, and dance garters with bells worn below the knees. These Sac and Fox men's straight dancers present a classic Eastern Woodlands appearance. Stroud, Oklahoma, 1983. (R. Shanks)

From the earliest days Christian clergymen worked among Indian people. A Jesuit priest talks with Indian and non-Indian parishioners as enacted at Sainte-Marie among the Hurons. Sainte-Marie recreates the 17th Century French and Indian life of this settlement. (Sainte-Marie among the Hurons)

A conical Algonquin birch bark wigwam and a Huron longhouse have been reconstructed at the historic Jesuit mission of Saint-Marie among the Hurons at Midland, Ontario. They are good examples of Eastern Woodlands dwellings. The Catholic mission church stands in the background. (Sainte-Marie among the Hurons)

Ojibwa and Algonkin staff members demonstrate Canadian Indian birch bark basketry and pottery making techniques for visitors at Sainte-Marie among the Hurons. Indian and Inuit staff are indispensable to museum programs that interpret Native North American culture and history. (Sainte-Marie among the Hurons)

ern Woodlands mortars and pestles, fish traps, storage huts, stretching racks for drying meat, storage pit granary, sweat bath, and an arts and crafts area. Outside the palisade is a deer run with long fences used to trap deer, an important but rarely seen Indian hunting device. There is also a maple sap works for processing this important Indian food. An agricultural area demonstrates how Indian foods such as corn squash and sunflowers were grown.

A Resource Centre has interpretive exhibits and a slide show to help you understand life in an Iroquois village.

There is picnicking and several log cabins to see and enjoy, too. Ska-Nah-Doht is generally open daily mid-May through August and weekdays year around. It is also open weekends in January and February when snow shoeing and cross-country skiing are in season. Closed holidays. Special events, school programs, group workshops, and guided tours can all be arranged in advance. Highly recommended.

ONTARIO—DESERONTO
MARACLE MOHAWK CENTRE INDIAN GIFT SHOP
TYENDINAGA MOHAWK INDIAN RESERVE
Box 202
Deseronto, Ontario
(613) 396-2431
Located at the Junction of Hwys 2 and 49 near Deseronto. Indian arts and crafts from the Tyendinaga Reserve and 50 other reservations across North America. Mohawk baskets and much more.

ONTARIO—KEENE
SERPENT MOUNDS PROVINCIAL PARK
3 miles S of Keene, Ontario
The park contains interesting Indian mounds dating back 2000 years.

ONTARIO—KENORA
LAKE OF THE WOODS OJIBWA CULTURAL CENTRE
Box 1720
Airport Rd at Rabbit Lake Rd
Kenora, Ontario P9N 3X7
(807) 548-5744
The Cultural Centre is open weekdays and provides a good introduction to Ojibwa culture. Fourteen different reserves participate in the programs at the Centre. The Centre is very active with school programs available locally, programs for the Indian Reserve communities, and research work on Ojibwa and Cree culture and history. Visitors may see display cases exhibiting arts and crafts produced by Indian people working at the Centre. A slide presentation is shown, teaching visitors about Ojibwa arts, crafts, and traditional dancing. Arts and crafts are sold.

A highlight of the year is the Annual Festival held in June at the recreation center in Kenora. People of many ethnic groups have booths offering foods, crafts, and explaining their cultures. The Ojibwa people have their popular booth with demonstrations of arts and crafts. What is done varies from year to year, but you may see moose hair embroidery, beadwork, quill work, birch bark work, looming, etc. The booth also offers traditional dried meat and fish dishes for you to try. Ojibwa dancing is performed including the beautiful jingle dress dancing done by women. Small metal cones sewn to the women's dresses make a pleasing jingling sound as the dancers move gracefully in time to the singing. The men's grass dance is done, along with other excellent dances.

If you visit the Centre itself, you may be lucky enough to see special projects in progress—perhaps moose quill embroidery or birch bark canoe construction.

From June through September there is a pow-wow almost every weekend somewhere in the Lake of the Woods area. The public is welcome and the Cultural Centre can provide information and directions to these events. Two types of pow-wows are held: traditional and contest. You may see the traditional moccasin game being played, an Eastern Woodlands guessing game. There is Ojibwa and Cree dancing and singing and occasionally events involving canoes. If the canoe events are held you'll see expert canoe handlers perform feats of fine canoemanship. Sometimes even logs are carried in the canoe demonstrations. The Islington Indian Band at Whitedog, Ontario, is particularly well known for its canoe events.

Lake of the Woods Cultural Centre provides a good orientation to the area's Indian cultures and an excellent service to both the Indian and non-Indian members of the community.

LAKE OF THE WOODS MUSEUM
Main St
Kenora, Ontario
(807) 468-8865
Displays Eastern Woodlands Indian artifacts.

ONTARIO—LONDON
MUSEUM OF INDIAN ARCHEOLOGY
1600 Attawandaron Rd
London, Ontario
(519) 473-1360
Indian archeological site over 10,000 years old. The

museum has displays and an audio-visual presentation.

ONTARIO—MANITOULIN ISLAND
OJIBWE CULTURAL FOUNDATION
West Bay Indian Reserve
Hwy 540, SW from Little Current
Manitoulin Island, Ontario
(705) 377-4902
The Ojibwa Cultural Foundation maintains a Centre where traditional and contemporary arts and crafts from 14 Indian Reserves are exhibited and sold. Quillwork, birch bark and sweetgrass baskets, pipes, and jewelry can be seen and purchased. Anishnabe (Ojibwa) language materials and posters are available, too. Educational, audio-visual, arts and crafts, and elders programs are offered. The Centre serves both Indian and non-Indian people with its programs. The annual WIKWEMIKONG INDIAN DAYS is a major event usually held around the first of August. The Foundation is to be congratulated in its work of revitalizing Ojibwa culture and promoting cross-cultural appreciation.

ONTARIO—MIDLAND
HURON INDIAN VILLAGE and HURONIA MUSEUM
Little Lake Park
Midland, Ontario
(705) 526-7009
This is a reconstructed Huron Eastern Woodlands Indian village within a traditional log palisade wall. Buildings include a longhouse, a shelter structure, and a medicine man's lodge. Pottery making, fish drying, meat curing, and other Indian activities are demonstrated. HURONIA MUSEUM is located here too, and has exhibits interpreting Huron Indian culture.

SAINTE-MARIE AMONG THE HURONS
Box 160
Hwy 12, 4.75 km E of Midland, Ontario L4R 4K8
(705) 526-7838
Construction of Sainte-Marie among the Hurons began in 1639, and was the central headquarters of the Jesuits' mission to the Huron Indians. After years of struggle, both French and Huron Christians succeeded in creating a community which housed one-fifth of the European population of New France. In addition, many Huron Christians lived here as well.

But European diseases and a disastrous war with the Iroquois crippled the Huron and French efforts to control the region. In 1649 after years of disease, war, and starvation, the French decided to abandon Sainte-Marie. The Jesuits sadly burned the community to the ground and along with their Huron friends eventually retreated to Quebec. Both French and Hu-

ron control of the area had been broken. To this day, Huron Indian people live in Village-des-Hurons, Loretteville, Quebec. They are the descendants of those who fled Sainte-Marie with the Jesuits long ago.

For centuries Sainte-Marie remained an archeological ruin until excavations and reconstruction finally began. Today Sainte-Marie is reconstructed and again provides an authentic mixture of 17th Century French and Indian cultures. Over two dozen buildings now stand and may be toured. Of special interest is a HURON LONGHOUSE and an ALGONKIN BARK CONICAL WIGWAM, both excellent reconstructions of traditional Eastern Woodlands homes typical of the area. The longhouse interior is nicely done with cooking fires, shelf-like sleeping platforms, food hanging from rafters, baskets, and more. Ojibwa and Algonkin staff members serve as guides for the Indian portion of your tour and often demonstrate pottery-making, birch bark basketry, and tell of Eastern Woodlands Indian traditions. The presence of Indian people on the staff adds an entirely new dimension to the experience of visiting Sainte-Marie and will make your visit even more worthwhile. The Georgian Bay Tribal Council has helped fund part of the Indian staff and both they and the Sainte-Marie administrators are to be congratulated.

A special event of interest is SHONDECTI, usually held in July. Ojibwa, Algonquin, Huron and other Native Canadian Indian people join together to share their rich traditions and cultures. This is an outstanding annual event.

Various special programs are offered, including classes for young and old in Woodlands Indian culture and archeology. Some of these are taught by Indian teachers. Contact Sainte-Marie for information and dates of these and other programs.

In September 1984, Pope John Paul II visited Sainte-Marie among the Hurons and was especially pleased to meet the Indian staff members. This is fitting for Sainte-Marie not only commemorates the trials of the French in Canada, but of the ordeal many Indian people suffered to be Christians.

SEE: QUEBEC—VILLAGE DES HURONS

ONTARIO—OTTAWA
INDIAN AND NORTHERN AFFAIRS
Government of Canada
Ottawa, Ontario
(819) 997-0380 publications
(613) 994-2822 office
The Indian and Northern Affairs Department administers services to Indian and Inuit people throughout Canada in a somewhat similar fashion to the US Bu-

The Micmac Association of Cultural Studies actively pursues understanding and appreciation of Micmac culture and history. A young Micmac stands watch as a scout during a portrayal of a historical event in eastern Canada. (Micmac Assoc. of Cultural Studies—Peter Christmas)

reau of Indian Affairs. Indian and Northern Affairs is usually very helpful. They have excellent publications available. Their magazine, INUIT ART AND CRAFTS provides fascinating, up to date coverage of Eskimo arts. Write for information: Inuit Art Section, Dept of Indian & Northern Affairs, Les Terrasses de la Chaudiere, Room 921, Ottawa, Ontario KIA OH4. Besides fine publications, Indian and Northern Affairs also has a library with a knowledgeable staff.

INUIT TAPIRASAT OF CANADA
176 Gloucester St, 3rd floor
Ottawa, Ontario K2P OA6
(613) 238-8181
This organization is a major force working for improved social and political conditions for Inuit people.

NATIONAL INDIAN ARTS & CRAFTS CORPORATION
604—141 Laurier W, Suite 604
Ottawa, Ontario K1P 5J3
(613) 232-2436
Helps promote and coordinate Canadian Indian and Eskimo arts and crafts. Excellent source of information. Has provincial corporations with offices across Canada. Also assists Native craftspeople with training, marketing information, grants, etc.

NATIONAL MUSEUM OF MAN
Victoria Museum Building
McLeod & Metcalfe St
Ottawa, Ontario
(613) 992-3497
Ottawa has a number of interesting museums. The National Museum of Man contains fine collections of Canadian Indian and Eskimo materials. Check also for special programs and exhibits.

ONTARIO—PETROGLYPHS PROVINCIAL PARK
NE of Lakefield, Ontario via Hwy 28 & 6
Algonkian Indian Rock Art approximately 1000 years old is found here.

ONTARIO—ST. REGIS INDIAN RESERVE
THE NORTH AMERICAN INDIAN TRAVELING COLLEGE, THE LIVING MUSEUM and WOODLANDS INDIAN VILLAGE
RR 3, Cornwall Island
Cornwall, Ontario K6H 5R7
(613) 932-9452 or 932-9445
Iroquois and other Indian people have joined together to create this important Eastern Woodlands cultural and education center. During summers you may visit the Indian village, from May through September and see traditional bark longhouses and other structures important to Woodlands culture.

The village is part of the NORTH AMERICAN INDIAN TRAVELING COLLEGE whose staff and elders are Cree, Ojibwa, and Iroquois. The College promotes appreciation and understanding of native heritage and culture.

The North American Indian Traveling College has a Travel Troupe of Woodlands Indian singers, dancers, speakers, and technicians who bring their unique culture and dance to audiences in the US and Canada. They may be contacted for dates and locations of performances. Booking arrangements and other information are available from the College. You will appreciate the magnificent traditionally beaded leggings and skirts with old time Woodlands designs.

The College has a library and media center with books, films and slides on Eastern Woodlands Indian cultures. Tours can be arranged in advance. The College is normally closed weekends, but often special weekend events are held that you may attend. Contact them for special programs and events.

A highlight of the year is AKWESASNE FRIENDSHIP DAY, usually the second weekend in July. Traditional Iroquois dances are done along with explanations of their significance and meaning. Besides the dances, there is also an Iroquois fashion show, baby clothing fashions, canoe racing, and arts and crafts sales. Phone for date and time.

Workshops and classes are held at this cultural center generally from January through March and include gus-to-weh making (the traditional Iroquois man's headdress), quilting, traditional Iroquois clothing, beading, and dugout canoe making.

Cornwall Island is located in the St. Lawrence River on the US-Canadian border between Cornwall, Ontario and Hogansburg, New York. Take the bridge across the river and turn just north of the Canadian customs facility. Go east along the road over two hills and then turn right to the Woodlands Indian village and the North American Traveling College. The College can also be contacted by mail at the address above or at Box 273, Hogansburg, New York 13655.

Two important Mohawk reservations are also in the area. St. Regis Reservation is at Hogansburg, NY, and St. Regis Reserve is here on Cornwall Island and adjacent lands in Canada. The two reservations actually border one another, separated by the Canadian—US boundary. Other Mohawk Reserves are Caughnawaga and Oka Reserves in Quebec and Gibson, and Tyendinga Reserve in Ontario.

Rita Joe, a Micmac from eastern Canada, is a poet and author of the acclaimed book, "Poetry of Rita Joe" (Abanaki Press). She writes so others may understand the rights of Indian people to dignity and quality education. (Micmac Association of Cultural Studies—Peter Christmas)

Iroquois lacrosse sticks made by Mohawk craftsman Matthew Etienne of Oka Reserve, West Oka, Quebec. Mr. Etienne's lacrosse sticks are used by several professional teams in the US and Canada. (Assoc. for the Advancement of Native North American Arts and Crafts)

Distinguished Onondaga artist Arnold Jacobs of Six Nations Reserve in Ontario, Canada. Many North American Indian artists rank among the most acclaimed painters in the world. (Assoc. for the Advancement of Native North American Arts and Crafts)

ONTARIO—SERPENT RIVER INDIAN RESERVE
SERPENT RIVER TRADING POST
Trans-Canada Hwy (Local Hwy 17)
Located midway between Sault Sainte Marie and Sudbury
Serpent River Indian Reserve, Ontario P0P 1B0
(705) 844-2864
The Serpent River Trading Post is Indian owned and operated. It carries a good selection of local Ojibwa arts and crafts plus the work of other tribes such as the Mohawk, Cree, and Micmac. Extended summer hours.

ONTARIO—THUNDER BAY
NATIONAL EXHIBIT CENTRE FOR INDIAN ART
Confederation College campus
Keewatin & Red Lake St
Thunder Bay, Ontario
(807) 577-6427
Contemporary and traditional Indian art in a wide range of media is exhibited. Check for special programs and events.

THUNDER BAY MUSEUM
219 S May St
Thunder Bay, Ontario
(807) 623-0801
Among the collections are Indian art exhibits. Thunder Bay is in Ojibwa Indian country.

ONTARIO—TIMMINS
OJIBWA AND CREE CULTURAL CENTRE
59—79 Third Ave
Timmins, Ontario
(705) 267-7911
The Centre serves 40 Indian communities locally plus Cree students from James Bay. A variety of services are provided for Indian people in the area. Among the programs are an Ojibwa-Cree media production program, educational program development for schools, a resource center, and a library.

PRINCE EDWARD ISLAND

PRINCE EDWARD ISLAND—CHARLOTTETOWN
MICMAC INDIAN VILLAGE
12 km W of Charlottetown, Prince Edward Island
(902) 675-3800 summer, 675-2971 winter
Reconstructed Eastern Woodlands Indian village of the Algonquian speaking Micmac tribe. Craft shop and visitor center.

QUEBEC

QUEBEC—CHICOUTIMI
MUSEUM OF THE SAGUENAY-LAC ST. JEAN
534 Rue Jacques Cartier
Chicoutimi, Quebec
(418) 545-9400
Eastern Woodlands Indian and Eskimo artifacts are displayed.

QUEBEC—KAHNAWAKE
SHRINE OF KATERI TEKAKWITHA
Saint-Francois Xavier Mission
Kahnawake Indian Reserve, Quebec
(514) 632-6030, call for directions to the mission
This famous Iroquois Indian woman has been beatified by the Catholic Church as a major step toward sainthood. Tours of the shrine and mission may be arranged. This is a Mohawk reserve.

QUEBEC—ODANAK
ABENAKIS MUSEUM
Abenaki Indian Reserve
Odanak, Quebec
(514) 568-2600, 568-2822 after 5
The Abenaki Indian people own this museum which interprets their history and culture. This Algonquian-speaking tribe once owned nearly all of Vermont and New Hampshire as well as a large area of southern Quebec. The community of Odanak (Saint Francis) is an Abenaki town resembling other nearby non-Indian villages. However, the Abenaki people still retain much of their rich culture and occasional performances of both social and ceremonial dances are presented. This is a chance for New Englanders and Canadians to meet the descendants of the first families of the region. Check with the museum for dates of Abenaki dances. The museum is generally open May 1 to September 10. SEE: TRIBAL LISTINGS—ABENAKI.

QUEBEC—OKA INDIAN RESERVE
KANESATAKE INDIAN ARTS & CRAFTS
113 Rue St—Jean Baptiste
Oka, Quebec J0N 1E0
(514) 479-8530 or 479-6555
The Mohawk Indian people offer a wide variety of woven, beaded, and leather arts and crafts along with Mohawk splint baskets, birch bark baskets and much more.

QUEBEC—VILLAGE DES HURON
THE INDIAN CRAFTSMEN & ARTISTS OF QUEBEC
540 Max-Gros Louis St
Village des Hurons, Quebec GOA 4VO
(418) 845-2150

Founded in 1974, the Corporation of Indian Craftsmen and Artists of Quebec has as its objective to maintain the production of authentic arts and crafts of the nine Indian bands of Quebec. These nine are the Abenaki, Algonquin, Attikamek, Cree, Micmac, Montagnais, Naskapi, Huron, and Mohawk. Their products include many fine items including Huron canoes, Micmac and Abenaki ash splint baskets, Huron pottery, Montagnais and Attikamek birch bark baskets, moccasins made by the Montagnais, Huron, Algonquin, Naskapi, Cree, Abenaki and Mohawk. Snowshoes of white birch and caribou hide made by the Montagnais are offered as well as Huron snowshoes of ashwood and cowhide. Dresses, jewelry, and much more are offered. Etched birch bark baskets are beautiful and Cree tamarack duck decoys are fascinating. Mail order.

SASKATCHEWAN

SASKATCHEWAN—BATOCHE
BATTLEFIELD NATIONAL HISTORIC SITE
32 km W of Domremy, Saskatchewan
(306) 423-6100

There were many marriages between French voyageurs (traveling woodsmen and fur traders) and Indian women during the adventurous days of the fur trade. The mixed French and Indian children soon formed a distinct cultural group in Canada called the Metis. The Metis people led a good life hunting, trapping, and farming until settlers began taking their land and game, thus threatening Metis survival. Finally, pushed to the limit in 1885, the Metis rebelled under the leadership of Louis Riel. War broke out after all requests for land rights had long been ignored by the English government, which ruled Canada at the time. The Metis' goal was to create an independent nation for themselves in western Canada. The Metis, however, were no match for the military power of Great Britain and were ultimately defeated. Batoche Battlefield National Historic Site preserves the site of Riel's major defeat. Here you will find a museum with displays, historical artifacts, and a Metis cemetery. Many Metis survive today and continue to work to achieve a rightful position in Canadian society.

SASKATCHEWAN—REGINA
PLAINS HISTORICAL MUSEUM
1801 Scarth St
Regina, Saskatchewan
(306) 352-0844

The museum contains exhibits on the culture of the Metis and their leader Louis Riel. Also Plains Indian exhibits on display.

SASKATCHEWAN INDIAN FEDERATED COLLEGE
127 College West Bldg
University of Regina
Wascana Parkway
Regina, Saskatchewan S4S OA2
(306) 584-8333

This is the only Indian operated, degree granting college in Canada. The Saskatchewan Indian Federated College is open to both Indian and non-Indian students and offers degrees in Indian Studies as well as other academic subjects. Students attend from across Canada and from other countries, too. Very worthwhile course studies are offered.

Each March the annual CULTURAL WEEK is held. The event features interesting speakers on contemporary Indian issues, a pow-wow, and arts and crafts sales. Check with the college for exact dates.

YUKON

YUKON—KLUANE
KLUANE MUSEUM OF NATURAL HISTORY
Km Post 1769 Alaska Hwy
Burwash Landing, Yukon

Among the collections are Indian arts and crafts. Craft shop.

YUKON—WHITEHORSE
NORTHERN IMAGES ARTS AND CRAFTS STORE
Canadian Arctic Co-operative Federation
311 Jarvis St at 4th Ave
Whitehorse, Yukon
(403) 668-5739

Eskimo (Inuit) and Indian arts and crafts co-operative offering fine work from the Far North. Carvings, sculpture, ivory and bone jewelry, garments of native animal skins, prints from Cape Dorset, Baker Lake, Holman, and Pangnirtung. Owned and operated by the Native people of Canada. Extended hours during the summer months.

YUKON NATIVE PRODUCTS
4230 4th Ave
Whitehorse, Yukon Y1A 1K1
(403) 668-5935
Specializing in Athabaskan and Tlingit Indian arts and craft items with high quality moccasins, parkas, mukluks, mitts, porcupine quill and beaded jewelry, and much more. Traditional Indian tanning on most products. Indian owned. Mail order ($1.00 for catalog).

SKOOKUM JIM FRIENDSHIP CENTRE
3159—3rd Ave
Whitehorse, Yukon
(403) 668-4465
The Friendship Centre offers various special events during the summer months. The biggest event is YUKON INDIAN DAYS, which features excellent attractions such as the Teslin Tlingit dancers with their traditional carved or woven head gear, button blankets, and other colorful Tlingit clothing. Arts and crafts are sold, and local Native craftspeople and artists are represented. Check with the Centre or Visitor Bureau for dates.

The Centre, incidentally, is named in honor of Skookum Jim, who first discovered gold in the famed Klondike gold rush. Two of the three men who originally discovered gold were Tagish Indians. Many of the ill prepared white men who later rushed to the Klondike strike had their lives saved by local Indian people on Chilkoot Pass and elsewhere. Many Tagish people are active in the Centre's programs.

THE MACBRIDE MUSEUM
First Ave between Steele & Wood St
Box 4037
Whitehorse, Yukon
Located along the Yukon River, the museum has a special section on Indian artifacts.

Model Margaret MacKenzie, a Dene', presents a lovely picture in her Dene' caribou hide dress with floral designs. She holds a birch bark basket, yet another product of Canadian Indian artists. (Dept. of Information, Govt. of Northwest Territories—Tessa Macintosh)

Two proud Cayuga brothers hold their father's lacrosse sticks made for this traditional Iroquois game. Their father, Alex N Jameson, is a fine craftsman in Ontario. (Association for Advancement of Native North American Arts & Crafts)

TRIBAL LISTINGS

The word "tribe" refers to any organized Native North American people. Many tribes use the terms nation, pueblo, band, rancheria, village, or colony to refer to themselves. We have tried to use the term preferred by each group. In Canada, Indian reservations are called reserves. Tribes are often called "bands" and tribal offices are termed "band offices." The TRIBAL LISTINGS section provides a great deal of additional information for our readers. It is cross indexed with the geographical section. Phone numbers are those of tribal offices. These do change from time to time, so you would be wise to check with directory assistance.

ABENAKI
The Abenaki once owned much of New England and are an important Eastern Woodlands tribe. The Abenaki today live primarily in Quebec, mostly on the Odanak (Pierreville) Reserve. Some arts and crafts are still made and traditional dances are occasionally performed. These dances include Abenaki dances, Iroquois eagle dance and women's blanket dance, Huron knife dance, Mesquakie pipe dance and others. SEE: QUEBEC—ODANAK. (Penobscot in Maine are considered to be eastern Abenaki by some authorities. SEE: PENOBSCOT.)

AHTNA
SEE: ALASKA—GLENNALLEN. Also see DENE. The tribally owned corporation Ahtna, Inc. may be contacted at Drawer G, Copper Center, AK 99573. Phone (907) 822-3476 or 822-3486.

ALABAMA (Alibamu)
The state of Alabama is named in honor of this tribe. Today most Alabamas live in Texas and the tribe operates extensive visitor attractions at their reservation in the scenic Big Thicket Wildlife Area. For the Texas branch of the tribe SEE: TEXAS—LIVINGSTON.

Other Alabamas live in Oklahoma among the Creek Nation. The Alabama-Quassarte tribal town is their main community and may be contacted through the Muscogee, OK, office of the Bureau of Indian Affairs.

ALGONKIN
The Algonkin people live primarily in Quebec on the Barriere Lake, Grand Lac Victoria, Lac Simon, and River Desert Reserves. They still make high quality birch bark canoes and other arts and crafts as well. SEE: ONTARIO—BRANTFORD and QUEBEC—VILLAGE DE HURONS. The Algonkin have given their name to the Algonquian language group which includes tribes from Nova Scotia to California.

ALEUT
The Aleut are the native people of Alaska's Aleutian Islands and the nearby mainland. Nearly 2000 Aleuts live on the islands and even larger numbers have migrated to mainland Alaska. Anchorage has a particularly large Aleut community. SEE: ALASKA—PRIBILOFF ISLANDS.

APACHE
There are several major groups of Apache people in Arizona, New Mexico, and Oklahoma. The most important annual events are girl's coming of age rites. These include colorful and moving rituals often with mountain spirit dancing (also called Crown dances). Apache events feature distinctive music and some of the most impressive costumes of all American Indians.

MESCALERO APACHE RESERVATION
Mescalero, NM
(505) 257-5141 or 671-4495
Gahan Ceremonial with girl's rites and mountain spirit dancing over Fourth of July weekend. SEE: NEW MEXICO—MESCALERO

JICARILLA APACHE RESERVATION
Dulce, NM
(505) 759-3242 or 759-3362
Tribal holiday around September 14 and 15 annually. Girls' rites, bear dances, and ceremonial races held periodically. SEE: NEW MEXICO—DULCE

WHITE MOUNTAIN APACHE RESERVATION
Whiteriver, AZ
(602) 338-4346
Apache Tribal Fair is usually held Labor Day weekend and has mountain spirit dancing. Girls' puberty rites and other dances are held most weekends during July and August. Check for events open to the public. SEE: ARIZONA—WHITE MOUNTAIN APACHE INDIAN RESERVATION.

White Mountain Apache high school students usually dance during the Malki Museum Fiesta in California on Memorial Day weekend. SEE: CALIFORNIA—MORONGO INDIAN RESERVATION.

SAN CARLOS APACHE RESERVATION
San Carlos, AZ
(602) 475-2361
During summer weekends girls' rites and mountain spirit dances are held. Check with the tribal tourism office for public events. The tribal fair is usually held over Veterans Day weekend and generally includes traditional dancing.

CAMP VERDE APACHE, (602) 567-5276 at Camp Verde, AZ, and the TONTO APACHE at Payson, AZ,

(602) 474-5000, have recently joined together to present some beautiful public dance performances in Flagstaff, AZ, during Fourth of July at the Coconino Center for the Arts. SEE: ARIZONA—CAMP VERDE

FORT SILL APACHE holds a festival in Apache, OK, in September and also appear at the Anadarko American Indian
Exposition, OK. Tribal office phone number is (405) 247-9493. SEE: OKLAHOMA—ANADARKO

ARAPAHOE
Wind River Indian Reservation
Arapahoe, WY
(307) 255-8265
Wyoming Arapahoe hold their sacred sun dance annually in July. Over Labor Day there is usually a celebration in Ethete, WY, on the Wind River Reservation. Check with the Arapahoe Tribal Office for details.

Southern Arapahoe today live in Oklahoma. They hold their Veterans Day pow-wow in Geary, OK, generally over Labor Day. Southern Arapahoe share a tribal office with the Cheyenne in Concho, OK, (405) 262-6332. SEE: WYOMING—WIND RIVER and OKLAHOMA—ANADARKO.

ARIKARA
SEE: HIDATSA

ASSINIBOIN (Stoney)
There is a Stoney Encampment held on the Stoney Reserve in Alberta in August. The Red Bottom Assiniboin pow-wow is held in August at Frazer, Montana. The Fort Peck (Assiniboin and Sioux) Tribal Office in Poplar, Montana should also know of other Assiniboin pow-wows. Phone (406) 768-5155.

ATHABASKAN
The name Athabaskan refers to both a group of languages and to subarctic tribes of the Yukon, Northwest Territories, and interior Alaska. These tribes of the Far North refer to themselves as Dene'. SEE: DENE'.

ATSUGEWI
The Atsugewi live largely along Hat Creek between Burney and Lassen National Park in California. SEE: CALIFORNIA—LASSEN.

AZTEC
There are several dance groups from this famed Mexican tribe that perform at various events in the United States. Aztec dancing features traditional costumes with the classic tropical bird feathers characteristic of their culture. Men carry a round shield

covered with beautiful featherwork. These dancers often wear rattles around their ankles, adding a pleasing traditional sound to the vibrant music.

Aztec dancers perform all over the US. They have appeared at the Malki Museum Fiesta (SEE: CALIFORNIA—MORONGO), Stand Rock Ceremonials (SEE: WISCONSIN—WISCONSIN DELLS), the Indian Pueblo Cultural Center (SEE: NEW MEXICO—ALBUQUERQUE), and at many other celebrations.

BLACKFEET
Blackfeet Indian Reservation
Browning, MT
(406) 338-7522 or 423-2544
The Blackfeet Tribal Council hosts North American Indian Days annually during July in Browning, MT. The celebration is held at the Blackfeet Tribal Fairgrounds, adjacent to the Museum of the Plains Indian. There are four days of traditional dancing, an encampment with many tepees, Indian handgames, parades, and more. This is one of the largest Native American events and draws people from tribes in both Canada and the US. Check with the Blackfeet Tribal Office or Museum for exact dates. SEE: MONTANA—BROWNING.

Reminders of the early traditional life of the Blackfeet and other Montana Indians can be seen at three unusual places. ULM PISHKIN STATE MONUMENT (12 miles W of Great Falls near Ulm, MT) preserves a Buffalo Jump where Plains warriors stampeded buffalo over a cliff for harvest. There is a self guided trail. MADISON BUFFALO JUMP STATE MONUMENT is south of Logan, MT, seven miles S of Hwy I-90 via a gravel road. Displays vividly show the technique of stampeding buffalo over a cliff. MEDICINE LAKE NATIONAL WILDLIFE REFUGE, (406) 789-2305, three miles SE of Medicine Lake, MT, includes the TEPEE HILLS NATURAL AREA. You can see many TEPEE RINGS, circles of rocks that once helped hold tepee covers down. The tepee rings preserved here date back many years.

CADDO
Caddo Tribal Office Center
Binger Y
Binger, OK
(405) 656-2344
Caddo music is among the most beautiful in Native America. The Caddo people have done an outstanding job of preserving their music and dance and know hundreds of songs. In late Spring the summer's schedule of dances is determined. The season begins in mid-June and usually runs through September. Three days of dancing occur over Labor Day, and occasional weekend dances occur on Friday and Saturday. Caddo people also participate in the American

Indian Exposition in Anadarko annually. SEE: OKLA-HOMA—ANADARKO.

Dancing usually begins about four in the afternoon with turkey dances, a dance done only during daylight hours. Around six there is a break for a meal; then the evening continues with social stomp dancing. The dancing may continue late into the night as the Caddo enjoy the music. (Canyon Records has two excellent records on Caddo music, SEE: ARIZONA—PHOENIX.)

Dances are held east of the modern tribal office building that stands on a wooded hill. The Caddo women wear lovely long dresses and beautiful hair ornaments with long flowing ribbons. Men often wear distinctive handsome Caddo ribbonshirts. Courteous, quiet, and respectful visitors may attend the Caddo dances by prior arrangement with the Caddo Tribal Office.

CAHTO (Kato)
The Cahto live on a reservation just west of Laytonville, California. Tribal office phone is (707) 984-6197.

CAHUILLA
The Cahuilla annually sponsor the Malki Museum Fiesta on the Morongo Indian Reservation near Banning, California. Held over Memorial Day, there is dancing, food, arts and crafts, peon hand games, and more. SEE: CALIFORNIA—MORONGO.

The Malki Museum Press publishes a fine selection of California Indian books. Write for their list: 11-795 Fields Road, Morongo Indian Reservation, Banning, CA 92220.

CATAWBA

The Catawba live in the vicinity of Rock Hill, South Carolina. The Catawba continue to make pottery, an art they have long been known for. Their mailing address is: Route 3, Box 324, Rock Hill, SC 29730.

CAYUGA
SEE: IROQUOIS

CAYUSE
SEE: UMATILLA

CHEHALIS
The Chehalis have an annual Tribal Day celebration, usually in late May on their reservation near Chehalis, Washington. Phone (205) 273-5911 for information.

CHEMEHUEVI
The Chemehuevi have recently taken steps to develop the recreational potential of their reservation on the Colorado River in California. Financing has been secured with the goal of developing recreational facilities across the river from Lake Havasu City, Arizona. Their goal is to allow Chemehuevi people to move back onto their desert reservation. Phone (714) 858-4531.

CHEROKEE
The Cherokee people have done an impressive job of presenting their culture to the public. Both the western Cherokee (SEE: OKLAHOMA—TAHLEQUAH) and the eastern Cherokee (SEE: NORTH CAROLINA—CHEROKEE) operate high quality, extensive facilities of interest to all visitors.

The Cherokee National Holiday is celebrated in Tahlequah, Oklahoma, usually in early September and offers an especially fine opportunity to participate in Cherokee culture. The Cherokee Fall Festival is usually held in Jay, Oklahoma around October.

An outstanding place to see traditional Cherokee stomp dancing is the Red Bird Smith ceremonial grounds near Vian, Oklahoma. Stomp dances are held here each August 17th, honoring the birthday of this great Cherokee traditional leader. (The two Cherokee cultural centers occasionally have traditional Cherokee stomp dancing, too.)

The Eastern Cherokee usually hold their annual fair in late September or early October. This fair includes traditional stickball games and offers Cherokee food for sale. SEE: NORTH CAROLINA—CHEROKEE.

CHEYENNE
Northern Cheyenne live in Montana today. A pow-wow is usually held in July, often with stickgames. SEE: MONTANA—LAME DEER and CUSTER BATTLEFIELD.

Southern Cheyenne live in western Oklahoma. They participate in the American Indian Exposition each year. SEE: OKLAHOMA—ANADARKO. The southern Cheyenne share a tribal office with the southern Arapahoe. SEE: ARAPAHOE. Also SEE: OKLAHOMA—CHEYENNE.

CHICKAHOMINY
The Chickahominy sponsor an annual fall festival with dancing, speeches, and other activities. The tribe's mailing address is: Chickahominy Indian Tribe, RFD 1, Box 226, Providence Forge, VA 23140. The state of Virginia serves Virginia Indian reservations, not the federal government which is common in most states.

The Seneca-Cayuga Tribal Office in Miami, Oklahoma, features wampum belt figures along the upper walls. (R. Shanks)

Many Indian tribes have architecturally exciting tribal office buildings. The Creek Nation in Okmulgee, Oklahoma, has an extensive complex, including the Independent Agencies building shown here. This striking auditorium is in the shape of a mound and earthlodge built by the Creek in Georgia 1000 years ago. The chiefs of the Five Civilized Tribes often meet here. (Creek Nation—Gary Robinson)

The Chumash Tribal Office at Santa Ynez, California, opts for contemporary California ranch-style architecture. (R. Shanks)

The Pomo people of the Elem Rancheria on the shores of Clear Lake in central California have a new tribal office. It features basketry designs along the roof tops that resemble the communal tule houses of old. (L. Shanks)

CHICKASAW

For the Chickasaw Nation SEE: OKLAHOMA—ADA, SULPHUR, and TUSKAHOMA for details.

CHINOOK

The Chinook people live in both Washington and Oregon today. There is a Chinook Tribal Office in Ilwaco, Washington, phone (206) 777-8303. They sponsor salmon bakes during special occasions and are actively working toward full Federal recognition of the tribe. Other Chinook live on Shoalwater Bay Reservation at Tokeland, Washington. (207) 267-6766.

CHIPPEWA

SEE: OJIBWA

CHITIMACHA

The Chitimacha have long been known for their fine baskets made of cane. Chitimacha people live around Charenton, Louisiana, and maintain a tribal office there. Phone (318) 923-4973.

CHOCTAW

Today the Choctaw live primarily in Oklahoma and Mississippi. For the Oklahoma Choctaw SEE: OKLAHOMA—DURANT and TUSKAHOMA. The Mississippi Choctaw sponsor an annual fair with stickball games and many other traditional activities. This is a colorful and interesting event. For the Mississippi Choctaw SEE: MISSISSIPPI—CHOCTAW INDIAN RESERVATION.

COSTANOAN

SEE: OHLONE

CHUMASH

The Chumash live primarily in Santa Barbara County, California. They have a modern reservation at Santa Ynez with a new tribal office building, a thriving bingo enterprise, and many nice, new homes. There is also a popular campground on the reservation. Phone the tribal office at (805) 688-7997 for details.

The Santa Ynez Dolphin dancers have revived some Chumash dances, including the impressive crane dance. Recently, Chumash men sailed one of their plank canoes (a unique Chumash type) along the Santa Barbara Channel, a tremendous feat on the open ocean. The Coastal Band of Chumash have been making efforts to organize in the Santa Barbara area.

A major Chumash activity has been the struggle to preserve sacred Point Conception in Santa Barbara County. This is one of the most sacred Native American sites in California. From Pt. Conception the souls of the dead traditionally depart on their journey to the Chumash spirit world. The Point is rich in early California and maritime history as well. It is hoped that the Chumash and their friends will be successful in preserving this important place. Another major concern has been ending the desecration of Indian burials both on the mainland and the Channel Islands.

The Chumash descendants today probably number in the thousands; one estimate is as high as 8000 survivors. Despite missionization and a terrible toll from early diseases, the Chumash people survive and are growing strong again. SEE: CALIFORNIA—SANTA BARBARA and CHANNEL ISLANDS.

COAST MIWOK

The Coast Miwok are the Indians of Marin and southern Sonoma counties in California. They are a branch of the Sierra Miwok of interior California. The Coast Miwok were taken to Mission San Rafael (SEE: CALIFORNIA—MISSIONS) where diseases devastated the Indians. Surviving Coast Miwok generally married into the Pomo tribes in Sonoma County or into some Anglo ranching families in Marin County. Coast Miwok people still live in the area today. Some Coast Miwok songs survive among the Kashaya Pomo and a reconstructed village has been built (SEE: CALIFORNIA—POINT REYES).

COAST SALISH

Many Coast Salish tribes sponsor special public events. Some Coast Salish tribes are also involved in the Spirit Dancing religion. Spirit Dancing is not intended to be a public event, although if you have friends who are active you may be invited. See Pamela Amoss' excellent book, "Coast Salish Spirit Dancing" for detailed information on this major Northwest Coast religion.

It is hoped that more Coast Salish people will follow the lead of the Lummi, Suquamish, Songhees and others in sponsoring annual events to share their rich cultures with all of us. SEE: LUMMI, SUQUAMISH, and SONGHEES. Also SEE: WASHINGTON—OLYMPIA.

COCOPAH

SEE: ARIZONA—SOMERTON

COEUR D'ALENE

The Coeur d'Alene hold three annual pow-wows in northern Idaho. The tribal office number in Plummer, Idaho, is (208) 274-3101.

COLVILLE

A number of different Plateau area tribes live on Washington's Colville reservation. They sponsor Indian Fairs, pow-wows, horse events and other activities during the late spring, summer, and fall. There is a tepee encampment with dancing, stick games, and more at Omak, Washington, usually in August during Stampede Days. Many tepees are pitched here and make an impressive sight. The Omak Chamber of Commerce can provide information and dates. Phone (509) 826-1880.

COMANCHE

The Comanche live in the vicinity of Lawton, Cache, and Apache, Oklahoma. The Comanche people hold frequent pow-wows during the year. The annual Comanche Homecoming Pow-wow is held in Sultan Park, Walters, OK, during July. This event originally celebrated the return of the Comanche warriors and its highlight is the Black Crow Society's dances. These are spectacular traditional Comanche dances. Another unique Comanche tradition are the Little Pony Society dances held around April at Apache Park in Apache, OK. Medicine men's dances are done at this time and the Little Pony Society's dances are also very impressive.

For exact dates of these and other dances check with the Comanche Tribal Office in Lawton, phone (405) 248-7724.

Although there is no Comanche Tribal Museum at present the tribe hopes to establish one.

COOS

SEE: OREGON—COOS BAY

COUSHATTA (Koasati or Quassarte)

The Coushatta live today in Texas, Oklahoma, and Louisiana. In Texas and Oklahoma they are closely associated with the Alabama. SEE: tribal listing—ALABAMA. Also SEE: TEXAS—LIVINGSTON for the visitor facility they operate.

COW CREEK BAND OF UMPQUA

SEE: UMPQUA

COWICHAN

The Nanaimo Cowichan in British Columbia sometimes sponsor races using fine dugout canoes at Nanaimo. The Songhees from Victoria and the Lummi from Washington state often compete in these events. A salmon bake is often held, too. There are other events sponsored by Cowichan bands that local Indian Centers will know about. The Cowichan weave beautiful hand spun wool sweaters for sale.

CREE

Cree groups participate and sponsor many pow-wows and other celebrations across central Canada. Among them is the Ermineskin Pow-wow at Hobbena, Alberta. Phone (403) 420-0008 for the band office. The MASKWACHEES CULTURAL COLLEGE in Hobbena, has a living history video program, library, and classes, phone (403) 585-3925. For the James Bay Cree Indian Days Committee (Box 374, Moose Factory, Ontario POL 1WO), phone (705) 658-4518. A good source of information on Cree and Ojibwa events is the Lake of the Woods Cultural Centre, SEE: ONTARIO—KENORA and TIMMINS; MANITOBA—WINNIPEG; and MONTANA—BOX ELDER.

CREEK (Muscogee)

The Creek Nation is organized into approximately 19 towns. Many of these towns still carefully maintain traditional Creek religion. The Creek ceremonial season runs from about May until September. It opens with weekend stomp dances. Some Creek people may spend their weekends camping at the town's ceremonial grounds. Many families have a camp with a small cooking shed, arranged about the grounds much as thatched roof houses were in ancient times. These serve as a social center and cooking place and many pleasant moments are spent here. Dancing usually begins late at night, often between 10 pm and 1 am and then continues until dawn. Creek people dance all night and the stomp dancing continues until sunrise. After some weeks of stomp dancing on weekends, Green Corn Ceremonial approaches. Its exact date is determined by lunar calculations and varies each year.

At Green Corn there are daytime sacred dances and nighttime social stomp dances. The ceremonial grounds of each town is arranged in a rectangle with three or four arbors around the edge where designated people sit. At the center of the ground is the sacred fire which the stomp dancing revolves around, sometimes in complicated and beautiful patterns. During Green Corn there is fasting, ceremonial drinking of the sacred drink and ritual scratching—all for purification and health. Green Corn is the peak of Southeastern Indian religious ceremonies and is deeply meaningful and special to the people. During the Green Corn ceremonies the beautiful women's ribbon dance is performed along with the impressive men's feather dance. In the ribbon dance the Creek women wear lovely ribbon dresses and hair trailers. During the feather dance, men carry long cane poles with white feathers attached and dance in careful patterns. After these and other rites are completed, a feast is enjoyed and the healing and healthful benefits of Green Corn are completed. The prayers of the people are for the benefit of all.

These stomp dances and Green Corn ceremonies are conducted by many towns and policies on visitors vary. Many of the best welcome visitors, but prior arrangement should be made for a visit either through Creek friends or by contacting the Communication Department of the Creek Nation.

Stomp dancing by Creek and other Southeastern Indian people is sometimes done after Plains Indian dancing concludes nightly at eastern Oklahoma pow-wows. Yuchi and Seminole ceremonial seasons follow the above description closely, although the Yuchi also have an Arbor Dance the week before Green Corn.

Other Creeks are Christians and attend "Indian Church". These are Christian churches where services are conducted in the Creek's Muscogee language. Visitors are normally welcomed to these services as at any other Christian church.

Some Creek people attend both traditional Creek ceremonies and Christian services. The traditional ceremonies date back to the days of the mound builders and are meaningful and moving. The Creek Indian Churches also have a long history and sacred services, too. If you are fortunate enough to attend either or both, you'll be impressed with the sincerity and character of the Creek people.

Today the Creek are also one of the leaders among North American Indian tribes in their medical, dental, communications, educational and other programs. Some programs once administered by the federal government are now very effectively run by the Creek Nation. A good way to keep up with Creek activities as well as national Native American news is to subscribe to the MUSCOGEE NATION NEWS, a monthly publication of the Muscogee (Creek) Nation. Phone (918) 756-8700 or write Box 580, Okmulgee, OK 74447. For more Creek events and information SEE: OKLAHOMA—OKMULGEE.

CROW

The Crow live in Montana, their land surrounding the site of Custer's defeat at the Battle of the Little Bighorn (SEE: MONTANA—CUSTER BATTLEFIELD). In fact, the Visitor Center of Custer Battlefield is a good place to buy traditional Crow arts and crafts.

Each year the Crow Indian people sponsor one of the largest and most popular Native American events on the northern Plains. This is the Crow Fair and it draws thousands of Indian and non-Indian people. There is an impressive tepee encampment, traditional dancing, Indian foods, arts and crafts sales, and more. You'll see Crow dancers with their distinctive flattened hair roach headpieces, a fine looking unique Crow style. Other tribes join the Crow for dancing and many people, both Indian and non-Indian, camp during the celebration. Crow Fair is generally held in August at Crow Agency, Montana. Check with the Crow Tribal Office for details, phone (406) 638-2671.

CUPEÑO
SEE: CALIFORNIA—PALA

DELAWARE (Lenni Lenape)

The original homeland of the Delaware includes New York City and much of New Jersey, Delaware, and western Pennsylvania. Today some Delaware people still live in their traditional homeland. (SEE: PENNSYLVANIA—ALLENTOWN for the Lenni Lenape Historical Society.) But most now live in Ontario, Oklahoma, and Wisconsin.

In Canada, some Delaware live on the Six Nations Reserve (SEE: ONTARIO—BRANTFORD) while others live at Moravian of the Thames Indian Reserve, Thamesville, Ontario. The annual Moravian Pow-wow is held in the Moravian Ball Park usually in early September. Band office phone number is (519) 692-3936.

Oklahoma has two major Delaware groups. One lives around Copan, Oklahoma, and sponsors an annual Delaware Pow-wow in late May or early June. The Western Delaware live at Anadarko, Oklahoma and participate in Indian celebrations nearby, phone (405) 247-2448. SEE: OKLAHOMA—ANADARKO. A tribal museum is being developed.

Wisconsin Delaware live among the Stockbridge and go by the name Munsee. Munsee and Unami are the two principal language groups of the Delaware people. For Wisconsin Delaware, SEE: WISCONSIN—STOCKBRIDGE-MUNSEE INDIAN RESERVATION.

DENE'

As we use the name here, Dene' refers to the Athabaskan speaking tribes of Northwest Territories, the Yukon, and interior Alaska such as the Slavey, Ahtna, Dogrib, Kutchin, Tanana, Tanaina, Tutchone, Kaska, Han and others.

The DENE' NATION organization has its headquarters in Yellowknife, and works for the political and social progress of the Dene' people. The Dene' Nation may be reached at Box 2338, Yellowknife, NWT X1A 2P7, Canada. Phone (403) 873-4081.

Doyon Limited, a native owned corporation manages the business affairs of many Alaskan Dene' people. Doyon Limited's address is: 201 First Ave, Fairbanks, AK 99791.

For Dene' bands and their activities see listings in NORTHWEST TERRITORIES, YUKON, and ALASKA.

DIEGUEÑO
SEE: TIPAI-IPAI

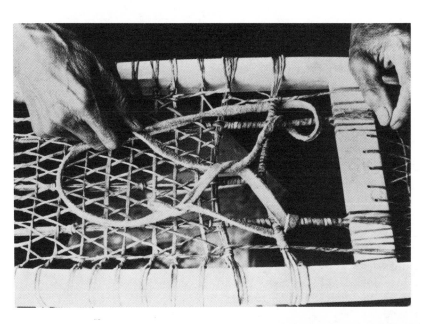

Snowshoes are indispensable in the Far North. Craftsman Johnny Neyelle, a Dene', works at Fort Franklin, Northwest Territories. (Dept. of Information, Govt. of Northwest Territories—Tessa Macintosh)

Johnny Neyelle weaves the finishing touches on a traditional Indian snowshoe. These high quality products are popular with Indians and non-Indians alike. (Dept. of Information, Govt. of Northwest Territories— Tessa Macintosh)

DOGRIB
SEE: NORTHWEST TERRITORIES—RAE-EDZO. Also SEE: DENE'.

ESKIMO (Inuit)
Many Eskimo people prefer the name "Inuit" when referring to themselves. Inuit people today live all across the Far North—from Siberia, across Alaska and Canada to Greenland. They are becoming increasingly important politically and economically in decision making processes regarding the future of the Arctic.

The life of the Inuit has changed greatly and visitors will see more snowmobiles than dog sleds. The Inuit are managing the all important skill of retaining what is good of their traditional culture while learning what is useful from the non-Eskimo. The Inuit people operate many businesses and Eskimo owned hotels, stores, and many other enterprises are now found across the North. You can also see fascinating traditional games, competitions, dance and music, kayaks, and ancient hunting and fishing skills. Arts and crafts of the highest quality are still made and can be purchased in many places.

SEE: NORTHWEST TERRITORIES, ALASKA, and YUKON. Also SEE: GREENLANDER this section.

FLATHEAD
Each Fourth of July weekend the Confederated Salish and Kootenai tribes of the Flathead Reservation sponsor their ARLEE POW-WOW. Held in Arlee, Montana, the pow-wow is famed for its high quality stick games. The traditional Indian guessing games involves soft, beautiful singing, guessing, and much fun. Teams sit facing one another along two parallel logs. Sticks are tapped on the logs in time to the singing. One team holds a pair of bones, one marked and the other plain. The opponents try to guess in which hand the white bone is held. If they guess correctly, they obtain possession of the bones. If they guess wrong, the other team gains a counting stick. Each counting stick is worth one point. The first team to win all the counters wins the game. Often the teams are evenly matched and the lead goes back and forth from one team to another. A particularly good game might go on all night. Eventually, one team gains possession of all the counters and wins. I can sit and listen to the gentle music for hours, watching the handling of the bones and the careful guesswork.

Stick games are common at pow-wows, particularly in the Plateau and Great Basin areas. But groups such as the Pawnee of Oklahoma and the Miwok of California still play the game, too. In various parts of the country, stick games are also called hand games, grass games, or peon.

But back to the Flathead. The Arlee Pow-wow also has Salish and Kootenai dancing and singing, arts and crafts sales, a rodeo, carnival, and rock music. You'll probably see tepees pitched right beside new RV's. This is a popular, well established pow-wow and it draws Indian and non-Indian people from both Canada and the US. For more information, contact the Confederated Salish and Kootenai Tribe in Pablo, MT at (406) 675-2700.

Also on the Flathead Reservation is the Flathead Indian Museum, in St. Ignatius, MT. The museum is also an arts and crafts supply store catering to Indian artisans over a wide area. Phone (406) 675-2700. Mail order. Periodic auctions sponsored.

FOX
SEE: MESQUAKIE

GABRIELIÑO
The original people of Los Angeles, CA. SEE: CALIFORNIA—ARCADIA and MISSIONS.

GRAND RONDE, CONFEDERATED TRIBES OF
The Grand Ronde Indian Reservation was terminated by the federal government in 1954. Termination of federal responsibility meant land loss, loss of services, and human suffering to the Oregon coastal tribes of Grand Ronde. The Grand Ronde Confederated tribes reorganized in 1974 and are working as a non-profit organization. Solar energy projects, arts and crafts enterprises and the like are being researched as possible endeavors. Many different tribes live on Grand Ronde and the neighboring Siletz reservation. These groups include the Kalapuya, Tillamook, Alsea, Takelma, Molala, Siletz, Tututni, Yaquina, and others. SEE: SILETZ.

GROS VENTRE
The Gros Ventre are also known as the Hidatsa. SEE: HIDATSA.

GREENLANDER (Inuit or Eskimo)
This is the name of the Eskimo people of Greenland, although "Inuit" is also used. For those interested in Greenlander culture and activities, write the Inuit Institute or the Government of Greenland at Godthab. Greenland is the only predominately Eskimo country in the world and is now fairly autonomous from Denmark, having achieved Home Rule on May 1, 1979. Incidentally, about six thousand Greenlanders have migrated to Copenhagen, Denmark. SEE: KANSAS—LAWRENCE.

HAIDA
SEE: BRITISH COLUMBIA—QUEEN CHARLOTTE ISLANDS, ALASKA—PRINCE OF WALES ISLAND and KETCHIKAN.

HALIWA-SAPONI

Haliwa-Saponi Tribal Pottery and Arts (Box 99, Hollister, NC 27844) is located on Hwy 561, twenty miles west of Hollister. Call for hours, (919) 586-4017. Pottery, quilts, beadwork, and stonework are offered. Mail order.

HAVASUPAI

The Havasupai live on a spectacular reservation in the bottom of the Grand Canyon The Havasupai hold an annual Peach Festival, usually in August. Dances are often held over Memorial Day weekend, too. SEE: ARIZONA—GRAND CANYON.

HIDATSA

Today the Hidatsa share North Dakota's Fort Berthold Reservation with the Arikara and Mandan. Known as the Three Affiliated Tribes, they have a fine museum and many interesting cultural activities. SEE: NORTH DAKOTA—FORT BERTHOLD INDIAN RESERVATION.

HOH

The Hoh live near the mouth of the Hoh River in Washington's Olympic Peninsula. Some of the Hoh participate in motorized canoe races using traditional type canoes (but with high powered engines added) to race along the rivers of the Olympic Peninsula. It is a highly skilled, risky sport as competitors speed past boulders and snags. The Hoh often race at Chief Taholah Days against the Quinault and Quileute. SEE: WASHINGTON—QUINAULT INDIAN RESERVATION and OLYMPIA.

HOPI

The Hopi are very traditional and deeply religious people, yet at the same time many are well educated, widely traveled, and very knowledgeable. Visiting these friendly, dignified Native Americans in their villages atop high desert mesas is a real thrill. There are dances many weekends during the summer, including the famous Snake Dance in August. You'll find a cultural center, a very good motel, restaurant, and shops all atop Second Mesa. SEE: ARIZONA—HOPI INDIAN RESERVATION.

HOUMA

The Houma have lost most of their culture but are working hard to better the lives of their people. The Houma Nation office is: Star Route, Box 95-A, Golden Meadow, Louisiana 70357. There is a Houma Indian Crafts Co-op based in Dulac, LA.

HUALAPAI (Walapai)

The center of the Hualapai Reservation is at the tribal administration center in Peach Springs, Arizona. There is usually a Hualapai pow-wow in August.

Sometimes Hualapai bird dancers appear at celebrations in Flagstaff, AZ, and elsewhere. Watching the Hualapai women dance is very impressive as they are exceptionally graceful dancers and seem to float as they move forward, then backwards during bird songs. SEE: ARIZONA—PEACH SPRINGS and FLAGSTAFF.

HUPA

Northwestern California's Hupa Indian people proudly continue many traditional activities on their reservation in Humboldt County. There is a fine tribal museum and periodic traditional dances such as the White Deerskin Dance, brush dance, and jump dance. SEE: CALIFORNIA—HOOPA INDIAN RESERVATION.

HURON

The Huron operate major canoe, snow shoe and other production facilities at their reserve in Quebec. SEE: QUEBEC—VILLAGE DES HURONS. SEE: ONTARIO—MIDLAND for a restored Huron village, museum, and cultural activities at both Sainte-Marie among the Hurons and at the Huronia Museum. Also SEE: WYANDOT.

The Huron address in Quebec is: Bande Indienne de la Nation Heronne-Wendat. 145 rue Chef Aime' Romain, Village des Hurons, Quebec GOA 4VO. Phone (418) 843-3767.

ILLINOIS (Peoria)

Today the Illinois call themselves the Peoria and live in northeastern Oklahoma. The Peoria Tribe Office is: Box 939, Miami, OK 74354, phone (918) 540-2535. Peoria Indian people are very much a part of the American mainstream life, but the tribe participates in and helps sponsor Indian Heritage Days in Miami, OK, which is usually held in June. SEE: OKLAHOMA—MIAMI. Some individual Peorias participate in local stomp dances, such as those that occur after Plains-style dancing ends late at night at the Quapaw Pow-wow. SEE: QUAPAW.

INUIT

SEE: ESKIMO and GREENLANDER

IOWA

The Iowa live today primarily in two locations. Some Iowa people live in Oklahoma. The Tribal Council's address is: Box 190, Perkins, OK 74059. Phone (405) 547-2402. Other Iowas live on a reservation on the Kansas-Nebraska border, which they share with the Sac & Fox. Although no separate Iowa tribal office is listed, the Sac & Fox Tribal office at Reserve, Kansas, is on the same reservation. Their number is (913) 742-7471. The Iowa participate in the Ameri-

One of the most widespread Indian games is called the handgame, stickgame, or grassgame. Teams face one another from behind small logs. A team holds a pair of bones or sticks, one of them marked. The opposing team must guess in which hand the marked bone is held. The team holding the bones sings gentle, beautiful songs. The singing is accompanied by rhythmically beating sticks on the logs in time to the music. This is a Miwok team from California playing a Paiute team from Nevada and eastern California shown on the opposite page. The woman in the center holds the bones in her left hand. (R. Shanks)

In a scene that could have taken place centuries ago, the Coastal Pomo Dancers of Point Arena, California, warm up before entering the dance area. Lead dancer is David Smith. (R. Shanks)

The leader of the Paiute team serves as the "pointer" and guesses which hand the marked bone is held in by his Miwok opponents. Teams compete to win a set of counting sticks—once a team has won all the sticks, the game is concluded. Games may go on all night and there are interesting variations in rules, music, and styles from one tribe to another. Handgames are fascinating to watch and offer beautiful music to listen to. Chaw-se Big Time Celebration, Pine Grove, California. (R. Shanks)

The joy of being a California Indian is evident in the faces of these Pomo dancers performing a social dance. Point Arena Coastal Pomo Dancers at Pt. Reyes National Seashore, 1982. (R. Shanks)

can Indian Exposition, SEE: OKLAHOMA—ANADARKO.

IROQUOIS

The Iroquois, or Six Nations, comprise of the Cayuga, Mohawk, Oneida, Onondaga, Seneca, and Tuscarora tribes.

These six nations joined together centuries ago to form what became the most powerful Indian confederation in the Eastern Woodlands. Their well organized republic was much admired by the founding fathers of the United States and some historians believe the US constitution was partly modeled after the Six Nations. Through the centuries, the Iroquois have maintained their political structure, arts and crafts, religion, dances and songs, and more. At the same time they have produced many outstanding individuals who have made significant achievements in the larger society of present day North America.

Originally from New York state, today the Iroquois live in New York, Wisconsin, Oklahoma, Ontario, and Quebec. All of these areas have fine artists and craftspeople and interesting special events. In addition, there are reconstructed villages, culture centers, and museums devoted to Iroquoian culture.

There are many listings in this book relating to the Iroquois and their events. SEE: NEW YORK—AUBURN, BASON, BUFFALO, FONDA, HOGANSBURG, IRVING, ONCHIOTA, SALAMANCA, SCHOHARIE, and NEDROW; WISCONSIN—ONEIDA; OKLAHOMA—MIAMI; ONTARIO—BRANTFORD, DELAWARE, DESERONTO, MIDLAND, and ST. REGIS; QUEBEC—KAHNAWAKE, OKA, and VILLAGE DES HURONS.

In addition, the annual Green Corn religious ceremony is held at many reservations. At some reservations, the public is allowed to attend these important ceremonies. The Seneca-Cayuga in Miami, OK, hold their Green Corn ceremony in July or August. Green Corn is a sacred ceremony and not for show, but the Seneca-Cayuga generally allow respectful guests. Phone (918) 542-6609. The Tuscarora Nation at Lewiston, NY, holds an annual fair, usually in August. Phone (716) 297-2053.

KARUK

The Karuk have very beautiful traditional ceremonies which they continue to hold along the Klamath River at Katamin, near Somes Bar, California. Odd numbered years have more events than do even numbered years as the ceremonial calendar is on a two year cycle. There are brush dances, jump dances, and white deerskin dances. These are sacred events but usually courteous visitors are welcome. Check with the Karuk Tribal Office in Happy Camp, California,

for information, (916) 493-5305. "Indian cards" is sometimes played (no cards are used), a traditional guessing game unique to Northwestern California. Occasionally Karuk groups also do public performances at colleges or Indian celebrations in northern California.

KALISPEL

The Kalispel or Pend d'Oreille have a Tribal Office and reservation near Usk, north of Spokane, Washington. There is an annual pow-wow here. Phone (509) 445-1147.

KAW (KANSAS)

The Kaw, or Kansas, now live in Oklahoma. Their tribal office address is: Box 78, Kaw City, OK 74641. Phone (405) 269-2552.

KICKAPOO

The Kickapoo are organized in three bands and vary greatly from one to another in their attitude toward outsiders. The southernmost branch now lives in Eagle Pass, Texas, and generally excludes outsiders, even other Indians. The Oklahoma Kickapoo have no public ceremonies, although some participate in other tribes' public events. The Kansas Kickapoo, however, graciously sponsor a public pow-wow on their reservation. SEE: KANSAS—HORTON and TEXAS—EAGLE PASS.

KIOWA

The Kiowa are prominent at many pow-wows in Oklahoma and even some in California. Many Kiowa still live in their western Oklahoma homeland, around Carnegie and Anadarko. The Kiowa Tribe has its Kiowa Tribal Museum (SEE: OKLAHOMA—CARNEGIE) which is a must for anyone interested in Kiowa culture and history. They also sponsor special events that are located at the tribal complex. There are many Kiowa dances during the year including some at the tribal complex. Check with the museum or tribal office for specific events and dates. The Kiowa Tribal Museum and Office number is (405) 654-2300.

KLAMATH

Under strong pressure from certain government and commercial interests, the large Klamath Indian Reservation in Oregon was broken up and sold off in 1954. Although tribal members received cash payments, the long term results were catastrophic. The tribe's land base was gone and government health and education benefits lost. Death and alcoholism rates soared, and a sense of tribal membership was lost. This dismal experience was the result of the Termination Act which aimed to curtail government social programs and legal responsibilities to Indian people. The Menominee in Wisconsin, Siletz and Grand Ronde of Oregon, Catawba of South Carolina, and numerous tribes in northern California and eastern Oklahoma suffered as well from the vicious Termination Act.

No one seems to have been hurt more than the Klamath, Modoc and Paiute people who make up the Klamath Tribe. According to the Klamath Tribe's report, during the period from 1966-1980, some 28% of the tribe died before reaching the age of 25, and over half were dead by age 40. Nearly half of all these deaths were due to alcohol or were alcohol related.

But many Klamaths refused to give up. They began fighting to restore the tribe and rebuild a future for their young. Gorden Bettles, a Community Services Liaison and a Klamath, began a program aimed at reducing juvenile delinquency at the old reservation town of Chiloquin. Since he began his work, delinquency rates have fallen 35 percent. Other Klamaths, lead by Marie Norris, formed the Organization for the Forgotten American to provide human services for those left destitute by the Termination Act. Francis Harjo, a Creek, and other dedicated workers at the office of the Klamath Tribe in Chiloquin are struggling to get Klamath Tribe restored to full Federal recognition by Congressional Act. The Menominee and others have already achieved this admirable goal and the Klamath can use the support of others sympathetic to this goal. The eloquent tribal publication, "Klamath Tribune" (Fall-Winter, 1985), explains the issue in detail. SEE: OREGON—CHILOQUIN.

KOOTENAY
The Kootenay hold an annual summer pow-wow at Fort Steele Heritage Park near Cranbrook, British Columbia, on Hwy 93/95. Contact the park for dates at (604) 489-3351. There is also a museum at the park with some Kootenay material displayed. Also SEE: FLATHEAD.

KUTCHIN (Loucheux)
The Kutchin or Loucheux live in northern Yukon and Northwest Territories today. Many traditional activities are continued by the Loucheux in their Far North homeland. SEE: YUKON and NORTHWEST TERRITORIES. Also SEE: DENE'.

KWAKIUTL
SEE: BRITISH COLUMBIA—QUADRA ISLAND and ALERT BAY.

LUISEÑO
Some years the Rincon Luiseño of Valley Center, San Diego County, California sponsor a fiesta with fes-

tivities and peon games, a southern California style of hand game. Tribal Hall phone number is (619) 749-1051. The Rincon Tribal Education Center is also located here and is a good resource for those interested in Luiseño culture.

LUMBEE
SEE: NORTH CAROLINA—ROBESON COUNTY

LUMMI
SEE: WASHINGTON—LUMMI INDIAN RESERVATION

MAIDU
The Maidu people of California's Sierra Nevada Mountains still do their outstanding traditional bear dance, both at Janesville and near Greenville. The Susanville Tribal Office often has information on these events, usually held in early June. Phone (916) 257-6264.

There is also a Maidu Dance Group under the leadership of two Native American Studies instructors from California State University, Sacramento. This fine group's members are Maidu, Wintun and Pomo and they do traditional Maidu dancing and singing at Indian Grinding Rock State Park's Chaw-se Big Time and other events. The Maidu Dancers may be contacted through the University's Native American Studies program. SEE: CALIFORNIA—PINE GROVE.

MAKAH
SEE: WASHINGTON—NEAH BAY

MALISEET
The Maliseet of New Brunswick are very closely related to the neighboring Passamaquoddy tribe of Maine. Traditional dancing is occasionally done at Tobique and Kingsclear, New Brunswick. Ash basketry is produced for sale, and various other cultural activities continue. An impressive Passamaquoddy-Maliseet Bilingual Program works to preserve the culture and educate the young. SEE: MAINE—PASSAMAQUODDY INDIAN RESERVATION.

MENOMINEE
SEE: WISCONSIN—MENOMINEE

MAHICAN
Most Mahican now live in Wisconsin on the Stockbridge-Munsee Reservation with the Delaware. The Mahican now prefer the name Stockbridge. SEE: WISCONSIN—STOCKBRIDGE-MUNSEE.

MANDAN
SEE: NORTH DAKOTA listings.

MARICOPA

Most Maricopa live with the Pima today in Arizona. The Maricopa are famed for their magnificent pottery.SEE: ARIZONA—SACATON.

MATTAPONI

SEE: VIRGINIA—MATTAPONI.

MESQUAKIE (FOX)

During the second weekend in August, from Thursday through Sunday, the Mesquakie people host an annual pow-wow. A traditional Mesquakie village is built for the occasion with wigwams and tepees. On the reservation near Tama, Iowa, you'll see some excellent Eastern Woodlands floral beadwork costumes and traditional men's hair roaches. High quality arts and crafts are produced and some are offered for sale. The Mesquakie are also called the Fox (of the Sac & Fox), but prefer to be known as Mesquakie. For more information, call the Tribal Office at (515) 484-4678.

METIS

The Metis are the mixed European and Indian descendants of early fur traders and their wives. They are an important ethnic group in Canada with a rich and interesting heritage. The METIS NATIONAL COUNCIL is located at 5-501 45th Street W. in Saskatoon, Saskatchewan. Phone (306) 933-3055.

MIAMI

The Miami live in Oklahoma and Indiana. They often get together during the Quapaw pow-wow and help sponsor Indian Heritage Days, both in Miami, OK. An excellent senior citizens project under Miami leadership has helped restore traditional crafts in the area. The Miami Office is in Anadarko, OK, phone (918) 542-1445. SEE: OKLAHOMA—MIAMI.

MICCOSUKEE

The Miccosukee are closely related to the Seminole in Florida. They retain much of their traditional life style and operate an excellent tourist center which draws people from all over the world. SEE: FLORIDA—MICCOSUKEE INDIAN VILLAGE.

MICMAC

One of the most important tribes of the Northeast. Over 12,000 Micmac live in Canada's maritime provinces and in Boston, MA. SEE: NOVA SCOTIA and PRINCE EDWARD ISLAND.

MISSION

This is a term applied to several tribes in coastal southern California, including the Diegueño (Ipai-Tipai), Luiseño, Cahuilla, Juaneño, Gabrieliño, and Cupeño. Most have reservations in San Diego County and adjoining counties. Incidentally, rather than using the term tribal office for their administration buildings, many southern California tribes prefer the term "tribal hall". The BIA office in Sacramento has a "Tribal Information Directory" which gives the addresses of California Indian Reservations, phone (916) 484-4682. The BIA's Palm Springs Office may be reached at (619) 325-2086. Also see individual listings for most of the tribes mentioned above. SEE: CALIFORNIA listings.

MIWOK

Miwok (MEE-wok) elder Bill Franklin and his family and friends have done an outstanding job of bringing Miwok culture to countless Indian and non-Indian people. This fine dance group does traditional Miwok dancing, complete with flicker feather orange and black headbands. Mr. Franklin's group dances at Chaw-se Big Time in late September and occasionally at such other locations such as the California State Indian Museum (SEE: CALIFORNIA—SACRAMENTO).

A major Miwok sponsored event is Chaw-we Big Time at Indian Grinding Rock State Park. (SEE: CALIFORNIA—INDIAN GRINDING ROCK).

The MI-WUK INDIAN ACORN FESTIVAL is held annually at Tuolumne Indian Rancheria (Reservation) near Tuolumne, California. Usually held in September it is a good opportunity to sample authentic California Indian foods such as acorn bread and acorn soup, two favorites. Miwok and Plains Indian dancing are both done during the festival. Call the Tuolumne Tribal Office for dates and details. Phone (209) 928-4277 or 928-4265.

MISSOURI

The Missouri have merged with the Otoe. SEE: OTOE—MISSOURI.

MODOC

SEE: OREGON—CHILOQUIN and FORT KLAMATH; CALIFORNIA—LAVA BEDS; and OKLAHOMA—MIAMI. Also SEE: Klamath.

MOHAWK

SEE: IROQUOIS

MOJAVE

The Mojave live along the California-Arizona border. Some live on the Fort Mojave reservation near Needles while others live on the Colorado River reservation at Parker, AZ. SEE: ARIZONA—COLORADO RIVER.

MONACHE (Western or Sierra Mono)

SEE: CALIFORNIA—NORTH FORK

MONTAGNAIS

The Montagnais live in Quebec on reserves administered under the Pointe Bleue, Bersimis, and Seven Islands agencies of Canada's Indian and Northern Affairs Department. The Montagnais are noted for fine moose hide moccasins, oval snow shoes, and other arts and crafts. The Naskapee have largely merged with the Montagnais today. SEE: QUEBEC listings.

NANTICOKE

The Nanticoke Indian Association's address is: Route 4, Box 170B, Millsboro, DE 19966.

NARRAGANSETT

Annually in August the Narragansett and other Algonquin people gather at Charlestown, Rhode Island, for an annual meeting and pow-wow. *Eagle Wing Press* is an Indian newspaper covering Indian events in New England and elsewhere. A subscription will help keep you up to date on this region's Indian activities. Their address is Box 579, Naugatuck, CT 06770.

NATCHEZ

Surviving Natchez are inter-married with the Creek and Cherokee in Oklahoma and participate in their ceremonies.

NAVAJO

The Navajo Nation and its many points of interest are discussed under ARIZONA—NAVAJO INDIAN RESERVATION. However, a major issue of the mid-1980's should be mentioned. For some years there has been a dispute between some Hopi and Navajo groups over legal rights to a portion of shared Navajo-Hopi land called the Joint Use Area. This is a large area, comprising of 3000 square miles. In 1974 Congress passed public law 93-531 which divided the joint use area and called for the removal of thousands of Navajo from Hopi portions of the land and a lesser number of Hopi from portions assigned to the Navajo.

This may have sounded reasonable at the time, but the actual implementation of the program has resulted in an enormous and tragic disruption of the lives of thousands of traditional Navajo people. Many have been removed to off reservation sites where it is impossible to live a traditional lifestyle. Opponents of relocation have charged that energy companies have been a major force behind the removal with an eye for usurping Indian mineral and energy resources. The land is reported to be rich in coal and uranium. What is clear is that the forced removal of Navajo traditional people is creating a heavy toll in human hardship. The Big Mountain Legal Defense/Offense Committee is working to repeal public law 93-531 and to divert appropriate removal funds to meet the needs of those already hurt by the removal program. For more information the Committee may be reached at 124 N San Francisco, Suite B, Flagstaff, AZ 86001.

NEZ PERCE

SEE: IDAHO—LAPWAI

NIPMUK

The Nipmuck Tribal Council of Massachusetts has its headquarters on the Hassanamico Indian Reservation in Grafton, MA. SEE: MASSACHUSETTS.

NOOTKA

Distinctive and dramatically impressive, Nootka music and dance is a real pleasure to listen to and see. The Canadian Department of Indian and Northern Affairs should have information on performances. There is a need in British Columbia to encourage regular public presentations of the unique classical music of Nootka Indian people.

OHLONE (Costanoan)

The Ohlone were the original inhabitants of most of San Francisco Bay south to Monterey Bay. Missionized at an early date, most of Ohlone culture has been lost until recently. A new interest in Ohlone culture has surfaced and villages have been reconstructed, and old crafts taught once again. The United Ohlone Cultural Association has been working to revive cultural activities and to protect historic burials from disturbance.

Ohlone basketry was among the finest in the world. They made tightly woven coiled baskets decorated with oval-shaped olivella shell beads arranged in downward pointing triangles. Tiny red feathers were sewn in to complement the beads. Another basket, a scoop-shaped winnower called a walexin (wahl-uh-HEEN) was the most complex and subtly woven of all Native American baskets. Perhaps someone will revive the weaving of these two basket types. SEE: CALIFORNIA—CARMEL, FREMONT, SUNOL and MISSIONS (Mission San Jose has an Ohlone priest on the staff).

OJIBWA

There are many excellent opportunities to attend Ojibwa cultural events. The Ojibwa, also known as the Chippewa, live in both Canada and the US, centering around Wisconsin, Minnesota and Ontario. There are 160,000 Ojibwa making them the second largest Indian tribe in the US and Canada. Wild rice harvesting, drum dances, moccasin games, birch bark basketry, moose hair tufting, Catlinite pipe-making, and many other Ojibwa traditions continue today.

Some of the Ojibwa bands own and operate impressive, efficient businesses. In reading the activities of

A Minnesota Ojibwa business, the Che-Wa-Ka-E-Gon Shopping Center on the Leech Lake Reservation. (Minnesota Chippewa Tribe—Betty Blue)

The Potawatomi of Shawnee, Oklahoma, operate a modern convenience store as one of their business enterprises. (Citizen Band of Potawatomi Tribe—Pat Sulcer)

the various Ojibwa reservations listed here you'll be impressed with the economic progress being made, especially in Minnesota. The Ojibwa have produced high quality Indian leadership, well run tribal offices, effective reservation business committees, and increased job opportunities.

At the same time, the Ojibwa work carefully to preserve their traditional culture, language, and arts and crafts. Every reservation and reserve we contacted had some traditional Ojibwa event of value to both the Ojibwa people and the interested public.

In Minnesota, six of the seven largest Ojibwa bands are members of the Minnesota Chippewa Tribe. Their address is: Box 217, Cass Lake, MN 56633. Phone (218) 335-2252. The tribe publishes, OURSELVES, an informative newspaper covering the six member reservations. They also have a good selection of publications for sale. Many of these books are aimed at elementary and middle school age youngsters, but some are of interest to people of all ages.

Like the Navajo, the Ojibwa have both a population and land base that exceeds some member countries of the United Nations. The Navajo are perceived as much larger because they live primarily on a single reservation in the Southwest. The Ojibwa, on the other hand, live in two countries and occupy dozens of reserves and reservations from the Great Lakes to Montana. The Ojibwa economic, political, and cultural potential rivals that of the Navajo. The combined population of the two tribes is over one-third of a million people. They are truly nations.

Incidentally, we have used the term "Ojibwa" rather than the better known "Chippewa" because many Ojibwa people told us they prefer it. SEE: MINNESOTA—FOND DU LAC, DULUTH, GRAND PORTAGE, MILLE LACS, BOIS FORT, PIPESTONE, and WHITE EARTH; WISCONSIN—BAYFIELD, HAYWARD, LAC DU FLAMBEAU, and ODANAH. There are also North Dakota and Montana Ojibwa reservations, too. You may also want to contact the Red Lake Ojibwa at Red Lake, MN. Phone (218) 679-3341.

For Canadian Ojibwa activities, SEE: ONTARIO—KANORA, TIMMINS, CURVE LAKE, SERPENT RIVER, and MANITOULIN.

OMAHA
The Omaha have a reservation in northeastern Nebraska. SEE: NEBRASKA—BANCROFT.

ONEIDA
SEE: IROQUOIS

ONONDAGA
SEE: IROQUOIS

OSAGE
The Osage have a number of celebrations in northeastern Oklahoma. Among them are the Osage Ceremonial Dances in Hominy in June, the Osage Tribal Ceremonial Dances in Pawhuska also held in June, and the Kiehkah Steh Club Pow-wow in Skiatook in August. SEE: OKLAHOMA—PAWHUSKA.

OTO-MISSOURIA
The Oto and Missouri people are so closely related that they share an office in Red Rock, Oklahoma, phone (405) 723-4334. They co-sponsor an annual pow-wow at the tribal grounds at Red Rock, usually in July.

OTTAWA
Today the Ottawa live from Canada to Oklahoma. There is a large annual Ottawa Pow-wow in August which brings to a close the summer pow-wow season around Miami, OK. The Oklahoma Ottawa office is in Miami. Phone (918) 540-1536 for information on the pow-wow held annually near Quapaw. The most traditional Ottawa communities are those around Wikwemikong, Manitoulin Island, Ontario where pow-wows are held annually in August. SEE: ONTARIO—MANITOULIN.

PAIPAI
The Paipai live in the mountains of northern Baja California, Mexico. Some still live in traditional jacales, reed houses once common from here north into southern California. A donation to the town headman may be requested of visitors.

PAIUTE
The Paiute people of the Great Basin sponsor a number of interesting events annually. Many are held in western Nevada around Schurz, Reno, Sparks, or Fallon. The *Native Nevadan*, an outstanding Indian news magazine lists most of these events. (To subscribe write: 98 Colony Road, Reno, NV 89502, phone (702) 329-2936.) Besides dancing, the Paiute (together with Shoshone and Washo people) usually include hand games at their events. These are ancient guessing games accompanied by very beautiful songs. A rodeo and crafts sales often are held simultaneously.

Particularly well known is Fallon Days which has an excellent parade, and you may see a young girl in traditional sagebrush clothing, a man in a bear skin robe, or a mother with her child in a beautiful Paiute cradle. This is a big event. The Fallon Chamber of Commerce can provide information and dates, phone (702) 423-2544.

The Walker River Paiute tribe annually sponsors its Pinenut Festival at Schurz in October with circle dancing, eating of delicious pinenuts, hand games, a barbecue and other events. Phone the tribal office at (702) 773-2306 for dates. Check the *Native Nevadan* for other events, including the annual Sparks pow-wow held in late summer. SEE: NEVADA listings.

PAMUNKEY

Once a part of the Powhattan Confederacy of Pocahontas fame, the Pamunkey live in Virginia. Virginia Indian reservations are administered by the state of Virginia, not by the federal government. SEE: VIRGINIA listings.

PAPAGO (Tohono O'Odham)

The Papago have a graceful and interesting traditional dance called the skipping or scraping dance. In Papago, it's the chelkona. It is one of the most distinctive and beautiful North American Indian dances with young women in flowing white dresses and young men in white shirts and pants. Most participants hold clouds, sea gulls, and other symbols above their heads as they dance. It is usually performed at the Malki Museum Fiesta at Morongo Indian Reservation. SEE: CALIFORNIA—MORONGO. In Arizona, contact the Papago Tribal Office in Sells, for information on performances, phone (602) 383-2221.

The Papago also participate in the O'ODHAM TASH Indian celebration at Casagrande, Arizona, in February. This is an opportunity to see "taka", traditional Indian field hockey, played by Papago and Paiute teams. Chicken Scratch dancing, a modern type dance enjoyed by the Papago, is done here, too. You'll see two days of dancing, a rodeo, hear contemporary Indian bands, and shop for arts and crafts. There is also a parade and barbecue. Contact the Casagrande Chamber of Commerce for this major event: Box 1014, Casagrande, AZ 85222 or phone (602) 836-2125.

Mission San Xavier del Bac also holds an annual pageant, usually on the Friday following Easter Sunday. The mission is on the San Xavier Papago Indian Reservation and there is Papago and Yaqui dancing among the activities. The mission is about ten miles south of Tucson on San Xavier Road, just off Hwy I-19. Phone the mission at (602) 294-2624 for details.

At San Xavier some Papago are both practicing Christians and believe in the effectiveness of traditional Indian doctors as well. There has recently been a shared respect between the Catholic priests and the Indian doctors as both provide spiritual support for the people.

Some Papago and Pima people attend the old Indian Fiesta of Saint Francis of Assisi in Magdalena, Sonora, Mexico held annually on or about October 4. Yaqui, Opata, Mayo, Cora, and southern Pima from Mexico also attend.

PASSAMAQUODDY

The Passamaquoddy from Pleasant Point, Maine (near Eastport) and the Maleseet from Tobique and Kingsclear, New Brunswick perform traditional Eastern Woodlands dancing at public celebrations periodically SEE: MAINE—PASSAMAQUODDY.

The Indian Township Passamaquoddy also sponsor an Indian pageant in summer. The office number is (207) 796-5420 in Princeton, Maine. There are occasional celebrations with Passamaquoddy dancing.

PAWNEE

The Pawnee sponsor one of the oldest and best established pow-wows in the United States. It is the annual Pawnee Homecoming held over the Fourth of July weekend in Pawnee, Oklahoma. The four bands of the Pawnee Nation join together for four days and nights of dancing, hand games, an arts and crafts show, and more. The friendly and dignified Pawnee people are a pleasure to be with as they annually don their traditional hair roaches, fur turbans, shawls, etc., for this major event. Visitors will also see the new Pawnee roundhouse built to resemble the traditional earthlodges of long ago. Ceremonies and meetings are held here today. Note, too, the fine old stone Pawnee Indian Agency buildings and tribal offices. For exact dates contact the Pawnee Tribal Office at (918) 762-3624. SEE: OKLAHOMA—PAWNEE.

PENOBSCOT
SEE: MAINE- OLD TOWN

PEORIA
SEE: ILLINOIS

PIMA
SEE: ARIZONA—SACATON

PIT RIVER (Achomawi)
The Pit River Indian people of northeastern California waged a well known struggle with Pacific Gas & Electric Company for the return of tribal lands during the 1970's. Today there is a tribal office at Burney, CA, phone (916) 335-5421 or 335-3353. There is also the Pit River Home and Agricultural Society in Alturas, CA, phone (916) 233-2584.

POMO
The Pomo are among the finest and most distinctive Indian dancers in North America. Best known for their brilliant orange flicker feather headbands,

Pomo music is unique to California. As with many other Native American groups, Pomo dancing is part of a living religion yet is also performed for the public. The Kashaya Pomo, Elem Pomo, Big Valley (Mission) Pomo, Coyote Valley Pomo, and Point Arena Pomo all have outstanding dance groups. Most do both ceremonial dancing and public performances as well. Most commonly seen are the type of dances the Clear Lake Pomo call "Shake head dancing" and the Pt. Arena Pomo call "Feather dancing." Dancers wear beautiful orange and black flicker feather headbands, wide beaded belts and dance skirts of fur or tule reeds. The spectacular "Big Head" dance is occasionally performed publicly and is unsurpassed in its impressive costume. The Big Head costume features a headdress of up to 75 wooden spines tipped with feathers. The headdress is five feet in diameter and very beautiful. This is probably the most sacred of Pomo dances. The Pomo people are to be congratulated for keeping California Indian dancing alive and well. SEE: CALIFORNIA—CLEAR LAKE, FORT ROSS, INDIAN GRINDING ROCK STATE PARK, POINT REYES, POINT ARENA, SANTA ROSA and UKIAH. In August, the City of Cotati, California also annually sponsors an Indian Day and the Pomo dance here. Phone the City of Cotati at (707) 795-5478. Pomo dance groups have participated in San Francisco's elite annual Ethnic Dance Festival.

PONCA

The Ponca people of Oklahoma hold annual pow-wows in Ponca City and at White Eagle Tribal Park with colorful dancing and a fair. The Ponca Tribal Office phone is (405) 762-8104.

POTAWATOMI

Today there are Potawatomi reservations and communities in Oklahoma, Kansas, Wisconsin, Michigan, and Ontario. Much of the tribe was driven from its homeland in the Great Lakes area around 1838. Oklahoma Potawatomi recall this event as the "Trail of Death" because so many people perished.

Fortunately, the tribe survived and is growing stronger each year. The Potawatomi are organized into widely scattered bands, but recently have held gatherings aimed at renewing ancient ties between the bands. The Pokagon and Huron Bands from the Great Lakes, the Prairie Band from Kansas, and the Citizens Band from Oklahoma are among those active in bringing the tribe together again.

Periodic pow-wows and gatherings are held. The Citizen Band publishes an excellent newspaper, *HowNiKan*. It covers contemporary Potawatomi activities with an emphasis on the Citizens Band, and gives a good understanding of the activities of a progressive, modern tribe which is seeking to strengthen its Potawatomi roots. The "People of the Fire" look to a brightening future. SEE: OKLAHOMA—SHAWNEE for information on the Citizen Band Potawatomi and their many activities.

The Prairie Potawatomi near Holton, Kansas, hold an annual pow-wow during the summer. Canadian Potawatomi participate in Ojibwa and Ottawa events there. There are also Potawatomi reservations at Wabeno, Wisconsin and near Escanaba, Michigan.

THE PUEBLO

The 19 Pueblos of New Mexico hold public events that include fine dancing, colorful costumes, and moving ceremonial rites. The Indian Pueblo Cultural Center (SEE: NEW MEXICO—ALBUQUERQUE) is the best place to visit before going to any Pueblo event. They can help you find out which pueblos are holding a celebration or ceremony, offer advice and guidance, and generally orient you. The Cultural Center also sponsors events on Fourth of July weekend and at other times. Check for their programs.

Because there are so many events at so many different pueblos we are listing them by dates. Occasionally, dates are changed so it is always best to check with the Pueblo or the Cultural Center before going. SEE: NEW MEXICO listings under the section TODAY'S PUEBLOS for information on individual communities. All 19 pueblos are covered along with phone numbers and directions for finding them. For those unfamiliar with the pueblos' names they are: ACOMA, COCHITI, ISLETA, JEMEZ, LAGUNA, NAMBE, PICURIS, POJOAQUE, SAN FELIPE, SAN ILDEFONSO, SAN JUAN, SANDIAN, SANTA ANA, SANTA CLARA, SANTO DOMINGO, TAOS, TESUQUE, ZIA, and ZUNI. (Also SEE: TEXAS—EL PASO).

NOTE: Dates are subject to change and some Pueblo's may be closed to the public for several days annually to observe certain sacred rites.

NEW MEXICO PUEBLO DANCES and OTHER EVENTS

January 1
TAOS TURTLE DANCE
SAN JUAN has a CLOUD DANCE about this time.

January 3
ISLETA CORN, TURTLE and other DANCES

January 6
TAOS BUFFALO or DEER DANCE
SAN ILDEFONSO EAGLE DANCE
Also ACOMA, COCHITI, LAGUNA, SAN FELIPE, SANTA ANA, SANTO DOMINGO, and ZIA usually hold dances this day.

A member of Bill Franklin's Miwok dancers stands beside a traditional Miwok bark house. Such houses were built of redwood by Pomo along the California coast and of incense cedar by the Miwok in the Sierra Nevada Mountains. Today all California Indian people live in contemporary houses, but old style villages have been reconstructed. (R. Shanks)

A lovely member of the Coastal Pomo Dancers models a traditional California Indian women's dress. She stands beside an old time California Indian house made of tule reeds. Pt. Reyes National Seashore. (R. Shanks)

January 23
SAN ILDEFONSO fiesta day and COMANCHE DANCE

February 2
SAN FELIPE BUFFALO DANCE

February 15
SANTO DOMINGO EAGLE DANCE
SAN JUAN DANCES
Sometimes a TURTLE DANCE at TAOS

Late February
ISLETA EVERGREEN DANCE

Palm Sunday in March or April
Many pueblos have GREEN CORN DANCES and ceremonial FOOT RACES.

March 19
LAGUNA dances and fiesta.

EASTER WEEK
Dances held at many pueblos. A few pueblos hold irrigation ditch opening ceremonies because they are
agricultural people and insuring good crops is important. Others hold ceremonial shinny games.
Check with the Indian Pueblo Cultural Center for information. SEE: NEW MEXICO—ALBUQUERQUE.

March 27
Dances are usually held at ACOMA, COCHITI, JEMEZ,
LAGUNA, SAN FELIPE, SANTA ANA, SANTO DOMIN-
GO, and ZIA.

April 1
CORN or TABLITA DANCES at many pueblos.

May 1
SAN FELIPE CORN DANCE

May 3
COCHITI CORN DANCE
TAOS CEREMONIAL FOOT RACES in the morning and
TABLITA DANCE.

May 14
TAOS BLESSING OF THE FIELDS

May 15
TAOS candle light procession.

Late May or early June
TESUQUE DANCE and BLESSING OF THE FIELDS

June 6
ZUNI RAIN DANCE

June 8
SANTA CLARA BUFFALO DANCE

June 13
SANDIA FEAST DAY
TAOS CORN DANCE
COCHITI, SAN JUAN, SAN ILDEFONSO and SANTA
CLARA hold dances.

Mid-June
ISLETA DANCE

June 24
Dances, chicken pulls, and ceremonial races at
ACOMA, COCHITI, SAN FELIPE, SAN JUAN, SANTA
ANA, and SANTO DOMINGO.

June 29
Fiesta, chicken pulls, and dances at ACOMA, CO-
CHITI, SANTA ANA, SANTO DOMINGO and others.

July 4
NAMBE CEREMONIAL at Nambe Falls.

July 14
COCHITI TABLITA DANCE

July 25
ACOMA, COCHITI, LAGUNA, and TAOS DANCES and
RABBIT HUNTS.

July 26
SANTA ANA FEAST DAY with CORN DANCES
TAOS DANCES

Late July
SANTA CLARA PUYE CLIFF DWELLING CEREMON-
IALS with DANCES, etc. Very popular event with pho-
tography permitted.

August 2
JEMEZ OLD BULL DANCES. These ancient dances
originated at the now abandoned pueblo of Pecos.
The handful of Pecos survivors left their war torn
home and fled to safety at Jemez. To this day, their
Old Bull Dance is still performed at Jemez. Thus,
even though Pecos is in ruins, one of its dances may
still be seen.

August 4
SANTO DOMINGO CORN DANCE

August 10
ACOMA CORN DANCES (held nearby at Acomita)
LAGUNA CORN DANCE
PICURIS CORN DANCE

August 12
SANTA CLARA CORN DANCE

August 15
ZIA CORN DANCES
LAGUNA HARVEST DANCE at Mesita Village.

Late August
ISLETA DANCES

September 2
ACOMA CORN DANCES atop the giant mesa.

Early September
ISLETA HARVEST DANCE

September 8
LAGUNA RESERVATION HARVEST DANCE at town of Encinal.
SAN ILDEFONSO CORN DANCE

September 19
LAGUNA HARVEST DANCE

September 29
TAOS SUNDOWN DANCE

September 30
TAOS CEREMONIAL RELAY RACES and POLE CLIMBING

October 4
NAMBE DANCES

November 12
JEMEZ CORN DANCES
TESUQUE ANIMAL DANCES

November or December
ZUNI SHALAKO DANCES with huge ten-feet high masked dancers representing spirits in ceremonies. This is one of the most impressive of all Native American dances. Check with the Zuni Pueblo Office for dates, SEE: NEW MEXICO—ZUNI.

December 12
JEMEZ and TESUQUE DANCES

December 25
TAOS DANCES

December 26
SAN JUAN TURTLE DANCES

December 31
Late evening dances at LAGUNA, SAN FELIPE, SANDIA, SANTO DOMINGO, etc.
SANDIA DEER DANCE.

PUYALLUP

The Puyallup maintain a tribal office in Tacoma, Washington. SEE: WASHINGTON—OLYMPIA.

QUAPAW

The Quapaw sponsor a large enjoyable pow-wow annually over Fourth of July weekend outside of Quapaw, Oklahoma. There are evenings of Plains-style dancing including a number of dances where visitors are invited to join in (a kind and pleasant gesture some other Native American groups do also). Most of the time you sit and watch beautifully dressed Quapaw, Osage, and other Indian groups join together for a variety of dances. Occasionally a traditional Quapaw dance such as a turkey dance is held.

Late in the evening after the Plains type dancing is over, there is usually some wonderful stomp dancing that goes on all night. Shawnee and Peoria leaders (helped by their wives, relatives, or girl friends who shake terrapin shell or milk can leg rattles) sing Eastern Woodlands and Southeastern stomp dance songs.

During the day the Quapaw hold a traditional Indian football game where men play against women. Unlike conventional football, a stuffed ball is kicked by the men but can also be thrown or run with by the women. The sport is great fun to watch and I have never seen anyone enjoy themselves as much as Indian football participants. Among some eastern Oklahoma tribes (such as the Seneca-Cayuga) if a man gets too rough, the next year he has to wear an apron and play on the women's team. A traditional ceremonial foot race is also sometimes held. Incidentally, the Quapaw are sometimes called the Arkansas and originally came from that state. The Quapaw Tribal Office's phone number is (918) 542-1853. SEE: OKLAHOMA—MIAMI.

QUECHAN (YUMA)

Once commonly known as the Yuma, the tribe prefers the name Quechan. They live on a reservation near Yuma, Arizona. SEE: ARIZONA—YUMA for details.

QUILEUTE

The Quileute of Washington's Olympic Peninsula have a few members who race powerful motorized canoes in river races with the Hoh and Quinault at Taholah and elsewhere. SEE: WASHINGTON—QUINAULT and OLYMPIA.

QUINAULT

SEE: WASHINGTON—QUINAULT and OLYMPIA.

SAC & FOX

The annual Sac & Fox Pow-wow is generally held the weekend after Fourth of July south of Stroud, Okla-

homa. The location is at the beautiful Sac & Fox Tribal Campground (RV and tent camping) amid pastoral woodlands in some of the most scenic country around. Since the days of the earliest explorers, visitors to the Sac & Fox have praised the exceptionally beautiful tribal costumes of this people. Today guests at the pow-wow will still see the reason for such high praise as Sac & Fox take no less pride in their dress today. The dancers grand entry is unexcelled. The straight dancers hair roaches and other apparel is particularly unforgettable. A number of interesting dances are done, including the warriors' sneak dance which acts out sneaking up on an enemy. There is a great arts and crafts sale with fine Sac & Fox, Pawnee, and other work offered.
Often Creeks and others come for late night stomp dancing after the pow-wow ends.

While here be sure to note the campground's store designed in the style of a traditional Sac & Fox summer lodge. Crafts are sold along with other items. The tribal museum and cultural center is open weekdays. Incidentally, these are the Sac portion of the Sac & Fox, while the Fox live in Iowa. Tribal Office can be contacted at: Route 2, Box 246, Stroud, OK 74079, phone (405) 275-4270 or (918) 968-3526. SEE: OKLAHOMA—STROUD.

Other Sac & Fox live in a reservation along the Kansas-Nebraska border. Their tribal office is Box 38, Reserve, KS, (913) 742-7471. Also SEE: MESQUAKIE.

SALINAN
The Salinan Indians of Monterey and San Luis Obispoe. Survivors tended to marry into Anglo and Hispanic families and some Californians proudly trace their ancestry to the Salinans. SEE: CALIFORNIA—JOLON and MISSIONS.

SALISH
SEE: COAST SALISH, FLATHEAD, COLVILLE, LUMMI, SONGHEES, and SUQUAMISH listings.

SARCEE
The Sarcee people live in and around Calgary, Alberta. They have some fine singers and drummers and have made commercial recordings of their music. The Sarcee Indian Band Office is at: 3700 Anderson Rd SW, Box 69, Calgary, Alberta, Canada T2W 3C4. Phone (403) 281-4455. They hold periodic celebrations and events, including a pow-wow near the end of June.

SEMINOLE
Today most Seminole people live in Florida and Oklahoma. Oklahoma Seminole live in the vicinity of Wewoka where the Seminole Nation's office and museum are located. The museum is a good place to find out about Seminole culture and events open to the public. SEE: OKLAHOMA—WEWOKA. Stomp dances are held regularly and some are open to visitors. There is an annual Seminole Nation Days in the town of Seminole with unforgettable stomp dances, crafts, and other events, usually held in September. Check with the Seminole National Museum, (405) 257-5589, or the Seminole Nation Office, (405) 257-6291 for dates of this and other public events. Oklahoma Seminole today live in modern houses and often are community leaders, but some still practice traditional activities.

Florida Seminole are famous for their thatch houses, colorful clothing, and traditional life style in the Everglades of Florida. The Seminole Okalee Village on the Seminole Reservation west of Dania, near Hollywood, FL, offers tours. Tribal Office phone number is (305) 583-7112. An annual pow-wow is also held here, usually in February. A Seminole Fair is generally held the forth weekend in December. The Seminole Arts & Crafts Center, 6073 Sterling Rd, Hollywood, FL, is at Hwy 441 and Sterling Road, four miles west of Dania, phone (305) 583-3590. Many arts and crafts items are sold. SEE: MICCOSUKEE. Also SEE: FLORIDA listings.

SENECA
SEE: IROQUOIS

SERI
About 500 Seri live in Sonora, Mexico, on the coast west of Hermosillo. The Seri once lived on Tiburon Island in the Gulf of California where armed resistance continued at least as late as 1904. Today Tiburon is a game refuge and the Seri live on the mainland. Their reservation or ejido is along the coast just east and north of Isla Tiburon. They also have a school at Punta Chueco. Four public ceremonies still continue today, including a girl's puberty fiesta.

The Seri are famed for their fine coiled basketry and exquisite carvings of desert ironwood. Dealers periodically visit the Seri and their art can be purchased in the US.

SERRANO
Serrano people of southern California usually participate in the Malki Museum Fiesta. A few Seranno cradles are still made today. San Manuel Reservation near San Bernardino, CA, is a Serrano community. The tribal office address is: 5771 N. Victoria, Highland, CA 92346. Phone: (714) 862-2439. SEE: CALIFORNIA—MORONGO INDIAN RESERVATION.

SHASTA
Tragically, not many Shasta people survive today in California and Oregon. The Quartz Valley Reserva-

The late Miriam Lee, Seneca, was an artist, teacher, clan mother, and respected member of the Allegany Indian Reservation in New York state. Here, she works on a basket that will be used for processing corn for soup and hominy. (Assoc. for the Advancement of Native North American Arts and Crafts)

This Plains couple is dressed for an Arapaho or Shoshone pow-wow in Wyoming. The elders are often honored at these events. (Wyoming Travel Commission)

tion, last of the Shasta land, was terminated in 1967 by the government's ill advised "Termination Program". Some Shasta history may be found at the Siskiyou County Museum, 910 S. Main in Yreka, CA, (916) 842-3836.

SHAWNEE

The three branches of the Shawnee people live in Oklahoma today. Many Shawnee are leaders in their communities in Oklahoma and are highly successful. Among Native American people the Shawnee are renowned for their knowledge and skills in traditional ceremonial life and dancing. Shawnee stomp dance leaders and shell shakers are prominent during the stomp dance competition held late at night during the Quapaw pow-wow. SEE: QUAPAW.

Many traditional Shawnee dances and ceremonies are still held, but they are not primarily public performances and are religious rites. If you attend any of these be sure to understand that they are sacred events. Read James Howard's wonderful book *Shawnee!*, before attending Shawnee events so you will understand their religious significance. Both the Absentee Band of Shawnee and the Cherokee (or Loyal) Shawnee bands have traditional ceremonies today. The Absentee Shawnee Tribal Office is in Shawnee, OK, (405) 275-4030. The Eastern Shawnee usually participate in the events around Miami, OK. The Eastern Shawnee's Tribal Office is in Seneca, Missouri, phone (918) 666-1435. SEE: OKLAHOMA—MIAMI.

SHINNECOCK

Shinnecock Indian people of Long Island, New York, host an annual pow-wow usually held over Labor Day weekend. The location is at the Shinnecock Reservation along Route 27A, Montauk Hwy, Southampton, New York. Traditional Eastern Woodlands Indian foods are sold including Shinnecock succotash and chowder. There are arts and crafts sales by Eastern Woodland Indian people from the US and Canada. Traditional dances are performed. Admission proceeds benefit the Shinnecock Tribe and Church. Phone the Shinnecock Community Center for information, (516) 283-9266. SEE: NEW YORK—SOUTHAMPTON.

SILETZ

The Confederated tribes of Siletz, Oregon, suffered "termination" in 1954 as part of an ill conceived government plan to no longer recognize the existence of many tribes. Government services and land were both lost. Social problems increased dramatically, but the Siletz struggled to come back. They reorganized the tribe, formed a non-profit corporation, restored the tribal cemetery, developed alcoholism and man-power programs, and fought for political

recognition. In 1977, after a long struggle, tribal status and government recognition was restored. The tribe was given federal land in Lincoln County, Oregon, to replace lost reservation lands. A tribal office has been established in Siletz, OR, and there are occasional traditional celebrations. SEE: GRAND RONDE and OREGON—COOS BAY.

SLAVEY

SEE: DENE'. Also see various listings under NORTHWEST TERRITORIES.

SONGHEES

The Songhees Indian Reserve sponsors annual dugout canoe races and other activities at their new reserve near Victoria, British Columbia, Canada. These are usually held in June or July. The Reserve Office number is (604) 386-1043.

SHOSHONE

There are a number of Shoshone groups in Nevada, Idaho, and Wyoming. The Wind River Shoshone live on a large reservation near Lander, WY. The Wind River people sponsor Indian Days at Fort Washakie generally in late June, sun dances in late July, an Indian Fair in August, Christmas dances in December, plus other events. The Shoshone Nation Office can provide help, phone (307) 255-8265.

The Fort Hall Shoshone and Bannock people in Idaho near Pocatello have the Shoshone-Bannock Festival in August (sometimes called Fort Hall Indian Days), phone (208) 234-3800. Duck Valley Reservation usually has a rodeo over Fourth of July. It is held at Owyhee, Nevada. Western Shoshone are major participants in many of the activities listed under PAIUTE. The *Native Nevadan* newsmagazine often lists Western Shoshone events. SEE: PAIUTE for address.

SIOUX (DAKOTA or LAKOTA)

One of the largest Native American groups today, the Sioux are actually a number of tribes spread over reservations in North and South Dakota, Nebraska, and elsewhere. Some live in Canada as well. The Sioux are great singers and dancers and some of their culture has spread to other Native American groups. The average American or Canadian often stereotypes other tribes as dressing in the Dakota traditional manner and as a result some groups have dropped their own traditions to imitate the Sioux. The Sioux don't imitate anybody and you can see some fine events in their lands. Listed below are a few of the better know celebrations and ceremonies.

During early May, Sioux encampments (tepee communities) are held on Pine Ridge Reservation at several locations. In June more dances are held here as well as at the Rosebud Reservation. In July, the Santee Sioux have their pow-wow at Flandreau, South Dakota. The same month, the Sioux Ceremonial is held at Sesseton, SD. Standing Rock reservation holds its' pow-wow at Little Eagle, SD, during this time. In August, the famous Sun Dance is held at Pine Ridge; the Spotted Tail Pow-wow is at Rosebud; and the Rosebud Tribal Fair is held.

Ft. Randall Pow-wow is held at Lake Andes around the first of August. The Lower Brule Sioux Pow-wow and the Rosebud Pow-wows are usually held in August. Over Labor Day, there is the Eagle Butte Pow-wow. Pow-wows continue on into the fall. The South Dakota Dept. of State Development, 221 South Central, Pierre, SD 57501, phone (800) 843-1930 publishes an annual Schedule of Events which lists the dates of some pow-wows. The Bureau of Indian Affairs in Aberdeen, SD, (605) 225-0250 and various tribal offices can provide dates and details. SEE: SOUTH DAKOTA listings.

SPOKANE
SEE: WASHINGTON—WELLPINIT

SUQUAMISH
SEE: WASHINGTON—SUQUAMISH

SUSQUEHANNOCK
Also known as the Conestoga. Supposedly extinct, some descendants are among the Seneca-Cayuga in Oklahoma. The Seneca-Cayuga were the westernmost branch of the conquering Iroquois as they expanded over Erie, Neutral, and other tribal territories. Survivors of many of these groups were incorporated into Iroquoian culture. Some of the songs and ceremonies of these groups may have influenced traditions and may be present among the Seneca-Cayuga and other Iroquois.

TARAHUMARA
The Tarahumara live in the high mountain country in the Mexican state of Chihuahua and still lead a very traditional life. They are famous for their ability to run amazing distances at very high altitudes. Baskets, woven sashes, and wood carvings are among the arts and crafts sold to visitors.

The Chihuahua al Pacifico Railway makes a brief stop at Copper Canyon in the Sierra Madre Mountains and passengers may get off the train and buy Tarahumara baskets and other products. Tarahumara villages can also be visited by road from Creel, Chihuahua. During Easter Week there are celebrations in the Indian communities. This is rugged, isolated country and visits should be well researched before going.

TIGUA
The Tigua welcome visitors to their cultural center with many activities. SEE: TEXAS—EL PASO.

TIPAI and IPAI (DIEGUEÑO)
The Tipai and Ipai people live primarily in San Diego County, California, and own a number of reservations. Some of the reservations hold annual public fiestas which include Indian games and foods. Most participate in the general social and economic life of the region, but some traditional memorial services are still privately held with traditional singing and ceremonies. SEE: MISSION this section.

TLINGIT
The Tlingit are justly famous for their totem poles, Chilkat blankets, button blankets, masks, carvings, baskets and other arts. Today, there are fine opportunities to see rich dances, carvings, and other examples of Tlingit culture in their southern Alaska homeland. SEE: ALASKA—ANGOON, HAINES, KAKE, KETCHIKAN and SITKA. Also SEE: WASHINGTON—SEATTLE under Daybreak Star Arts Center's Indian Dinner Theater.

TOLOWA
The Tolowa have had a cultural and dance program at Redwood National Park sponsored in part by College of the Redwoods. Worthwhile sessions in Northwestern California Indian culture are conducted over a period of weeks during the summer. For details contact Redwood National Park, 1111 Second St, Crescent City, CA 95531. Phone (707) 464-6101.

TONKAWA
The Tonkawa hold their annual pow-wow at Tonkawa, Oklahoma, during the summer. Phone (405) 628-2561.

TSIMSHIAN
The Tsimshian are world famous for their wood carvings, including totem poles and masks. SEE: BRITISH COLUMBIA—HAZELTON and ALASKA—MATLAKATLA and KETCHIKAN.

TULALIP
The Tulalip live northwest of Everett, Washington, on a beautiful, forested reservation. Economic development is under way and a bingo enterprise is thriving here. Tribal offices are at Marysville, WA, phone (206) 653-4585.

TUNICA-BILOXI
The Tunica and Biloxi tribes recently achieved formal legal recognition as a tribe from the Federal government. The tribal office is in Marksville, Louisiana, phone (318) 253-9763.

TYGH
The Tygh (pronounced "tie") Indian people hold a Tygh Valley Indian Celebration north of Warm Springs, Oregon, generally in May. The Warm Springs

Tribal Office should have information since some Tygh live on that reservation. SEE: OREGON—WARM SPRINGS.

TUSCARORA
SEE: IROQUOIS

UMPQUA
The Umpqua are organized into two bands: the Cow Creek (or Upper Umpqua) and the Lower Umpqua. The bands are named for their locations along the Umpqua River. For the Lower Umpqua SEE: OREGON—COOS BAY.

The Cow Creek Umpqua live around Canyonville, Oregon, and participate in the Canyonville Pioneer Days celebration and also sponsor an annual pow-wow. The Cow Creek people have been working for economic progress, preservation of archeological sites, and with local history groups to help preserve their culture.

UMATILLA
Umatilla, Cayuse, and Walla Walla people live on Oregon's Umatilla Reservation. SEE: OREGON—PENDLETON.

UTE
The Ute, especially in Colorado, have visitor oriented parks, recreational opportunities, and wilderness expeditions. The Ute people also hold annual dances and fairs, most of which are open to respectful guests. SEE: COLORADO—IGNACIO and TOWAOC; UTAH—FORT DUCHESNE.

WAILAKI
The Wailaki settled on the Round Valley Indian Reservation at Covelo, California, where they live today. Recently the Round Valley people initiated a new arts and crafts program with an emphasis on beadwork. Phone (707) 983-6126 for the Round Valley Tribal Office. SEE: YUKI.

WALAPAI
SEE: HUALAPAI

WAMPANOAG
The Wampanoag of Martha's Vineyard, Massachusetts, have been working to regain a portion of tribal lands on their island homeland. SEE: MASSACHUSETTS—MARTHA'S VINEYARD.

WAPPO
Wappo people of central California have intermarried with the more numerous Pomo. Laura Fish Somersall still weaves traditional Wappo baskets of the highest quality and a few other women who are at least part Wappo weave, too. An exhibit of Mrs. So-

mersall's basketry is on display at the Warm Springs Dam Visitor Center, 3333 Skaggs Springs Rd, Geyserville, CA, (707) 433-9483. Although labeled Pomo baskets in the display, Mrs. Somersall is a fluent Wappo speaker who has been a consultant on scholarly studies of the tribe. Modern Wappo sometimes participate in Kashaya Pomo dances.

WARM SPRINGS
The Wishram, Warm Springs, Paiute and other tribes of the Warm Springs Indian Reservation in Oregon hold dances Sundays during summer at their magnificent resort. There is usually an enjoyable Fourth of July celebration here as well. A major pow-wow is generally held in June while the important and traditional Root Festival falls in mid-April. The Warm Springs people rent authentic tepees as accommodations at their tribal campground (completely modern facilities), call (503) 553-1112. Incidentally, the movie, "Three Warriors", was filmed here. SEE: OREGON—WARM SPRINGS.

WASHO
The annual La Ka Le'l Ba Pow-wow at Carson City, Nevada, is sponsored in the fall by the Carson Indian Colony. There is traditional and fancy Indian dance competition, hand games, Indian food, and arts and crafts. Phone (702) 883-7442 or 883-1446 for dates and information. In recent years the Washo have been known for their business and educational progress. Also SEE: NEVADA—CARSON CITY.

WICHITA
The Wichita often join with the Caddo and Delaware in pow-wows in the Anadarko, OK area. Check with the Wichita Tribal Affairs Office for information on events. Phone (405) 247-2425. SEE: OKLAHOMA—ANADARKO.

WINNEBAGO
The Winnebago today live in Nebraska and Wisconsin. The Nebraska Winnebago hold an annual pow-wow, usually in late July. The Tribal Office number in Winnebago, NE, is (402) 878-2272. For Wisconsin Winnebago, SEE: WISCONSIN—WISCONSIN DELLS. Winnebago craftspeople produce very fine beadwork.

WINTUN
There are three major divisions of Wintun people in California's Sacramento Valley and surrounding hills. The southern Wintun or Patwin suffered great population loss and most survivors merged with Wintun people to the north at Rumsey and Colusa. The Cache Creek bingo enterprise is offered to the public at Rumsey Rancheria, phone (916) 796-3182. Central Wintun or Nomlaki live primarily around Elk Creek, CA, and have a ceremonial roundhouse that is

active on the Grindstone Rancheria. Exquisite California Indian dancing is performed here, although it is primarily religious and seldom seen by other than local Indian people. Consideration has been given by the tribe to exchanging the reservation for agricultural land. Northern Wintun or Wintu formed the Toyon-Wintu Center near Redding, CA, with the goal of providing help for the Wintu people in the area.

WISHRAM
SEE: WARM SPRINGS

WIYOT
Today the Wiyot live largely in their Humboldt County, California, homeland primarily at Blue Lake, on the Table Bluff Rancheria near Loleta, and around the mouth of the Mad River. It is a miracle that anyone survives today. Groups of "volunteers" roamed California's North Coast massacring Indian people during the 1860's. The Wiyot suffered particularly. Take the bridge across Humboldt Bay from Eureka to Samoa and the second island you cross is Indian or Gunther Island. Here a major portion of the Wiyot—from infants to grandparents—were massacred by a few vigilantes. Author Bret Harte was shocked and outraged at the carnage and said so in print. He was driven from the area. The Wiyot as a tribe have never fully recovered from such genocide, but the warm kindness and strength of character of the Wiyot people remains to this day.

WYANDOT
Oklahoma Wyandot participate in Indian Heritage Days at Miami, OK. SEE: OKLAHOMA—MIAMI. The tribal office number is (918) 540-1541.

YAHI
A branch of California's Yana tribe, the Yahi are famous because of Theodora Kroeber's books on Ishi, the last "wild" Indian in the US. A few Yana people survive today, but the Yahi are gone. SEE: CALIFORNIA—BERKELEY.

YAKIMA
SEE: WASHINGTON—YAKIMA

YAQUI
The Yaqui were originally Mexican Indians, but during long conflicts with the Mexican government many have resettled in Arizona. Most live in or near Tucson and Phoenix. At Holy Week, the Yaqui people perform a number of colorful and distinctive dances. Some ceremonies are a mixture of Indian and Spanish influences, but the blending is a pleasing one. The Deer Dance is truly Indian and features deer impersonators with Southwestern Indian gourd hand rattles and Mexican Indian leg rattles.

The Pascua-Yaqui Tribal Council Offices are at 7474 Camino de Oeste in Tucson, phone (602) 883-2338. They operate a landscape nursery, charcoal packing business, and a bingo enterprise on their reservation. Arts and crafts products include Deer Dance statues and cultural paintings. For dates and locations of dances contact: the Tucson Visitors Bureau, Box 27210, Tucson, AZ 85726, phone (602) 791-4768; the Phoenix Visitors Bureau, 2701 E Camelback Rd, Suite 200, Phoenix, AZ 85251, phone (602) 957-0700; or the Pascua Yaqui Tribe. SEE: PAPAGO.

YAVAPAI
Some traditional life still exists among Arizona's Yavapai people along side a modern approach to progress in their communities. Work is beginning on a Yavapai Community College at Prescott where hopefully some traditional cultural activities will be among the subjects taught. For information check with the Tribal Office, (602) 445-8790.

YOKUTS
The Tache Yokuts of Lemoore, California, sponsor an annual celebration in late August that includes a newly formed dance group that sings traditional Yokuts songs. The Tribal Office number is (209) 924-3487. Also in late August, the Tule River Yokuts hold a spiritual gathering for their community and respectful guests. The Tule River Reservation is east of Porterville, CA, and the Tribal Office's number is (209) 781-4271.

YUCHI
The Yuchi hold stomp, arbor, and Green Corn dances at their ceremonial grounds near Kellyville, Oklahoma, late spring and summer. The music and dancing is outstanding and deeply religious. The Yuchi are administratively part of the Creek Nation. SEE: CREEK.

YUKI
The Yuki were subject to one of the worst genocides of all North American Indians. A group of greedy land settlers in Round Valley, California, decided to exterminate the tribe to steal their land. The government tried to protect the Yuki, even stationing troops for Indian protection. But a genocidal "war" was waged and the peaceful Yuki all but destroyed. A few survivors live on the Round Valley Indian Reservation at Covelo, CA. See Virginia Miller's heartbreaking book, "Ukomno'm: The Yuki Indians" for the full story. SEE: WAILAKI.

YUMA
SEE: QUECHAN

Traditional Iroquois clothing is modeled by the children of craftswoman and teacher Florence Brant, a Mohawk. Thanks to their mother these youngsters will know their heritage. They stand beside a corn field, the most important Iroquois traditional food. (Association for Advancement of Native North American Arts and Crafts)

YUROK

Some traditional activities are still practiced among the Yurok and elders sometimes conduct classes or lecture locally to help educate Indians and non-Indians about Yurok culture. Two traditional Yurok plank houses still stand near Requa at the north side of the mouth of the Klamath River. These are private residences. The Yurok's Resighini Business Council is located in Klamath, CA, phone (707) 482-3371.

ZUNI

SEE: PUEBLO. Also SEE: NEW MEXICO—ZUNI.

ACKNOWLEDGEMENTS

It is due to the kindness, generosity and helpfulness of the following people and organizations that this book could be written. All helped in different ways. Some shared cultural knowledge, some shared photographs and information on events or places, many graciously posed for pictures or took time to talk, others reviewed portions of the manuscript and offered suggestions. Writing this book was much like a journey, and whenever the task seemed too large the words of many of these people offered encouragement and inspiration. Whether by phone, letter, or in person, their spirits reached out and helped create this book. A little bit of the heart of each person who helped is in this book. Thank you, to each and everyone.

Some people went out of their way to help and deserve special mention for their effort. They include: Jesse, Dan and Jackie Frank, David Smith and all of the Coastal Pomo Indian Dancers of Pt. Arena, CA; Milton "Bun" Lucas, Clarence Carillo, and Lanny Pinola of the Kashaya Pomo; Jim Brown, Malvina Brown, Ken Fred, and Nelson Hopper of the Clear Lake Pomo; Mable MacKay of Rumsey Rancheria; Laura Fish Somersall, Wappo; Bill Franklin and family, Miwok; Geneva Mattz, Yurok; and the late Henry Azbill, Maidu; Lyle Marshall, Hupa Tribal Museum; The Creek Nation, esp. Communications Center staff Gary Robinson, Rob Trepp, and Helen Chalakee; all six of the Ojibwa Reservation Business Committee offices and other branches of the Minnesota Chippewa Tribe, esp. Dave Danz, Dave Villebrun, Betty Blue, Floyd Ballinger, Dick Hoaglund, Dennis Maddox, Norma Felty, and Frank Michaud, Jr. The Chickasaw Nation, esp. Governor Overton James and Pat Gover; the Seneca-Cayuga Tribe of Oklahoma, esp. Chief James Allen, Leroy Howard, and Sue Nuckles; Peggy Sweeney, Yuchi; the Pawnee Tribal Office, esp. Alvin Echohawk; the Inter-Tribal Ceremonial Assoc. of Gallup, esp. Larry Linford; the Mississippi Band of Choctaw, esp. Julie Kelsey; Alaska Indian Arts, esp. Jim Heaton; Yakima Nation Cultural Center, esp. Vivian Adams and Sheryl Antelope; Northwest Indian Fisheries Commission, esp. Steve Robinson; Schoharie Museum of the Iroquois Indian, esp. Christina Johannesn; Ska-Nah-Doht, esp. Janet Cobban; Prince of Wales Northern Heritage Centre, esp. Lynette Harper; U'Mista Cultural Centre, esp. Gloria C. Miller; Lake of the Woods Cultural Centre, esp. Maria Seymore; Native American Rights Fund; Miccosukee Tribe; Mattaponi Indian Museum, esp. Norman Custalow and the late Chief O.T. Custalow; Indian & Northern Affairs Dept. of Canada, esp. the library and Inuit Arts Section staff; Lenni Lenape Historical Society, esp. Carla Messinger; Ute Mountain Ute Tribal Park, esp. Arthur Cuthair; Alabama-Coushatta Tribal Office; Kiowa Tribal Museum, esp. Geneva Emhoolah; Passamaquoddy-Maliseet Bilingual Program, esp. Joseph A. Nicholas; Micmac Assoc. of Cultural Studies, esp. Peter Christmas; Iroqrafts, esp. Wm Guy Spittal; Delf Norona Museum; Canyon Records, esp. Raymond Boley; Choctaw Nation esp. Frank Watson; Choctaw Nation Museum, esp. Donna Jo Williams; Indian Arts & Crafts Board, esp. Myles Libhart; Malki Museum, esp. Katherine Siva Saubel; Superintendent of Cahokia Mounds State Historic Site; Dept of Culture, Govt. of Northwest Territories, esp. Tessa Macintosh; Oneida Nation Museum, esp. Bob Smith; Sainte-Marie among the Hurons, esp. Shirley Whittington; Citizen Band Potawatomi Tribes, esp. Patricia Sulcer; Tillicum Village; and the Assoc. for the Advancement of Native North American Arts & Crafts.

The following tribal offices and institutions also helped greatly by providing information on events: Cocopah Elder Center, esp. Mrs. Frances Evanston; Hualapai Tribe; Kaibab Paiute Tribe; Navajo Nation, esp, Kee Long; Kwakiutl Museum, esp. Estelle Inman; Menominee Tribe; United Indians of All Tribes, Daybreak Star Center; Inter-Tribal Friendship House of Oakland, CA, esp. Nancy Scott; Quechan Museum, esp. Pauline Jose; Klamath Tribe; Stockbridge-Munsee Tribal Office, esp. Molly Shawano; Comanche Tribal Office, esp. Jeroux Navaquaya; Ojibwa Cultural Foundation; Sac & Fox Tribe of Oklahoma, esp. the RV Park Store staff; Quapaw Tribe; Absentee Shawnee Tribe, esp. JD Little Jim; Seminole Nation Historical Society; Penobscot Tribe, esp. Carol Dana; Saskatchewan Federated Indian College, esp. Stephanie Rogers; Caddo Tribe, esp. Tony Williams; White Mtn. Apache Tribe Quinault Nation; Suquamish Museum, esp. Marilyn Jones; Kickapoo Tribe of Kansas, esp. Fred Thomas; Nez Perce Tribe; Spokane Tribe, esp. Georgia Peone; Cheyenne River Sioux Tribe, esp. Don Eagle Chasing; Fort Berthold Tribal Office, esp. Pam Yellowbird; American Indian Exposition, esp. Miles Stevenson; Lower Brule Sioux Office; Tonawanda Seneca Office; North American Indian Traveling College; esp. Barbara Barnes; Bad River Ojibwa Tribe, esp. Jim Thannum; Mesquakie Tribe, esp. Chris Youngbear; Woodlands Indian Cultural Center; Songhees Band Office; Indian Pueblo Culture Center; Apache Cultural Center; Susanville General Council Office; Southern Ute Tribe; Umatilla Tribe; Warm Springs Tribe; Karuk Tribal Office; Quileute Nation; Aztec Dancers; Ralph Aguilar, Paiute; Anita Chisholm, Shawnee; Tammy Lucas and many other tribal offices and individuals.

Other very helpful organizations were the Travel and Economic Development offices of the following states: Oklahoma Tourism, esp. Fred Marvel; Alaska Division of Tourism; Iowa Development Comm.; Florida Dept. of Commerce; Montana Dept. of Commerce; Wyoming Travel Comm. esp. Cindy Hendrickson; Colorado Tourism Board; New Mexico Economic Development Office, esp. Frank Anaya; Ohio Dept of Tourism; South Dakota Dept of Development; Wisconsin Dept. of Tourism; and Minnesota Office of Tourism.

We would also like to thank: the National Park Service; Lowie Museum, esp. Frank Norick; Craig Bates of Yosemite National Park; Point Reyes National Seashore; Oregon Historical Society; Santa Barbara Museum of Natural History esp. Jan Timbrook and the late Travis Hudson; Wisconsin Historical Society; Rev. Ralph Shanks, Sr., Viola Shanks, Laurel, Torrey, and Don Shanks.

The author would like additionally to thank four teachers who especially influenced my academic work. Dr. Sherri Cavan, who chaired my thesis committee at San Francisco State University and who taught me to analyze and to develop my own understanding of human behavior; Larry Dawson of Lowie Museum of Anthropology who imparted invaluable and unique insights into anthropology and natural science; Miss Ford, my Blue Lake, Calif., elementary school teacher who first sparked an interest in human culture and local history; and the late Dr. James H. Howard of Oklahoma State University whose writings opened up a new world of understanding linking traditional and contemporary Native American cultural life.

For production of the book we would like to thank Frank Gaynor of the Graphics Group; Marie Pence of Miller Freeman Publications; North Bay Photo; B and B Photo; and the late Jack Mason.

Finally, I would like to thank my loving wife, Lisa, for her interest and dedication to this book. Although she refused to accept a title other than editor, she truly deserves to be promoted to co-author.

ABOUT THE AUTHOR

Ralph Shanks is a teacher in the public schools and Native American Studies is among the many subjects he has taught. He has a lifelong interest in North American Indian cultures which has resulted in this book. Mr. Shanks has done post-graduate studies and research at the University of California's Lowie Museum of Anthropology and has served as Research Associate in Anthropology for the Santa Barbara Museum of Natural History. He has been a consultant on Native American cultures for the National Park Service and various museums including the British Museum in London and the Museum of Man in Paris.

Mr. Shanks feels he is a student of Indian cultures and that the real teachers are the cultural and spiritual leaders of the tribes. It is through their teaching and example that he has learned, and he hopes this book reflects their wisdom and kindness.

Mr. Shanks is also a maritime historian and has written two books on the subject: "Lighthouses of San Francisco Bay" and "Lighthouses and Lifeboats of the Redwood Coast". His articles on the US Life-Saving Service have been published by the National Maritime Museum. Editor Lisa Shanks is the author's wife and they have two daughters, Laurel and Torrey.

ABOUT THE EDITOR

Lisa Woo Shanks hold a degree in Natural Resource Planning and Interpretation. She previously worked for the National Park Service as a planner and park ranger. Currently, she is a soil conservationist for the USDA Soil Conservation Service where she has authored technical material for the vineyard industry. Her background in publication planning, writing, and production has been indispensable to the completion of this book. Lisa Shanks has managed the computer word processing and editing of this volume. Both she and her husband have spent the last seven years traveling throughout North America researching "The North American Indian Travel Guide".

Large Pomo seed gathering basket, California.

Back cover photo: Sioux dancer (South Dakota Tourism)